AF573685

Step-by-step Recipes

for the complete cook

Judy Brown

Lecturer in Advanced Domestic Cookery
Guildford County Technical College
City & Guilds Examiner in Cookery

Mollie Chitty

Lecturer in Domestic Cookery and Teaching Methods
Guildford County Technical College

PITMAN PUBLISHING

First published 1971

SIR ISAAC PITMAN AND SONS LTD
Pitman House, Parker Street, Kingsway, London, WC2B 5PB
P O Box 6038, Portal Street, Nairobi, Kenya
SIR ISAAC PITMAN (AUST) PTY LTD
Pitman House, Bouverie Street, Carlton, Victoria 3053, Australia
PITMAN PUBLISHING COMPANY S A LTD
P O Box 11231, Johannesburg, South Africa
PITMAN PUBLISHING CORPORATION
6 East 43rd Street, New York, N Y 10017, U S A
SIR ISAAC PITMAN (CANADA) LTD
THE COPP CLARK PUBLISHING COMPANY
517 Wellington Street, Toronto 2B, Canada

G.1 - (G.3352)

ISBN: 0 273 31421 1

IBM Typeset by H. Charlesworth & Co. Ltd., Huddersfield
Printed by G. A. Pindar & Son Ltd., Scarborough
Bound by Hunter & Foulis Ltd., Edinburgh

Foreword

Step-by-Step Recipes has been written by two Domestic Subjects Lecturers in this College who have wide and varied experience of teaching Cookery in School, Training College and Technical College. They have taught vocational and non-vocational students of all age groups and at present are responsible for students taking City and Guilds Food and Family and Further Education Teachers' Courses.

The authors have for some considerable time been conscious of the need for a recipe book which students could use for reference in class and they have to some extent overcome the problem by producing recipe "hand-outs" for use in all the Cookery classes in the College. *Step-by-Step Recipes* began at this point and will replace the hand-outs by providing a *fully comprehensive* range of recipes—a particular feature of this book since the recipes in each section are graded to suit the needs of all from the beginner to the "Cordon Bleu" student.

There is no doubt that this book will be invaluable to teachers and students in all educational establishments where Cookery is taught—Schools, Colleges and the Adult Education Service. Students in recreational classes will find the book as useful as will those who are preparing for examinations such as City and Guilds 471, Parts I and II, G.C.E. "O" and "A" level and others.

Special features include the total average times needed to prepare the various dishes—practical information which the housewife will appreciate and which will assist the examination student who is concerned with work study and job evaluation. The Metric System is of course included to ensure the continued usefulness of the book in the years to come.

I am particularly glad to have the opportunity to introduce *Step-by-Step Recipes.* This is a book for which there has long been a need and which will be welcomed by all who enjoy good food and cookery.

NANCY BRIEN
Head of Homecraft and Catering Department
Guildford County Technical College

Contents

3 FISH *26*

4 MEAT, POULTRY AND GAME; STUFFING *42*

Meat

Salads

Salad Dressings

20 FILLINGS *254*

21 ICINGS *258*

22 PETITS FOURS *261*

Useful information

MEASUREMENTS

A Spoonful

As much *above* as in the *bowl* of the spoon

One standard tablespoonful (tbsp)	=	approx 30g/1 oz flour or similar ingredient
One standard teaspoonful (tsp)	=	approx 5g/¼ oz as above
One 5 ml teaspoonful	=	approx 1 very large teaspoonful

½ lit/1 pt = 4 gills or 20 fluid oz
⅛/¼ pt = 1 gill or 5 fluid oz

Conversions to Metric Measure

Weight		*Length*		*Liquid*	
½ oz	15 grammes	½ in	10 millimetres	⅛ litre	125 millilitres
1 oz	30 grammes	1 in	25 millimetres	¼ litre	250 millilitres
2 oz	60 grammes	2 in	50 millimetres	⅜ litre	375 millilitres
4 oz	110 grammes	3 in	75 millimetres	½ litre	500 millilitres
8 oz	230 grammes	4 in	100 millimetres		
12 oz	340 grammes	12 in	300 millimetres		
1 lb	450 grammes				

Note

1 Weights are correct to ¼ oz
2 Length is almost exact, except for ½ in
3 ½ lit = 1 pt *less* 3 tablespoonfuls

TEMPERATURES

OVEN SETTING	APPROX. TEMPERATURE IN THE CENTRE OF THE OVEN	
	Degrees Fahrenheit	*Degrees Centigrade*
¼	240	115
½	265	130
1	290	140
2	310	155
3	335	170
4	355	180
5	380	190
6	400	205
7	425	220
8	445	230
9	470	240
Electric cookers can be brought up to a higher temperature –		
	500	260
	550	290
Self-cleaning oven	900	480

MISCELLANEOUS PROCESSES

Seasoned Flour

Flour with salt and pepper added in the proportion of 1 tbsp flour, 1 tsp salt, ¼ tsp pepper.

Bacon Rolls

1 Remove rind and any bone from the rasher **2** Stretch with a knife–cut into 3 **3** Roll and put on to a skewer **4** Grill or bake. Use to garnish or as part of a mixed grill

To chop parsley

1 Wash the parsley–dry **2** Remove stalks–chop finely **3** Put into muslin and hold under running cold water. Squeeze lightly

To fry parsley

1 Wash parsley–dry **2** Pick off sprigs **3** Hold in a frying-spoon and immerse in hot deep fat for about 3 seconds; remove **4** Immerse a second time and remove **5** Immerse a third time and hold in fat until all sizzling ceases **6** Drain well
NB This is usually cooked after using deep fat for frying and the heat should be turned off

To skin tomatoes

1 Impale on a fork 2 Dip into a pan of boiling water, count slowly to 4–remove 3 Remove skin with a vegetable knife
NB If required for salads, plunge into cold water before skinning to prevent further cooking

Lemon Butterflies

1 Cut a thin slice of lemon, cut in half across 2 Cut again from skin edge almost to the centre–open out to form wings 3 Remove pips

Lemon Wedges

1 Cut the lemon into quarters (across and lengthwise) 2 Cut each quarter into 3 3 Remove pips

To whip cream

1 Pour cream into a basin–add a little castor sugar and flavouring
2 Whip with a fork to stiffness required

To chop jelly

1 Turn set jelly on to damp kitchen paper and chop quickly. The jelly must be very firm
Use as a garnish for cold sweets and savoury dishes that have been masked and coated with jelly
NB Jelly may be piped through a plain tube

To unmould jellies and creams

1 Put the mould quickly through hot water twice. Wipe. 2 Shake the mould sharply on to the hand and slip the jelly or cream on to a wet dish
NB The water should be a comfortable heat for the hand

Glaze (made with good stock)

1 Strain stock–reduce to a syrupy consistency

Glaze substitute

⅛lit/ ¼ pt water
30g/1 oz gelatine
1 tsp marmite or Oxo cube
1 Heat together and use as for glaze

Jam Glaze

1 Sieve apricot jam 2 Heat until clear 3 Add water if too thick 4 Colour if necessary

Arrowroot Glaze

⅛ lit/ ¼ pt water or fruit syrup
1 tsp arrowroot (scant)
colouring
1 Mix ingredients and bring to the boil 2 Stir all the time until mixture clears 3 Add colouring

Gelatine Glaze

⅛ lit/ ¼ pt syrup
1 tsp gelatine
colouring
1 Heat gelatine in syrup 2 Add colouring 3 Leave until nearly set

Clarifying Fat

Trimmings of fat
1 Put into a pan 2 Cover with water and boil with lid on for 20 minutes 3 Remove lid and allow water to evaporate 4 Reduce heat and continue to cook fat until skins only remain 5 Strain through muslin–leave to cool
NB Dirty fat may be cleansed in the same way

To colour desiccated coconut

1 Colour a small amount of warm water with pink or green colouring 2 Pour this over some coconut and stir to mix thoroughly 3 Allow to steep until colour is correct 4 Press out water 5 Dry coconut thoroughly and store
NB Chopped almonds may be coloured in the same way, and coloured green are used as mock pistachios

To make coconut infusion

1 Soak 30 grammes or 1 oz desiccated or fresh coconut in ¼ litre or ½ pt water 2 Bring slowly to the boil and infuse for 10 minutes 3 Wring in a piece of muslin to extract the liquid

Melba Toast

1 Cut very thin slices of bread and remove the crusts and cut diagonally 2 Put on to a baking tray in a slow oven and bake till pale brown–10–15 minutes 3 Serve in a basket in a folded napkin

To boil rice

1 Wash rice, put into a large pan of boil salted water with 1 tsp lemon-juice 2 Boil quickly–no lid, 10–12 minutes until *just* tender 3 Strain–run cold water through the rice 4 Spread on a plate or dish–cover and dry in a warm place turning occasionally

1

Starters

FRUIT JUICES

Orange, Lemon or Grapefruit Juice

1 orange, 1 lemon or 1 grapefruit
sugar

to serve: 1
time: 15 minutes
squeezer or juice-extractor

1 Wash the fruit **2** Squeeze or extract juice **3** Sweeten to taste **4** Chill **5** Serve in a glass

NB The juice may be served strained or unstrained.

Pineapple Juice

1 small pineapple
sugar

to serve: 2–3
time: 15 minutes
squeezer or juice extractor

1 Peel pineapple–remove 'eyes' and cut up, removing the hard core **2** Extract juice and sweeten to taste **3** Chill **4** Serve in a glass

Tomato Juice

230g/½ lb fresh or tinned tomatoes
1 tbsp vinegar
1 dessertsp sugar
1 tsp lemon-juice
salt
black pepper
Worcester sauce

to serve: 2–3
time: ½ hour
sieve or liquidizer

1 Wash tomatoes–pulp and strain **2** Add all ingredients, except Worcester sauce **3** Check seasoning **4** Add sauce to taste **5** Chill **6** Serve in a glass

FRUIT

Grapefruit

1 grapefruit
sugar
cherry

to serve: 2
time: 15 minutes
2 grapefruit glasses
grapefruit-knife

1 Cut grapefruit in half, remove the pips **2** Cut round inside skin and take out the core **3** Loosen the segments making sure they will come out easily **4** Sprinkle with a little sugar and flavour with sherry if liked—chill **5** Serve very cold in the skins, decorate with a cherry except when served for breakfast

Grapefruit Cocktail

1 grapefruit
melon
pineapple
orange
maraschino cherries
1 sprig mint
sherry or maraschino

to serve: 2
time: 15 minutes
2 grapefruit glasses

1 Prepare the grapefruit as usual **2** Remove the fruit and mix with the other fruit cut into suitably-sized pieces **3** Sweeten, but do not make too sweet **4** Add sherry or maraschino and put into glasses and chill **5** Top with a cherry and mint

Melon

1 honeydew or cantaloup melon

to serve: 4—8 according to size of melon
time: 10 minutes
small plates

1 Cut in slices, remove seeds, leave whole or cut in sections—chill **2** Serve garnished with thin slices of orange. Sugar and ground ginger are served separately

Melon Cocktail

1 honeydew or cantaloup melon
port wine or liqueur
stock syrup (page 315)

to serve: 4—8
time: 20 minutes
goblets
ball-cutter

1 Cut the flesh of a ripe melon into balls with the cutter **2** Macerate in a little syrup with port wine or a liqueur—chill thoroughly **3** Serve in the goblets

Melon en Surprise

1 melon
fresh fruit, e.g. pineapple, banana, peach, pear, grapes
stock syrup (page 315)
liqueur

to serve: 4
time: ½ hour
ice
1 plate

1 Cut the top off a ripe melon 2 Remove seeds and scoop out the flesh—cut into dice 3 Mix with cut fresh fruit 4 Moisten with syrup and liqueur 5 Fill the melon with this and serve on the plate surrounded with crushed ice

Small Melons with Water Ice

1 small melon
water ice (page 190)

to serve: 2
time: 1½ hours
2 small plates

1 Cut melon in half crosswise—remove seeds—chill 2 Fill centre with a water ice 3 Serve on the plates

Cantaloup Special

1 small cantaloup melon
1 tsp curry-powder
½ tsp ground ginger
½ wineglass full port
2 tbsp whipped cream
½ tbsp apricot purée
lemon-juice

to serve: 2
time: ½ hour
muslin
ball-cutter
1 plate

1 Cut melon in half, cut flesh into balls with a ball-cutter 2 Mix curry-powder, ginger and port, and strain through muslin 3 Add cream, apricot and lemon-juice 4 Pile the flesh of the melon back into the skins and pour the dressing over 5 Chill and serve

Avocado Pears

1 ripe avocado pear

1 The avocado pear may be served in the following ways—

Plain *(a)* Cut the pear in half and remove stone.

(b) Serve on a piece of lettuce very cold with a French dressing flavoured with Worcester sauce.

2 As above with a highly-seasoned tomato sauce

3 *(a)* Cut the flesh into small balls with a ball-cutter.

(b) Toss the balls in a little well-seasoned mayonnaise, French dressing or tomato sauce.

(c) Put back into the skin and serve as before: serves 2.

4 Fill the centres:
(a) With a mixture of shrimps and mayonnaise.
(b) With crab meat and French dressing.
(c) With prawns and mayonnaise.
Serve as before.

Avocado and Melon

ball-cutter

5 *(a)* Cut the avocado flesh into medium-sized balls with the cutter.
(b) Cut the same size and quantity from a ripe melon.
(c) Toss in a little French dressing.
(d) Serve very cold in glasses topped with chervil.

Green Prawn and Avocado

1 ripe avocado pear
6–8 prawns
mayonnaise (page 131)
1 tbsp spinach purée (frozen)
seasoning and lemon-juice
parsley, etc., to garnish

to serve: 2
time: 10 minutes
2 small plates

1 Cut pear in half and remove stone 2 Remove flesh and cube—stand in lemon juice 3 Mix mayonnaise and spinach, season, and add to pear—add prawns 4 Pile into pear skins and garnish with heads and cress

HORS-D'ŒUVRE

hors-d'œuvre dishes

Hors-d'œuvre Variés

Beetroot	(page 124)
Potato	(page 126)
Cucumber	(page 124)
Tomato	(page 125)
Mixed vegetables	(page 126)
Carrot	(page 125)

Mushrooms in White Wine (Champignons au vin blanc)

110g/¼ lb button mushrooms
1 tsp lemon-juice
oil
4 tbsp white wine
1 tbsp vinegar
seasoning

to serve: 3
time: 10 minutes
1 hors-d'œuvre dish

1 Wipe the mushrooms and sauté in a little oil 2 Cover with the other ingredients adding a little sugar if necessary 3 Cook for a few minutes 4 Cool and serve in the juices

Artichoke Bottoms (Fonds d'artichauts)

to serve: 3
time: 10 minutes
1 hors-d'œuvre dish

Marinade the bottoms for about 1 hour in oil or lemon-juice, seasoning and a little grated onion or crushed garlic. They may be finished in various ways–

1 With pimento, tomato and potato, bound with thick mayonnaise, piled on the fonds and sprinkled with chopped chives.
2 With salmon and mayonnaise, sprinkled with hard-boiled egg mixed with parsley.
3 With lobster, prawn or shrimp with mayonnaise, garnished with a small piece of the meat.
4 With vegetable salad with mayonnaise, garnished with a tiny ball of cauliflower.

Beetroot Cassolettes (Cassolettes de betterave)

1 large cooked beetroot
6 anchovy fillets
2 gherkins
1 hard-boiled egg
1 tsp chopped parsley
1 tsp chopped chives
pinch of mixed herbs
French dressing (page 131)
seasonings

to serve: 6 or 8
time: 25 minutes
25 mm/1 in. or 10 mm/½ in. cutters
1 hors-d'œuvre dish

1 Cut 6–8 small cassolettes from the beetroot, and marinade in the French dressing for 15 minutes **2** Cut the anchovy fillets, gherkins and white of egg into thin strips **3** Sieve the yolk and add the parsley, chives and herbs **4** Season well and moisten with a little dressing **5** Drain the cassolettes and fill them with the savoury mixture **6** Dish and garnish with the sieved yolk

Anchovy Fillets and Potato Salad

3 tbsp potato salad
6 anchovy fillets
1 hard-boiled egg
1 firm skinned tomato

to serve: 3
time: 15 minutes
1 hors-d'œuvre dish

1 Pile the salad in the dish and arrange the fillets in large rings on the top **2** Fill the rings with chopped egg **3** Cut the tomatoes in thin slices, cut these in half and arrange overlapping round the edge of the dish

Anchovy Fillets Mimosa

3 tbsp potato salad
6 anchovy fillets
1 hard-boiled egg
parsley

to serve: 3
time: 15 minutes
1 hors-d'œuvre dish

1 Put the potato salad in the dish and flatten slightly 2 Cut the fillets in half lengthways and arrange as lattice-work over the salad 3 Chop white of egg and sieve yolk 4 Put a border of the white round the edge of the dish and a border of the yolk inside–garnish with parsley

Anchovy Rolls (Paupiettes d'anchois)

1 cucumber
French dressing (page 131)
6 anchovy fillets
3 stuffed olives
2 tbsp crab, lobster or prawn meat
mayonnaise (page 131)
parsley

to serve: 6
time: 30 minutes
1 hors-d'œuvre dish

1 Peel the cucumber and cut into 25 mm/1 in. slices 2 Cut out the centre and marinade in the French dressing for 15 minutes 3 Chop up the meat and moisten with mayonnaise 4 Drain the cucumber and dish 5 Fill the cavity with the fish mixture 6 Twist an anchovy fillet round each and place a slice of stuffed olive on top and garnish with parsley.

Indian Pineapple Salad (Salade d'ananas à l'indienne)

1 small pineapple or a small tin
1 sour apple
1 small head celery
pimento or red pepper
mayonnaise (page 131)
seasoning

to serve: 3
time: 10 minutes
1 hors-d'œuvre dish

1 Cut pineapple into small pieces and cut apple and celery into shreds 2 Mix the three together, season and moisten with mayonnaise 3 Pile into the dish and garnish the top with thin strips of pimento and fine sprigs of celery 4 Serve very cold

Smoked Salmon

slices of thin smoked salmon
lemon
brown bread and butter

to serve: 1 slice per person
time: 5 minutes
1 small plate

1 Place a slice of salmon on a plate either flat or rolled up lightly 2 Garnish with small wedges of lemon 3 Serve rolls of very thin brown bread and butter.

Prawn Cocktail

4 prawns
1 tbsp mayonnaise (page 131)
1 tsp tomato purée
Worcester sauce
1 tsp mixed vinegars (tarragon, chilli, garlic)
seasoning, salad

to serve: 1
time: 10 minutes
1 goblet

1 Wash salad and reserve some small leaves for decoration 2 Break up the rest and put into the goblet 3 Add the prawns 4 Add seasonings to the mayonnaise and coat the prawns 5 Decorate with salad and prawn heads and serve very cold

NB Lobster may be used instead of prawns. Garnish with lobster claws.

Shrimps or Prawns Stanley (Crevettes à la Stanley)

⅛ lit/¼ pt pickled shrimps or prawns
4 tbsp mayonnaise
curry-powder or paste
lemon-juice
seasoning
hard-boiled egg

to serve: 3
time: 10 minutes
1 hors-d'œuvre dish

1 Season the mayonnaise with the curry and lemon-juice and add the shrimps or chopped prawns, keep a few for garnish 2 Pile in the dish and garnish with sliced egg and pieces of fish

Shrimp or Prawn Salad (Salade de crevettes)

⅛ lit/¼ pt pickled shrimps or prawns
mayonnaise or French dressing or tartar sauce (page 95)
chopped parsley

to serve: 3
time: 5 minutes
1 hors-d'œuvre dish

1 Mix the shrimps or chopped prawns with the chosen dressing keeping a few for garnish 2 Pile in the dish and garnish with chopped parsley and pieces of the fish

Scampi meunière

⅛ lit/¼ lb fresh or frozen Dublin Bay prawns
60g/2 oz butter
lemon
seasoning
brown bread and butter

to serve: 3
time: 10 minutes
3 small plates

1 Heat the butter and cook the prepared prawns for about 5 minutes 2 Put on to a hot dish, or the plates 3 Add seasoning and lemon-juice to the butter, heat and pour over the prawns 4 Garnish with lemon butterflies and parsley 5 Serve with brown bread and butter.

Asparagus Salad with Shrimps

½ bundle of asparagus or small tin of asparagus tips
⅛ lit/¼ pt picked shrimps
mayonnaise
paprika

to serve: 3
time: ½ hour
1 hors-d'œuvre dish

1 Cook and drain the asparagus, and lay in French dressing (page 131). 2 Moisten the shrimps with mayonnaise **3** Arrange the tips in a circle or ½ circle **4** Pile the shrimps in the centre or within the ½ circle **5** Sprinkle with paprika

Rollmop Herrings

2 fresh herrings
2 tsp salt } marinade
⅛ lit/¼ pt water } marinade
⅛ lit/¼ pt vinegar } marinade
1 small onion
1 bay-leaf
1 gherkin
chillies
pickling-spice

to serve: 4
time: 3 days
jars
cocktail-sticks

1 Fillet the herrings (page 31) and marinade for 2 hours 2 Put into a shallow dish, cover with vinegar and leave for a further 2 hours **3** Chop the onions, drain the fillets and put a little onion on each (keep the vinegar) **4** Roll up the fillets firmly and secure with wooden cocktail-sticks **5** Put into a jar with bay-leaf, chilli and gherkin **6** Boil the vinegar with the pickling-spice–cool, and strain over herrings 7 Cover jar and keep in a cool place
NB 1 The herrings are not cooked 2 The fillets may be divided into half for part of an hors-d'œuvre varié

2

Stocks and soups

STOCKS

Bone Stock

2 kg/4 lb beef bones
4 lit/4 qt cold water
1 carrot
1 turnip
1 onion
½ tsp salt
bay-leaf
10 peppercorns

time: 7 hours
stock pot or large saucepan

1 Wipe bones, trim off fat and marrow, chop or saw into small lengths 2 Soak in water 1 hour 3 Bring slowly to boil–skim off white scum–leave brown scum 4 Simmer 2 hours–add prepared vegetables in large chunks, herbs and salt 5 Simmer for a further 4 hours 6 Strain–allow to cool 7 Remove fat the following day 8 Store in a refrigerator or cold larder

Household or Second Stock

left-over bones, carcasses
cooked and uncooked meat, gristle, giblets
fresh vegetables
salt
peppercorns
bay-leaf
water

time: 2¼ hours
large pan or stock pot

1 Remove fat–put into the pan with vegetables and seasonings 2 Cover with cold water 3 Bring to the boil–skim–simmer 2 hours 4 Strain–remove fat when set

NB Avoid: foods containing starch, green vegetables, fat foods, cheese.

Brown or White Stock (First)

2 kg/4 lb shin beef or knuckle of veal, poultry or rabbit
4 lit/4 qt cold water
1 tsp salt
1 carrot
1 onion
celery
bay-leaf

time: 6½ hours
stock pot or large saucepan

1 Wipe meat and cut into cubes removing fat but not gristle or bones **2** Cover with cold water and allow to stand ½–1 hour **3** Bring slowly to boil and remove white scum **4** Add salt, flavourings and vegetables **5** Simmer gently 4–5 hours, skimming as necessary **6** Strain through sieve and throw away vegetables **7** When cold skim and use.

Meat Glaze

Any kind of stock; if very white colour with Marmite, Oxo, etc.

1 Strain and put in a large pan, removing any trace of fat **2** Boil hard with lid off, skimming if necessary **3** Reduce to the consistency of treacle, taking care not to burn **4** Pour into a small jar and keep in a cool place **5** When required for use, heat by standing in a pan of water. Use for glazing galantines, etc., and for enriching sauces and gravies.

Substitute glaze—dissolve 15g/½ oz gelatine in ⅛ lit/¼ pt of emergency stock and use when on the point of setting.

Vegetable Stock

450g/1 lb mixed vegetables
1 lit/1 qt water (cold)
bay-leaf
peppercorns
salt

time: 1 hour
large pan or stock-pot

1 Prepare the vegetables and cut up roughly **2** Put into the pan with water and seasonings **3** Simmer for approx. ¾ hour **4** Strain **5** Use as required

NB Vegetable stock must always be freshly made.

Fish Stock (1)

fish trimmings, e.g. fins, bones, heads (no eyes), skins
bay-leaf
parsley stalks
peppercorns
salt
cold water

time: 20 minutes
saucepan

1 Put fish into the pan with seasonings and cover with cold water
2 Simmer 10–15 minutes 3 Strain 4 Use as required
NB Fish stock must always be freshly made.

Fish Stock (2)

450g/1 lb whitefish bones and skins e.g. sole, haddock (not plaice)
60g/2 oz chopped onion
15g/½ oz parsley stalks
2 tsp lemon-juice
1 lit/2 pts water
4 tbsp white wine
30g/1 oz margarine
1 tsp salt
6 peppercorns

time: ¾ hour
strainer
large saucepan

1 Sauté the onions and bones in the fat–add the parsley 2 Add the wine and reduce to half–add water and salt 3 Bring to the boil and simmer for 20 minutes–add the lemon-juice 4 Skim and strain
Use as required
NB This stock can be reduced and used as fish glaze.

Court Bouillon (Stock used for cooking fish)

1½ lit/3 pt water
4 tbsp vinegars (mixed)
1 onion
1 carrot
bouquet garni (parsley, thyme, tarragon, bay-leaves, cloves, peppercorns)
salt

to make bouillon: 45 minutes
large pan

1 Slice onion and carrot 2 Put all ingredients into the pan and allow to simmer gently 30–40 minutes. Cool 3 Place fish in this liquid, cover and allow to poach in the oven or on top heat 4 If to be served cold, allow to cool in the liquid

NB
1 Wine may be used instead of vinegar, or mixed with vinegar.
2 Cider may be substituted.
3 The remaining liquid may be strained and used as the basis of a sauce for the fish, or as the liquid in Aspic Jelly.

Stock Substitutes

1 Water and Marmite or Bovril, Oxo, etc. 2 Stock cubes, e.g. beef, chicken, mushroom or vegetarian cubes 3 Vegetable water 4 Mix and use as a substitute for fresh stock

SOUPS

Mutton Broth

230g/½ lb scrag end neck mutton or veal, chicken or rabbit
½ lit/1 pt water
1 small carrot
1 turnip
1 onion
15g/½ oz pearl barley or rice
1 tsp chopped parsley
seasoning

to serve: 3
time: 2 hours
saucepan
soup-tureen

1 Blanch the barley to whiten and soften 2 Cut wiped meat into joints and remove as much fat as possible 3 Put into water with a little salt–bring to the boil, skim off white scum–leave brown 4 Prepare the vegetables and dice finely 5 Add vegetables, barley or rice and simmer gently 1½ hours 6 Take out the meat, remove it from the bone, cut into small pieces–return to the pan–reheat–check seasoning and consistency 7 Pour into a hot dish–if greasy run kitchen paper over the top to remove grease 8 Sprinkle chopped parsley on top

Scotch Broth

Use 230g/½ lb lean beef instead of mutton

Minestrone

2 tomatoes
230g/½ lb carrots
a small piece of turnip
2 stalks of celery
1–2 leeks or onions
1 rasher of streaky bacon
30g/1 oz butter or oil
1 clove of garlic
1 lit/1 qt of stock
seasoning
bouquet garni
30g/1 oz spaghetti
small cabbage heart
2 tbsp chopped parsley
cheese

to serve: 3–4
time: 2 hours
saucepan
soup-tureen
cheese-dish

1 Prepare the vegetables and cut into small pieces, dice or strips
2 Remove the rind and dice the bacon 3 Heat the fat and sauté the

bacon and vegetables for 7–10 minutes **4** Add the crushed garlic, stock, seasoning and bouquet garni, cover and simmer about 1 hour **5** Add the spaghetti and shredded cabbage heart and cook for a further ½ hour or until the vegetables are tender **6** Remove the bouquet garni and check the seasoning. Just before serving add parsley **7** Hand grated cheese separately

Mulligatawny Soup (Potage à la Mulligatawny)

340g/¾ lb lean beef
1 small carrot
1 small onion
30g/1 oz butter
30g/1 oz flour
¾ lit/1½ pt stock or 2 beef stock cubes
1 tsp curry-powder
1 tsp curry-paste
½ sour apple
bouquet garni
1 tbsp chutney
lemon-juice–seasoning
60g/2 oz cooked Patna rice

to serve: 3–4
time: 2½ hours
saucepan
liquidizer
soup-tureen
plate and paper

1 Cut up meat and vegetables in small pieces **2** Sauté in the butter and bacon pieces **3** Add flour, curry-powder and paste and cook for a few minutes **4** Add stock, chopped apple, bouquet garni, chutney, a little salt **5** Simmer for 1½–2 hours skimming when necessary **6** Take out a few pieces of meat to serve in the soup **7** Liquidize the remainder **8** Reheat–add lemon-juice and pieces of meat **9** Pour into a hot bowl and serve the rice separately on a plain paper sprinkled with paprika
NB 4 tbsp of cream or coconut milk is a great improvement to this soup.

Chicken Purée (Purée à la princesse)

15g/½ oz butter
15g/½ oz flour
½ lit/1 pt chicken stock or (1 chicken stock cube)
60g/2 oz cooked chicken
2 tbsp cream
seasoning
Melba toast (see Misc. Processes)

to serve: 3–4
time: 20 minutes
saucepan
liquidizer
soup-tureen
plate for toast

1 Make a roux with butter and flour **2** Add stock gradually and boil well **3** Cut up chicken and liquidize with some of the liquid **4** Add to rest of liquid and bring to the boil **5** Add cream and reheat without boiling **6** Serve with Melba toast **7** A *little* chopped parsley or chives may be sprinkled on top if liked

Kidney Soup

110g/¼ lb ox kidney

to serve: 3–4

110g/¼ lb lean beef
½ lit/1 pt brown stock or 1 beef stock cube
1 small onion
chopped parsley
45g/1½ oz butter
seasoning

time: 2¼ hours
saucepan
liquidizer
soup-tureen

1 Steep kidney for 10 minutes in tepid salted water **2** Cut kidney and beef into small pieces **3** Chop onion roughly **4** Sauté both in the butter for 10 minutes **5** Add stock and rice and simmer gently until tender–about 1½ hours **6** Liquidize and reheat–check seasoning and consistency **7** Pour into a hot bowl and sprinkle with the parsley

Oxtail Soup

½ oxtail (tail end)
1 lit/1 qt stock
30g/1 oz dripping
30g/1 oz flour
1 stalk celery or celery salt
carrot
turnip
onion
seasoning
bouquet garni and 6 peppercorns
lemon-juice
parsley

to serve: 4–6
time: 4½ hours; leave overnight; to finish–10 minutes
saucepan
liquidizer
soup-tureen

1 Divide the tail into joints–wash. blanch and dry **2** Melt the fat–fry the joints and vegetables–remove joints **3** Add the flour and make a brown roux **4** Add stock–boil–skim–add joints and simmer with bouquet and seasonings for 4 hours **5** Strain–remove fat when cold **6** Return to the pan and boil **7** Cut up some of the meat for garnish–liquidize the remainder in the soup **8** Season with lemon, salt, pepper, add meat and reheat **9** Serve in a hot bowl sprinkled with parsley

Consommés

1 lit/1 qt stock (⅓ white, ⅔ brown)
110g/¼ lb lean beef
4 tbsp cold water
carrot, turnip, onion
white and shell of one egg
bay-leaf, mace, peppercorns
salt as required
sherry

to serve: 3–4
time: 1½ hours
saucepan
liquidizer
jelly-cloth
soup-tureen or soup-cups

1 Liquidize meat and cold water and allow to stand for a short time **2** Remove all fat from stock **3** Cut vegetables into large pieces, and put all ingredients into the scalded pan **4** Whisk until boiling and allow to boil up three times **5** Infuse over *low heat* with lid half on for at least 1 hour **6** Strain through the cloth, three times or until clear, adding sherry during the straining **7** Reheat and pour over garnish

NB Consommé takes its name from its garnish. It may be served chilled, in which case serve in glasses topped with a small piece of parsley or chervil.

Garnishes

A la Julienne

1 dessertsp carrot
1 tsp turnip
1 tsp leek
1 tsp celery
1 tsp lettuce-leaf
15g/½ oz butter
⅛ lit/¼ pt stock
salt

time: 20 minutes

1 Shred all vegetables *very* finely, all the same length **2** Sauté in butter (not lettuce) **3** Cook in the boiling stock, adding lettuce for 1 minute **4** Strain–put into a hot bowl and pour the consommé over

A la Célestine

½ egg
15g/½ oz flour
2 tbsp milk
seasoning
chopped parsley
1 tsp parmesan (grated)
pinch mixed herbs (small)
15g/½ oz butter

time: 20 minutes
kitchen paper
omelet pan

1 Make a batter in the usual way (page 153) **2** Add other ingredients and seasoning **3** Melt some butter and fry batter as for pancakes **4** Drain thoroughly on paper **5** Cut into very thin and even shreds **6** Put into bowl and pour the consommé over

A la royale

1 yolk egg
2 tbsp stock
salt

time: ½ hour
muslin
dariole-mould
foil
bain-marie
small cutters

1 Strain stock through muslin–heat **2** Pour on the yolk–season **3** Strain into well-greased dariole-mould–cover **4** Steam or cook in bain-marie in the oven until firm **5** Turn out and cut into small fancy shapes–pour the consommé over

A la Carmen

1 tsp boiled Patna rice
1 tsp red sweet pepper (or tinned) cut into Julienne strips

time: 10 minutes

1 If fresh pepper–parboil **2** Put into bowl and pour the consommé over

A la Jardinière

1 tsp peas (cooked)
1 tsp carrot (cooked) and cut into balls
1 tsp turnip (cooked) and cut into balls
1 tsp cauliflower sprigs

time: 20 minutes
ball-cutter

1 Cook in stock and put into the bowl 2 Pour the consommé over

Consommé à la Mulligatawny

To main recipe add 1 tsp curry-powder
1 tsp lemon-juice
Cooked chicken

plate for rice

1 Mix curry powder with meat and water–liquidize–stand for 15 minutes 2 Proceed as in main recipe 3 Serve with a garnish of neatly-cut cooked chicken in the soup and Patna rice served separately

Chilled Consommé

Consommé served chilled in glasses topped with parsley or chervil

Potato Soup

450g/1 lb potatoes
1 onion
1 celery stalk or celery salt
30g/1 oz margarine
1 tsp flour
seasoning
½ lit/1 pt white stock or chicken stock cube
parsley
⅛ lit/¼ pt milk
croûtons of toast or fried bread

to serve: 3–4
time: 50 minutes
saucepan
liquidizer
soup-tureen
croûton-dish

1 Prepare vegetables and chop roughly 2 Sauté in the melted fat 3 Add stock and seasoning–simmer till vegetables are tender–sieve or liquidize 4 Blend flour with a little milk–add to purée with remaining milk 5 Bring to the boil–check seasoning and consistency 6 Serve in the hot bowl, sprinkled with parsley 7 Serve croûtons separately

Lentil Soup

110g/4 oz lentils
½ lit/1 pt water or stock
1 small onion
30g/1 oz dripping or bacon rinds
a piece of celery
bouquet garni

to serve: 3–4
time: 2 hours
saucepan
liquidizer
soup-tureen
croûton-dish

tomato (optional)
salt and pepper
croûtons
chopped parsley

1 Wash lentils, chop vegetables roughly 2 Melt fat or extract fat from bacon 3 Add onion and lentils and sauté 7–10 minutes 4 Add liquid, bring to the boil and simmer 1½ hours adding tomato and bouquet garni 5 Remove bouquet garni and sieve or liquidize 6 Reheat, season and check consistency, thin down with stock if necessary 7 Cream may be added if liked 8 Serve sprinkled with parsley and hand croûtons separately

Onion Soup

450g/1 lb onions
30g/1 oz margarine
30g/1 oz flour
⅛ lit/¼ pt milk
seasoning
½ lit/1 pt light stock or chicken stock cube
4 tbsp cream
chopped parsley
grated cheese

to serve: 3–4
time: 45 minutes
saucepan
liquidizer
soup-tureen
cheese-dish

1 Melt fat–chop onions roughly and sauté 2 Add stock and boil till the onions are tender 3 Sieve or liquidize 4 Reheat–blend flour with milk and add to purée–boil 5 Add cream–reheat and serve in the hot bowl sprinkled with parsley 6 Serve grated cheese separately

Leek Soup

Use the white part of leeks instead of onions

Tomato Soup

½ lit/1 pt tinned tomatoes and ¼ lit/½ pt stock
or
450g/1 lb fresh tomatoes and ½ lit/1 pt stock
1 small carrot
1 small onion
30g/1 oz bacon or margarine
pinch of mixed herbs
15g/½ oz cornflour
seasoning–sugar
croûtons of toast or fried bread

to serve: 3–4
time: 1¼ hours
saucepan
muslin
liquidizer
strainer
soup-tureen
croûton-dish

1 Prepare carrot and onion–chop roughly 2 Sauté with the bacon or margarine for 10 minutes 3 Add tomatoes (if fresh washed and cut up) stock, herbs tied in muslin and a little salt 4 Bring to boil–cook for ¾ hour 5 Remove bouquet and liquidize and strain 6 Blend cornflour

with a little cold water and add to the above 7 Bring to the boil, stirring and boil for a few minutes 8 Pour into the hot bowl and garnish with parsley 9 Serve the croûtons separately
NB For cream of tomato soup add 4 tbsp of cream or evaporated milk–heat, but do not boil.

White Vegetable Soup

1 carrot
1 turnip
1 onion
1 cabbage-leaf
a small leek
1 small stick celery
bay-leaf
30g/1 oz flour
30g/ 1 oz margarine
¼ lit/½ pt milk
¾ lit/1½ pt boiling water
salt and pepper
chopped parsley

to serve: 4
time: 1 hour
saucepan
shredder
soup-tureen

1 Prepare vegetables, shred finely 2 Melt margarine, add vegetables, sauté 7–10 minutes–shake occasionally 3 Pour ¾ lit/1½ pt boiling water on to vegetables–add seasoning and bay-leaf 4 Boil until vegetables are tender and volume reduced by half–remove bay-leaf 5 Blend flour with milk–add and stir until boiling–check seasoning and consistency 6 Pour into the hot dish, sprinkle with parsley

Mushroom Soup

230g/½ lb mushrooms or stalks (half stalks and half mushrooms)
½ lit/1 pt light stock or stock cube
30g/1 oz butter
30g/1 oz flour
⅛ lit/¼ pt milk
½ onion
½ stick celery or celery salt
lemon-juice
1 tsp chopped parsley
4 tbsp evaporated milk or cream
croûtons

to serve: 3–4
time: 1 hour
saucepan
liquidizer
soup-tureen
croûton-dish

1 Wash stalks and mushrooms 2 Melt butter and add stalks, onion, celery and mushrooms, chopped roughly (save 2 mushrooms for garnish) 3 Sauté for a few minutes–pour on stock 4 Simmer until stalks are soft–liquidize 5 Rinse pan and return purée, adding blended flour and milk 6 Stir until boiling–simmer for a few minutes 7 Sauté whole mushrooms in a little extra butter 8 Season, add cream, parsley and lemon-juice just before serving–add sautéd mushroom cut in strips–*do not let the soup boil after these have been added* 9 Serve with croûtons of fried bread

Cream of Celery Soup (Potage crème de céleri)

1 good head of celery
1 medium-sized onion
60g/2 oz butter
½ lit/1 pt milk or milk and stock
1 blade mace
1 bay-leaf
6 peppercorns
30g/1 oz flour
1 yolk of egg
4 tbsp cream
seasoning–croûtons of fried bread
chopped parsley

to serve: 3–4
time: 50 minutes
saucepan
strainer
liquidizer
soup-tureen
croûton-dish

1 Wash celery, chop onion and sauté in the butter **2** Add the flour and cook for a few minutes without browning **3** Bring milk slowly to the boil with the spices and bay-leaf–strain **4** Add gradually to the celery and simmer gently until tender **5** Liquidize and add yolk of egg and cream and heat without boiling–dish and sprinkle with parsley **6** Serve with croûtons

Green Pea Purée (Purée de pois verts)

½ lit/1 pt peas or a medium packet frozen peas
small bunch of parsley
small bunch of mint
½ lit/1 pt white stock or 1 chicken stock cube
4 tbsp cream
seasoning
fried croûtons

to serve: 3–4
time: 35 minutes
saucepan
liquidizer
soup-tureen
croûton-dish

1 Bring the stock to the boil **2** Add a little salt, peas, parsley and mint **3** Cook until tender–liquidize **4** Reheat–add cream and check seasoning and consistency **5** Pour into the hot bowl and serve croûtons separately

NB If using fresh peas, include the pods, but in this case the soup must be sieved and not liquidized

Cream of Watercress Soup

2 bunches watercress
1 leek
½ lit/1 pt light stock–or a chicken stock cube
4 tbsp cream or evaporated milk
salt, cayenne pepper
30g/1 oz butter
30g/1 oz flour
croûtons

to serve: 3–4
time: 1 hour
saucepan
liquidizer
soup-tureen
croûton-dish

1 Wash watercress, remove stalks **2** Chop leek and sauté in the butter with watercress 3 Add stock and seasonings and simmer for 30 minutes 4 Liquidize and reheat–adjust seasonings and consistency 5 Add cream–do not reboil 6 Serve with fried croûtons

Asparagus Purée (Purée d'asperges)

450g/1 lb Jerusalem artichokes
1 onion
30g/1 oz butter
½ lit/1 pt light stock or stock cube
salt and pepper
15g/½ oz flour
¼ lit/½ pt milk
4 tbsp cream
croûtons of fried bread
chopped parsley

to serve: 3–4
time: 1 hour 40 minutes
saucepan
liquidizer
soup-tureen
croûton-dish

1 Wash and peel the artichokes very thinly adding lemon juice or vinegar to the water to preserve the colour 2 Melt the butter and sauté the chopped onion and sliced artichokes 3 Add stock, season and cook for about 1 hour–liquidize 4 Add flour blended with the milk and cook for a few minutes 5 Add cream and reheat without boiling–dish and sprinkle with parsley 6 Serve with the croûtons

Cream of Cucumber Soup

1 large cucumber
½ lit/1 pt boiling light stock or stock cube
30g/1 oz margarine or butter
30g/ 1 oz flour
⅛ lit/¼ pt milk
4 tbsp evaporated milk or cream
green colouring
salt and pepper
croûtons

to serve: 3–4
time: 50 minutes
saucepan
liquidizer
soup-tureen or soup-cups
croûton-dish

1 Wash cucumber, remove skin and cut into pieces 2 Bring stock to boil, add the cucumber–cook until tender, 10–15 minutes–liquidize 3 Melt butter, add flour, then the purée by degrees, and boil well 4 Add milk and seasoning, then evaporated milk or cream–reheat *Do not boil* 5 Add colouring to give cucumber shade–check consistency–dish 6 Serve with croûtons
NB This soup may be served chilled with a thin slice of unpeeled cucumber on top.

Asparagus Purée (Purée d'asperges)

1 tin asparagus or 230g/½l fresh asparagus–see note
½ lit/1 pt white stock or chicken stock cube

to serve: 4–5
time: 35 minutes
saucepan
liquidizer

15g/½ oz butter
15g/½ oz flour
¼ lit/½ pt milk
4 tbsp cream
seasoning
croûtons of fried bread or Melba toast
(see Misc. Processes)

soup-tureen
croûton dish

1 Make a roux with the butter and flour **2** Add stock and milk and bring to boil **3** Add asparagus, reserving a few tips for garnish **4** Simmer until tender–about 10–15 minutes–liquidize **5** Heat and add cream **6** Season and add green colouring if necessary, adjust consistency–dish, add garnish **7** Serve with the croûtons or Melba toast

NB If fresh asparagus is used allow extra time for cooking.

Cream of Cauliflower Soup (Crème de choux-fleurs or Crème Dubarry)

1 medium cauliflower
30g/1 oz butter
½ lit/1 pt white stock or 1 chicken stock cube
15g/½ oz cornflour
⅛ lit/¼ pt milk
4 tbsp cream
1 yolk of egg
seasoning
croûtons of fried bread or Melba toast
(see Misc. Processes)

to serve: 4
time: 40 minutes
saucepan
liquidizer
soup-tureen
croûton-dish

1 Prepare cauliflower and divide into sprigs **2** Sauté in the butter **3** Add the stock and a little salt and cook until tender **4** Keep back a few sprigs for garnish and liquidize the remainder **5** Blend the cornflour with the milk and add to the purée and bring to the boil **6** Mix yolk and cream and add to the soup–check seasoning and consistency and heat without boiling–dish **7** Add the sprigs divided into very small pieces **8** Serve with croûtons or Melba toast

Hollandaise Soup

30g/1 oz butter
30g/1 oz flour
½ lit/1 pt white stock or chicken stock cube
salt and pepper
1 egg-yolk
¼ pint milk
4 tbsp cream

to serve: 4
time: 30 minutes.
saucepan
strainer
ball-cutter
soup-tureen

Garnish
1 tbsp peas
1 tbsp carrot
1 tbsp cucumber
} cut with the ball-cutter

1 Cook the vegetables in boiling salted water, drain 2 Make a roux with butter and flour, add stock and boil well 3 Mix the yolk, cream and milk together and strain into the soup 4 Reheat gently to cook the yolk and until vegetables are suspended 5 Check seasoning and dish

Crème Solférino

1 small carrot
1 onion
1 leek
60g/2 oz tomato pureé
230g/½ lb potatoes
30g/1 oz fat bacon
15g/½ oz flour
bouquet garni
salt and pepper
⅛ lit/¼ pt milk
½ lit/1 pt white stock or chicken stock cube
croûtons

to serve: 4
time: 1 hour
saucepan
liquidizer
soup-tureen
croûton-dish

1 Extract fat from the bacon 2 Sauté roughly chopped vegetables (except potatoes) 3 Add flour–cook for 2 minutes 4 Add stock, tomato purée, seasoning, bouquet garni–bring to the boil–add sliced potatoes 5 Simmer till tender 6 Remove bouquet garni–liquidize 7 Bring to the boil–add milk and check seasoning and consistency 8 Serve in the hot bowl–handing croûtons separately

Brown Vegetable Soup

1 carrot
1 turnip
1 onion
1 small head celery or celery stalks
2 tomatoes, fresh or tinned
¾ lit/1½ pt stock or 2 stock cubes
30g/1 oz flour
30g/1 oz dripping
seasoning
chopped parsley
croûtons

to serve: 4–5
time: 1 hour
saucepan
liquidizer
soup-tureen
croûton-dish

1 Prepare vegetables, cut into large pieces and dry as much as possible (not tomatoes) 2 Melt dripping–when smoking add the vegetables and fry till light brown–turn on to a plate 3 Add flour to fat in pan–make a brown roux 4 Add stock–bring to the boil–return vegetables, add skinned tomatoes and salt and cook quickly until vegetables are tender 5 Liquidize–return to the rinsed pan–heat–check seasoning and consistency 6 Serve soup in the hot dish and sprinkle with parsley

Chestnut purée (Purée de marrons)

230g/½ lb chestnuts

to serve: 4

1 onion (small)
15g/½ oz butter
½ lit/1 pt white stock or 1 chicken stock cube
4 tbsp cream
seasoning
fried croûtons or Melba toast (see Misc. Processes)

time: 1¼ hours
saucepan
liquidizer
soup-tureen
croûton-dish

1 Slit the chestnuts and boil for 10 minutes **2**Remove the skins and break in pieces **3** Melt the butter and sauté chestnuts and chopped onion **4** Add stock and simmer until chestnuts are tender–liquidize **5** Add cream and check seasoning and consistency–reheat without boiling–dish **6** Serve with the croûtons or Melba toast

Lobster Bisque (Bisque d'homard)

lobster shell
a little of the cooked meat
½ lit/1 pt fish stock (page 10)
30g/1 oz butter
30g/1 oz ground rice
1 small onion
1 small piece carrot
1 bay-leaf
spring parsley
salt
cayenne
lemon-juice
1 tsp anchovy essence
4 tbsp cream
4 tbsp sherry
15g/½ oz coral or paprika butter

to serve: 4
time: 1¼ hours
saucepan
strainer
soup-tureen

1 Wash and break up the shell **2** Melt butter, sauté onion, carrot, bay-leaf and parsley **3** Add ground rice and shell and stock **4** Simmer 40 minutes **5** Strain, add anchovy essence, cream, sherry and lemon juice **6** Reheat without boiling **7** Whisk in the butter and add lobster meat **8** Check seasoning and consistency–dish

Crème Vichyssoise

6 small leeks
15g/½ oz butter
1 potato (fairly large)
½ lit/1 pt white stock or chicken stock cube
⅛ lit/¼ pt cream or evaporated milk
salt and pepper
chopped chives

to serve: 4
time: 3 hours
saucepan
liquidizer
soup-tureen or soup-cups

1 Cut the white part of leeks in thin slices **2** Prepare and chop potato **3** Cook leeks and potato very slowly in the butter without browning **4** Add stock and a little salt and cook gently until tender–liquidize **5** Cool, add cream and check seasoning and consistency **6** Chill and

serve sprinkled with chopped chives
NB This soup may be served pale green by adding a small packet of frozen peas, with leeks and potatoes, i.e. vichyssoise verte.

Summer Pea Soup

230g/½ lb shelled peas (290g/10 oz packet frozen peas)
1 lettuce
½ lit/1 pt chicken stock or stock cube
salt and pepper
1 medium potato
1 medium onion
⅛ lit/¼ pt cream or evaporated milk
juice of ½ lemon
mint

to serve: 4
time: 3 hours
saucepan
liquidizer
soup-tureen or soup-cups

1 Put peas, sliced onions and potato, quartered lettuce and half chicken stock into the pan–bring to boil **2** Cover–simmer 15 minutes–liquidize **3** Add remaining stock and simmer 5 minutes **4** Add cream, lemon-juice and seasoning–check seasoning and consistency–chill **5** Dish–sprinkle with chopped mint

Chilled Spanish Soup (Gazpacho)

450g/1 lb tomatoes–fresh or tinned
1 green pepper
1 onion
¼ cucumber
1 tbsp vinegar
1 tbsp oil
60g/2 oz fresh breadcrumbs
1 clove of garlic
⅛ lit/¼ pt tomato-juice
seasoning and lemon-juice
chopped parsley or chives

to serve: 4–5
time: 2 hours
liquidizer
soup-cups or glasses

1 Skin the fresh tomatoes and cut up removing hard centre **2** Remove seeds from pepper and blanch **3** Skin cucumber **4** Put all ingredients into the liquidizer–liquidize and strain **5** Correct consistency, adding a little more tomato-juice if necessary **6** Season and add lemon juice **7** Chill and serve in glasses sprinkled with chopped parsley or chives

Avocado Pear Soup (Chilled)

1 ripe avocado pear
⅜ lit/¾ pt white stock or chicken stock cube
⅛ lit/¼ pt cream
seasoning
lemon-juice
paprika

to serve: 4–5
time: 2 hours
liquidizer
soup-cups or glasses

1 Cut the pear in half, remove stone and scoop out all the flesh **2** Put into the liquidizer with the stock and liquidize for 1 minute 3 Add the cream and liquidize for ½ minute 4 Turn into a jug or basin and add salt, pepper and lemon-juice to taste–check consistency 5 Chill thoroughly 6 Serve in cups or glasses with a sprinkle of paprika

3
Fish

Poached Fish

230g/½ lb fresh white fish fillet
⅛ lit/¼ pt milk and water or fish stock
bay-leaf
salt and pepper
lemon-juice

to serve: 2
time: ½ hour
Yorkshire-pudding tin
foil or greaseproof paper
oven No. 3 or 170 °C/335 °F

1 Wash, dry and skin the fish **2** Put in the tin and add the liquid seasoning **3** Cover and bake 15–20 minutes **4** Drain and use as required–use the liquid to make sauce
NB White wine may be used as part of the liquid.

To Poach Smoked Fish

time: 40 minutes

1 Wash the fish **2** Soak for ten minutes in cold water **3** Drain and poach as white fish

White Fish Dishes

230g/½ lb fillet of white fish (plaice, haddock, etc.)
or
2 fish cutlets

to serve: 2
time: 30–40 minutes

1 Poach the fish–drain (page 26) **2** Arrange on a hot dish **3** Coat with the sauce **4** Garnish according to the kind of sauce

Sauce	Garnish
⅛ lit/¼ pt white	parsley, lemon butterflies, grapes, paprika
⅛ lit/¼ pt cheese	raspings, parsley
⅛ lit/¼ pt parsley	lemon butterflies
⅛ lit/¼ pt shrimp	parsley, paprika
⅛ lit/¼ pt tomato	parsley, potato balls, raspings
⅛ lit/¼ pt brown	raspings, potato balls, parsley, lemon butterflies

Steamed Fish

230g/½ lb white fish
salt and pepper
butter
lemon-juice
lemon
parsley

to serve: 2
time: ½ hour
saucepan of boiling water
covered plate
foil or greaseproof paper

1 Wash, dry and skin the fish—cut into portions 2 Season, place on the plate, add butter and lemon juice 3 Cover and put on pan and, if using greaseproof, cover with a lid or basin 4 Steam for 15–20 minutes 5 If serving plain—pour liquid round or serve as for white fish dishes (page 26)

Fish Pie

230g/½ lb cooked white fish, e.g. cod, haddock, etc.
230g/½ lb mashed potato mixture (page 107)
⅛ lit/¼ pt coating sauce
seasoning
lemon butterflies
parsley

to serve: 2
time: ½ hour
pie-dish
grill

1 Flake up the fish 2 Put into the hot sauce—season well and put into the dish 3 Spread hot potato mixture on top 4 Decorate with a fork 5 Brown under the grill 6 Serve on a dish on a plain paper with parsley and lemon butterfly garnish

Russian Fish Pie

110g/¼ lb rough puff or puff pastry (page 229) or frozen pastry
110g/¼ lb white or smoked fish—cooked (page 26)
⅛ lit/¼ pt white sauce
1 hard-boiled egg
chopped parsley
egg for glazing

to serve: 3
time: 1 hour
baking-tray
oven No. 7 or 220 °C/425 °F

1 Roll pastry into a 200 mm/8 in. square—turn over and put on the dry baking tray 2 Flake fish and mix with the sauce—season well. Set aside to cool 3 When quite cold—place mixture on pastry, cover with sliced egg 4 Damp edges of pastry—fold corners to centre and pinch edges together. Glaze with egg 5 Roll out pastry trimmings and cut into leaves—attach to joins—glaze 6 Bake for 20 minutes. Reduce to oven No. 4 or 180 °C/355 °F—leave for a further 10–20 minutes 7 Serve hot—on a plain paper, garnished with parsley 8 Serve accompanied by a colourful vegetable

Kedgeree

110g/¼ lb cooked smoked fish
60g/2 oz patna rice
60g/2 oz margarine or butter
salt and nutmeg
cayenne pepper
1 hard-boiled egg
1 tsp chopped parsley
1 tbsp milk

to serve: 2
time: 25 minutes

1 Cook the rice in boiling water for 12–15 minutes **2** Rinse and dry **3** Chop white of egg and sieve yolk **4** Melt the fat, add milk, rice, flaked-up fish and chopped white **5** Put into a small vegetable dish and decorate with the yolk and parsley **6** Stand on a plate on a plain paper
NB Tinned or white fish may be used as an alternative.

Scalloped Fish

⅛ lit/¼ pt coating sauce
110g/½ lb mashed potatoes
110g/¼ lb cooked fish
seasoning
raspings and cheese

to serve: 2
time: 25 minutes
scallop shells
or individual dishes
grill
nylon bag
No. 8 vegetable-forcer

1 Pipe mashed potato round edge of scallop shells **2** Flake fish, add to the sauce, season **3** Put this mixture into the border of potatoes **4** Sprinkle with raspings and cheese **5** Brown under the grill **6** Serve on plain paper on a plate, garnish with parsley
NB White or smoked fish may be used.

Fish Cakes

110g/¼ lb cooked potato
110g/¼ lb cooked fish, e.g. smoked or fresh (page 26)
a little egg for binding
pinch nutmeg
seasoning
30g/1 oz margarine
egg and raspings
parsley

to serve: 2
time: 1 hour
deep-fat pan
thermometer (optional)

1 Sieve potato **2** Flake up fish, removing skin and bones **3** Melt margarine–add fish and potato **4** Add about 1 dessertspoon of egg and heat thoroughly **5** Add seasonings and turn on to a plate to cool **6** Divide into four **7** Shape into cakes–egg and crumb–reshape **8** Fry in hot fat 180 °C/355 °F for 3–4 minutes–drain well **9** Serve on an oval dish on a plain paper and garnish with parsley **10** Serve tomato sauce separately
NB These may be fried in shallow fat if liked.

Grilled Sole

1 medium sole
30g/1 oz maître d'hôtel butter (page 102)
lemon
salt and pepper
butter or lard for brushing

to serve: 1
time: 20 minutes
kitchen roll
grill

1 Wash fish–dry–remove fins **2** To remove skin–*(a)* Cut across skin at tail end *(b)* 'Thumb' up the sides *(c)* Ease skin from tail cut, and pull off from tail to head *(d)* repeat on second side *(e)* Trim tail to a point **3** Remove head and gut–wash, dry **4** Brush with melted fat–season **5** Make three incisions across fish to bone on either side of fish (not opposite each other) **6** Place on the greased grill and grill the better side second, for approx. 3–4 minutes each side **7** Serve on an oval dish with maître d'hôtel butter on fish and lemon wedges at head end

Fried Fish

230g/½ lb fresh white fish fillet
seasoned flour
egg
raspings
lemon

to serve: 2
time: 25 minutes
deep-fat pan
thermometer
kitchen roll

1 Wash fish and dry, skin and cut into portions **2** Dip in seasoned flour **3** Brush with egg–coat with raspings–firm on the raspings and re-shape the fish **4** Fry at 180 °C or 350 °F for 3–6 minutes according to the thickness of the fish **5** Drain very well **6** Serve on an oval dish and plain paper–garnish with lemon wedges and parsley
NB Cutlets or whole small fish may be served this way.

Fried Plaice Fillets

1 plaice
egg
raspings
1 tbsp seasoned flour
lemon
parsley

to serve: 2–4
time: 50 minutes
kitchen roll
deep fat
thermometer (optional)
filleting-knife

1 Wash fish–dry **2** Remove head close to bone–cut off fins **3** Remove gut and clean–wash and dry

To fillet **1** With dark side uppermost cut across the tail skin to the bone **2** Cut down centre back line to the bone **3** Remove left fillet–stroking the knife against the bone **4** Reverse fish–remove remaining fillet **5** Turn fish over and repeat Nos. 3–4

To skin **1** Place fillet skin side down on a board **2** Push flesh off skin with the knife

To coat 1 Dip fillets in the seasoned flour 2 Brush with egg 3 Toss in crumbs 4 Firm-on crumbs and reshape

To cook 1 Fry in deep or shallow fat at approx. 180 °C/360 °F until golden brown 2 Drain well 3 Serve garnished with lemon wedges and parsley

Fried Sole

1 medium sole
seasoned flour
egg and raspings
lemon
parsley
tartar sauce (page 95)

to serve: 2
time: 50 minutes
filleting-knife
kitchen roll
deep-fat pan
thermometer (optional)

1 Prepare sole–*(a)* skin as for grilled sole (page 29)–gut *(b)* fillet as for plaice (page 29) 2 Dip fillets in seasoned flour, coat with egg and raspings–firm on crumbs–reshape 3 Lower into fat pan at 180 °C/ 355 °F, twisting each fillet 4 Fry for approximately 3 minutes 5 Drain well 6 Serve on plain paper on an oval dish with lemon wedges 7 Hand tartar sauce separately

Whitebait

110g/¼ lb whitebait
3 tbsp seasoned flour
lemon
brown bread and butter

to serve: 1
time: 15 minutes
kitchen roll
deep-fat pan and basket
thermometer (optional)

1 Wash the whitebait and put on the paper to dry 2 Toss a few at a time in the flour 3 Put into the frying basket 4 Heat the fat to at least 205 °C or 400 °F 5 Cook for 1 minute 6 Drain well, and serve very hot piled on a plain paper with wedges of lemon and brown bread and butter

Fried Fish in Batter

230g/½ lb white fish fillet
⅛ lit/¼ pt coating batter (page 153)
parsley
lemon
seasoned flour
⅛ lit/¼ pt suitable sauce, e.g. tomato

to serve: 2
time: 20 minutes
skewer
kitchen roll
deep or shallow fat
thermometer (optional)

1 Skin fish–cut into portions 2 Coat with the flour 3 Dip in batter–drain on a skewer 4 Fry in deep fat 170 °C or 350 °F for 4–5 minutes 5 Drain well 6 Serve on a plain paper on an oval dish garnished with lemon wedges and parsley 7 Serve sauce separately
NB If fried in shallow fat the fish must be turned during cooking.

Baked Stuffed Cod Cutlets

2 tail-end cod cutlets
1 tbsp breadcrumbs
½ tbsp suet
1 tsp parsley–chopped
salt and pepper
lemon-rind and -juice
egg to bind
(1 tbsp breadcrumbs to egg to bind: stuffing)
butter

to serve: 2
time: 45 minutes
kitchen roll
baking-tin
oven No. 4 or 180 °C/355 °F

1 Wash fish, wipe–bone 2 Mix stuffing ingredients with egg to a soft consistency 3 Stuff the cutlets 4 Sprinkle with lemon-juice, salt and pepper and put a knob of butter on top 5 Bake on the greased tin until cooked–20-25 minutes 6 Serve on an oval dish with plain paper–garnish with parsley 7 Hand tomato, parsley or tartar sauce separately

NB 1 May be served on a dish with sauce poured round
2 Any white fish cutlets may be used.

Fish Mould

230g/½ lb white fish
2 tbsp fresh breadcrumbs
2 tbsp suet
4 tbsp milk or milk and fish stock
½ tsp chopped parsley
1 egg
seasoning
⅛ lit/¼ pt coating sauce

to serve: 2
time: 1 hour; in dariole-moulds ½ hour
foil
steamer
125 mm/5 in. greased pudding-basin or tin or 4 dariole-moulds

1 Skin, bone and flake up the fish finely 2 Put in a bowl and add the suet, parsley, breadcrumbs, liquid and beaten egg 3 Season and mix very thoroughly 4 Put into the prepared tin and cover with foil 5 Steam ¾ hour or until firm (in dariole-moulds approx. 15 minutes) 6 Turn out and coat with sauce

NB The sauce may be egg, parsley, shrimp, etc.

Herrings

time: 10 minutes
kitchen roll
salt

To prepare

1 Wash well

2 Remove scales from tail to head using a knife (preferably in a bowl of water)

3 Remove fins from tail to head

4 Remove head–make a slit 50 mm/2 in. long in underside of fish

5 Draw out the gut and break the blood clot–save the roe

6 Wash very well–dry

To bone

time: 5 minutes

1 Cut to tail on underside
2 With skin uppermost press the backbone with thumb and finger and press fish flat–turn over
3 Lift the tail end of the backbone with a knife and pull it out from tail to head removing any small bones that are left
4 Remove black internal skin by rubbing with salt

Fried Herring

1 herring
seasoned flour
egg
raspings or oatmeal
lemon
parsley
mustard sauce (page 90)

to serve: 1
time: 25–30 minutes
kitchen roll
deep or shallow-fat pan
thermometer (optional)

1 Prepare the herring (page 31) 2 Bone–season–fold in half 3 Dip in seasoned flour 4 Coat with egg and raspings or oatmeal–firm on the coating 5 Fry in deep fat 170 °C/350 °F for 4–5 minutes 6 Drain well 7 Serve on a plain paper on an oval dish with lemon wedges and parsley garnish 8 Hand mustard sauce separately
NB If using shallow fat turn after 3 minutes

Grilled Herrings

1 herring
maître d'hôtel butter (page 102)
seasoning
seasoned flour
lemon

to serve: 1
time: 25–30 minutes
kitchen roll
greased grill

1 Prepare herring–bone (page 31) 2 Sprinkle with salt and pepper and fold in half 3 Dip in seasoned flour 4 Grill for approx. 4 minutes each side 5 Serve on an oval dish with maître d'hôtel butter and garnished with parsley and lemon wedges

Baked Stuffed Herrings

2 herrings
stuffing:
1 dessertsp chopped or shredded suet
1 tbsp breadcrumbs
grated rind of lemon
egg
salt and pepper
pinch of mixed herbs,
½ tsp chopped parsley

to serve: 2
time: 1 hour
kitchen roll
foil
baking-tray
oven No. 3 or 170 °C/335 °F

1 Prepare and bone herring (page 31) 2 Mix dry stuffing ingredients and bind into a soft mixture with egg 3 Open out herring, place stuffing

inside—fold herring over, wrap loosely in greased foil **4** Place on the tray—cook 15 minutes **5** Turn on to a hot dish—Garnish with parsley and lemon butterflies

Soused Herrings

3 herrings
4 tbsp water
4 tbsp vinegar
2 slices onion
bay-leaf
1 tsp pickling spice
parsley stalks
salt, pepper

to serve: 3, or 6 if for hors-d'œuvre
time: 1¼ hours; cold, 3 hours
kitchen roll
casserole
oven No. 3 or 170 °C/335 °F

1 Put spices and flavourings into the dish with salt, vinegar and water **2** Bone herrings (page 31), cut lengthwise, season and roll up from head to tail—Place in liquid, cover and bake for ¾ hour **3** Serve hot in strained liquid—Garnish with parsley **4** To serve cold, allow to cool in the liquid—Serve with salad or as hors-d'œuvre

Filets de sole à la rouennaise

1 sole
60g/2 oz lobster farce (see lobster cutlets, page 40)
⅛ lit/¼ pt cardinal sauce (page 90)
fish stock (page 10)
chopped black olives
seasoning—lemon-juice
paprika butter (page 102)

to serve: 2–4
time: 40 minutes
foil
kitchen roll
Yorkshire-pudding tin
oven No. 3 or 170 °C/335 °F

1 Skin and fillet the sole (page 29) season with salt and lemon juice **2** Spread fillets with lobster farce—fold in half, place on the tin—pour over a little fish stock **3** Cover with foil and poach about 15 minutes **4** Make the sauce, add the cream and colour with paprika butter—check seasoning **5** Arrange the fillets, overlapping down the centre of a hot dish **6** Coat with the sauce **7** Garnish with olives in a line down centre of fillets

Sole bonne femme

1 medium sole
4 tbsp white wine
small piece carrot and onion
pinch mixed herbs
seasoning
hollandaise sauce (page 95)
2 small mushrooms
30g/1 oz butter
lemon juice
1 dessertsp finely chopped parsley
seasoning

to serve: 2–4
time: 1¼ hours
foil
kitchen roll
Yorkshire-pudding tin
oven No. 3 or 170 °C/335 °F
nylon bag
No. 8 vegetable forcer
grill

230g/½ lb duchess potato mixture
(page 108)
egg for glazing

1 Wash and fillet the sole (page 29)–season and fold in half, skinned side inside–make stock using fish skins, etc. 2 Put fillets in the tin, add carrot, onion, herbs 3 Pour over the wine and 4 tbsp stock 4 Cover with foil and poach 10–15 minutes 5 Sauté chopped mushrooms in butter and lemon juice 6 Make hollandaise sauce using 2 tbsp of stock as a base 7 Add to it the mushrooms and parsley 8 Put fish on a hot dish with fillets overlapping 9 Strain liquid into a pan and reduce quickly to 2 tbsp and add to the sauce 10 Coat the fish 11 Pipe the potatoes round the edge–glaze 12 Brown lightly under a very hot grill

Sole à la Mornay (Sole with Cheese Sauce)

1 medium sole
⅛ lit/¼ pt coating sauce–made with
fish stock
2 tbsp grated parmesan cheese
½ lb duchess potato mixture
(page 108)
4 tbsp single cream or evaporated milk
seasoning

to serve: 2
time: 1 hour
kitchen roll
foil
Yorkshire-pudding tin
oven No. 3 or 170 °C/335 °F
grill
nylon bag
No. 8 vegetable forcer

1 Fillet the sole (page 29)–make fish stock 2 Fold fillets, season and poach 10–15 minutes 3 Put on to a hot dish overlapping down the centre 4 Add cream and two thirds of the cheese to the sauce–season 5 Coat the fish and sprinkle with remaining cheese 6 Pipe the potato round the outside 7 Brown under the pre-heated grill

Sole véronique

1 medium sole filleted (page 29)
2 heaped tbsp green grapes
⅛ lit/¼ pt coating sauce made with
fish stock
seasoning
1 tbsp single cream
1 tbsp white wine
lemon-juice

to serve: 2
time: 1 hour
foil
kitchen roll
Yorkshire-pudding tin
oven No. 3 or 170 °C/335 °F

1 Make fish stock with the pieces of fish left after filleting 2 Fold fillets in half after seasoning–skinned side inside 3 Put into the tin with the wine, a little stock and lemon juice 4 Cover and bake 10–15 minutes 5 Remove the pips from the grapes and heat in a little wine–lid on 6 Arrange the fillets, overlapping on a hot dish 7 Strain the liquid and add to the sauce 8 Add the cream, heat and check consistency and seasoning 9 Coat the fillets and garnish with the grapes

Fish à la meunière

Fillets of sole (4), fresh haddock, plaice, etc., or 2 small trout
1 dessertsp seasoned flour
60g/2 oz butter
1 lemon
chopped parsley

to serve: 2
time: ½ hour
kitchen roll
frying-pan

1 Dry the fish and coat in the seasoned flour 2 Fry until golden brown in *half* the butter 3 Put on to a hot dish 4 Skim the butter and add the remainder to it–heat 5 Add 1 tsp of lemon-juice and the chopped parsley 6 Pour over the fish and garnish with lemon butterflies

Filets de sole à la merluche fumée

1 medium sole
salt, pepper
lemon-juice
fish stock

Smoked Haddock Farce
2 tbsp cooked, smoked haddock
knob butter
1 tsp flour
2 tbsp fish stock
seasoning
Sauce: ⅛ lit/¼ pt hollandaise sauce (page 95)

to serve: 2
time: 1¼ hours
kitchen roll
Yorkshire-pudding tin
foil
deep/or shallow-fat pan
oven No. 3 or 170 °C/335 °F

1 Make a sauce with butter, flour and liquid 2 Add the haddock finely flaked–season 3 Fillet the sole (page 29) 4 Spread the fillets with some of the farce and fold in half 5 Put in the tin, add fish stock and cover 6 Bake 10–15 minutes 7 Use remaining farce to make very small balls 8 Coat with egg and raspings–fry (in butter if using shallow fat) 9 Dish the fillets, overlapping down the centre of a hot dish 10 Coat with the hollandaise sauce 11 Garnish with the fried balls
NB Any white fish may be used to make a more economical dish, e.g. fillet of fresh haddock. A less rich hollandaise sauce may be used, i.e. one which has a base of white sauce (page 89).

Sole à la Colbert

1 medium sole
30g/1 oz maître d'hôtel butter (page 102)
parsley
egg and raspings
1 dessertsp seasoned flour
lemon wedges (3) for garnish

to serve: 1
time: ½ hour
kitchen roll
scissors
deep-fat pan
thermometer (optional)

1 Skin the sole, remove head and trim off tail and fins 2 Half fillet on one side 3 Coat with seasoned flour, egg and raspings 4 Turn back flaps on half-filleted side 5 Cut through bone at top and bottom and down sides, using scissors 6 Fry 3–4 minutes at 170 °C/340 °F
7 Remove the bone and put on a dish, on a plain paper 8 Put maître

d'hôtel butter in the centre **9** Pile fried parsley on top **10** Garnish with lemon at head end

Sole in Aspic

1 sole
aspic jelly (page 209) or
1 packet aspic
cucumber, red pepper, black olives, etc. } for decoration

to serve: 2
time: 1½ hours
foil
kitchen roll
Yorkshire-pudding tin
4 dariole-moulds
oven No. 3 or 170 °C/335 °F

1 Fillet the sole (page 29) season–roll up–poach **2** Set a layer of aspic jelly in the moulds–set a layer of decoration–cover with a thin layer of aspic jelly **3** Place one rolled fillet in the mould–set in aspic **4** Fill the mould with aspic–set **5** Turn out **6** Serve on a dish with salad garnish and surround with chopped aspic jelly

"Boiled" Salmon

450g/1 lb tail-end salmon

time: 25 minutes
fish-kettle or large saucepan

1 Wash thoroughly in salted water **2** Plunge into boiling water to cover **3** Reduce heat and simmer allowing 10 minutes per 450g/1 lb plus 10 minutes–if very thick allow a little longer **4** Drain very thoroughly **5** If using frozen salmon add 1 tbsp oil to the water

To boil salt fish
1 Put into cold water and bring to the boil
2 Simmer till tender

Grilled Salmon

1 salmon steak
pat of maître d'hôtel butter (page 102)
oil
vinegar
seasonings
cucumber salad (page 124)

to serve: 1
time: 45 minutes
kitchen roll
greased grill

1 Wash the fish **2** Make a marinade with the oil, vinegar and seasonings **3** Allow the fish to lie in this for about ½ hour turning several times **4** Grill 4–5 minutes on each side **5** Dish on a hot dish adding the maître d'hôtel butter and garnishing with parsley and cucumber **6** Serve with cucumber salad

Salmon Mousse

230g/½ lb cooked salmon
or tinned salmon
1 tbsp tomato purée

to serve: 4–5
time: 1½–1¾ hours
liquidizer

⅛ lit/¼ pt aspic jelly
2 tsp gelatine
⅛ lit/¼ pt coating white sauce
⅛ lit/¼ pt cream or evaporated milk
2 whisked egg whites
Decoration: cucumber skin, black olives, etc.
Accompaniments: green salad, cucumber salad (pages 126, 124)

110 mm/4½ in soufflé-mould
foolscap paper
rubber band

1 Prepare the mould by putting the paper round the outside–keep in place with the rubber band 2 Liquidize the salmon and sauce 3 Put into a bowl and add the tomato purée, half-whipped cream and seasoning 4 Dissolve the gelatine in the aspic jelly 5 Add to salmon mixture and stir until on point of setting 6 Fold in the whisked whites and pour into the prepared mould–set 7 When set cover top with a thin layer of aspic–set 8 Decorate and cover with a layer of aspic jelly–set 9 Remove the paper and dish on a plate with a plain paper 10 Serve with salad and cucumber

Salmon Mayonnaise

450g/1 lb tail-end salmon cooked (page 36) or 1 salmon steak
aspic jelly (page 209) or 1 packet aspic jelly
mayonnaise (page 131)
salad garnish
cucumber cornets
black olives, cucumber-skin, red pepper, lemon
cucumber salad (page 124)

to serve: 4 or 1
time: 1 hour
muslin

1 Bone and skin the cold salmon and reshape 2 Coat with a mixture of ⅔ mayonnaise and ⅓ aspic jelly (tammied) allow to set 3 Decorate 4 Coat with a layer of aspic jelly–set 5 Place on a bed of lettuce on an oval dish 6 Decorate with cress and cucumber cornets 7 Serve with the cucumber salad

Prawns in Aspic

18 prawns, picked
aspic jelly (page 209) or 1 pkt aspic jelly
decorations (pepper, cucumber, etc.)
1 hard-boiled egg
2 tbsp cream
2 tbsp mayonnaise
cress

to serve: 3–4
time: 1–1¼ hours
110 mm/4 in charlotte-mould
75 mm/2½ in diameter dariole-mould
ice

1 Decorate the bottom of the mould 2 Set a layer of prawns, etc 3 Stand a dariole-mould in the centre 4 Fill the mould in layers as the first layer 5 Mix cream and mayonnaise, add a few chopped prawns and 2 tbsp aspic–stir, until on point of setting 6 Remove the dariole-mould by filling with a little hot water 7 Fill the space with cream

mixture 8 When set turn out on an oval dish and garnish with chopped aspic–prawn-heads and cress

Trout Caprice

2 rainbow trout
1 tbsp chopped fresh herbs
1 tbsp fresh breadcrumbs
egg to bind
1 tbsp melted butter
seasoned flour
60g/2 oz butter for frying
½ orange
½ lemon
1 banana
chopped parsley

kitchen roll
frying-pan

1 Clean fish and remove backbone (see herring, page) **2** Make a farce with the breadcrumbs, herbs, egg and melted butter. Season **3** Fill the fish with this farce **4** Roll in seasoned flour **5** Using half the butter, fry the fish until golden brown–keep warm **6** Cut banana in half lengthwise and fry in the remaining butter **7** Cut some round of orange and lemon, with the skin on **8** Squeeze the juice from the remaining fruit **9** To dish, put the fish on a hot dish, place a banana on each **10** Add chopped parsley and fruit-juice to the fat left in the pan **11** Heat and pour over fish **12** Decorate with the rounds of orange and lemon

Crabe garni (Dressed Crab)

1 medium-sized crab
2 tbsp French dressing (page 131)
1 tbsp fresh breadcrumbs
seasoning
1 tsp finely chopped parsley
½ hard-boiled egg
large pat green or coral butter

to serve: 1–2
time: 1¼ hours
skewer
a weight
oil
paper forcing-bag
No. 8 icing-forcer

1 Wash crab and twist off claws and feelers **2** Separate upper from lower shell and keep latter intact for dishing **3** Remove and discard *(a)* Spongy gills[1] *(b)* Stomach–hard sac near the head **4** Remove meat from the body and break off shell at natural line **5** Wash the shell and oil the outside **6** Crack the claws and remove all the meat **7** Mix white meat with the dressing and dark meat with the breadcrumbs–season **8** Fill the shell, putting the dark meat at the bottom and white meat on top *or* dark meat in the centre and white meat each side **9** Decorate with chopped parsley, sieved yolk and finely chopped white **10** Pipe with coloured butter **11** Serve on a plain paper and garnish with the small feelers

NB If hot crab is preferred, use white sauce instead of dressing, sprinkle breadcrumbs on top–heat and brown under a grill. Garnish with parsley and feelers.

[1] "Dead men's fingers."

To Prepare a Lobster

1 boiled lobster

time: ½ hour
kitchen roll
weight
skewer

1 Twist off the claws and feelers–crack and remove the flesh 2 Split the lobster down the back lengthways–open out. Remove the 'dead-men's-fingers,' the hard stomach sac (just below the head) and discard 3 Take out all the flesh 4 Keep claws for garnish 5 Use as required

Lobster Borealis (Homard Boréalis)

1 cooked lobster
30g/1 oz butter
4 tbsp sherry
1 tsp tomato purée
⅛ lit/¼ pt coating white sauce
2 tbsp thin cream
Garnish
230g/½ lb duchess potato mixture (page 108)
1 hard-boiled egg
4 medium mushrooms
beaten egg

to serve: 2–3
time: 1¼ hours
kitchen roll
weight
skewer
nylon bag
No. 8 vegetable-forcer
No. 8 icing-forcer
grill

1 Prepare the lobster (page 39) 2 Cut up the flesh into fairly large pieces 3 Pipe the duchess potato mixture round an entrée dish 4 Glaze and brown in the oven or under the grill 5 Sauté the lobster meat in the butter 6 Add sherry, tomato purée, sauce and some of the cream–season 7 Prepare and cook mushrooms (whole) 8 Sieve the egg yolk and bind with a little cream–season 9 Put lobster mixture inside potato border 10 Pipe egg yolk round mushrooms and fill the centre with chopped whites 11 Garnish the lobster with these mushrooms and the claws

Lobster Thermidor

1 cooked lobster
⅛ lit/¼ pt coating sauce
4 tbsp cream
¼ tsp dry mustard
1 tsp Worcester sauce
1 tbsp sherry
1 tbsp grated parmesan cheese
paprika, butter, seasoning
watercress

to serve: 1–2
time: 1 hour
kitchen roll
weight
skewer
grill

1 Prepare lobster and keep the shell (page 39) 2 Cut meat into large

cubes 3 Add cream to sauce 4 Combine the mustard with the Worcester sauce and sherry 5 Add to sauce and check seasoning 6 Add lobster meat 7 Fill the shell with this mixture 8 Sprinkle with the parmesan cheese and dot with butter 9 Brown under the grill–sprinkle with paprika 10 Dish on a plain paper 11 Garnish with watercress and the lobster claws

Lobster Cutlets (Côtelettes d'homard)

110g/4 oz lobster meat
30g/1 oz butter
30g/1 oz flour
⅛ lit/¼ pt fish stock or water
1 yolk of egg
seasoning–lemon-juice
egg and raspings
fried parsley

to serve: 3
time: 1¼ hours
deep-fat pan
thermometer (optional)

1 Make a sauce with the butter, flour and liquid **2** Add lobster meat finely chopped **3** Add yolk and heat gently **4** Season and turn out on a plate to cool **5** Divide into six even-sized pieces **6** Shape into cutlets and coat with egg and raspings twice **7** Fry at 180 °C/360 °F for 3–4 minutes **8** Place a lobster claw to simulate the bone in each cutlet **9** Dish on an oval dish with a plain paper 'bone' to the left **10** Garnish with fried parsley

Lobster Newburg

1 cooked lobster
  or tinned lobster
60g/2 oz butter
1 tbsp brandy
4 tbsp cream
1 yolk of egg
paprika
seasoning
90g/3 oz cooked patna rice

to serve: 3
time: 1¼ hours
kitchen roll
weight
skewer

1 Prepare lobster (page 39) **2** Sauté lobster pieces in the butter for a few minutes **3** Add heated brandy **4** Combine egg yolk and cream in a basin **5** Heat gently over a pan of hot water until mixture coats the spoon **6** Add lobster and season **7** Add paprika **8** Serve on the rice **9** Garnish with watercress and lobster claws
NB This mixture may be used to fill bouchée-cases.

Savoury Cream

110g/¼ lb lobster, crab, prawn or fish
  of any kind

to serve: 3–4
time: 2 hours

$\frac{1}{8}$ lit/¼ pt cream or evaporated milk
4 tbsp aspic jelly
1 dessertsp mayonnaise
4 tbsp tomato juice
1 tsp gelatine
ice
175 mm/7 in border-mould

To decorate: aspic jelly—salad, black olives, cucumber skin, etc.

1 Mask a border mould with aspic jelly **2** Decorate with neatly-cut pieces of olive, cucumber skin and small pieces of fish used if suitable, e.g. prawn **3** Dissolve the gelatine in the tomato juice **4** Whip cream or evaporated milk **5** Add aspic jelly, mayonnaise and fish cut into small pieces **6** Season and add gelatine mixture **7** Stir until on point of setting—mould and turn out when set **8** Decorate with salad, chopped aspic and suitable pieces of fish used, e.g. prawn heads, lobster claws, etc.

NB Serve as a cold fish entrée, or as a buffet dish made in dariole-moulds.

4
Meat, poultry and game; stuffings

MEAT

Beef
2 kg/4 lb boned sirloin
1 kg/2 lb topside of beef
1½ kg/3 lb rolled ribs

Lamb
1½–2 kg/3–4 lb leg of lamb
1 kg/2 lb best end of neck of lamb
1½ kg/3 lb shoulder of lamb
1 kg/2 lb loin of lamb

Pork
2 kg/4 lb leg of pork
1 kg/2 lb loin of pork
1 kg/2 lb pork shoulder

kitchen roll
roasting-tin
trivet
oven No. 6 or 205 °C/400 °F

Veal
1½ kg/3 lb leg of veal
1 kg/2 lb loin of veal
1 kg/2 lb fillet of veal

General method (1) **1** Wipe the meat–prepare–tie or skewer (metal) if necessary **2** Place on a trivet pouring 4 tbsp of oil on top **3** Put into the preheated oven for 15 minutes to seal **4** Reduce to No. 4 180 °C/355 °F and cook required time–basting every 20 minutes **5** Serve on a large oval dish **6** Hand gravy separately

Preparation of meat **1** Meat may be cooked on the bone or boned and rolled
For beef and lamb and veal Rub cut surfaces with salt
For pork Rub crackling with salt, sugar and oil–score well
Cooking time
Beef–on the bone: 15 minutes per ½ kg/lb and 15 minutes over
Beef–boned: 20 minutes per ½ kg/lb and 20 minutes over
Lamb–on the bone: 20 minutes per ½ kg/lb and 20 minutes over
Lamb–boned: 25 minutes per ½ kg/lb and 25 minutes over
Pork–on the bone: 25 minutes per ½ kg/lb and 25 minutes over
Pork– boned: 30 minutes per ½ kg/lb and 30 minutes over

Veal—on the bone: 25 minutes per ½ kg/lb and 25 minutes over
Veal—boned: 30 minutes per ½ kg/lb and 30 minutes over
NB Beef may be cooked 'rare,' or moderately well done or well done.
Oil may be used instead of dripping.

Accompaniments

Beef—Yorkshire pudding and/or horse-radish sauce Lamb—mint sauce or mint jelly, red-currant jelly Pork—apple sauce, sage jelly Veal—lemon—bacon rolls	} Thin gravy

Stuffed joints **1** Add 5 minutes per ½ kg/1 lb to the cooking time

Accompaniments

Pork—sage-and-onion stuffing Veal—veal force-meat Lamb—veal force-meat or sage-and-onion stuffing	} Thickened gravy

General method of roasting (2)

Joints as previously	kitchen roll foil oven No. 7 or 220 °C/425 °F

1 Pre-heat oven **2** Wipe the meat—prepare as before **3** Place meat in centre of oiled foil on a roasting-tin—wrap in a *loose* parcel—press edges lightly together to prevent opening **4** Roast according to time **5** 15 minutes before the end of the cooking time remove from the oven and turn back the foil—return to oven to brown

For pork—open 20–25 minutes before cooked to give crisp crackling.

Roasting times

	Approx. weight		*Approx time per ½ kg/lb*	
Beef	1 kg/2–2½ lb	Rare	25–30 mins	No. 7 or 220°C/425°F
		Med.	30–35 mins	
		Well done	35–40 mins	
	2 kg/4–4½ lb	Rare	20 mins	
		Med.	20–25 mins	No. 7 or 220 °C/425 °F
		Well done	25–30 mins	
Lamb	1–2 kg/2½–4½ lb		35 mins	No. 7 or 220 °C/425 °F
Rolled stuffed joints	1 kg/2 lb		40 mins	No. 7 or 220°C/425 °F
Pork	1 kg/2 lb		40–45 mins	No. 7 or 220°C/425 °F
	2 kg/4½ lb		35 mins	No. 7 or 220°C/425 °F

NB1 The flavour is retained and the meat is more tender
2 The shrinkage is reduced
3 The meat does not require basting
4 The oven remains clean

Boned, Stuffed Best End Neck Lamb

680g/1½ lb best end neck lamb

farce:
- 2 tbsp fresh breadcrumbs
- ½ tbsp suet or margarine
- pinch mixed herbs
- 2 tsps chopped parsley
- grated lemon-rind
- salt, pepper
- egg to bind

dripping or oil

to serve: 3–4
time: 1¾ hours
oven No. 7 or 220 °C/425 °F
roasting-tin
trivet
string

1 Remove skin **2** Remove bones–starting at top of ribs and working to vertebrae (use bones for stock) **3** Spread stuffing from below 'eye.' **4** Roll from thick to thin end–Tie and weigh **5** Cook as for roast, stuffed joints **6** Serve with thick gravy

NB Breast of lamb may be used instead of best end of neck

Braised Lamb or Veal

680g/1½ lb best end neck of lamb or veal

Farce. Mix all together and bind with egg:
- 2 tbsp breadcrumbs
- 1 tbsp suet
- ½ tsp chopped parsley
- pinch mixed herbs
- ¼ lemon (grated rind)
- egg–seasoning

mirepoix:
- 1 tbsp chopped bacon pieces
- 1 tbsp oil
- 1 carrot
- 1 onion
- peppercorns–mace-cloves

about ¾ pt stock
espagnole sauce (page 92)
macédoine of vegetables:
peas, carrot balls cut from above
button mushrooms

to serve: 3–4
time: 2 hours
kitchen roll
oven No. 3 or 170 °C/335 °F
braising-pan
string
foil
ball-cutter

1 Remove skin and some fat from meat **2** Bone, stuff, roll and tie in shape–weigh **3** Put oil in braising pan and when very hot, fry meat quickly, to brown evenly all over **4** Fry mirepoix and bones of meat **5** Pour off all fat **6** Put meat on top of mirepoix **7** Pour on stock to come to top of mirepoix–cover top of pan with foil **8** Put on lid and cook gently for time calculated by weight (half that time stewing on top and half that time in oven) **9** Place meat on a hot dish and strain liquid in pan **10** Reduce this to a glaze–brush meat **11** Pour the espagnole sauce round **12** Garnish with the macédoine sautéd in butter

Mixed Grill

1 lamb's cutlet
1 sausage or 2 chipolatas
1 bacon rasher
1 sheep's kidney
1 tomato
1–2 mushrooms
Garnish
watercress,
maître d'hôtel butter (page 102)
potato crisps (page 111)

to serve: 1
time: ½ hour
kitchen roll
skewers
grill

1 Wipe tomato–cut in half 2 Wipe or peel mushrooms 3 Prick sausages 4 Make bacon rolls (see Misc. Processes) 5 Steep kidney, skin, open and core 6 Wipe cutlet–trim off surplus fat–taper, or bone and roll 7 Brush all ingredients with oil or fat and season–brush the grid 8 Have grill on full, put grid in lower position 9 After calculating cooking time, grill in sequence 10 Serve on hot oval dish–no paper, cutlet bone to the left 11 Garnish with watercress and maître d'hôtel butter and potato crisps

Liver and Bacon

230g/½ lb calf's or pig's liver
2 rashers bacon
⅛ lit/¼ pt stock
seasoned flour
dripping if necessary

to serve: 2
time: ½ hour
kitchen roll
frying-pan
strainer

1 Steep liver in tepid salt water for 7–10 minutes 2 Remove rind and any bone from bacon and fry (dry fry), add rinds to extract fat 3 Remove bacon from pan and put on heated oval dish 4 Dry liver, cut into thin slices. Coat in the seasoned flour 5 Put into the pan–fry quickly on either side–reduce heat and cook very gently till cooked through–put on dish 6 Remove any bits from the pan–add 1 tsp flour–brown–add stock–boil–season –taste 7 Arrange liver neatly on the hot dish, bacon on top–and strained gravy round 8 Serve with potatoes and a colourful vegetable

Stuffed Liver

230g/½ lb sliced liver (pig's, calf's or lamb's)
3–4 streaky rashers
¼ lit/½ pt stock or stock cube
1 tbsp seasoned flour
2 tbsp breadcrumbs
1 tsp chopped parsley
1 tbsp chopped onion
lemon rind
salt and pepper
egg to bind
(farce: the seven items above, seasoned flour to egg to bind)
parsley to garnish

to serve: 2
time: 1¼ hours
kitchen roll
oven No. 4 or 180 °C/355 °F
roasting-tin

1 Steep liver in tepid salt water for 10 minutes 2 Mix ingredients for farce–

bind loosely with egg **3** Dry liver, trim, dip in seasoned flour–place in the tin **4** Put a little farce on each slice of liver–put a rasher of bacon on top **5** Pour on the stock and cook for ¾ hour **6** Place meat on an oval dish, thicken stock and pour round–garnish with parsley

Irish Stew

230g/½ lb middle neck mutton, or breast
450g/1 lb potatoes
1 large onion
salt and pepper
stock or chicken-stock cube
chopped parsley

to serve: 2–3
time: 2 hours
kitchen roll
meat-saw

1 Wipe and joint the meat, remove fat and gristle **2** Put in a pan and cover with stock **3** Bring to the boil, skim **4** Prepare vegetables, slice half potatoes and all onions, add to the meat with seasoning **5** Simmer gently 1½ hours **6** Half an hour before dishing add remaining potatoes, whole or halved and steam on top of stew

To serve Make a border of the whole potatoes, pile meat in centre, pour liquid over, sprinkle meat with chopped parsley. Excess liquid may be served in a sauce-boat.

Fricassée of Veal, Chicken or Rabbit

230g/½ lb lean veal, chicken or rabbit joints
1 onion
salt and pepper
8 button mushrooms
bay leaf, mace, peppercorns
30g/1 oz butter
30g/1 oz flour
⅛ lit/¼ pt liquid from veal or chicken or rabbit
⅛ lit/¼ pt milk
lemon-juice
1 yolk of egg
4 tbsp cream or evaporated milk
fried croûtons
bacon rolls
lemon butterflies
parsley

to serve: 2
time: 1 hour 40 minutes
a heavy pan
frying-pan
strainer

1 Cut veal into moderate-sized pieces, onions into chunks–leave rabbit or chicken as joints **2** Put meat into pan with ⅜ lit/¾ pt water–bring slowly to boil–skim well **3** Add onion, herbs, mushrooms, salt and pepper–simmer till tender (1 hour) **4** Prepare bacon rolls (see Misc. Processes) **5** Strain off stock remove herbs and onion **6** Make sauce in rinsed pan with butter, flour, milk and stock–add meat **7** Correct seasoning, add lemon-juice, cream or evaporated milk and yolk **8** Grill bacon rolls or cook in oven–fry triangular croûtons **9** Serve on an oval dish–meat and mushrooms in centre, sauce strained round–bacon rolls in piles at either end–place croûtons round the edge–butterflies down the centre–garnish with parsley in the centre of butterflies

Summer Stew

230g/½ lb middle neck of lamb
450g/1 lb small new potatoes
4 new carrots
110g/¼ lb peas
stock or chicken stock cube
chopped parsley–seasoning

to serve: 2
time: 2 hours
meat-saw
kitchen roll

1 Wipe meat and cut into joints and remove as much fat as possible **2** Put into a pan with 3 or 4 sliced potatoes, 1 sliced carrot, and a little salt **3** Cover with stock and bring to boil–skim and simmer 1½ hours **4** Add peas, remaining carrots and potatoes half an hour before dishing **5** To dish, make a border of the whole potatoes, pile meat and other vegetables in the centre–sprinkle with parsley

Brown Stew

450g/1 lb chuck steak, skirt, flank or shin
30g/1 oz flour
30g/1 oz dripping
1 carrot
1 turnip
1 onion
½ lit/1 pt liquid (stock or beef stock cube)
seasoning
parsley

to serve: 3–4
time: 2½ hours
kitchen roll
strong pan
wooden spatula or spoon

1 Wipe, trim and cut meat into cubes **2** Fry meat in smoking dripping–stir **3** Remove meat leaving fat in pan–add flour and make a brown roux (i.e. fry slowly till chestnut brown) add more dripping if necessary **4** Add stock–bring to the boil, stirring, skim. Add meat, chopped onion, half carrot and half turnip cut roughly **5** Simmer gently for 2 hours stirring and skimming occasionally **6** Dice remaining vegetables and boil as a garnish **7** Season, taste, check consistency **8** Serve in an entrée-dish, meat down the centre and sauce poured over–garnish with piles of cooked vegetables sprinkled with chopped parsley

Beef Olives

340g/¾ lb top side or buttock steak
1 medium onion
1 medium carrot
1 stick celery *or* celery salt
30g/1 oz dripping

to serve: 3
time: 2½ hours
kitchen roll
string or cotton
strong pan

30g/1 oz flour
⅜ lit/¾ pt stock or stock cube
salt and pepper

deep-fat pan
thermometer
strainer

Farce
1 tbsp fresh breadcrumbs
1 tbsp chopped suet or prepared suet
2 tsp chopped parsley
pinch of mixed herbs
lemon-juice
½ egg
salt and pepper

1 Make farce by mixing all the dry ingredients together–season and bind with egg **2** Cut meat into thin slices across the grain **3** Spread each slice thinly with stuffing, roll and tie **4** Prepare and slice vegetables **5** Melt fat and fry meat, remove and fry vegetables **6** Remove vegetables and add flour to fat and make a brown roux **7** Add stock, bring to boil and season **8** Replace meat and vegetables, simmer till tender, approx. 1½ hours **9** Remove tie from meat and arrange on serving dish **10** Strain sauce and pour round meat **11** Garnish with forcemeat balls, coated and fried in deep fat at 180 °C/355 °F

NB Espagnole sauce may be used (page 92)

Ragoût of Veal, Chicken or Rabbit

450g/1 lb lean veal, chicken or rabbit joints
4 rashers
4 small carrots
2 small onions
30g/1 oz flour
⅜ lit/¾ pt stock
1 slice of bread for triangular croûtons
seasoning

to serve: 4
time: 2½ hours
kitchen roll
1 heavy pan
deep-fat pan
thermometer

1 Cut meat into large squares–leave joints whole **2** Prepare rashers and fry lightly–put on a plate **3** Fry meat in the bacon fat **4** Add flour and make a brown roux (it may be necessary to add a little extra fat) **5** Add stock, bring to boil and skim **6** Add meat and whole vegetables **7** Simmer gently for 1½ hours, skimming when necessary **8** Ten minutes before dishing, stan the plate of rashers on top of the pan to heat **9** Pile meat in the centre of a hot dish, arrange vegetables at each end and pour the sauce over **10** Place bacon on top and fried croûtons round the edge

NB Croûtons may be fried in shallow fat

Hot Pot

230g/½ lb chump chops or lean beef
e.g. topside or buttock steak
1 tbsp seasoned flour
¼ lit/½ pt stock or beef stock cube

to serve: 2
time: 2½ hours
kitchen roll
foil

2 small onions
340g/¾ lb potatoes
parsley
dripping

oven No. 3 or 170 °C/335 °F
casserole

1 Wipe the meat–trim and cut into neat joints 2 Dip in seasoned flour 3 Arrange in a casserole in layers with the sliced vegetables–finish with a layer of sliced potatoes 4 Pour in stock and place shavings of dripping over potatoes 5 Cover with foil and cook for 1½ hours–remove foil and cook for further ½ hour to brown potatoes 6 Serve in the casserole on plain paper on a plate or dish–garnish the top with parsley

NB Last layer of potato may be in knobs instead of slices

Goulash

230g/½ lb stewing steak or pie veal
30g/1 oz dripping or butter
1 onion
30g/1 oz flour
bouquet garni
1 dessertsp paprika
⅜ lit/¾ pt stock
1 dessertsp tomato purée
seasoning
230g/½ lb fresh tomatoes or ¼ lit/½ pt tinned
2 tbsp white wine
Garnish
4 tbsp cream or evaporated milk
spaghetti, macaroni or noodles

to serve: 2–3
time: 3¼ hours
kitchen roll
foil
oven No. 4 or 180 °C/355 °F
thick saucepan

1 Cut meat into large cubes, slice onion 2 Melt the fat and cook onion until soft (not brown)–remove 3 Reheat fat and fry meat 4 Add flour, onion, bouquet garni, paprika and stock–bring to the boil–add tomato purée and seasoning 5 Cook gently for 30 minutes–add chopped tomatoes (skinning if fresh) 6 Cover with foil and lid and cook over gentle heat or in the oven for 2 hours 7 Remove bouquet garni–adjust seasoning and consistency–add wine and cream 8 Serve very hot in an entrée-dish, garnished with boiled pasta at either end

Casserole of Beef

340g/¾ lb buttock or chuck steak
230g/½ lb carrots
1 onion
1 tbsp tomato purée
60g/2 oz flour
60g/2 oz dripping
clove of garlic
¾ lit/1½ pt stock or stock cube
1 tbsp Marmite
salt and pepper
triangular croûtons
peas for garnish

to serve: 3
time: 2½ hours
kitchen roll
oven No. 4 or 170 °C/335 °F
casserole or braising-pan
thermometer (optional)

1 Melt dripping–sauté onion and half carrots and meat cut in cubes–remove to a plate 2 Add flour and make a brown roux–add stock and bring to the boil, and add meat and vegetables 3 Cook for 2 hours 4 Fry the croûtons, and prepare and cook the garnish 5 Serve in an entrée dish, meat in the centre, croûtons round the edge, vegetables at each end

NB Croûtons may be fried in deep or shallow fat at 180 °C/355 °F.

Oxtail Stew

½ oxtail
1 onion
2 carrots
small piece swede
1 turnip
bouquet garni
1 tsp salt
pepper
30g/1 oz flour
30g/1 oz dripping
stock or stock cube
parsley

to serve: 3
time: 3 hours and overnight
kitchen roll
a heavy pan

1 Wipe the tail–cut into joints–remove excess fat **2** Blanch the joints **3** Put into the pan, add one carrot and onion and swede **4** Cover with stock, add bouquet and seasoning **5** Bring to the boil–skim **6** Simmer 2–3 hours–leave to cool overnight in a bowl **7** Remove surface fat **8** Melt dripping in the pan–add flour and make a brown roux **9** Add stew, boil–taste–correct seasoning **10** Cook remaining vegetables, diced, in boiling salted water. Drain **11** Serve in an entrée dish, joints in the centre, vegetables at either end **12** Garnish with chopped parsley

Mince

230g/½ lb minced beef
1 small onion
15g/½ oz flour
15g/½ oz dripping
⅛ lit/¼ pt stock or stock cube
seasoning
triangular croûtons
parsley

to serve: 2
time: 1 hour
a thick saucepan
thermometer (optional)

1 Chop onion finely–mix with the meat **2** Fry meat and onion in hot dripping **3** Take out of the pan–add extra fat, add flour and make a brown roux **4** Add stock and make the sauce **5** Add meat and seasoning and simmer very gently for about ½–1 hour–adjusting seasoning **6** Serve on an oval dish with fried or toasted croûtons round the edge **7** Garnish with parsley

NB Croûtons may be fried in deep or shallow fat at 180 °C/355 °F.

Curry of Fresh Meat

230g/½ lb chuck steak, rabbit, chicken or lean veal
30g/1 oz dripping
1 onion
½ apple *or* rhubarb stick
30g/1 oz flour
2 tbsp curry powder
30g/1 oz sultanas
1 tbsp coconut
½ lit/1 pt stock or stock cube
lemon-juice
1 tbsp jam or 1 tbsp chutney
1 dessertsp treacle
salt
110g/4 oz boiled rice (patna)
1 gherkin

to serve: 2
time: 2¼ hours
kitchen roll
heavy pan
deep or shallow fat pan
thermometer

1 Prepare meat–cut into cubes and fry in hot fat **2** Add chopped onion –cook for a few minutes **3** Add flour and curry powder–cook a few minutes **4** Add liquid and chopped apple **5** Bring to the boil–add salt, sultanas, coconut, jam or chutney and treacle, and simmer gently for 1½ hours **6** Add lemon-juice–check seasoning and consistency **7** Serve in an entrée-dish–meat in the centre–sauce round, garnish with gherkin

Accompaniments

1. Rice–serve separately on an oval dish on plain paper with a dash of paprika as garnish.
2. Puppadoms–plain or flavoured.
   (a) Fry in deep or shallow fat 3–4 minutes at 170 °C/335 °F.
   (b) Serve on an oval dish–plain paper.
3. Orange.
   (a) Skin–cut in thin slices.
   (b) Arrange in overlapping layers in a small dish–sprinkle with salt and lemon.
4. Tomato. Skin–cut in slices–serve as orange sprinkled with lemon.
5. Banana.
   (a) Skin, cut in slices.
   (b) Dip in lemon.
   (c) Serve as orange.
6. Nuts–serve in a small dish.
7. Toasted coconut–as above.
8. Mango chutney–as above.

Kidneys Sautés Turbigo (Rognons sautés Turbigo)

4 heart-shaped fried croûtons
4 sheep's kidneys
⅛ lit/¼ pt espagnole sauce (page 92)
30g/1 oz butter or dripping

to serve: 2
time: 1 hour
kitchen roll
shallow-fat pan

6 small button mushrooms
4 small grilled or fried chipolatas
2 tbsp cooked and sautéd peas
parsley

thermometer

1 Steep kidneys for 10 minutes in tepid salt water 2 Skin, halve, remove sinew and cut each half into three pieces–season 3 Fry quickly for approx. 4–5 minutes–drain, return to the pan and add the espagnole sauce 4 Sauté mushrooms, add to sauce, simmer for 20 minutes 5 Serve in an entrée-dish 6 Garnish with the croûtons which have been fried in butter, chipolatas and peas

Boiled Meat

Beef–Topside, silverside, brisket, thick flank
Mutton–Leg, best end neck
Pork– Belly–fresh or pickled
Boiling salt water
Root vegetables for flavouring
Boiled vegetables for garnish

kitchen roll
a large saucepan

1 Prepare the meat, remove excess fat and spinal cord–tie or skewer into a good shape 2 Put into boiling water–boil 10 minutes to seal–add vegetables in large chunks 3 Reduce heat and simmer for required time 4 To serve–drain well–absorb fat on joint with kitchen paper 5 Place on a large dish and garnish with the vegetables 6 Serve liquor in a sauce-boat 7 To serve cold–cool in liquor, drain–wrap in foil and press on a flat surface under a weight on a plate

Cooking time

As for roast meat plus five minutes per ½ kg/lb (page 42).
Dumplings may be added to liquor 20 minutes before serving.
NB Mutton may be served with caper sauce (page 89).
Boiled salt meat, e.g. brisket.

1 Steep overnight in cold water.
2 Put prepared joint into cold water, bring slowly to the boil–pour off liquid.
3 Cover with cold water–bring to the boil and proceed as for fresh meat.

Boiled Mutton and Caper Sauce

680g/1½ lb best end neck of mutton or ½ leg mutton
carrot
turnip
onion
¼ lit/½ pt caper sauce (page 89)
boiling salted water

to serve: 3–4
time: 1½ hours approx.
kitchen roll
large saucepan
saw
string

1 Wipe meat–remove spinal cord–chine 2 Remove skin from back 3 Saw through cutlet bones at about half way–fold top section under and tie the

joint—weigh **4** Boil for 10 minutes—reduce heat and simmer allowing 20 minutes per ½ kg/lb plus 20 minutes for thin joints and 25 minutes per ½ kg/lb plus 25 minutes for thick joints—add turnip and onion whole and carrot cut in strips ½ hour before serving **5** Make the sauce, season well **6** Remove string, absorb fat on joint with kitchen paper **7** Place joint on a large oval dish—coat with the sauce and pile vegetables at either end

To Boil Ham

large pan or fish-kettle

1 Steep 24 hours in cold water **2** Scrub off 'bloom' in warm water **3** Weigh soaked ham **4** Bring slowly to the boil in fresh water **5** Simmer gently for 25 minutes per ½ kg/lb of ham and 25 minutes extra **6** Allow to cool in the cooking water

To serve hot Allow to cool for 1 hour—remove skin—score fat criss-cross, stick with cloves, sprinkle with brown sugar and toasted crumbs, brown in oven 15 minutes at No. 6 or 205 °C/400 °F

To serve cold **1** After cooling in water—remove skin and dress with toasted breadcrumbs **2** Place a ham frill on the knuckle

NB 1 To add flavour, vegetables, cloves, cider and/or beer may be added to the cooking water.

2 Cold ham is best left in a cool larder for 24 hours before skinning to prevent loss of weight and juices by evaporation.

To Bake Ham

kitchen roll
shallow roasting-tin
water paste or foil
oven No. 3 or 170 °C/335 °F

1 Steep overnight at room temperature **2** Criss-cross skin **3** Wrap completely in water paste i.e. flour, salt and water, or foil and place skin side up in the roasting-pan **4** Roast 25–28 minutes per ½ kg/lb **5** Remove covering 20 minutes before the end of cooking time **6** Sprinkle well with brown sugar and glaze at No. 5 or 190 °C/380 °F for 20 minutes **7** Serve with cinnamon added to apple-sauce (page 98)

Reheated Dishes

Meat Basic mixture

230g/½ lb cold meat
⅛ lit/1½ pt stock
2 tsp flour
30g/1 oz dripping

time: 20 minutes

1 small chopped onion
1 tsp parsley (chopped)
nutmeg
seasoning
mushrooms (optional)

1 Mince meat 2 Melt dripping–fry onion without burning 3 Add flour–brown slightly–add stock and mushrooms–bring to the boil–cool 4 Add meat and seasonings–mix well–use as required

Shepherd's Pie

230g/½ lb meat mixture
230g/½ lb mashed potato
parsley garnish

to serve: 2
time: 20 minutes
grill

1 Put the mixture into a pie-dish 2 Spread or pipe with potato 3 Brown under the grill or in the oven 4 Serve with sauce or gravy, on an oval dish with plain paper 5 Garnish with parsley

Meat Croquettes

230g/½ lb meat mixture
egg–raspings
parsley

to serve: 2–3
time: 20 minutes
deep-fat pan
thermometer (optional)

1 Shape mixture into corks 2 Coat with egg and raspings–firm on 3 Fry in hot deep fat 2–3 minutes to crisp at 180 °C/355 °F 4 Drain well 5 Serve on an oval dish with plain paper, piled like logs, garnished with parsley 6 Hand a good sauce separately

Rissoles

230g/½ lb meat mixture
230g/½ lb shortcrust pastry (page 229)
egg
raspings or vermicelli

deep fat-pan
thermometer (optional)
100 mm/4 inch plain cutter

1 Roll pastry very thinly, into rounds, or cut with the cutter 4 Enclose meat mixture in pastry 3 Coat with egg and raspings or vermicelli, firm-on 4 Fry in deep fat at 170 °C/335 °F for 6 minutes–drain well 5 Serve on an oval dish–plain paper 6 Garnish with parsley 7 Serve sauce separately

Dresden patties

110g/¼ lb meat mixture
2 slices bread (very thick)
egg
raspings
parsley

50 mm/2 inch round cutter
25 mm/1 inch round cutter
deep fat pan
thermometer

1 Cut bread into rounds with the larger cutter 2 Cut out centre using smaller cutter 3 Cut a thin lid from the removed centre piece 4 Brush case and lid with egg and coat with raspings–firm on 5 Fry quickly at 190 °C/380 °C 6 Drain well and fill with hot meat mixture and place lid at an angle 7 Serve on an oval dish with plain paper, garnished with parsley 8 Serve a sauce separately

Galantine of Beef

230g/½ lb fresh minced beef
110g/¼ lb bacon
6 tbsp fresh breadcrumbs
pinch mixed herbs
salt and pepper
1 egg
stock or stock cube

to serve: 3–4
time: hot 2¼ hours; cold 2¼ hours plus cooling time
foil
large pan
liquidizer

1 Blanch bacon and mince or liquidize with crumbs–add beef and seasonings **2** Bind with egg and stock to give a slack mixture **3** Wrap in the foil **4** Put into boiling water–boil for 10 minutes, simmer for 1½ hours

Serving
To serve hot Coat with crumbs, put on to an oval dish–pour tomato sauce round (page 99)
To serve cold Trim ends and brush or coat with glaze (page) When set, pipe with seasoned butter and serve on a plain paper garnished with salad or parsley

Liver Pâté

340g/¾ lb pigs' liver
110g/¼ lb bacon pieces
1 clove garlic
5 anchovy fillets
3–4 thin streaky rashers
¼ lit/½ pt white coating sauce
seasoning

to serve: 4–6
time: 1½ hours plus cooling time
bain-marie
foil
liquidizer
bread-tin 160 x 85 x 50 mm/7½ x 3½ x 2 in.

1 Blanch bacon pieces, cut up and mix all ingredients and liquidize **2** Line the bread-tin with the rashers **3** Check the seasoning of the mixture and put into the prepared tin **4** Cover with the foil, place in the bain-marie and bake for about 1 hour **5** Press lightly and cool **6** Serve in slices with hot buttered toast **7** If not for immediate use cover with a little clarified butter
NB Chicken liver may be used instead of the pigs' liver.

Pâté of Veal and Beef

230g/½ lb each of lean veal and buttock steak
45g/1½ oz butter
1 bay-leaf
salt, pepper, ground mace

to serve: 4–6
time: 5¼ hours plus cooling time
foil
liquidizer
casserole
bread-tin 160 x 85 x 50 mm/7½ x 3½ x 2 in.
bain-marie
oven No. 3 or 170 °C/355 °F

1 Cut up the meat and put into a casserole with one third of the butter, bay-leaf and seasonings **2** Cover, stand in bain-marie and put into the oven for about 5 hours–remove the bay leaf **3** Melt the remaining butter and add to meat–liquidize **4** Check seasoning and press into the tin, or a glass mould may be used **5** Run some clarified butter over the top and use as required

Wet Pickle for Meat

450g/1 lb coarse salt
170g/6 oz brown sugar
30g/1 oz saltpetre
4 lit/1 gall water

large pan
plastic or china bowl or bucket
strainer

1 Put all these ingredients into the large pan, bring to the boil and boil for 5 minutes, skimming frequently **2** Strain into a large basin or bowl or plastic bucket **3** Use when cool **4** This pickle will keep indefinitely
To use Rub surface of meat to be pickled with salt and allow to stand for 1 hour–place in the pickle
Time in pickle 7–10 days, turning each day
Suitable joints Silverside, brisket, belly of pork, ox tongue, sheep's tongues, etc.

Brawn

½ pig's head (salted)
1 onion
bouquet garni
40 peppercorns
2 blades mace
4 cloves

to serve: approx 20
time: salted 3 hours plus cooling time; unsalted, 5 days
large pan
suitable moulds

1 Wash the pig's head, remove the brains and cut out veins and bone splinters **2** Salt the head in the pickle (page 56) for 3–4 days–wash **3** Put into cold water, bring to boil and simmer for 1½ hours **4** Take out of water and remove all the meat from the bones–cut into dice **5** Return bones to liquid in which the head was boiled, and add onion and spices **6** Boil for ¾ hour–strain **7** Using 1 lit/1 qt of above, put it in a pan and add the meat **8** Season and bring to the boil **9** Put into wet moulds **10** When cold turn out and use as required

Tongues

If a tongue has not been salted by the butcher, it may be done at home (see Wet Pickle, page 56) and will take 5–10 days, according to size.

To cook an ox tongue **1** Wash tongue **2** Cover with cold water, adding a bouquet garni, 1 bay-leaf, 6 peppercorns and a blade of mace **3** Simmer gently for 4–5 hours or until tongue is very tender

For a round **1** Curl tongue and put into a suitably sized pan **2** Proceed as above **3** Remove skin, trim root and remove all bones **4** Curl tightly and put into a cake-tin or pyrex dish **5** Strain over enough of the liquid in which the tongue has been cooked, to cover–press with a heavy weight **6** When cold, turn out and use as required

NB If weather is very hot 1 tsp gelatine may be added to the liquid before pressing

For a glazed arched tongue To cook, put a skewer through root, attach a tape or string to the skewer and pass it over the tongue to the tip and tie firmly just above the tip drawing the tongue into an arched position. Cook according to directions in a pan large enough for it to be covered with water.

To finish 1 Skin the tongue, trim root and remove bones 2 Place on a board and fasten root with a skewer 3 Cover a weight with foil and put it on the tip to keep the whole in an arched position 4 When firm, tape may be removed 5 Leave overnight on board 6 Glaze 7 Move on to a suitable dish and decorate with piped butter and pieces of cut aspic

Tongues may be served fresh or salted and may be–

Ox tongues	average	4–5 lb/approx. 2 kg
Calves' or pigs'	average	1–2 lb/approx. 450g–1kg
Lambs' or sheeps'	average	8–12 oz/approx. 230g–340g

Tongue with Almonds and White Grapes

1 calf's tongue (fresh or slightly salted)
15g/½ oz butter
60g/2 oz shredded almonds
110g/¼ lb green grapes
¼ lit/½ pt espagnole sauce (page 92)
1 tsp tomato purée
4 tbsp madeira or sherry
lemon-juice
seasoning
fleurons of puff pastry

to serve: 4–6
time: 2½ hours
frying-pan
large pan

1 Cook the tongue as directed (page 56) 2 Cool, then trim, skin and cut into slices 3 Pip the grapes 4 Fry the almonds in the butter and add the grapes–add some lemon juice 5 Put sauce in a pan, add tomato purée, grapes, almonds and wine 6 Adjust seasoning and consistency 7 Arrange slices of tongue overlapping on a hot dish 8 Pour sauce over, arranging grapes and almonds down the centre 9 Garnish with the fleurons

Savoury Roll

110g/¼ lb suet crust pastry (page 229)
savoury filling (see over)

to serve: 2–3
time: 2 hours
steamer
foil

1 Roll pastry into an oblong 2 Turn over and turn up the sides 3 Spread with the chosen filling 4 Damp the bottom edge and roll

the pastry down 5 Wrap loosely in foil 6 Steam 1½ hours 7 Turn out and serve with a suitable sauce

Fillings

1 Mince, see shepherds' pie (page 54)

2 110g/4 oz chopped bacon or ham
60g/2 oz chopped tomato
1 tsp chopped parsley
pinch mixed herbs

3 60g/2 oz chopped tomato
60g/2 oz chopped mushrooms (sautéd in butter or margarine)
1 hard-boiled egg (chopped)
seasoning

All the above should be served with a brown or tomato sauce

Steak and Kidney Pudding

110g/¼ lb suet-crust pastry (page 227)
230g/½ lb stewing steak
60g/2 oz ox kidney
1 small onion
1 small potato
1 tbsp seasoned flour
parsley
stock or stock cube

to serve: 2–3
time: 4½ hours
a steamer
a greased basin
foil

1 Make the pastry–roll out as for fruit pudding and line basin (page 157) **2** Prepare the filling as for steak and kidney pie (page 59) and fill basin–add 4 tbsp stock **3** Draw up the pastry and seal over filling **4** Cover with greased foil **5** Put into the steamer and cook for four hours **6** Serve in the basin on a plate with a plain paper and with a table napkin pinned round **7** Hand gravy separately

NB The pudding may be filled with hot stock before serving.

Cornish Pasties

110g/¼ lb buttock steak
1 onion
1 medium potato
piece swede
seasoning
170g/6 oz shortcrust pastry (page 227)
egg to glaze

to serve: 2
time: hot 1¼ hours; cold 1¼ hours plus cooling time
greased and floured baking tray
oven No. 6 or 205 °C/400 °F

1 Make pastry **2** Prepare vegetables–cut into small pieces **3** Prepare meat–cut into cubes **4** Divide pastry into four and knead, roll into rounds–turn over **5** Place potato, swede, onion and meat on pastry–season–add 1 tsp water **6** Damp edges–draw together across filling to form a boat shape–flute and brush with egg **7** Put onto the tray and bake till golden–reduce to Reg. No. 3 or 170 °C/335 °F and bake

in all 35–40 minutes
To serve cold Cool–serve on an oval dish, plain dish paper with parsley garnish accompanied by salad or *To serve hot* Serve as above with a brown or tomato sauce *or* Serve as a picnic food

Steak and Kidney Pie

110g/¼ lb rough puff pastry (page 229)
230g/½ lb stewing steak
60g/2 oz ox kidney
1 small potato
1 small onion
1 tbsp seasoned flour
egg for glazing
parsley
stock or stock cube

to serve: 2–3
time: 2½ hours if using ready-made pastry
½ lit/1 pt pie-dish
oven No. 7 or 220 °C/425 °F

1 Steep kidney in tepid salted water **2** Cut trimmed meat into thin strips, toss in seasoned flour **3** Cut up kidney and wrap a piece in each strip of meat–put into the dish **4** Add remaining flour, chopped onion and sliced potato–add 4 tbsp stock **5** Roll out pastry just larger than the dish **6** Line the edge of the pie dish–damp the pastry **7** Cover with pastry–trim **8** Knock up edges and flute with large firm flues–brush with egg **9** Roll out the trimmings and make pastry leaves **10** Make a hole in the centre of the pie–arrange leaves round hole–brush with egg **11** Bake for 25 minutes to cook pastry, reduce to No. 3 or 170 °C/335 °F for a further 1¼–1½ hours–cover with paper if necessary **12** To serve, fill with hot stock and serve on a plain paper on an oval dish. Garnish with parsley

Sausage Rolls

110g/¼ lb flaky pastry or rough puff pastry (page 229)
110g/¼ lb sausage meat
egg to glaze

to make: 8 large or 16 cocktail size
time: using ready-made pastry 1 hour
baking tray
oven No. 7 or 220 °C/425 °F

1 Make the pastry **2** Divide sausage in two–roll into two long sausages **3** Roll pastry into an oblong the length of sausage rolls and about 150 mm/6 in. wide–turn over **4** Place meat on pastry edges–cut pastry down the centre **5** Damp pastry edges–roll round sausage, join underneath **6** Mark–divide into eight rolls–glaze **7** Put on to the dry baking tray **8** Bake for 15–20 minutes then reduce to No. 3 or 170 °C/335 °F for further 15–20 minutes **9** Serve on an oval dish with a plain paper–garnish with parsley **10** Sausage rolls should always be served heated unless to be used for a picnic

Veal and Ham Patties

110g/¼ lb rough puff pastry (page 229)
110g/¼ lb lean pie veal
30g/1 oz bacon pieces

to serve: 3–6
time: using ready-made pastry 1¼ hours
6 deep patty-tins

parsley
pinch of mixed herbs
lemon-juice
white stock or stock cube
seasoning
egg for glazing

plain cutter
oven No. 7 or 220 °C/425 °F

1 Roll out the pastry large enough to cut 6 rounds–re-roll trimmings and use to line the patty tins 2 Cut up veal, blanch and cut up bacon 3 Add chopped parsley, herbs seasoning and lemon-juice 4 Fill the patty-tins–add 1 tsp stock 5 Cover with pastry from first rolling and brush with egg 6 Bake for 15 minutes–reduce to No. 3 or 170 °C/335 °F and bake for a further 15 minutes 7 Serve on a plain paper on an oval dish–garnish with parsley or cool and serve, as above, cold

Vol-au-vent

110g/¼ lb puff pastry (page 229)
⅛ lit/¼ pt coating sauce
4 tbsp cream
filling
parsley

to serve: 2
time: 1¼ hours using ready-made pastry
baking tray
175 mm/7 in. and 125 mm/5 in. oval-cutters, or sideplate and smaller cutter, or cut into an oblong
oven No. 7 or 220 °C/425 °F

1 Roll the pastry out to the size of the larger cutter–cut 2 Cut halfway through the centre of the pastry using the smaller cutter 3 Put on to the dry tray–chill thoroughly 4 Glaze the top 5 Roll some of the remaining pastry very thinly and cut out an oval with the smaller cutter–glaze and place on ton with the vol-au-vent 6 Bake at top of oven for 20–30 minutes 7 Take off the top and remove doughy material–put back in the oven to dry off 8 Prepare filling by chopping the chosen meat and adding to the sauce–add cream and seasoning 9 Dish on a plain paper topping with the separate top 10 Garnish with parsley, or lobster claws, prawn heads, etc.

Fillings

1. 110g/¼ lb cooked chicken and ham
2. 110g/¼ lb cooked veal and ham
3 110g/¼ lb cooked lobster
4. 110g/¼ lb cooked prawn or shrimp
5. 110g/¼ lb cooked oyster, salmon, etc.

Veal and Ham Pie

110g/¼ lb hot-water crust (page 230)
110g/¼ lb lean pie veal
60g/2 oz bacon pieces (blanched)
salt and pepper
1 tsp chopped parsley
grated lemon-rind
1 hard-boiled egg

to serve: 2
time: hot 2¼ hours; cold 2¼ hours plus cooling time
pan of hot water and bowl
oblong tin 125 x 75 x 50 mm/ 5 x 3 x 1 in.
10 mm/½ in plain cutter
oven No. 6 or 205 °C/400 °F

1 Cut veal into small pieces 2 Cut up bacon and add to veal with seasoning, chopped parsley and lemon-rind 3 Grease and flour tin and line with 2/3 pastry–leave 1/3 in the warm bowl 4 Add egg and filling and cover with remaining pastry 5 Glaze–decorate with pastry circles 6 Make a hole in centre–decorate and glaze 7 Bake for 30 minutes–reduce to Reg. 3 or 170 °C/335 °F for 1 hour, total 1½ hours 8 Fill with hot stock 9 Serve on plain paper–parsley garnish

To serve cold Add 1 tsp gelatine to ⅛ lit/¼ pt stock. Fill cold pie and allow to set. Serve with salad accompaniment.

Toad-in-the-Hole

⅛ lit/¼ pt pancake batter (page 153)
110g/¼ lb sausage-meat or sausages
30g/1 oz dripping
parsley to garnish

to serve: 2
time: 45 minutes
oven No. 6 or 205 °C/400 °F
Yorkshire-pudding tin, 8½ x 5½ in. 210 x 135 mm

1 Melt dripping in the tin till really hot–add sausages 2 Pour batter over 3 Bake 30–35 minutes 4 Serve on plain paper on an oval dish, cut into portions 5 Garnish with parsley 6 Serve a suitable sauce separately

Kromeskis à la Russe

⅛ lit/¼ pt white coating sauce
90g/3 oz cooked chicken or veal
30g/1 oz cooked ham
2 cooked mushrooms
3 rashers
yeast batter (page 154)

to serve: 2–3
time: 45 minutes
deep-fat pan
thermometer (optional)

1 Chop chicken, ham and cooked mushrooms and put into the sauce–season 2 When cold shape into small corks 3 Roll each in a piece of bacon 4 Coat in the batter 5 Fry at 180 °C/355 °F for about 2 minutes–drain 6 Dish on an oval dish on a plain paper 7 Garnish with parsley and serve tomato sauce separately (page 99)
NB These may be made using cooked fish instead of meat.

Veal Quenelles

230g/½ lb veal fillet
⅛ lit/¼ pt light stock } sauce
30g/1 oz flour } sauce
30g/1 oz butter } sauce
1 egg
1 tbsp cream
salt and pepper
⅜ lit/¾ pt béchamel sauce (page 90)
green peas

to serve: 3
time: 45 minutes
kitchen roll
sauté-pan
liquidizer

1 Liquidize veal and sauce 2 Add egg, seasoning and cream 3 Form into quenelles with dessert spoons 4 Poach in salted water in the pan

till set, approx. 10 minutes 5 Drain on the paper. Dish on an oval dish, coated with Béchamel sauce and garnished with peas
NB Chicken or rabbit or pork may be substituted for veal.

Rabbit or Veal Quenelles Virgil (Quenelles de lapin ou Veau à la Virgile)

90g/6 oz veal or rabbit meat
⅛ lit/¼ pt sauce
60g/2 oz butter
2 yolks of egg
1 dessertsp cream
pinch nutmeg
salt and cayenne
small tin asparagus tips
1 tbsp thick white sauce
lemon-juice

to serve: 3–4
time: 1½ hours
6–8 85 mm/3½ in. boat-moulds
ball-cutter
liquidizer
sauté-pan

1 Drain and chop 6 asparagus tips 2 Mix with the thick white sauce–season and put on a plate to cool 3 Cut up the rabbit or veal removing any skin or gristle 4 Liquidize with half the sauce, butter and yolks–season and add cream 5 Line the greased boat-moulds ¼ in./5 mm thick with the quenelle mixture 6 Fill centres with the asparagus mixture 7 Cover over with the quenelle mixture–smooth with a wet knife–cool 8 Prepare a garnish of carrot balls and peas–sauté 9 Thin down ⅛ lit/ ¼ pt white sauce–add the cream, a few drops of lemon-juice and seasoning 10 Poach the quenelles in the pan until firm (about ¼ hour) (they will come out of the moulds and rise to the top of the water) 11 Drain on the paper 12 Arrange, overlapping, on a hot dish 13 Coat with sauce and garnish with the peas and carrots
NB If using hare or other game, substitute espagnole for the white sauce.

To Prepare Cutlets

4 bones best end neck (small meat)

time: 20 minutes
kitchen roll
saw

1 To get length of cutlets–twice the length of the noisette plus 10 mm/ ½ in. for frill–saw across 2 Saw off the chine bone 3 Divide the cutlets, cutting between the bones 4 Trim the cutlets–removing excess fat and tapering towards the bone 5 Bone for frill must be scraped bare
6 Cutlets should be seasoned 7 Fry or grill with bone facing right first
8 Dish with bone facing left and curve inwards

Noisettes de mouton à la Maintenon

4 bones best end neck of lamb
For coating: beaten egg
raspings
For dishing: round croûtons of fried bread (1 for each noisette)

to serve: 2
time: 45 minutes
sauté-pan

Garnish: tinned artichoke bottoms or
mushrooms (1 for each)
1 tbsp peas
For serving: ¼ lit/½ pt tomato sauce
(page 99)

1 Bone the best end neck and divide into four—trim and roll up—skewer in place—coat and fry in 2/3 butter 1/3 oil, 4 minutes each side 2 Heat the garnishes in butter 3 Dish each noisette on a croûton of fried bread 4 Place an artichoke bottom or mushroom on each, and fill with peas 5 Pour the sauce round

Côtelettes à la Soubise

4 bones best end neck of lamb
⅛ lit/¼ pt espagnole sauce (page 92)
4 tbsp thick soubise sauce (page 89)
glaze (page 10)

to serve: 2
time: 45 minutes
kitchen roll
saw
sauté-pan
cutlet-frills

1 Divide the cutlets and trim carefully (page 62) 2 Prepare the sauces—the espagnole should be of a flowing consistency and the soubise coating 3 Using a frying-medium of 2/3 butter and 1/3 oil, fry the cutlets quickly on both sides 4 Place on a hot dish in a semicircle and glaze each cutlet 5 Pour the espagnole round and put the soubise in the curve of the cutlets 6 Put a frill on each cutlet

Côtelettes de mouton à la milanaise

4 bones best end neck (small meat)
beaten egg } for coating
white raspings }
1 tbsp strips of ham or tongue } for garnish
½ tbsp black olives cut in strips }
1 tbsp cooked spaghetti }
knob butter }
⅛ lit/¼ pt espagnole or tomato sauce (pages 92, 99)

to serve: 2
time: 1 hour
kitchen roll
saw
sauté-pan
cutlet-frills

1 Prepare and trim the cutlets—season 2 Coat with egg and raspings 3 Heat the garnish in butter 4 Heat the sauce and check consistency 5 Fry the cutlets in a frying-medium of 2/3 butter and 1/3 oil about 3 minutes on each side 6 Put on a hot dish bones to the left and pour the sauce round 7 Place the garnish inside the curve of the cutlets 8 Put a frill on each cutlet

Côtelettes de mouton à la réforme

4 bones best end neck (small meat)
1 tbsp chopped ham
beaten egg } to coat
white raspings }

to serve: 2
time: 1 hour
kitchen roll
saw

½ tbsp strips carrot
½ tbsp strips black olive
½ tbsp strips white of egg
½ tbsp strips mushroom
} garnish
1 dessertspoon sherry
⅛ lit/¼ pt réforme sauce (page 94)

sauté-pan
cutlet-frills

1 Prepare and trim cutlets (page 62)–season–coat 2 Fry in the usual frying-medium 3 Put on a hot dish 4 Have ready the heated sauce and garnish heated in a dessertsp of sherry 5 Arrange the cutlets, bones to the left, pour the sauce round 6 Add the garnish inside the curve of the cutlets 7 Place a frill on each cutlet

Côtelettes à l'ambassadrice

4 bones best end neck
stock or stock cube
15g/½ oz butter
1 tsp finely-chopped onion
1 tsp finely chopped mushroom
½ tsp finely-chopped parsley
15g/½ oz flour
4 tbsp stock
30g/1 oz chopped marrow
½ yolk egg
lemon-juice
seasoning
} farce
egg and raspings
⅛ lit/¼ pt ambassadrice sauce (page 92)

to serve: 2
time: 1½ hours
kitchen roll
deep-fat pan
thermometer
saw
cutlet frills

1 Melt butter and sauté onion and mushroom until soft 2 Add flour and liquid and cook for a few minutes 3 Add yolk and marrow a little at a time–season and cool 4 Divide and trim cutlets as usual (page 62) 5 Cook them in a little stock–cool and trim if necessary 6 With the bone facing left, coat top and sides with the cool farce 7 Coat with egg and raspings twice 8 Fry in deep fat at 180 °C/355 °F 9 Dish in a semicircle and pour the ambassadrice sauce round 10 Put a frill on each cutlet

Lamb Cutlets Saint-Germain

4 bones best end neck (small meat)
small tin of foie-gras or pâté
Green Chaud-froid
4 tbsp green pea purée
1 tbsp white sauce
4 tbsp aspic jelly (page 209)
or 1 packet aspic
1 tbsp cream
green colouring
Decoration white of egg
aspic jelly
Dishing salad and aspic jelly

to serve: 2
time: 1½ hours
kitchen roll
saw
sauté-pan
cutlet-frills
muslin

1 Divide the cutlets and trim (page 62) 2 Fry—cool—and retrim if necessary 3 Coat the cutlets on one side with the foie-gras or pâté 4 Mix ingredients for chaud-froid and tammy through muslin—colour if necessary 5 When mixture thickens, coat the cutlets 6 Decorate with neatly-cut pieces of white of egg 7 Glaze with liquid aspic 8 Dish on salad, put a frill on each cutlet, and decorate with chopped or cut aspic jelly

Veal Cutlets Viennoise (Escalopes de veau à la viennoise)

230g/½ lb fillet veal (cut very thin)
1 hard-boiled egg
1 lemon
olives
anchovy fillets
15g/½ oz butter
egg and raspings
chopped parsley

to serve: 2–3
time: 45 minutes
kitchen roll
sauté-pan

1 Trim the cutlets and marinade them in beaten egg, seasoning, parsley and mixed herbs, for 10–15 minutes 2 Coat with raspings 3 Fry in butter and oil for 6–8 minutes 4 Dish on a hot dish and garnish with stoned olives and an anchovy fillet on each cutlet 5 Pour the remaining butter and oil over the cutlets 6 Decorate with lemon butterflies, chopped egg-white, parsley and sieved egg-yolk

Côtelettes de veau

340g/¾ lb fillet veal (cut thin)
1 tsp chopped parsley
pinch mixed herbs
15g/½ oz butter
lemon-rind and juice
1 egg-yolk
white raspings
seasoning
bacon rolls (grilled)
lemon butterflies
vegetable garnish (peas or macédoine)
tomato sauce (page 99)

to serve: 2–3
time: 1 hour
kitchen roll
sauté-pan
cutlet-bat

1 Trim cutlets neatly but sparingly and beat well 2 Mix parsley, herbs, lemon rind/juice and seasoning with beaten egg 3 Add melted butter and marinade the meat in this mixture (10 minutes) 4 Coat with white raspings 5 Fry in a mixture of 2/3 butter, 1/3 oil (about 4 minutes each side) 6 Arrange on a hot dish 7 Put a lemon butterfly and small bacon roll on each cutlet 8 Pour the tomato sauce round 9 Garnish with the cooked vegetables sautéd in butter

Veal Cutlets à la Talleyrand

230g/½ lb fillet of veal (cut thin)
1 dessertsp clarified butter
1 dessertsp chopped mushroom
½ tsp chopped onion
salt and pepper
¼ lit/½ pt pouring white sauce
1 egg-yolk
lemon-juice
chopped parsley

to serve: 2–3
time: 1½ hours
kitchen roll
sauté pan

1 Cut the fillet into neat rounds or pieces **2** Fry lightly on one side–turn –sprinkle with onion and mushroom–fry **3** Pour off any surplus fat–add sauce and simmer gently for about 1 hour or until tender **4** Lift out the cutlets on to a hot dish **5** Add yolk, parsley and lemon-juice to the sauce–cook very gently without boiling **6** Coat cutlets with the sauce

Filets viennoise

230g/½ lb minced beef
1 tsp chopped parsley
1 tsp flour
1 egg
1 tsp grated onion
espagnole or tomato sauce (pages 92, 99)
2 tbsp vegetable garnish
onion rings
white of egg
2 tsp flour

to serve: 2
time: 45 minutes
deep fat
thermometer
sauté-pan

1 Mix minced beef, parsley, flour, grated onion and seasoning **2** Bind with the egg **3** Divide into four and shape into rounds about 10 mm/½ in. thick **4** Cut four onion rings and dip in white of egg and flour **5** Fry onion rings in deep fat at 180 °C/355 °F till crisp **6** Heat sauce and check consistency **7** Heat vegetable garnish in butter **8** Fry fillets in 2/3 butter and 1/3 oil, for about 4 minutes each side **9** Place on a hot dish **10** Pour the sauce round, put an onion ring on top of each and the vegetable garnish at each side

Filets de bœuf aux bananes

230g/½ lb thick fillet of beef
230g/½ lb duchess potato mixture (page 108)
1 banana
⅛ lit/¼ pt espagnole or tomato sauce (pages 92, 99)
glaze (page 10)
butter and oil for frying
egg and raspings for coating

to serve: 2
time: 45 minutes
kitchen roll
sauté-pan
thermometer
deep-fat pan

1 Trim the meat into neat fillets (about 4) 2 Divide the duchess potato mixture into four and shape the same as the fillets 3 Coat twice and fry at 180 °C/355 °F until golden 4 Cut banana in half, and then in quarters lengthwise–coat and fry 5 Fry the fillets in the frying medium (2/3 butter 1/3 oil) for 8 minutes 6 Place on a hot dish on top of a potato cake 7 Glaze each fillet 8 Pour the sauce round and put a banana on each fillet

Filets de bœuf a la bearnaise

230g/½ lb fillet of beef (thick)
⅛ lit/¼ pt espagnole sauce (page 92)
4 tbsp béarnaise sauce (page 95)
chopped tarragon
butter and oil
glaze (page 10)

to serve: 2
time: 50 minutes
kitchen roll
sauté-pan

1 Prepare the meat and trim sparingly–they should be 25 mm/1 in. thick–season 2 Check consistency and seasoning of the espagnole sauce 3 Make the béarnaise sauce 4 Fry the fillets in 1/3 oil and 2/3 butter, for 8 minutes 5 Dish on a hot dish and glaze each fillet 6 Pour the espagnole round 7 Put the béarnaise on top of each fillet 8 *Sprinkle* the chopped tarragon on the béarnaise sauce

Tournedos Henry IV

230g/½ lb fillet beef (2–3 tournedos)
larding bacon
croûtons
béarnaise sauce (page 95)
watercress
potato straws (page 111)

to serve: 2–3
time: 50 minutes
kitchen roll
sauté-pan

1 Trim the tournedos and wrap with larding bacon–tie, season 2 Cut croûtons to size and fry 3 Fry tournedos in usual frying-medium for 2–3 minutes each side 4 Dish on oval dish with watercress garnish and bundle of straws–pour béarnaise sauce on the tournedos

Filets de bœuf à la Pompadour

340g/¾ lb thick fillet beef
1–2 firm tomatoes
20g/1 oz mâitre d'hôtel butter (page 102)
espagnole sauce (page 92)
vegetable garnish
knob butter
croûtons of fried bread (one for each fillet)

to serve: 3
time: 45 minutes
kitchen roll
sauté-pan
greased baking-tray

1 Divide meat into at least 10 mm/½ in. fillets and trim sparingly–season 2 Skin tomatoes and cut into thick rounds–put on to the tray 3 Prepare croûtons (round or oval according to shape of fillets) 4 Heat sauce and

sauté garnish **5** Fry fillets in usual frying-medium (2/3 butter, 1/3 oil) about 3 minutes each side **6** Put on a hot dish and place a round of tomato on each fillet **7** Place a round of maître d'hôtel butter on top and pour the sauce round **8** Add the garnish

Sweetbreads Talleyrand

1 sweetbread
15g/½ oz butter
2 chopped mushrooms
small onion–chopped
⅛ lit/¼ pt white sauce
1 yolk egg
½ tsp chopped parsley
seasoning
fleurons of puff pastry

to serve: 1–2
time: 1 hour
foil
kitchen roll
sauté-pan
oven No. 4 or 180 °C/355 °F

1 Wash and steep the sweetbread for 5 minutes and blanch **2** Fry in the butter but do not brown **3** Add sauce, mushrooms and onion **4** Cover with foil and cook in the oven until tender (about 30 minutes) **5** Remove sweetbread from sauce and keep hot **6** Add yolk of egg, parsley and seasoning, and heat but do not boil **7** Coat the sweetbread and garnish with fleurons of puff pastry

Sweetbread à l'italienne (Ris de veau à l'italienne)

1 ox sweetbread
croûte of fried bread
30g/1 oz boiled macaroni
2 mushrooms
knob of butter
⅛ lit/¼ pt espagnole sauce (page 92)
30g/1 oz butter
15g/½ oz bacon
1 carrot
1 onion
blade mace
bouquet garni
stock
seasoning
} mirepoix

to serve: 1–2
time: 2½ hours
kitchen roll
braising-pan
oven No. 4 or 180 °C/355 °F

1 Steep sweetbread, blanch **2** Remove fat and press till cool **3** Prepare braising-pan, place the bread in it and cook 1–1½ hours **4** Put on a hot dish standing on the croûte **5** Strain liquid and reduce this to a glaze, and brush the bread **6** Pour the sauce round **7** Garnish with the mushrooms, sautéd, cut in strips and tossed with the macaroni

Sweetbread à la princesse

1 large ox sweetbread
¼ lit/½ pt coating sauce made with white stock or chicken stock cube
1 yolk of egg

to serve: 1–2
time: 1 hour
kitchen roll
oven No. 3 or 170 °C/335 °F

4 tbsp cream or evaporated milk
lemon-juice–seasoning
croûte
2 medium firm tomatoes
vegetable garnish
knob of butter

sauté-pan
strainer

1 Steep, blanch and press the sweetbread 2 Put in the pan with the sauce and simmer gently until tender (approx. 1 hour) 3 Lift on to the croûte 4 Add yolks and cream to the sauce, check consistency and seasoning 5 Strain over the sweetbread 6 Cut tomatoes in half–scoop out some of the pulp–bake until fairly soft 7 Arrange at each end of sweetbread and fill with sautéd vegetable garnish

Ham Mousse (Mousse de jambon Béchamel)

230g/½ lb cooked ham
1 tbsp tomato purée
⅛ lit/¼ pt aspic jelly
2 tsps gelatine
⅛ lit/¼ pt white coating sauce
⅛ lit/¼ pt cream or evaporated milk
2 whisked egg-whites
seasoning

to serve: 3–4
time: 1½ hours
rubber band
foolscap paper
110 mm/4½ in Soufflé-mould
liquidizer

DECORATION:
black olives, cucumber skin, peppers, aspic jelly (page 209) or packet aspic jelly
ACCOMPANIMENTS:
Cumberland sauce (page 98), green salad (page 126)

1 Prepare the soufflé-mould 2 Liquidize the ham, having cut it into small pieces leaving some of the fat 3 Mix with the sauce, cream and tomato purée 4 Add the gelatine dissolved in the aspic jelly–season 5 When beginning to set fold in the egg-whites and pour into the mould 6 When set, cover with a thin layer of aspic jelly–set and decorate 7 Coat with aspic jelly–set–remove paper 8 Stand on a plate with a plain paper 9 Serve with green salad and Cumberland sauce

NB Chicken or chicken and ham, veal, or veal and ham or game may be used.

POULTRY

Chicken

1 chicken

time: 30 minutes
kitchen roll
taper
skewer

Drawing

(a) Singe the bird if necessary.
(b) Have two bowls of tepid water, one for cleansing fingers and one for the giblets.

(c) Cut off head and slit up the skin at the back from base of neck.
(d) Remove crop, windpipe and neck joint.
(e) Cut skin round knee-joint, twist and pull out sinews—cut off feet.
(f) Cut between vent and tail (pope's nose).
(g) Putting fingers inside the bird, loosen the inside at both ends.
(h) Remove gizzard, intestines, heart and liver (with gall-bladder) from the tail-end.
(i) Wipe the bird.
(j) Cut gall-bladder away from liver taking care not to break it.
(k) Put liver, heart, gizzard (with bag removed) and neck in water—these are the giblets.
(l) The feet may be scalded and stripped and put with the giblets.

Stuffing

If the bird is to be stuffed, this is done before trussing.

Trussing (for roasting)

time: 10 minutes
trussing-needle
string

(a) Fold flap of skin over the back of the neck end, and fold the ends of the wings over it.
(b) Place bird on its back and press legs well down into sides. Pass the tail through the vent.
(c) Thread a trussing-needle with thin string.
(d) Put through the wing and out through the other wing.
(e) Cross at back (tie if liked).
(f) Put through the leg and out through the other leg.
(g) Re-thread the needle and repeat.
(h) Pull string firmly and tie underneath.

To truss (for boiling)

time: 10 minutes

(a) Cut off legs at knee.
(b) Loosen the skin round the legs and push the bone inside.
(c) Truss as for roasting.

Roast Chicken

1 roasting chicken 1½–2 kg/3–3½ lb
oil—sugar—salt
farce if required (veal force-meat page 86)
bacon rolls (see Misc. Processes)
sausages
bread-sauce (page 100)
thick gravy (if stuffed)

to serve: 4–5
time after drawing: 1½ hours plain or 1¾ hours stuffed
kitchen roll
oven No. 7 or 220 °C/425 °F if wrapped in foil
oven No. 6 or 205 °C/400 °F if plain
roasting-tin

thin gravy (if plain)
green salad (page 126)

trivet
trussing-needle
string

1 Draw and truss the bird according to directions (page 69) 2 Rub with oil, sugar and salt and put on to a large piece of foil—fold up loosely—turn in the edges 3 Put on to the trivet in the roasting-tin 4 Roast, allowing 15 minutes per ½ kg/1 lb and 15 minutes extra 5 Open foil 15 minutes before the bird is cooked, to brown 6 Take off the foil, remove string, put on to a large oval dish 7 Garnish with sausages and/or bacon rolls 8 Hand salad and bread-sauce separately 9 Make gravy in the roasting-tin and hand separately

Goose, Turkey, Duck are treated similarly—with the exception of accompaniments—

	STUFFING	SAUCE	GRAVY
GOOSE	Sage and onion	Apple	Thick
TURKEY	Veal force-meat or chestnut farce or sausage-meat	Bread Cranberry	Thick
DUCK	Sage and onion	Apple Orange sauce (see sauce bigarade, page 93)	Thick

NB Salad may be served with all roast birds—either green or orange.

Boiling Fowl

1 boiling fowl 2 kg/4 lb
Suitable sauce, e.g. egg, parsley

to serve: 6–8
time: 2½ hours
kitchen roll
a large pan

To draw as for roasting chicken (page 69)
To truss see chicken notes (page 70)

To cook
1 Bring salted water to the boil—immerse chicken—boil for 10 minutes.
2 Reduce heat—simmer until tender.

Time
Time varies according to the age of the bird.
For a very old bird allow 30–35 minutes per ½ kg/1 lb plus 30 minutes.
For a moderately old bird 20–25 minutes per ½ kg/1 lb plus 20 minutes.

To serve
1 Remove string—put on to a large oval dish.
2 Remove surface grease with paper.
3 Coat with sauce or serve sauce separately.
NB A young bird may be steamed (page 72).

To Steam Chicken

1 young chicken 1–1½ kg/2–3 lb
oil
salt

kitchen roll
steamer
foil

1 Truss chicken as for boiling (page 70) **2** Rub with oil and salt **3** Wrap loosely in foil and steam 1–1¼ hours **4** Use as required

To Bone a Chicken

time: 15–20 minutes
small sharp knife

1 Singe if necessary **2** Cut off head, draw sinews–cut legs off at knee-joint. Remove wings to 2nd joint **3** From neck end, remove neck-joint, windpipe and crop **4** Cut down centre back **5** Begin boning, using a small sharp knife, and removing 2 wings from inside **6** Remove the wish-bone and carry on down the body keeping close to the skeleton **7** Remove legs, 2 joints from each side **8** Continue boning to the parson's nose, cutting through this at the end

Chicken with Oranges

1 small roasting chicken or chicken joints
4 tbsp dry white wine
1½ oranges
1 dessertsp flour
1 dessertsp soft brown sugar
1 tbsp tarragon vinegar
½ tsp paprika
seasoning
oil
Garnish
½ orange
1 bunch watercress
90g/3 oz patna rice

to serve: 4
time: 1½ hours
kitchen roll
braising-pan

1 Joint the chicken, and fry in oil until brown **2** Remove joints and excess fat **3** Peel the rind off the oranges and cut into fine shreds **4** Squeeze out the juice and mix this with the vinegar and wine **5** Stir the flour and paprika in the pan and cook 1–2 minutes **6** Add the liquids and bring to the boil **7** Replace the chicken joints **8** Add the shredded orange rind and simmer gently for about ½ hour **9** Cut the orange for garnish into thin slices without removing the peel **10** Pile the chicken on a dish **11** Check seasoning of liquid and pour it over **12** Garnish with orange slices and watercress **13** Serve with a dish of plain boiled rice

Chicken with Almonds

4 chicken joints
15g/½ oz butter

to serve: 2–4
time: 1 hour

1 onion
2 tomatoes
30g/1 oz sultanas
15g/½ oz flour
4 tbsp white wine
4 tbsp stock
30g/1 oz almonds
pinch of cinnamon
seasoning–oil

kitchen roll
braising-pan

1 Fry the chicken joints in oil until brown–remove from pan **2** Cook the chopped onion in the remaining oil until soft but not coloured **3** Add flour and cook for a minute **4** Add skinned and chopped tomato wine and stock **5** Season and add cinnamon **6** Replace joints and simmer gently for 30 minutes **7** Add cleaned sultanas 5 minutes before dishing **8** Fry almonds in a little oil until pale brown **9** Pile joints on a dish **10** Reduce the sauce if necessary, pour it over the chicken and sprinkle with the fried almonds **11** A dish of rice may be served separately, plain or coloured with saffron

Chicken Marengo (Poulet à la Marengo)

1 small chicken
2 tbsp oil
⅛ lit/¼ pt espagnole sauce (page 92)
⅛ lit/¼ pt tomato sauce (page 99)
4 tbsp sherry
croûte of fried bread
1 tbsp strips of mushroom
fleurons of puff pastry

to serve: 3–4
time: 1 hour
kitchen roll
sauté-pan

1 Joint the chicken and fry in the oil **2** Have sauces boiling, add joints, and simmer gently until tender **3** Dish joints on the croûte **4** Check consistency of sauce and strain over the chicken **5** Garnish with strips of sautéd mushrooms and fleurons of pastry

Mediterranean Chicken

4 chicken joints
4 rashers streaky bacon
thyme (fresh if possible)
⅛ lit/¼ pt tinned tomatoes
1 onion
4 tbsp white wine
4 tbsp stock
1 tsp flour
1 tbsp oil
30g/1 oz butter
garlic–bay-leaf
1 green pepper
chopped parsley

to serve: 2–4
time: 1¼ hours
kitchen roll
braising-pan
string

1 Put a small piece of thyme on each joint **2** Wrap a rasher of bacon round each one and tie with string **3** Heat butter and oil together and fry the joints until they are brown **4** Remove joints and cook the chopped onion until soft but not coloured **5** Add flour and cook for a minute **6** Add tomatoes, stock and wine **7** Add peppers which have had all seeds removed and been cut into shreds, crushed garlic and bay-leaf **8** Put in the chicken joints and simmer gently for about 30 minutes **9** Remove bay-leaf and check seasoning **10** Pile joints on a hot dish and remove string **11** Reduce liquid and pour it over, and sprinkle with chopped parsley **12** A dish of plain boiled rice and a green salad are suitable accompaniments for this dish

Coq au vin

8 heart-shaped croûtons
1 roasting chicken (3–3¼ lb or 1½ kg)
1 tbsp flour
60g/2 oz butter
110g/¼ lb bacon pieces
⅛ lit/¼ pt red burgundy
2 cloves garlic or garlic salt
12 button onions
8 button mushrooms
bouquet garni
salt and pepper
⅛ lit/¼ pt chicken stock or chicken stock cube
chopped parsley

to serve: 4–8
time: 1¾ hours
kitchen roll
sauté-pan
braising-pan

1 Joint chicken–toss in seasoned flour **2** Melt butter, add bacon, and fry the chicken till brown **3** Transfer chicken and bacon to the pan **4** Fry onions and mushrooms in the fat and add to the pan **5** Pour off all but one tbsp fat–add flour and make a brown roux **6** Add wine and ⅛ lit/¼ pt chicken stock–bring to boil–pour over chicken, cover and cook ¾ hour **7** Serve on an oval dish, joints in the centre, sauce poured over, mushrooms piled at each end, onions and croûtons round sides–garnish with chopped parsley

Pilaff or Pilau of Chicken

1 small chicken or 4 chicken pieces (boiling chicken may be used)
water
bouquet garni
2 onions
1 carrot
30g/1 oz butter
60g/2 oz sliced almonds
60g/2 oz raisins
⅛ lit/¼ lb rice
seasoning

to serve: 2–4
time: 1½ hours
kitchen roll
oven No. 4 or 180 °C/355 °F
pan
sauté-pan

1 Cook the chicken in water to cover with bouquet garni, carrot, one onion and salt 2 Simmer gently until tender 3 Sauté sliced onion in half the butter and add half almonds and raisins 4 Add rice and cook for a few minutes 5 Add ⅜ lit/¾ pt of chicken stock 6 Season, bring to the boil and put in the oven until the liquid is absorbed and rice tender 7 Divide chicken into joints (unless pieces have been used) 8 Toss in remaining butter 9 Arrange on a dish and cover with the well-seasoned rice 10 Cover with remaining almonds and raisins (which have been heated in the butter used to fry chicken)

Chicken Chaud-froid

joints of cooked chicken (8 joints from 1 chicken)

chaud-froid sauce:
¼ lit/½ pt thick white sauce
⅛ lit/¼ pt aspic jelly (liquid)
1 tsp gelatine
seasoning
2 tbsp cream

Decorations
skin of sweet peppers, cucumber, tomato, black olives, etc.
aspic jelly for coating.

to serve: 4–8
time: 1½ hours
kitchen roll
muslin
cooler
ice

1 Arrange cold, trimmed and skinned joints on the cooler 2 Dissolve gelatine in aspic and add to sauce–add cream 3 Season and tammy through muslin and stir until thick 4 Coat each joint evenly–set 5 Decorate neatly–set 6 Glaze with cold liquid aspic–set 7 Arrange on a dish, flooded with aspic–set

NB A boned and stuffed chicken, pheasant, pigeon, etc., may be done in the same way. A brown sauce is used for game birds.

Chicken in Aspic

cooked chicken
peas
hard-boiled egg
cucumber
red pepper
aspic jelly (page 209)

to serve: 2–3
time: 1½ hours
100 mm/4 in. charlotte-mould
or
4–5 dariole-moulds

1 Cut the chicken into neat pieces 2 Cut some neat pieces of pepper, cucumber skin and white of egg for decoration 3 Set a little aspic in the bottom of the mould or moulds 4 Decorate and cover decoration with aspic 5 Fill up with chicken, vegetables, etc. 6 Cover with jelly and set each layer before starting the next 7 When mould is full allow to set 8 Turn out and garnish with chopped aspic, etc.

Galantine of Chicken

1 roasting chicken or boiling fowl
bouquet garni

to serve: 8
time: 3 hours and overnight

stock for cooking
Farce
340g/¾ lb sausage-meat
110g/¼ lb cooked tongue (or tinned)
1 hard-boiled egg
Glaze (page 10)
salad garnish
savoury butter

trussing-needle
string
large pan
cloth or foil
cooler

1 Prepare chicken by boning (page 72) **2** Open out and spread with half of the sausage-meat **3** Place tongue and egg on top and cover with remaining sausage-meat **4** Draw flesh over stuffing and sew with string up centre back **5** Tie firmly in a cloth or wrap in foil **6** Immerse in boiling water with giblets and carcass **7** Simmer for 1–3 hours depending on age of chicken **8** Drain and cool thoroughly

To glaze
1 Trim off ends and place chicken on the cooler.
2 Brush with glaze–set.
3 Pipe with savoury butter.
4 Serve on an oval dish with plain paper or on a dish flooded with aspic. Add salad garnish.

Chicken Soufflé (Soufflé de volaille)

110g/¼ lb cooked chicken
15g/½ oz butter
15g/½ oz flour
4 tbsp milk
4 tbsp cream
} sauce
2 eggs
seasoning and lemon-juice
⅛ lit/¼ pt coating white sauce
2 tbsp cream
seasoning
paprika pepper

to serve: 2–3
time: 1½ hours
¼ lit/½ pt charlotte-mould
large pan
lid and cutter
liquidizer
greased paper

1 Grease the mould and fit a disc of greased paper in the bottom **2** Chop the chicken finely, add to the sauce **3** Add eggs and liquidize **4** Season, add lemon-juice and fold in the half-whipped cream **5** Put into the prepared mould and cover with the greased paper **6** Place on the cutter in the pan with water reaching the top of the cutter **7** Steam *very gently* until firm–30–40 minutes **8** Add the cream to the white sauce **9** Turn the soufflé on to a hot dish **10** Coat with the sauce and decorate lightly with paprika
NB This soufflé may be made with veal, sweetbread, ham or fish.

Chicken and Ham Cutlets

230g/½ lb cooked chicken
60g/2 oz diced ham
⅛ lit/¼ pt thick white sauce

to serve: 3–4
time: 1 hour
deep-fat pan

½ tsp chopped parsley
salt and pepper
1 finely-chopped gherkin
white crumbs
egg for coating

thermometer

1 Dice chicken–add to ham **2** Add meat, salt, pepper, parsley and gherkin to sauce–check seasoning and turn on to a plate to cool **3** Divide into 6 or 8 **4** Roll in flour, shape into cutlets or corks **5** Coat with egg and white crumbs twice–firm on the crumbs and reshape the cutlets **6** Fry for 2 minutes at 180 °C/355 °F and drain well **7** Serve on an oval dish on a plain paper, garnished with fresh or fried parsley **8** Hand a piquant sauce or tomato sauce separately
NB Fish, shell fish, hard-boiled eggs may be substituted for chicken and ham.

Pigeon à la duchesse

1 pigeon
30g/1 oz butter
salt, pepper
macédoine of vegetables
60g/2 oz sausage-meat
egg
raspings
⅛ lit/¼ pt espagnole sauce (page 92)

to serve: 2
time: 45 minutes
kitchen roll
deep-fat
thermometer

1 Split pigeon in half, remove breast-bone and beat flat **2** Sauté in butter and press flat **3** When cold spread with the sausage-meat on cut side **4** Coat with egg and crumbs **5** Fry in deep fat at 180 °C/355 °F, for 3-4 minutes **6** Dish–pour sauce round and garnish with macédoine of sautéd vegetables

Pigeons farcis allemande

1 pigeon
1 tbsp oil
small carrot
small onion
¼ lit/½ pt stock
⅛ lit/¼ pt espagnole sauce (page 92)
farce:
2 oval croûtons of fried bread
1 tbsp fresh bread-crumbs
1 tsp chopped onion
1 tsp chopped parsley
30g/1 oz mushroom stalks
15g/½ oz butter
seasoning
pigeon liver
a little beaten egg
cherries or orange slices for garnish
red wine or italian vermouth

to serve: 2
time: 2½ hours
kitchen roll
braising-pan
trussing-needle and string
oven No. 3 or 170 °C/335 °F
foil

1 Bone the pigeon (page 72) **2** Sauté the onion, chopped mushroom stalks and chopped liver in the butter and add to the bread-crumbs **3** Add parsley and seasoning and bind with beaten egg **4** Stuff the pigeon with this farce and sew up neatly **5** Heat the oil in the braising pan and fry the pigeon quickly all over–remove **6** Brown the chopped vegetables and pigeon bones **7** Pour off any oil left and place pigeon on the mirepoix **8** Pour the stock over, cover pan with foil, put on the lid and cook gently for 20 minutes **9** Put into the oven for further 20 minutes **10** Take out the pigeon and cut in half **11** Place on a hot dish on the croûtons **12** Strain the stock, reduce and add to the espagnole sauce–season **13** Coat the pigeon and garnish with cherries or orange slices which have been heated in red wine or Italian Vermouth

NB Pheasant or grouse may be used.

Pilaff of Pigeon with Apricots and Nuts

to serve: 2
time: 2 hours
kitchen roll
sauté-pan

1 pigeon
60g/2 oz butter
1 medium onion
1 clove garlic
bouquet garni
½ lit/1 pt stock
170g/6 oz patna or Italian rice
1 tsp green or preserved ginger
pinch of saffron
4 dried apricots (soaked)
1 dozen raisins
12 almonds
6 pistachio nuts
1 dessertsp coconut
⅛ lit/¼ pt coconut milk–(fresh or dry)

1 Prepare coconut milk by pouring ⅛ lit/¼ pt boiling water on to 1 tbsp of desiccated coconut–allow to stand for ½ hour and squeeze through muslin **2** Shred the almonds and pistachio nuts **3** Heat half the butter and brown the pigeon–cut in half and put to one side **4** Chop onion and sauté half in the butter **5** Add garlic, pigeon, bouquet garni and stock to cover **6** Simmer gently for about 1 hour **7** Melt remaining butter and sauté the rest of the onion **8** Add rice and cook until slightly coloured **9** Add liquid (from pigeon) ginger, saffron, nuts, raising, coconut (dry), pigeon and apricots **10** Cook for 15 minutes–add extra stock if needed **11** Lastly add coconut milk and check seasoning **12** Serve piled up on a dish

NB If liked the nuts and raisins may be heated in wine and sprinkled on top and apricots may be used as a garnish.

Pigeon à la flamande

to serve: 2
time: 2 hours

2 young pigeons (or 2 legs of rabbit)
30g/1 oz butter

2 rashers of fat bacon
6–8 small onions
¼ lit/½ pt stock (chicken stock cube)
salt and pepper
60g/2 oz raisins
2 tbsp sherry
1 tbsp beurre manié (page 327)
mashed potatoes
parsley

kitchen foil
braising-pan
nylon bag
No. 8 vegetable-forcer
oven No. 4 or 180 °C/355 °F

1 Clean and halve pigeons and fry in butter until browned, remove **2** Fry onions (whole) and add bacon cut in strips–add pigeon **3** Pour on stock to come ¾ way up bird. Season. Cook for 1 hour **4** Add raisins which have been soaked in sherry **5** When cooked, remove bird and then thicken with beurre manié **6** Pile meat on a hot dish and coat with the sauce **7** Garnish with piped potatoes and parsley

Pigeon en cocotte normande

1 pigeon
30g/1 oz butter
30g/1 oz sliced onion
1 small apple
15g/½ oz flour
⅛ lit/¼ pt cider
¼ lit/½ pt stock or stock cube
bouquet garni
Garnish
1 apple
1 rasher bacon to make bacon rolls

to serve: 2
time: 2½ hours
kitchen roll
oven No. 4 or 180 °C/355 °F
braising-pan

1 Brown pigeon in butter. Remove **2** Brown onion slices and small apple slices **3** Sprinkle with the flour and cook for a few minutes **4** Pour in cider and stock and bring to the boil **5** Season with salt and pepper. Add bouquet garni and pigeon **6** Cook in tightly-covered pan for 1½–2 hours **7** When cooked, remove pigeon, strain sauce and, if necessary, reduce over quick heat **8** Arrange pigeon on dish, garnish with fried apple rings, fried bacon rolls and sauce

Pigeon and Mushroom Pie

110g/¼ lb stewing steak
1 pigeon
1 tsp chopped onion
1 dessertsp chopped parsley
rind and juice of ½ lemon
pinch of ground mace
60g/2 oz mushrooms
1 tbsp seasoned flour
110g/¼ lb rough puff pastry (page 229) or frozen pastry
egg for glazing
parsley

to serve: 3–4
time: 2¾ hours
oven No. 6 or 205 °C/400 °F for ½ hour
No. 3 or 170 °C/335 °F for 1¼ hours
pie-dish

1 Bone the pigeon, cut up (keep liver to one side) 2 Make stock with the bones and remainder of giblets adding a few vegetables, a bay-leaf, blade of mace and salt 3 Cut meat into squares and mix with pigeon and chopped liver 4 Add the onion, parsley, mace, grated rind and juice of the lemon, seasoned flour 5 Slice the mushrooms and add 6 Put into the pie-dish 7 Cover with the pastry, trim, decorate, glaze with egg and bake 8 Serve on a dish with a plain paper and garnish with parsley

NB 1 If liked the pigeon feet may be scalded, glazed and used as a garnish.
2 This pie may be served hot or cold
3 This mixture may be used in a raised pie–340g/¾ lb of hot-water crust will be needed.

Roast Duck with Cherries

1 duck 2–2½ kg/4–5 lb
2 tbsp oil–salt and sugar
1 tin cherries
3 tbsp Italian Vermouth
6 streaky rashers (for bacon rolls)
1 tbsp flour } for gravy
1 tbsp oil } for gravy
¼ lit/½ pt stock from giblets } for gravy

to serve: 4–5
time: 2½ hours
kitchen roll
oven No. 5 or 190 °C/380 °F
foil
meat-tin
trivet

1 Stuff duck if liked (page 71) 2 Rub over with the oil, salt and sugar and wrap in foil 3 Cook for 1½ hours 4 Remove the foil, baste duck and return to oven for about ½ hour to crisp 5 While duck is cooking, stone the cherries, put into a bowl with the syrup and vermouth 6 Make bacon rolls (these may be cooked in the oven or under the grill) 7 When duck is cooked lift on to a hot dish and keep warm 8 Make the gravy in the tin 9 Surround the bird with the cherries and bacon rolls 10 Serve gravy separately, accompanied with potatoes and vegetable or salad

Roast Duck

1 duck 2–2½ kg/4–5 lb
2 tbsp oil
1 tbsp honey–1 tbsp flour
stuffing if liked (page 71)
orange slices and watercress for garnish
orange sauce (optional) (page 94)

to serve: 4–5
time: 2½ hours
kitchen roll
meat-tin
trivet
oven No. 5 or 190 °C/380 °F

1 Rub the duck over with oil and stuff if liked–season 2 Wrap in foil and cook for 1½ hours 3 Remove foil and rub the duck with honey and flour 4 Return to oven for about ½ hour to crisp 5 Put on to a hot dish and garnish with watercress and sliced orange 6 Serve with a brown gravy made in the tin and using stock made from giblets, or orange sauce

Fruit Cocktail Duck

4 duck joints
1 orange
1 slice pineapple
60g/2 oz cherries
1 ripe pear
$\frac{1}{8}$ lit/¼ pt red wine
seasoning
a little garlic
oil
1 tsp cornflour

to serve: 2–4
time: 1¼ hours
kitchen roll
sauté-pan
oven No. 4 or 180 °C/355 °F

1 Prepare and mix the fruit, add wine, garlic, seasonings and grated orange-rind **2** Fry the joints lightly in the oil in the pan **3** Pour fruit over the duck **4** Cover the pan, put in the oven and cook until tender, about 30 minutes **5** Arrange the duck on a dish **6** Strain off the liquid and thicken with the cornflour **7** Correct seasoning, add the fruit and arrange round the duck **8** Garnish with watercress

GAME

Pheasant, pigeon, grouse, guinea-fowl, etc.
Venison and hare

General preparation of Game-birds **1** Allow to hang required time **2** Pluck **3** Singe–draw–follow instructions for roast chicken (page 69) **4** Use as required

Accompaniments
pheasant–brown crumbs–crisps–salad–bread sauce–thin gravy–watercress garnish

pigeon, grouse, guinea-fowl, partridge } as pheasant

For preparation, cooking of game-birds see "Chicken" (page 70)

Venison

Cook joints as for roast meat (page 42)

Accompaniments
Red-currant jelly (page 313)

Hare

Cook whole–as for roast meat (page 42)
Cook in joints as for jugged hare (page 83)

Accompaniments
Red-currant jelly
Force-meat balls (page 84)
Thick gravy

Salmis of Game

1 cooked pigeon–grouse, etc.
60g/2 oz butter
1 small onion } finely chopped
1 small carrot }
1 clove of garlic (chopped)
4 tbsp red wine
1 dessertsp flour
¼ lit/½ pt stock (from cube, or game stock)
60g/2 oz mushrooms
chopped parsley
bay-leaf–thyme–lemon-juice
triangular croûtons

to serve: 1–4, according to bird
time: 1¾ hours
sauté-pan

1 Joint the bird **2** Sauté mushrooms and remove **3** Sauté onions, carrot and garlic **4** Add wine and simmer for a few minutes **5** Blend flour and stock and add–boil **6** Add herbs, trimmings from bird and salt–cover and simmer for 1 hour **7** Strain to remove vegetables–return liquid **8** Add mushrooms and game and simmer for 5 minutes **9** Dish the salmis and garnish with the croûtons, which have been fried in butter, and the chopped parsley

Game Pie

Pastry
340g/¾ lb flour
90g/3 oz butter
yolk of egg
salt
⅛ lit/¼ pt milk

to serve: 4–5
time: 2¾ hours and overnight
kitchen roll
raised pie-mould, greased
bowl over a pan of hot water
oven No. 6 or 205 °C/400 °F

Filling
230g/½ lb pork sausage-meat or minced veal
1 pigeon or partridge or grouse or ½ pheasant
30g/1 oz chopped mushrooms
1 tsp parsley
⅛ lit/¼ pt stock–1 tsp gelatine
aspic jelly
glaze (page 10)

1 Melt butter, add milk, boil **2** Pour on to the sieved flour, salt and egg **3** Mix well, knead–keep warm **4** Line the pie-mould with ¾ of the pastry **5** Spread a layer of sausage-meat or veal round the sides and across the bottom **6** Fill the centre with fillets of game–add chopped mushrooms, parsley and seasoning **7** Cover with remaining sausage-meat or veal **8** Roll out remaining pastry, cover mould, and seal the edges–make a hole in the centre **9** Roll out trimmings and cut into leaves or rounds–decorate **10** Bake for 1½ hours reducing heat to No. 2 or 155 °C/310 °F, after 25 minutes **11** Fill with stock and gelatine **12** Remove mould and when cold brush with glaze **13** Decorate with glazed game legs and pieces of aspic

Jugged Hare

1 hare
1 onion stuck with 3 cloves
60g/2 oz butter
½ lit/1 pt stock or stock cube
bouquet garni
cayenne pepper and salt

Thickening
30g/1 oz butter
30g/1 oz flour
⅛ lit/¼ pt red wine
1 tbsp red-currant jelly

Garnish
fleurons of puff pastry
cherries
force-meat balls (page 84)

to serve: 6–8
time: 5 hours and overnight
kitchen roll
braising pan
deep-fat pan
thermometer
oven No. 4 or 180 °C/355 °F

1 Skin and paunch the hare–joint **2** Wipe the joints– do not wash **3** Fry in the butter **4** Add onion, seasoning and stock **5** Bake 2½–3 hours–cool, preferably overnight **6** Re-heat and cook 15–20 minutes **7** Knead together butter and flour and make into small balls (beurre manié) **8** Stir into the stew ½ hour before serving **9** Add wine and jelly–check seasoning **10** Cook pastry fleurons, heat cherries and fry force-meat balls **11** Arrange joints in the centre of a hot dish–pour the sauce over **12** Pile cherries on top of hare **13** Garnish with fleurons and force-meat balls **14** Serve additional red-currant jelly separately

Venison in Port

450g/1 lb venison steak
60g/2 oz butter, 1 tbsp oil
1 chopped carrot
1 chopped onion
1 clove garlic
bay-leaf
thyme
seasoning
⅛ lit/¼ pt port wine

to serve: 3–4
time: 2–2½ hours
kitchen roll
oven No. 4 of 180 °C/355 °F
braising-pan
frying-pan

1 tbsp butter } beurre manié
1 tbsp flour }
1 tbsp red currant jelly
glaze (page 10)
Garnish
6 chestnuts (cooked)
12 button onions
3 mushrooms
fried triangular croûtons

1 Put butter and oil in the pan—fry steak quickly and remove **2** Add carrot, onion, garlic and herbs **3** Place the steak on this mirepoix **4** Cover, and put into the oven for 20 minutes **5** Pour the port over and continue cooking until steak is tender **6** Remove the steak and keep warm **7** Strain sauce into a small pan and skim off any grease **8** Thicken by adding the beurre manié a little at a time **9** Add red-currant jelly and check seasoning **10** Strain over the steak **11** Garnish with glazed chestnuts, onions and sautéd mushrooms **12** Surround with croûtons

STUFFINGS

Savoury or Veal Stuffing (or Force-meat Balls)

2 tbsp fresh breadcrumbs
1 tbsp suet, margarine or butter
1 tsp chopped parsley
pinch of mixed herbs
¼ lemon (grated rind and juice)
seasoning
beaten egg
finely chopped or grated onion (optional)

time: 15 minutes
liquidizer

1 Mix all the dry ingredients, season and bind with the egg

NB **1** Melt butter or margarine before adding to dry ingredients.
2 Suitable to use with veal, lamb, chicken, turkey and fish.
3 Sometimes made into small balls, coated and fried and used as a garnish, e.g. hare.

Sage and Onion Stuffing

110g/¼ lb onions
6 sage-leaves (fresh or dried)
60g/2 oz fresh breadcrumbs
30g/1 oz butter
seasoning
cider or stock to bind
½ beaten egg

time: 25 minutes
liquidizer
(stuffing for goose, duck or pork)

1 Prepare and cook the onions and drain well—chop and liquidize **2** Add breadcrumbs, chopped sage and melted butter **3** Season well and add egg to bind **4** Add stock or cider if mixture is too dry

Variations
1 2 chopped pickled walnuts.
2 1 apple peeled, cored and diced.

Sausage Stuffing or Force-meat

230g/½ lb pork sausage-meat or
230g/½ lb minced pork
30g/1 oz fresh breadcrumbs
½ onion
½ beaten egg
seasoning

time: 15 minutes
liquidizer
(suitable for chicken and turkey)

1 Mix all ingredients together 2 Season well and bind with the egg

Sausage, Mushroom and Onion Stuffing

30g/1 oz dripping
1 large onion
450g/1 lb pork sausage-meat
seasoning
1 tsp chopped parsley
4 tbsp fresh breadcrumbs
½ tsp mixed herbs
110g/¼ lb chopped mushrooms

time: 20 minutes
liquidizer
(suitable for chicken and turkey)

1 Melt dripping–add chopped onion–fry lightly–add mushrooms
2 Add sausage-meat and seasonings and mix well, frying over low heat
3 Add crumbs–use as required

Stuffing for Turkey or Chicken

liver of the turkey or chicken
30g/1 oz butter
110g/¼ lb chipolata sausages
110g/¼ lb chestnuts (tinned)
3 large cooked prunes
2 small pears
4 tbsp white wine
seasoning

time: 12 minutes

1 Brown the liver in half the butter 2 Simmer the sausages in stock or water for 5 minutes 3 Cut sausages in 2 or 3 pieces 4 Dice fruit and liver 5 Mix all ingredients and add remaining melted butter 6 Season well and moisten with the wine

Gratin Force-meat

60 g/2 oz fat bacon pieces
110g/¼ lb chicken livers
15g/½ oz chopped onion or shallot
bay-leaf, thyme, garlic
15g/½ oz mushroom stalks

time: 10 minutes
liquidizer
(suitable for chicken and turkey)

seasoning
1 tbsp white crumbs
egg to bind

1 Sauté chicken livers and onion with the bacon 2 Add herbs, mushrooms and seasoning and brown quickly 3 Remove bay-leaf and thyme if fresh 4 Drain and liquidize 5 Add crumbs and bind with egg

Veal and Ham Stuffing

15g/½ oz beef marrow or suet
60g/2 oz fresh breadcrumbs
1 tsp grated onion
¼ tsp chopped sage
¼ tsp chopped parsley
lemon-rind
15g/½ oz chopped cooked ham
seasoning
egg to bind

time: 10 minutes
liquidizer
(suitable for beef olives and poultry)

1 Chop marrow or suet and mix with crumbs 2 Add grated onion and remaining ingredients 3 Season and bind with egg

Chestnut Stuffing

230g/½ lb chestnuts (weighed after peeling) or tinned
30g/1 oz fresh breadcrumbs
small onion
1 dessertsp chopped parsley
30g/1 oz melted butter
½ beaten egg
seasoning

time: 45 minutes (if tinned chestnuts 20 minutes)
liquidizer
(suitable for chicken and turkey)

1 Cook chestnuts in milk or stock until tender–drain and chop 2 Add grated onion, parsley, melted butter, egg and breadcrumbs–season 3 If too dry add some of the liquid in which the chestnuts were cooked

Apple and Prune Stuffing

60g/2 oz fresh breadcrumbs
4 cooked prunes
1 apple
30g/1 oz chopped nuts (any variety or mixed)
grated rind of ¼ lemon
1 dessertsp egg
30g/1 oz melted butter
seasoning

time: 10 minutes
liquidizer
(suitable for duck and goose)

1 Chop prunes, prepared apple and nuts 2 Mix all ingredients–season and bind with egg

Rice, Onion and Pineapple Stuffing

60g/2 oz cooked rice
1 onion
60g/2 oz chopped pineapple
pinch of mixed herbs or
½ tsp dried or fresh basil
seasoning

time: 15 minutes
(suitable for all poultry)

1 Mix rice and pineapple 2 Add mixed herbs and grated onion 3 Season and mix well

Raisin, Apricot and Almond Stuffing

15g/½ oz butter or goose or duck dripping
30g/1 oz raisins
30g/1 oz almonds (roughly chopped)
1 tsp chopped parsley
1 tbsp tinned apricots
rind and juice of ¼ lemon
seasoning

time: 15 minutes
(suitable for duck, goose, veal and pork)

1 Cook the corn, if fresh (page 116) 2 Chop the onion and fry in the lightly browned 2 Add raisins and almonds and cook for a few minutes 3 Add remaining ingredients and season well

Sweet Corn Stuffing

3 tbsp sweetcorn (fresh or tinned)
1 medium onion
30g/1 oz butter
1 tbsp chopped parsley
grated rind of ½ lemon
1 beaten egg
seasoning

time: 20 minutes
(suitable for chicken and turkey)

1 Cook the corn, if fresh (page 116) 2 Chop the onion and fry in the butter until cooked and lightly brown 3 Add corn and cook for a few minutes 4 Add parsley, lemon-rind and seasoning and bind with the egg

Duxelle Stuffing

30g/1 oz chopped onion or shallot
110g/¼ lb mushrooms
15g/½ oz butter
salt, pepper, nutmeg
1 tsp chopped parsley
1 tsp tomato purée
1 tbsp fresh breadcrumbs
1 tbsp white wine–optional

time: 20 minutes
liquidizer
(suitable for fish)

1 Sauté onion until tender 2 Add chopped mushrooms (with stalks) and stir until moisture has evaporated 3 Season and add remaining ingredients 4 Moisten with a little white wine if necessary

Ambassadrice Farce

15g/½ oz butter
1 tsp finely-chopped onion
1 tsp finely-chopped mushroom
½ tsp finely-chopped parsley
15g/½ oz flour
4 tbsp stock
30g/1 oz chopped marrow
½ egg-yolk
lemon-juice
seasoning

time: 15 minutes
(used for cutlets ambassadrice)

1 Melt butter and sauté onion and mushroom until soft **2** Add flour and liquid and cook for a few minutes **3** Add yolk and marrow a little at a time—season and cool

5
Sauces

White Sauce

Coating
$\frac{1}{8}$ lit/¼ pt milk
15g/½ oz margarine or butter
15 g/½ oz flour
seasoning

time: 10–15 minutes

Flowing
Use half the quantity of fat and flour

1 Melt the fat in a pan **2** Remove from heat–add flour–mix together to form a roux **3** Return to a low heat and cook for a few minutes **4** Remove from the heat, add liquid very gradually stirring continuously **5** When all liquid has been added return to the heat and bring to the boil stirring–boil 2 minutes **6** Season–check consistency
Use as required.

Additions

1 *Parsley.* Add 2 tsp finely-chopped parsley to cooked sauce and 1 tsp lemon-juice.
2 *Shrimp, prawn, lobster.* Add 1 tbsp chopped shrimp or prawn or lobster to cooked sauce and 1 tsp lemon-juice.
3 *Cheese.* Add 60g/2 oz finely-grated cheese to cooked sauce and re-heat gently–do not boil. (Mornay).
4 *Anchovy.* Add 2 tsp anchovy essence to cooked sauce. Omit salt. Colour if required.
5 *Caper.* Add 1 dessertsp capers, 1 tsp caper vinegar. The basic sauce may be made with half milk and half meat liquor or fish stock
6 *Onion.* Add 110g/¼ lb cooked chopped onion, to basic sauce made from ½ milk, ½ onion-water. Re-heat.
7 *Soubise.* Add 4 tbsp onion purée to basic sauce made with ½ milk, ½ onion-water. A little cream or evaporated milk improves the sauce.

8 *Egg.* Add half a hard-boiled egg to basic sauce–reheat.
9 *Cardinal.* Add lobster butter (page 102), or colour basic white sauce with pink or orange colouring. Add lemon-juice and 4 tbsp cream.

Béchamel Sauce

time: ¾ hour
strainer

1 small carrot
1 stick celery
1 small shallot
5 white peppercorns
blade of mace
piece of bay-leaf
¼ lit/½ pt milk
30g/1 oz butter or margarine
30g/1 oz flour
salt
4 tbsp cream

1 Make sauce with fat, flour, mustard and milk **2** Add chopped ingredients–season, add egg
bring to boil–simmer 10 minutes **4** Strain–reheat and season **5** Add cream–heat carefully **6** Use as required

Tartar Sauce (cooked) (1)

time: 25 minutes

⅛ lit/¼ pt milk
15g/½ oz flour
15g/½ oz butter or margarine
2 tbsp vinegar
1 tbsp sugar
¼ tsp mustard
1 tsp chopped parsley
1 tsp chopped gherkins
1 tsp chopped capers
1 egg-yolk
seasoning

1 Make sauce with fat, flour, mustard and milk **2** Add chopped ingredients–season, add egg

Mustard Sauce

time: 15 minutes

1 tsp flour
15g/½ oz margarine or butter
⅛ lit/¼ pt beef (or fish) stock
½ tsp mustard
1 tsp malt and tarragon vinegar mixed
1 tsp sugar

1 Make a roux sauce with flour, mustard and half the fat **2** Add liquid–boil and cook thoroughly **3** Add sugar and vinegar **4** Add extra fat in small pats, beating well. Do not allow to boil again

Lemon Sauce (Savoury)

⅛ lit/¼ pt white sauce made with stock, fish stock, or milk and stock (page 10)
½ lemon
1 tbsp cream
1 dessertsp chopped parsley (optional)

time: 30 minutes

1 Peel rind thinly and infuse in the liquid for 15 minutes **2** Make the sauce, using this liquid **3** Remove rind **4** Add the lemon-juice gradually **5** Add the cream and parsley (if liked) **6** Reheat, but do not boil **7** Season and serve with chicken, or fish

Fennel Sauce (Sauce fenouil)

⅛ lit/¼ pt white sauce (page 89)
1 dessertsp chopped green fennel
lemon-juice
seasoning

time: 20 minutes

1 Plunge the fennel into boiling water, drain, squeeze dry and chop finely **2** Add to the sauce **3** Add a few drops of lemon-juice—season **4** Serve with fish—especially good with mackerel

Hollandaise Sauce (mock) (1)

⅛ lit/¼ pt béchamel (page 90) or plain white sauce
1 yolk of egg
2 tbsp cream
lemon-juice
seasoning

time: 10–15 minutes

1 Heat the sauce **2** Add the yolk mixed with the cream **3** Reheat without boiling **4** Add lemon-juice and seasoning **5** Check consistency

Chaud-froid Sauce

¼ lit/½ pt white sauce
⅛ lit/¼ pt aspic jelly
1 tsp gelatine
1 tbsp cream
seasoning

time: 20 minutes
muslin

1 Dissolve the gelatine in the aspic jelly **2** Add to the sauce **3** Add cream and seasoning **4** Tammy through muslin **5** Use as required
NB A brown chaud-froid sauce may be made using espagnole instead of a white sauce and is used for game. A white chaud-froid may be coloured green by using green-pea purée and a little green colouring and may be used for coating fish dishes.

Caramel Sauce

⅛ lit/¼ pt flowing white sauce (page 89)
caramel
Caramel Recipe
30g/1 oz granulated sugar
2 tbsp water

time: 15 minutes

1 Boil sugar and water until a rich golden colour. Do not *stir* **2** Pour the hot sauce into the caramel and stir vigorously **3** Serve in sauce-boat

Basic Brown Sauce

1 small carrot
1 small onion
30g/1 oz flour
30g/1 oz dripping
⅜ lit/¾ pt stock or stock cube
seasoning

time: 1 hour
strainer

1 Prepare carrot and onion and chop roughly **2** Melt the dripping and sauté the carrot and onion without colouring **3** Add flour and make a brown roux slowly **4** Add stock and bring to boil **5** Simmer for 15–20 minutes **6** Season and strain
NB A little tomato or tomato purée improves the colour and flavour.

Espagnole Sauce (Brown)

1 carrot
1 onion
60g/2 oz flour
60g/2 oz butter
60g/2 oz bacon pieces
½ lit/1 pt stock
110g/¼ lb tomatoes
  or ⅛ lit/¼ pt tinned tomatoes
60g/2 oz mushroom stalks
seasoning

time: 4 hours

1 Prepare carrot and onion and chop roughly **2** Melt the butter and add bacon **3** Sauté carrot and onion for about 10 minutes without browning **4** Add flour and cook *very slowly* until a bright chestnut brown (about 2–3 hours) **5** Add liquid, tomatoes and mushrooms and simmer for about 1 hour **6** Strain. Season–use as required
NB The slower this sauce is made the better the flavour.

Ambassadrice Sauce

⅛ lit/¼ pt espagnole sauce (page 92)
1 tsp red-currant jelly
1 tsp lemon-juice
30g/1 oz blanched sultanas
seasoning

time: 10 minutes

1 Mix all these ingredients 2 Season and correct consistency 3 Use as required

Bigarade Sauce (1) (Sauce bigarade)

⅛ lit/¼ pt espagnole sauce (page 92)
½ small orange
¼ lemon
4 tbsp claret
pinch of sugar
seasoning

time: 20 minutes
strainer

1 Put the sauce into a pan and add the orange-rind and a strip of lemon-rind 2 Simmer gently for 10 minutes–strain 3 Add the orange-juice, 1 tsp of lemon-juice and wine 4 Season, add sugar and check consistency 5 Reheat and serve

Bigarade Sauce (2)

⅛ lit/¼ pt espagnole sauce (page 92)
1 onion finely chopped
15g/½ oz butter
4 tbsp red wine
1 small bay-leaf
rind and juice of one orange
1 tsp red-currant jelly
stock or stock cube

time: 30 minutes
strainer

1 Sauté onion in the butter (do not brown) 2 Add wine and bay-leaf 3 Reduce gently by about one-third 4 Add the juice and half the orange-rind to the espagnole sauce 5 Simmer gently for about 5 minutes 6 Shred remaining rind thinly–blanch and drain 7 Add 4 tbsp stock to the sauce 8 Strain, and add shredded rind and jelly 9 Check seasoning and consistency
NB This is a good sauce to serve with duck or game of any kind.

Cider Sauce

⅛ lit/¼ pt espagnole sauce (page 92)
4 tbsp cider
small bay-leaf
1 clove
seasoning

time: 10 minutes
strainer

1 Mix all the ingredients in a small pan 2 Simmer for 5 minutes 3 Check the consistency 4 Season and strain 5 Serve with ham, pork or duck

Demi-glace Sauce (Sauce demi-glace)

⅛ lit/¼ pt espagnole sauce (page 92)
4 tbsp good gravy from roast meat
or 2 tbsp of liquid meat glaze (page 10)

time: 20 minutes
strainer

1 Strain the gravy and remove any fat **2** Put in a pan with the sauce **3** Boil well for 15 minutes **4** Strain if necessary

Italian Sauce (Sauce italienne)

⅛ lit/¼ pt espagnole sauce (page 92)
15g/½ oz butter or 1 tbsp oil
small onion (chopped)
15g/½ oz chopped mushroom stalks
1 tbsp sherry
2 tbsp stock or stock cube
1 bay-leaf
seasoning

time: 45 minutes
strainer

1 Sauté the vegetables in the fat **2** Add stock and wine and boil until well reduced **3** Add sauce, bay-leaf and seasoning **4** Simmer for 10 minutes **5** Strain

Orange Sauce (Savoury)

⅛ lit/¼ pt espagnole sauce (page 92)
½ an orange
½ a lemon
4 tbsp red wine
1 tbsp of red-currant jelly
seasoning

time: 30 minutes
strainer

1 Remove the orange-rind very thinly and cut into fine strips **2** Cover with cold water and cook until just tender—strain **3** Add orange and lemon-juice and rind to the espagnole sauce **4** Heat—add wine and seasoning **5** Add red-currant jelly **6** Serve with roast duck, goose or wild duck

Piquante Sauce (Sauce piquante)

⅛ lit/¼ pt espagnole sauce (page 92)
small chopped onion
1 bay-leaf
4 tbsp vinegar
1 chopped gherkin
1 tsp chopped capers
seasoning

time: 30 minutes
strainer

1 Put onion and bay-leaf in a pan with vinegar **2** Boil and reduce to half the quantity **3** Add the sauce and simmer for 15 minutes **4** Strain, and add gherkin and capers **5** Check seasoning and consistency, reheat and serve

Réforme Sauce

⅛ lit/¼ pt espagnole sauce (page 92)
4 tbsp vinegar
2 tbsp port wine

time: 15 minutes
strainer

1 tsp red-currant jelly
6 peppercorns

1 Boil vinegar and peppercorns (reduce to about half) 2 Strain into the espagnole sauce 3 Heat and correct consistency and seasoning 4 Add jelly and wine—reheat and serve

Hollandaise Sauce (2)

2 tbsp white vinegar
2 yolks
60g/2 oz butter
seasoning

time: 20 minutes
whisk

1 Reduce the vinegar to half quantity 2 Add enough water to give 3 tbsp liquid 3 Cool and add yolks separately 4 Cook gently until it begins to thicken 5 Add butter a little at a time whisking continuously 6 Add seasoning and use as required

NB The sauce must not boil.

Béarnaise Sauce

4 tbsp mixed vinegars
1 tsp chopped onion
3 peppercorns
1 yolk of egg
30g/1 oz butter
seasoning

time: 20 minutes
strainer

1 Boil the vinegars with the onion and peppercorns until well reduced—strain 2 Add 1 tbsp of water 3 Add yolk 4 Cook very gently until thick 5 Add butter a little at a time 6 Season

NB Simple béarnaise sauce may be made using ⅛ lit/¼ pt white sauce.

Mousseline Sauce (Hot savoury)

2 yolks of eggs
4 tbsp csream
1 tbsp white stock
pinch of nutmeg
15g/½ oz butter
lemon-juice and seasoning

time: 20 minutes
whisk

1 Put all the ingredients except the butter and lemon-juice into a small pan 2 Whisk over gentle heat until thick enough to prevent separation 3 Whisk in butter a little at a time 4 Add lemon-juice and serve at once

Tartar Sauce (2)

⅛ lit/¼ pt mayonnaise (page 131)
2 tbsp vinegar
1 tsp chopped parsley
1 tsp chopped capers
1 tsp chopped gherkins
grated onion or crushed garlic (optional)

time: 15 minutes

1 Add ingredients to mayonnaise 2 Serve cold in a sauce-boat

Jam Sauce

$\frac{1}{8}$ lit/¼ pt water
1 dessertsp sugar
2 tbsp jam
colouring
1 tsp arrowroot
lemon-juice

time: 10 minutes
strainer

1 Blend arrowroot with the water 2 Bring to the boil 3 Add jam, lemon-juice, colouring 4 Heat, strain and use as required
NB Syrup and marmalade sauces are made by the same method.

Lemon Sauce

$\frac{1}{8}$ lit/¼ pt water
60g/2 oz sugar or golden syrup
juice of 1 lemon
rind of ½ lemon
1 tsp arrowroot

time: 25 minutes
strainer

1 Peel the rind thinly and infuse in the water for 15 minutes 2 Blend the arrowroot with a little cold water 3 Pour on the hot water and return to the pan 4 Bring to boil and boil for 2 minutes–strain 5 Add sugar or syrup, and lemon-juice 6 Colour if necessary

Butterscotch Sauce

110g/¼ lb dark moist sugar
$\frac{1}{8}$ lit/¼ pt water
30g/1 oz butter
rind of ½ lemon
1 tsp arrowroot
vanilla essence
lemon-juice

time: 20 minutes
strainer

1 Dissolve sugar in the water 2 Add butter and lemon-rind and boil gently for 5 minutes. Strain 3 Blend the arrowroot with the lemon-juice and a little cold water 4 Add to the sauce and boil to thicken 5 Add a few drops of vanilla essence

Wine Sauce

$\frac{1}{8}$ lit/¼ pt water } syrup
60g/2 oz sugar }
1 tbsp jam
4 tbsp sherry
1 tsp lemon-juice
colouring

time: 20 minutes
strainer

1 Make the syrup (page 164) 2 Add the jam and when well mixed add the remaining ingredients 3 Reheat and add colouring 4 Strain if necessary

Custard

⅛ lit/¼ pt milk
1 dessertsp sugar
1 tsp custard powder

time: 10 minutes

1 Blend custard powder with a little milk–pour into a pan–add remainder of milk **2** Bring to the boil stirring–boil 2 minutes **3** Add sugar **4** Serve in a sauce-boat

Chocolate Sauce

60g/2 oz plain cooking chocolate
⅛ lit/¼ pt syrup (page 164)
½ tsp instant coffee
2 tsp brandy or rum or a few drops of vanilla essence
1 tsp cornflour
1 tbsp milk
1–2 tbsp cream (optional)

time: 25 minutes

1 Make the syrup **2** Add coffee-powder and broken chocolate **3** When chocolate is thoroughly melted, bring to the boil–simmer 3 minutes **4** Blend cornflour in the milk, add to the chocolate mixture–bring to the boil **5** Stir in flavouring–add cream **6** Use as required

Egg Custard Sauce

⅛ lit/¼ pt milk
1 egg
1 dessertsp sugar
vanilla

time: 15 minutes
strainer
(whisk)

1 Heat the milk **2** Add to beaten egg **3** Strain into a small pan **4** Stir over very gentle heat until thick enough to coat the back of the spoon **5** Add sugar and a few drops of vanilla, or use vanilla sugar
NB If the custard should show signs of curdling, whisk holding the pan over cold water

Mousseline Sauce (Sweet)

2 eggs
4 tbsp cream
45g/1½ oz castor sugar
1 tbsp sherry

time: 10–15 minutes
whisk

1 Put all the ingredients into a small pan **2** Whisk over gentle heat until thick enough to prevent separation **3** Serve at once with hot soufflés, etc.

Apple Sauce

1 medium cooking apple
1 tsp sugar
grated rind of ¼ lemon
15g/½ oz butter

time: 15–20 minutes
liquidizer

1 Peel, core and slice apple **2** Put butter into a pan–add apple, sugar and lemon-rind **3** Cover and cook slowly till tender **4** Liquidize and re-heat **5** Serve in a sauce-boat

Cranberry Sauce

230g/½ lb cranberries
⅛ lit/¼ pt water
60g/2 oz sugar

time: 30 minutes
liquidizer
sieve

1 Stew cranberries and sugar in water till very tender (do not allow to boil dry) **2** Liquidize and sieve to remove seeds **3** Reheat

Cumberland Sauce

1 orange
1 lemon
4 tbsp port wine
2 tbsp red-currant jelly
small piece onion

time: ½ hour plus chilling time

1 Cut orange and lemon-rind into fine julienne strips and grate the onion **2** Put these into cold water–bring to boil and cook for about 15 minutes, or until water has nearly gone and peel is tender **3** Boil wine and jelly **4** Add to peel and heat throughly **5** Chill and serve
NB This sauce is always served chilled and improves if kept for a day or two–it may also be served with cold game, game pies and boar's-head

Chestnut Sauce

230g/½ lb chestnuts or tinned purée
⅜ lit/¾ pt stock or stock cube
30g/1 oz butter
pinch of cinnamon
grated lemon-rind (½ lemon)
4 tbsp cream
seasoning

time: fresh, 1 hour; tinned, 10 minutes
liquidizer

1 Slit the shells of the nuts and boil or bake them for 15–20 minutes
2 Remove shells and skins **3** Simmer in the stock with lemon rind–until tender–liquidize **4** Reheat and add butter a little at a time
5 Add cream, cinnamon and seasoning **6** Serve with roast chicken or turkey

Tomato Sauce

230g/½ lb tomatoes or ¼ lit/½ pt tinned tomatoes
1 small carrot
1 small onion
15g/½ oz bacon pieces or 15g/½ oz margarine
bouquet garni
¼ lit/½ pt stock (stock cube) or if tinned– ⅛ lit/¼ pt stock
seasoning
2 tsp cornflour
sugar if necessary

time: 1 hour
liquidizer
strainer

1 Extract fat from bacon **2** Add roughly cut onion and carrot, sauté 7 minutes **3** Add tomatoes (if fresh, cut roughly) stock, seasoning and bouquet **4** Boil till tender **5** Remove bacon and bouquet–liquidize and strain **6** Blend cornflour with little water **7** Add to purée–bring to the boil **8** Correct seasoning–adjust consistency **9** Serve in a sauce-boat or use as required

Curry Sauce (Sauce indienne)

1 small onion
30g/1 oz butter or margarine
1 small apple
15g/½ oz curry-powder
15g/½ oz ground rice or flour
¼ lit/½ pt stock or coconut infusion (see Misc. Processes)
1 tsp treacle
2 tsp lemon-juice
1 dessertsp chutney or jam
salt

time: ¾ hour

1 Chop the onion and sauté gently in the fat **2** Add flour and curry-powder and cook gently for 2–3 minutes **3** Add liquid–when boiling add all the other ingredients **4** Simmer gently for at least ½ hour **5** Use as required

Mint Sauce

2 tbsp finely-chopped mint
2 tbsp boiling water
2 tbsp vinegar
1 tsp castor sugar

time: 15 minutes

1 Dissolve sugar in the boiling water–add vinegar and allow to cool **2** Chop mint **3** Add to the cooled liquid **4** Serve in a sauce-boat

Horse-radish Sauce

⅛ lit/¼ pt white sauce or evaporated milk or cream
45g/1½ oz grated horse-radish
salt, cayenne, sugar
1 dessertsp white vinegar

time: 10 minutes
liquidizer

1 Peel horse-radish and cut up thickly and liquidize **2** Whip cream—add horse-radish, vinegar and seasoning. Taste **3** Serve in a sauce-boat; or add ingredients to white sauce or whipped evaporated milk

Walnut and Horse-radish Sauce

60g/2 oz shelled walnuts
2 tbsp fresh liquidized horse-radish
1 tsp sugar
juice of ½ lemon
⅛ lit/¼ pt cream
salt

time: 15–20 minutes
liquidizer

1 Chop the walnuts **2** Whip the cream **3** Stir in the walnuts and horse-radish **4** Lastly add lemon-juice and seasoning
NB This is a good sauce to serve with cold salmon or salmon trout.

Bread Sauce

90g/3 oz stale breadcrumbs
1 onion
1 blade mace
2 cloves
piece of bay-leaf
5 peppercorns
¼ lit/½ pt milk
15g/½ oz butter and/or 1 tbsp cream
seasoning

time: 30 minutes
strainer

1 Put onion and spices into milk—bring to the boil—infuse 20 minutes **2** Strain—return milk to the pan and add breadcrumbs—add butter **3** Reheat—season—stir in cream if used **4** Check consistency
NB The onion may be liquidized after removing the spices and added to the sauce.

SWEET BUTTERS

Brandy butter

90g/3 oz butter
170g/6 oz icing sugar or
150g/5 oz icing sugar plus 30g/1 oz ground almonds
3 tbsp brandy

time: 15 minutes
mixer
sieve

1 Cream the butter until soft 2 Work in the sieved icing sugar and beat until white and light 3 Add ground almonds if used 4 Beat in brandy gradually

NB This butter will keep well in an airtight jar.

Rum butter

60g/2 oz butter
110g/¼ lb moist sugar
4 tbsp rum

time: 30 minutes
mixer

1 Beat butter to soften 2 Add sugar and beat until light and creamy 3 Add rum gradually 4 Chill before serving

Sherry butter

As for rum butter, using sherry in place of rum and castor sugar in place of moist sugar.

SAVOURY BUTTERS

Anchovy butter

30g/1 oz butter
15g/½ oz anchovy paste or sieved anchovies
lemon-juice

time: 15 minutes
foil

1 Mix butter and paste 2 Blend in a few drops of lemon-juice and a little cayenne pepper 3 Wrap in foil and chill

Chutney butter

30g/1 oz butter
15g/½ oz chutney
½ tsp French mustard
lemon–seasoning

time: 20 minutes
sieve
foil

1 Mix butter and chutney 2 Add mustard, lemon-juice and seasoning 3 Sieve, wrap and chill

Curry butter

30g/1 oz butter
½ level tsp curry-powder
lemon-juice and salt

time: 15 minutes
foil

1 Cream butter and curry-powder 2 Mix in a few drops of lemon-juice and salt 3 Wrap and chill

Garlic butter

30g/1 oz butter
½ clove of garlic

time: 15 minutes
sieve

salt foil

1 Crush the garlic and cream with the butter 2 Add salt–sieve 3 Wrap and chill

Lobster butter

15g/½ oz lobster coral (spawn) (raw if possible)
30g/1 oz butter

time: 10 minutes
sieve

1 Mix coral until smooth 2 Work in the butter–season–sieve 3 Use for colouring sauces or bisques

Maître d'hôtel butter

30g/1 oz butter
1 tsp finely-chopped parsley
lemon-juice, salt and cayenne

time: 15 minutes
foil

1 Cream the butter and work in the parsley, lemon-juice and seasoning 2 Wrap and chill

Mustard butter

30g/1 oz butter
1 tsp French mustard

time: 15 minutes
foil

1 Cream the butter 2 Add the mustard and work it in 3 Wrap and chill

Paprika butter

30g/1 oz butter
1 tsp paprika pepper

time: 15 minutes
foil

As for mustard butter

6
Vegetables, Salads and Salad dressings

Cabbage, Spring Greens or Sprouting Broccoli

1 small savoy cabbage or
230g/½ lb spring greens
or sprouting broccoli
15g/½ oz butter

to serve: 2
time: 15 minutes

1 Remove outer leaves **2** Cut into quarters, wash quickly **3** Shred just before cooking **4** Put into a little boiling salted water–cover–cook until just tender **5** Drain well–add butter and toss **6** Serve in a hot vegetable-dish

Brussels Sprouts

230g/½ lb sprouts
15g/½ oz butter
salt

to serve: 2
time: 15 minutes

1 Remove outer leaves **2** Cut stalk at base to make a cross **3** Wash quickly in cold water **4** Put into a very little boiling salted water **5** Boil rapidly with lid on until just tender **6** Drain well **7** Add butter toss with a spoon **8** Serve in a hot vegetable dish, stalks downward

If frozen:
1 Melt butter in a pan.
2 Sauté the frozen sprouts, lid on, until tender.
3 Serve as for fresh sprouts.

Cauliflower

1 small cauliflower
⅛ lit/¼ pt coating white sauce seasoning

to serve: 2
time: 20 minutes

1 Divide the cauliflower into "flowerlets", or to cook whole, remove centre of stalk **2** Wash thoroughly–cook in a very small quantity of boiling, salted water **3** Drain and arrange in a vegetable dish **4** Coat with sauce

Cauliflower au gratin

As cauliflower
Add 60g/2 oz grated cheese

to serve: 2
time: 20 minutes
grill

1 Cook cauliflower (page 103) 2 Prepare white sauce, add 2/3 cheese 3 Arrange cauliflower in a dish–coat with sauce–sprinkle with remaining cheese **4** Grill **5** Serve on a plate on a plain paper
NB Leeks, marrow, chicory may be served as cauliflower or cauliflower au gratin.

Cauliflower French Fried

1 medium-sized cauliflower
1 egg
1 tbsp oil
raspings
seasonings
parsley

to serve: 3
time: 30 minutes
deep-fat pan
thermometer

1 Prepare and cook as for cauliflower (page 103) 2 Drain well and dip in the beaten egg, oil, and seasoning 3 Coat with raspings **4** Fry in the deep fat at 180 °C/355 °F till golden brown–drain **5** Serve in a vegetable-dish on a plain paper and garnish with parsley

Cauliflower Maltaise (Choux-fleur à la Maltaise)

1 medium-sized cauliflower
⅛ lit/¼ pt hollandaise sauce (1 or 2, pages 91, 95)
1 small orange
seasoning

to serve: 3
time: 30 minutes

1 Prepare and cook as for cauliflower (page 103) 2 Make the hollandaise sauce, but after adding the butter add strained orange-juice gradually and finally the grated rind–adjust the seasoning 3 Arrange in a hot vegetable-dish in a dome-shape **4** Coat with sauce, dish on a plain paper
NB This can be served with a plain hollandaise sauce.

Cauliflower Polonaise (Choux-fleur polonaise)

1 medium-sized cauliflower
90g/3 oz butter
2 tbsp fresh breadcrumbs
1 hard-boiled egg
1 tsp chopped parsley

to serve: 3
time: ½ hour
oven No. 3 or 170 °C/335 °F
baking-tray
sauté-pan

1 Prepare and cook as for cauliflower (page 103) 2 Put sprigs on the tray and place ½ the butter over the top, dry off in the oven 3 Arrange dome-shaped in a hot vegetable dish **4** Fry breadcrumbs in remaining butter **5** Mix fried breadcrumbs with the chopped parsley, sieved yolk and chopped white of egg **6** Sprinkle this over the cauliflower
7 Serve standing on a plain paper

Spinach

Allow 450g/1 lb spinach per helping.

450g/1 lb spinach
15g/½ oz butter
salt

to serve: 1
time: ½ hour

1 Wash spinach very well in several waters **2** Remove leaf from stalk **3** Put into a dry pan (cook in the liquid that adheres to the leaves) **4** Gradually add more washed spinach as the amount in the pan reduces—cook till tender **5** Drain very well **6** Add butter and salt—toss **7** Serve in a hot vegetable dish

Frozen spinach

1 Melt butter in pan—add spinach.
2 Sauté till tender.
3 Serve as for fresh spinach.

Broad Beans

230g/½ lb broad beans
15g/½ oz butter
salt

to serve: 1
time: 15 minutes

1 Shell the beans **2** Put into a little boiling, salted water—cover **3** Cook till tender **4** Drain well—add butter—toss **5** Serve on a hot vegetable dish

NB 1 If beans are coarse, the skin can be removed before serving
2 These can be served coated with parsley sauce

Frozen Beans

1 Melt butter—add beans **2** Sauté till tender **3** Serve as above

Runner or French Beans

230g/½ lb runner beans
15g/½ oz butter
salt
boiling water

to serve: 2
time: 15 minutes
bean-slicer

1 Wipe beans—cut off ends and slice thinly or put through a machine **2** Put into a little boiling, salted water—cover **3** Cook until just tender **4** Drain very well **5** Add butter and toss **6** Serve in a hot vegetable dish

NB 1 Runner beans, if old—string
2 French beans if very young may be cooked whole or cut in diamonds and used as a garnish

If frozen **1** Melt butter—add beans **2** Sauté till tender **3** Serve as for fresh or cook in a very little boiling, salted water and finish as above

Boiled Peas

230g/½ lb peas
15g/½ oz butter

to serve: 1–2
time: 20–30 minutes

salt
boiling water
mint
1 tsp sugar

1 Shell peas **2** Put into a little boiling, salted water to which a sprig of mint and the sugar has been added **3** Cook till tender–10–20 minutes according to age **4** Drain well–remove mint **5** Add butter–toss **6** Serve in a hot vegetable dish

Frozen peas

1 Melt butter in a pan–add peas and mint **2** Sauté till tender **3** Serve as for fresh peas

Petits pois à la française

450g/1 lb green peas or 1 pkt (large) frozen peas
⅛ lit/¼ pt boiling water
sprig of mint
sprig of parsley
small piece of onion (chopped)
salt
sugar
90g/3 oz cooked ham
15g/½ oz butter
1 tsp flour
fleurons

to serve: 4
time: 20 minutes

1 Cook the peas gently in the boiling water with salt, sugar, mint, parsley and onion added until tender–drain **2** Dice the ham and toss in the butter–add the flour **3** Add peas and heat together for a few minutes **4** Pile in a hot vegetable-dish–garnish with the fleurons
NB A dessertsp of cream may be added at the last minute if liked

Petit pois à la Chantilly

1 small packet frozen peas or 230g/½ lb young fresh peas
230g/½ lb young carrots
15g/½ oz butter
1 tbsp cream
salt
mint

to serve: 3
time: ½ hour

1 Cook the peas in the butter, mint and little salt, or as for fresh peas (page 105) **2** Cook carrots in a small quantity of boiling, salted water **3** Strain–sauté peas in butter and carrots in the cream **4** Make a border of the carrots in a hot dish and pile peas in the centre
NB Small carrots may be cooked whole. Larger carrots should be cut into logs.

Buttered Carrots

230g/½ lb carrots
15g/½ oz margarine or butter

to serve: 2
time: 20 minutes

1 tsp chopped parsley
salt
boiling water

1 Prepare carrots, cut into logs 2 Cook quickly in a small quantity of boiling salted water until tender 3 Strain–turn on to a plate 4 Melt fat–add parsley 5 Sauté carrots–serve in a hot dish arranged in a pile of logs.

Parsnips

Boiled: cook and serve as carrots (page 107)
Roast: cook and serve as potatoes (page 109)
Steamed: cook as potatoes (page 108)

Swedes, Turnips

230g/½ lb swedes or turnips
15g/½ oz butter
seasoning
parsley

to serve: 2
time: 25–30 minutes

1 Peel thickly–cut into pieces 2 Cook in boiling salted water till tender 3 Drain well–add butter and seasoning–mash 4 Reheat–serve in a hot vegetable-dish–garnish with parsley

NB 1 tbsp of cream improves the flavour

Boiled Potatoes

230g/½ lb old potatoes
salt

time: 25 minutes
vegetable-brush

1 Scrub and peel potatoes and cut into oven-sized pieces 2 Put into cold salted water to cover (just)–bring to the boil and boil about 15 minutes 3 Drain well, dry and use as required

Mashed or Creamed Potatoes

230g/½ lb potatoes
15g/½ oz margarine or butter
2 tbsp milk
salt and pepper
parsley

to ricer serve: 1–2
time: ½ hour

1 Prepare potatoes as for boiled potatoes (page 107) 2 Put through the ricer 3 Put fat and milk into a pan–boil, add potato and beat till white and fluffy–season 4 Serve in a hot dish, in a pyramid or rounded–garnish with a sprig of parsley

Potato Croquettes

230g/½ lb potatoes
egg
15g/½ oz butter
seasoning
parsley
egg and raspings

to serve: 2
time: 1 hour
deep-fat pan
thermometer
ricer

1 Cook potatoes–dry well (page 107), put through the ricer **2** Melt butter–beat in potatoes **3** Add 1 dessertsp egg, seasoning and flavouring **4** Cool on a plate **5** Shape into corks or balls **6** Coat *twice* with egg and crumbs–firm-on crumbs and re-shape **7** Fry in deep fat at 180 °C/355 °F for two minutes–fry parsley **8** Serve in vegetable dish on plain paper garnished with fresh or fried parsley

Flavourings: Grated cheese, chopped herbs, shrimps, etc., fried onion

Duchess Potatoes

to serve: 2
time: 45 minutes
greased baking-sheet
No. 8 vegetable star-forcer
forcing-bag
oven No. 7 or 220 °C/425 °F

Recipe: as for potato croquettes (page 107)
1 Prepare the mixture as for potato croquettes **2** Put into the bag and force on to the sheet in rounds, figure-S or hairpins **3** Bake 1 minute–remove from oven and brush *very* gently with egg **4** Return to the oven to brown for about 25 minutes **5** Serve in a vegetable-dish on a plain paper with parsley garnish
NB They may be browned under the grill

Potato Puffles (Pommes dauphine)

230g/½ lb mashed potato (page 107)
choux pastry (2-egg quantity) (page 232)
salt

to serve: 4
time: 1 hour
deep-fat pan
thermometer

1 Follow the method for choux pastry **2** Add the potato–mix and season well **3** Drop in teaspoonsful into fat at 170 °C/335 °F–cook for 4–5 minutes **4** Drain well and sprinkle with salt **5** Serve on a dish paper in a vegetable-dish; or put into a forcing-bag with a 10 mm/½ in. plain forcer and cut off in short lengths into the fat

Steamed Potatoes

230g/½ lb potatoes
seasoning

time: 30–35 minutes
steamer

1 Prepare potatoes **2** Cut into even-sized pieces **3** Place in the steamer–sprinkle with salt **4** Steam for 25–30 minutes or until tender **5** Use as required

Roast Potatoes

230g/½ lb potatoes
dripping or oil

to serve: 2
time: 1 hour 20 minutes

salt
flour

roasting-tin
trivet
oven No. 6 or 205 °C/400 °F

1 Prepare potatoes—cut into even-sized pieces if very large 2 Parboil 5 minutes 3 Dry—sprinkle with flour and salt 4 Put on to the trivet, baste with fat 5 Cook for ¾ to 1 hour—basting every 20 minutes 6 Serve in a hot vegetable-dish

Potatoes Château (Pommes château)

230g/½ lb medium-sized potatoes
60g/2 oz butter
chopped parsley
seasoning

to serve: 2
time: 1 hour
sauté-pan
roasting-tin
oven No. 6 or 205 °C/400 °F

1 Prepare the potatoes—cut into quarters and trim 2 Blanch and drain 3 Melt the butter—skim and toss the potatoes in this for a few minutes 4 Bake until golden brown, cooked and crisp on the surface 5 Drain and sprinkle with a little salt 6 Dish in a hot vegetable-dish and sprinkle with chopped parsley

Potatoes Anna

340g/¾ lb potatoes
30g/1 oz butter
seasoning
parsley

to serve: 2
time: 1¼ hours
mandolin (optional)
foil
small buttered fireproof dish or sandwich-tin
oven No. 4 or 180 °C/355 °F

1 Peel potatoes and trim—slice thinly 2 Arrange overlapping circles of potato in the tin or dish putting butter, salt and pepper between each layer 3 Cover with foil and bake for about ¾ hour 4 Turn on to a hot vegetable-dish 5 Sprinkle with parsley

Potatoes Baked in their Jackets

medium-sized old potatoes
oil
parsley

to serve: 1–2 potatoes per person
time: 1–1¼ hours
vegetable brush
oven No. 4 or 170 °C/355 °F

1 Scrub potatoes—prick well, rub with oil 2 Put on to the baking-sheet 3 Bake for ¾ hour or till soft 4 Serve in a vegetable-dish—garnish with parsley 5 Hand butter separately

Stuffed Potatoes

(1)

2 medium-sized potatoes
110g/¼ lb cooked sausages
parsley

to serve: 2
time: 1¼ hours
oven No. 4 or 170 °C/355 °F

1 Bake potatoes (page 109) 2 Cut the end off each potato 3 Slit potato and insert the sausages 4 Serve garnished with parsley

(2)

2 medium-sized potatoes
30g/1 oz butter or margarine
30–90g/2–3 oz of
(a) cooked minced ham
(b) cooked minced beef
(c) cooked minced chicken
(d) grated cheese
(e) cooked lentils
seasoning
parsley

to serve: 2
time: 1–1¼ hours

1 Bake potatoes (page 109) 2 Cut a round out of each potato 3 Scoop out the potato and mix with the chosen ingredients 4 Pack into the potatoes, piling the mixture up 5 Replace round and return the potatoes to the oven for a few minutes to reheat 6 Serve on a plain paper or folded table-napkin and garnish with parsley

Chipped Potatoes

large old potatoes
salt
parsley

time: 1 hour
deep-fat pan with frying-basket
thermometer
kitchen roll
tea-cloth

1 Peel the potatoes, dry them, and cut a slice off each end–straighten sides, top and bottom 2 Cut down the length of the potato in 10 mm/½ inch widths, holding potato firmly 3 Turn potato on side, and cut again in lengths about 75 mm/3 inches long 4 Soak the chips in cold water for 20 minutes 5 Wrap in the cloth to dry 6 Put into the frying-basket and cook till tender at 170 °C/335 °F 7 Remove from fat and heat the fat to 190 °C/380 °F 8 Return the chips and crisp quickly 9 Turn on to kitchen paper–sprinkle with salt 10 Serve in a vegetable-dish on a plain paper, garnished with parsley

Straws, Matchsticks (Allumettes)

As for chipped potatoes (page 110)

time: ¾ hour
deep-fat pan
thermometer
kitchen roll
tea-cloth

Prepare as for chips making: straws 50 mm/2 in. x 5 mm/¼ in.; or matchsticks match-size

To fry: fry in hot deep fat at 190 °C/380 °F till tender and crisp. Proceed as for chipped potatoes.

Game Chips or Potato Crisps

1 large potato
salt

time: 1 hour
deep-fat pan
thermometer
mandolin or slicer
tea-cloth
kitchen roll

1 Prepare potato–cut off one end 2 Slice very finely with a sharp knife or mandolin, or slicer on a machine 3 Soak in cold water–dry 4 Fry in deep fat at 180 °C/355 °F until golden brown and crisp. Turn with a spatula or frying-spoon 5 Drain well–sprinkle with salt 6 Serve on a plain dish paper in a vegetable-dish; or serve as a garnish; or serve as a cocktail snack

Gaufrette potatoes (Pommes gaufrettes)

1 large potato

time: 1 hour
mandolin
deep-fat pan
thermometer
kitchen roll
tea-cloth

1 Peel potato–cut a slice off one end 2 Set the ridged cutter finely 3 Cut one slice off potato–turn potato quarter turn–cut a second slice–this will be like lattice-work 4 Continue cutting, turning potato quarter each time 5 Soak in cold water 6 Dry in the cloth 7 Fry in hot fat at 190 °C/380 °F till crisp–about 2 minutes 8 Drain well–sprinkle with salt 9 Use as required

Parisian Potatoes (Pommes de terre à la parisienne)

large potatoes
butter

time: for 1 potato ½ hour
ball-cutter
sauté-pan
kitchen roll

1 Using the ball-cutter, scoop out balls from the potatoes 2 Blanch and drain well 3 Fry until brown in the clarified butter, turning frequently 4 Drain and sprinkle with salt
Use as a garnish, e.g. for fish dishes

New Potatoes

230g/½ lb even-sized new potatoes
mint
15g/½ oz butter
1 tbsp chopped parsley

to serve: 2
time: 25 minutes
vegetable-brush

1 Scrub potatoes 2 Put into boiling salted water with mint. Cook till tender. Test with skewer 3 Drain, turn on to a plate–remove skins

4 Melt butter, add parsley–turn potatoes gently in the butter 5 Serve in a hot vegetable-dish; or scrub and scrape potatoes before boiling

New Potatoes Alsacienne (Pommes de terre alsacienne)

450g/1 lb new potatoes
60g/2 oz lean bacon
6 spring onions
30g/1 oz butter
seasoning
chopped parsley

to serve: 3–4
time: 1 hour
foil

1 Wash and scrape potatoes 2 Put into boiling salted water 3 Boil for 10 minutes–drain–remove 4 Melt butter, add bacon cut in strips and spring onions left whole 5 Sauté 3–4 minutes 6 Add potatoes and seasoning, cover with foil and lid 7 Cook very slowly, shaking gently from time to time 8 When tender, add parsley, shake and dish

New Potatoes Hollandaise (Pommes de terre nouvelles à la hollandaise)

450g/1 lb new potatoes–seven sized
30g/1 oz butter
4 tbsp coating white sauce
½ yolk egg
lemon-juice
pepper
salt
nutmeg

to serve: 3–4
time: ½ hour

1 Prepare and cook the potatoes (page 111) 2 Arrange in a vegetable-dish 3 While potatoes are cooking, heat the sauce, and gradually beat in the butter 4 Add yolk of egg, lemon-juice and seasonings 5 Correct the consistency, coat the potatoes and serve very hot

Sauté Potatoes

230g/½ lb parboiled potatoes
30g/1 oz butter
1 tbsp oil
seasoning
parsley

to serve: 2
time: 20 minutes
heavy frying-pan

1 Slice potatoes 2 Heat butter and oil and put in all the potatoes–season 3 Allow to colour and turn occasionally and shake pan to prevent sticking 4 When golden brown, turn on to a hot dish and sprinkle with chopped parsley

Beetroot

2 small beetroot
⅛ lit/¼ pt coating white sauce

to serve: 1–2
time: 1–1¼ hours

1 Shake off the soil–cut off leaves leaving a small piece of stem. Do not break the skin 2 Put into a pan and cover with cold, salted water

3 Boil ¾–1¼ hours according to size **4** Peel off the skin and cut into slices **5** Serve on a hot dish coated with sauce

To Serve Cold–

time: 1–1¼ hours, and overnight

1 Allow to cool in the water **2** Skin **3** Cut in slices or strips **4** Coat with vinegar or French dressing (page 131)

Celeriac

230g/½ lb celeriac
⅛ lit/¼ pt coating white or egg sauce (page 89–90)

to serve: 2
time: 35 minutes
vegetable-brush

1 Wash and brush to remove outer skin **2** Cut into even-sized pieces **3** Cook in boiling, salted water 15–30 minutes **4** Drain well **5** Serve in a hot dish, coated with the sauce

NB To serve cold, cut into dice and toss in French dressing (page 131)

Artichokes

230g/½ lb Jerusalem artichokes
15g/½ oz butter
vinegar
boiling, salted water

to serve: 2
time: 30 minutes
vegetable-brush

1 Scrub, peel thinly in cold water, to which 1 tsp vinegar has been added **2** Cook in boiling, salted water till tender (about 20 minutes) **3** Drain well and toss in melted butter **4** Serve in a hot vegetable-dish

NB To fry, follow recipe and method for carrot fritters (page 123)

Onions

To boil–

230g/½ lb onions
⅛ lit/¼ pt white, cheese or tomato sauce (pages 88, 89, 99)

to serve: 1–2
time: 30 minutes

1 Skin the onions–leave whole **2** Blanch to soften the flavour **3** Boil in salted water till tender **4** Drain well **5** Serve in a hot dish coated with the sauce

To Braise–

1 Prepare and leave whole **2** Cook and serve as for braised celery (page 115)

To Bake–

time: ¾ hour
oven No. 3 or 170 °C/335 °F

baking-sheet or
fireproof dish

1 Choose large onions **2** Parboil **3** Put on to the greased baking-sheet **4** Bake till tender and brown **5** Serve as required

To Fry–

Shallow frying — *time:* ½ hour
frying-pan

1 Cut onion into thin slices **2** Fry in shallow fat for about 15–20 minutes **3** Serve as required

Onion Rings–

time: 25 minutes
kitchen roll
deep fat
thermometer

1 Cut into rings **2** Dip in egg white, toss in seasoned flour **3** Fry in deep fat till golden brown at 180 °C/355 °F **4** Drain well **5** Use as required

Leeks

450g/1 lb leeks — *to serve:* 2
⅛ lit/¼ pt white or cheese sauce (page 89) — *time:* ½ hour

1 Cut off roots and green ends and remove outer covering **2** Slit lengthwise and wash very thoroughly **3** Put into a small quantity of boiling, salted water and cook till tender **4** Drain *very* well **5** Serve in a hot dish coated with the sauce

To braise–

Cook for 20–25 minutes as for celery (page 115)

Leeks au gratin–

Add 60g/2 oz cheese to the sauce and finish as for cauliflower au gratin (page 104)

Celery

1 head celery — *to serve:* 1–2
⅛ lit/¼ pt coating white, parsley or cheese sauce (page 89) — *time:* ½ hour
vegetable-brush

1 Remove green tops (use for soups) **2** Divide stalks and scrub, cut into even-sized pieces **3** Put into boiling salted water and cook till tender–about 20 minutes–longer if very thick **4** Drain well **5** Serve in a hot dish coated with the sauce

To braise–

1 head celery
⅛ lit/¼ pt stock or stock cube
mirepoix (page 330)

to serve: 1–2
time: 1¼ hours
braising-pan
foil

1 Prepare as boiled celery (page 114) **2** Put on the mirepoix, add stock, cover with foil and tightly fitting lid–cook for ¾–1 hour **3** Strain off the liquid–reduce to 'glaze' **4** Put the celery into a hot dish, pour the 'glaze' over

Seakale and Chicory

Boil or braise as for celery (page 114)

Mushrooms

4 medium open mushrooms
melted fat
seasoning

time: 10 minutes
grill

1 Wash and wipe mushrooms–if very dirty, peel **2** Remove stalks (use for flavouring) **3** Brush with melted fat–sprinkle with salt and pepper **4** Grill under a medium grill for about 4–7 minutes **5** Use as required

To stew–

230g/½ lb mushrooms
⅛ lit/¼ pt milk or stock and milk
seasoning
30g/1 oz butter
chopped parsley
1 tbsp arrowroot
lemon-juice

to serve: 2
time: 20 minutes

1 Prepare mushrooms **2** Sauté in butter for 7 minutes **3** Add liquid and salt and simmer till mushrooms are tender **4** Blend arrowroot with a little water–add to stock–bring to the boil–boil 1 minute **5** Add lemon-juice, check seasoning **6** Serve sprinkled with chopped parsley

To sauté–

110g/¼ lb mushrooms
30g/1 oz butter
seasoning

time: 10 minutes

1 Prepare mushrooms **2** Melt fat **3** Add mushrooms and sauté till tender–5–7 minutes **4** Use as required

Tomatoes

To grill–

2 tomatoes

time: 10 minutes

seasoning
melted fat

grill

1 Wipe tomatoes and cut in half (as for squeezing a lemon) 2 Brush cut surface with fat–sprinkle with salt and pepper 3 Put under the grill at full heat 4 Cook till tender–about 5 minutes. Use as required
NB Tomatoes are never turned.

To bake–

2 tomatoes

time: 25 minutes
oven No. 3 or 170 °C/335 °F
greased baking-sheet

1 Wipe tomatoes, cut a cross in the skin on top and put on the baking-sheet 2 Bake for 15–20 minutes 3 Use as required

Marrow

1 young marrow
⅛ lit/¼ pt coating white sauce

to serve: 2–3
time: 25 minutes
steamer

1 Peel marrow thinly–cut in half 2 Remove seeds–cut into even-sized pieces 3 Put into the steamer and steam till tender 4 Lift carefully on to a hot vegetable-dish 5 Coat with the sauce
NB This may be served as for cucumber with sauce.

Cucumber with Sauce (Concombre à la poulette)

1 cucumber
15g/½ oz butter
1 tsp finely-chopped onion
⅛ lit/¼ pt coating sauce
1 small egg
½ tsp finely-chopped parsley
seasoning

to serve: 1–2
time: ½ hour
steamer

1 Peel cucumber, cut into 25 mm/1 in slices and steam until tender (about 20 minutes)–drain 2 Melt the butter and sauté the onion 3 Add cucumber and toss over heat for a few minutes 4 Stir in the white sauce 5 Add beaten egg and parsley 6 Heat without boiling 7 Season and serve very hot in a vegetable-dish
NB Marrow may be served in the same way.

Corn on the Cob

2 heads of young corn
60g/2 oz melted butter
boiling, salted water

to serve: 2
time: ½ hour
4 skewers

1 Remove the outer covering of the corn 2 Cook in plenty of boiling salted water until tender approx. 15–20 minutes 3 Drain, and stick a clean skewer in each end 4 Serve on a hot plate with melted clarified butter. These are often served as a 'starter' to a meal

Artichokes—Globe (Boiled) (Artichaut au naturel)

2 globe artichokes
salt
lemon-juice
⅛ lit/¼ pt hollandaise sauce (page 95)
tartar sauce (page 95) or French dressing (page 131)

to serve: 2
time: 2 hours
scissors
tea-cloth

1 Soak artichokes in cold salted water for at least 1 hour 2 Cut off tail, trim bottoms, cut off outer leaves and trim tops of remaining leaves with scissors 3 Put into boiling salted water to cover and add lemon-juice 4 Cook until tender 15–45 minutes according to size and freshness (when cooked leaves pull out easily) 5 Remove from water and drain well 6 Serve with the chosen sauce

Artichoke Bottoms Colbert (Fonds d'artichauts à la Colbert)

4 artichoke bottoms, tinned
30g/1 oz maître d'hôtel butter
4 croûtons of fried bread
egg and raspings
parsley or cress

to serve: 2
time: 20 minutes
deep fat
thermometer
50 mm/2 in. plain cutter
kitchen roll

1 Season the artichoke bottoms 2 Coat in egg and raspings 3 Fry at 180 °C/355 °F–drain 4 Place on the croûtons 5 Serve on a plain paper 6 Divide the maître d'hôtel butter between the four bottoms 7 Garnish with parsley or cress

NB To give extra flavour, a little meat glaze or marmite may be worked into the maître d'hôtel butter.

These may be served as a vegetable or a savoury.

Asparagus (Asperges au naturel)

1 bundle asparagus
salt
60g/2 oz butter
lemon-juice

to serve: 2
time: ½ hour

1 Trim ends of asparagus to a suitable size for serving 2 Scrape stalks and wash well 3 Tie in small bundles according to size 4 Cook gently in enough boiling, salted water to cover, putting in the large ones first to allow them a few minutes extra cooking and to ensure them all being cooked at the same time 5 When tender (15–20 minutes) dish on a large piece of toast to absorb water, or on a drainer, or use an asparagus-dish 6 Serve with skimmed melted butter, flavoured with lemon-juice

Asparagus Points (Pointes d'asperges)

asparagus

time: 15 minutes

melted butter
seasoning

1 Cut the asparagus into points **2** Cook as for plain asparagus allowing only 5–10 minutes **3** Drain and serve–*(a)* as a garnish; *(b)* as filling for omelets; *(c)* for asparagus rolls; *(d)* for hors-d'œuvre in a marinade
NB Tinned asparagus may be used for any of the above purposes.

Aubergine Fried (Aubergines frites)

1 aubergine
flour
salt and pepper
oil
parsley

to serve: 1
time: 45 minutes
frying-pan
kitchen roll

1 Wash aubergine and slice in 10 mm/½ in. pieces **2** Sprinkle with salt and leave to drain for about ½ hour turning from time to time **3** Wipe with paper and coat with seasoned flour **4** Fry in oil until brown on both sides **5** Dish in a hot-vegetable-dish sprinkled with chopped parsley **6** Serve with tomato sauce if liked (page 99)

Aubergine abignonaise

1 aubergine
2 firm tomatoes
60g/2 oz mushrooms
⅛ lit/¼ pt tomato sauce (page 99)
oil

to serve: 1
time: 45 minutes
oven No. 4 or 180 °C/355 °F
frying-pan
fireproof dish

1 Peel aubergine and cut into rounds 5 mm or ¼ in. thick–cover with salt–drain **2** Fry in oil and put into the fireproof dish **3** Cut off tops of tomatoes and scoop out inside **4** Slice mushrooms and cook in oil for 2–3 minutes–moisten with sauce–season **5** Fill tomatoes with this mixture and arrange on aubergine **6** Cook for about 7 minutes
7 Serve with tomato sauce

Stuffed Tomatoes

2 firm tomatoes
½ tsp chopped onion
1 tbsp fresh breadcrumbs
15g/½ oz margarine
15g/½ oz grated cheese
chopped parsley (optional)
parsley garnish
croûtons
seasoning

to serve: 1–2
time: 45 minutes
oven No. 3 or 170 °C/335 °F
greased baking-tray
50 mm/2 in. plain cutter

1 Wash and dry tomatoes **2** Cut small round from top of tomato and scoop out the centre–put into a basin **3** Melt margarine, fry onion, add crumbs, parsley, seasoning and sufficient pulp to bind **4** Fill tomatoes and replace lid **5** Bake for approximately 15 minutes–

remove lids **6** Sprinkle with cheese **7** Serve on rounds of buttered toast or fried bread on plain dish paper, garnished with parsley
NB Other fillings may be used, e.g. minced chicken, sausage-meat, etc.

Stuffed Marrow

1 small marrow
110g/¼ lb minced meat or savoury stuffing
brown or tomato sauce (pages 92, 99)
pinch mixed herbs
butter or margarine
seasoning

to serve: 2
time: 1½ hours
oven No. 6 or 205 °C/400 °F
greased baking-tin
foil

1 Peel marrow, cut off one end and scrape out seeds **2** Mix the meat with enough sauce to make a fairly soft mixture–add seasoning **3** Stuff the marrow with this mixture **4** Place back the end cut off, rub the surface with the fat and wrap in foil **5** Put on the greased tin, and bake for about 1 hour, removing the foil for the last 10 minutes to allow marrow to brown **6** Serve on a hot dish and pour the sauce round or serve separately
NB Alternatively the marrow may be cut in 35 mm/1½ in. slices and cooked as stuffed cucumber (page 121).

Aubergine Stuffed (Aubergines farcies)

1 aubergine
15g/½ oz cooked and chopped ham or tongue
15g/½ oz cooked and chopped meat, chicken or game
½ tsp chopped parsley
pinch of mixed herbs
seasoning
½ egg
1 tbsp fresh breadcrumbs
15g/½ oz butter or grated cheese

to serve: 1
time: 1¼ hours
oven No. 4 or 180 °C/355 °F
greased baking-tray

1 Wash the aubergine **2** Remove stalk and cut in half lengthwise–scoop out seeds and pulp **3** Chop pulp and add the other ingredients–bind with egg, season well **4** Put this mixture into the skins **5** Sprinkle with crumbs and butter or cheese **6** Place on the tray and bake for 30–40 minutes **7** Dish and garnish with parsley, serving a suitable sauce separately

Stuffed Sweet Peppers

1 sweet pepper
oil

to serve: 1
time: 45 minutes
oven No. 4 or 180 °C/355 °F
Yorkshire-pudding tin
kitchen roll

To prepare—Remove a slice from the stalk end and scoop out seeds **1** Cook in boiling salted water 10–15 minutes—dry **2** Fill with the stuffing—brush with oil **3** Put in the tin with a little water **4** Bake in a moderate oven

Stuffings—

1 Cooked mushrooms, breadcrumbs, softened onion, a little cooked rice and seasoning **2** Sweet corn, either tinned or fresh tossed in cream or sauce. Serve peppers on a bed of sautéd spaghetti, and peas, etc. **3** Hard-boiled egg, chopped fried bacon and white sauce **4** Minced, seasoned meats of different kinds

To serve—

1 On a croûte of fried bread—75 mm/3 in. round or oval cutter **2** On a bed of 45g/1½ oz of cooked spaghetti which has been sautéd in butter and finely-chopped parsley

Stuffed Onions

2 large onions
1 tbsp minced meat or sausage meat
1 tbsp fresh breadcrumbs
15g/½ oz butter
salt and pepper
30g/1 oz dripping
seasoning
brown or tomato sauce (pages 92, 99)

to serve: 2
time: 1½ hours
kitchen roll
oven No. 5 or 190 °C/380 °F
baking-tin

1 Parboil the onions **2** Drain and remove centres to give a hole big enough to take half the filling **3** Melt the butter, add meat, crumbs, seasoning and chopped onion centres—fill the onions with the mixture **4** Heat the dripping in the baking-tin, put in the onions and baste well **5** Bake about 1 hour until the onions are brown and tender **6** Serve on a hot dish with brown or tomato sauce

Stuffed Mushrooms

2 mushrooms
1 shallot or small onion
15g/½ oz butter
1 tsp chopped parsley
1 tbsp breadcrumbs
a little brown sauce (page 92)
salt and pepper
parsley or watercress
2 croûtes of fried bread

to serve: 1
time: ½ hour
oven No. 3 or 170 °C/335 °F
50 mm/2 in. plain cutter
greased baking-tray

1 Prepare mushrooms **2** Chop trimmings with shallot and parsley **3** Sauté in butter, add a little brown sauce, breadcrumbs, salt and pepper **4** Stuff mushrooms with this mixture **5** Put on the baking-sheet and bake for about 10 minutes 6 Place each mushroom on a croûte of fried bread 7 Dish on a plain paper 8 Garnish with parsley or watercress. Serve hot

Tomatoes–Stuffed Soubise

2 large tomatoes
30g/1 oz butter
30g/1 oz mushrooms
15g/½ oz grated cheese
1 large onion
15g/½ oz flour
⅛ lit/¼ pt milk
½ egg white
seasoned flour
fat for frying

to serve: 1–2
time: 1¼ hours
kitchen roll
liquidizer
deep-fat pan
thermometer (optional)
oven No. 4 or 180 °C/355 °F
greased baking-sheet

1 Chop mushrooms finely 2 Melt ¼ the butter–cook the mushrooms in this–add the cheese 3 Cut some rings from the onion and keep on one side–chop the remainder and cook slowly in a knob of the butter–liquidize 4 Make a sauce with the remaining butter and milk–add onion –season 5 Coat the onion rings in white of egg and flour–Fry in deep fat at 180 °C/355 °F 6 Wash tomatoes, cut off tops and scoop out inside–add to mushroom mixture 7 Fill with the mixture, replace tops and cook in oven 7–10 minutes 8 Serve with the soubise sauce round, the onion rings on top

Cucumber Stuffed

1 cucumber
filling:
- 60g/2 oz sausage meat
- 1 tbsp thick tomato sauce or ½ tbsp tomato purée
- 1 tbsp chopped mushroom
- pinch spice
- seasoning

4 croûtes of fried bread (size of cucumber rounds)
4 rounds of ham or tongue (same size as cutter)
chopped parsley
⅛ lit/¼ pt tomato sauce (page 99)

to serve: 2–3
time: 1 hour
steamer and small tin
plain cutter
plain:
- 50 mm/2 in. cutter
- 10 mm/½ in. cutter

10 mm/½ in. plain forcer
forcing-bag

1 Cut cucumber into 50 mm/2 in pieces–peel thinly 2 Remove seeds with the small cutter 3 Boil for 2–3 minutes in salted water 4 Mix ingredients for the filling 5 Pipe into each case allowing a little to stand above the case 6 Steam for 20–25 minutes standing on the tin 7 At the same time heat the two rounds of ham or tongue 8 Place the croûtes on a hot dish and cover with the meat 9 Stand the cucumber on these and pour the sauce round 10 Garnish with chopped parsley

NB 1 Any raw savoury mixture may be used **2** If a cooked farce is used, add hot after steaming.

Brussels Sprouts with Chestnuts (Choux de Bruxelles aux marrons)

450g/1 lb Brussels sprouts
12 cooked chestnuts
60g/2 oz ham
2 tbsp cream
salt and pepper

to serve: 3–4
time: ½ hour

1 Cook the sprouts (page 103)–drain well **2** Chop chestnuts roughly **3** Put sprouts, chestnuts and chopped ham in a pan **4** Add cream and seasoning **5** Reheat very gently **6** Serve in a vegetable-dish

Red Cabbage with Apples

1 small red cabbage
30g/1 oz butter or margarine
1 small onion
2 medium-sized cooking apples
1 tbsp golden syrup
lemon-juice
2 tbsp vinegar
seasoning

to serve: 2–3
time: 1½ hours

1 Melt the fat **2** Add finely-chopped onion and sauté until cooked **3** Add finely-shredded cabbage, peeled and sliced apples and syrup **4** Cook very gently for about 10 minutes, shaking frequently **5** Add lemon-juice, vinegar, and salt **6** Simmer for approximately 1 hour **7** Season, and serve in a hot vegetable-dish

Red Cabbage (Stewed)

1 small red cabbage
60g/2 oz cooked ham
15g/½ oz butter or margarine
½ lit/1 pt stock or stock cube
⅛ lit/¼ pt vinegar
1 tbsp sugar
seasoning

to serve: 2–3
time: 1½ hours

1 Wash cabbage and slice thinly **2** Put in a pan with diced ham, butter, ½ the stock and the vinegar **3** Stew very gently for 1 hour **4** Add remaining stock, sugar and seasoning **5** Stir and cook until all the liquid has dried off **6** Serve at once
NB This is a good accompaniment to sausages.

Carrottes d'automne

230g/½ lb carrots
60g/2 oz mushrooms
30g/1 oz butter

to serve: 2
time: 20 minutes

finely-chopped herbs
seasoning

1 Prepare the carrots and cut into julienne strips 2 Cook in a little boiling salted water until tender 3 Cut the mushrooms into dice and sauté in the butter 4 Add the carrots and cook together for a few minutes 5 Season and dish in a hot dish 6 Sprinkle with the herbs and serve

Spinach à la crème

450g/1 lb spinach or 1 packet frozen spinach
15g/½ oz butter
1 tbsp cream or white sauce
lemon-juice
seasoning
triangular croûtons

to serve: 1
time: ¾ hour
liquidizer

1 Prepare spinach, cook and liquidize (page 105) 2 Sauté in butter, add lemon juice and seasoning 3 Add cream or sauce 4 Put into a hot dish and surround with triangular croûtons which have been fried in butter

Carrot Fritters (Beignets de carottes)

230g/½ lb new carrots (small)
1 tsp oil }
1 tsp vinegar } marinade
pinch sugar }
½ tsp chopped parsley }
yeast batter (page 154)
fresh or fried parsley

to serve: 2
time: ¾ hour
kitchen roll
deep fat
thermometer

1 Prepare carrots and cook (page 106) 2 Soak in the marinade for 10 minutes 3 Make the yeast batter 4 Dip the carrots in the batter 5 Fry in the deep fat at 180 °C/355 °F for 2–3 minutes–drain 6 Dish in a vegetable-dish on a plain paper 7 Garnish with fresh or fried parsley

Corn Fritters

⅛ lit/¼ pt coating batter (page 153)
110g/¼ lb cooked fresh corn (page 116) or ½ tin plain corn
clarified butter
seasoning

to serve: 3–4
time: ½ hour
frying-pan

1 Prepare the batter 2 Add the well-drained corn 3 Heat the butter 4 Drop the mixture into the fat in small rounds 5 When cooked on one side, turn and cook on the other. Use to garnish Chicken Maryland

Corn Jardinière

110g/¼ lb fresh corn or ½ tin plain corn or frozen corn

to serve: 2
time: ½ hour

2 tbsp cooked peas
2 tbsp sliced cucumber
2 tbsp sliced green pepper
chopped chives
1 tbsp cream

1 If using fresh corn, cook and remove from the cob and drain, or drain tinned corn **2** Add the other vegetables **3** Season and toss in the cream **4** Serve as a vegetable or a garnish

NB The above may be served cold, substituting mayonnaise for cream and use as an hors-d'œuvre or a vegetarian dish.

If using frozen corn, sauté in butter and then add other vegetables.

Ratatouille à la niçoise

1 large aubergine
1 courgette
1 green sweet pepper
1 clove garlic
1 onion
2 medium tomatoes
bouquet garni
2 tbsp oil
chopped parsley
seasoning

to serve: 3–4
time: 1½ hours
kitchen roll

1 Cut up courgette (do not skin if very young)–sprinkle with salt **2** Peel aubergine, cut up and sprinkle with salt–do not remove seeds **3** Blanch pepper after removing seeds **4** Skin tomatoes, squeeze out pips, cut up **5** Slice onion and sauté in the oil **6** Dry courgette and aubergine **7** Add other ingredients, garlic (crushed with salt) and bouquet garni **8** Cook gently for ½ hour–remove bouquet **9** Put into a dish and sprinkle with parsley

NB Croûtons may be served round the edge.

SALADS

Beetroot Salad

1 medium-cooked beetroot
French dressing (page 131)
chopped chives

to serve: 1–2
time: 10 minutes

1 Peel the beetroot and cut into thin slices **2** Cut slices into strips **3** Toss in the French dressing **4** Arrange piled in a dish and sprinkle with the chopped chives

Cucumber Salad

½ cucumber
French dressing (page 131)
chopped parsley

to serve: 2–3
time: 15 minutes
mandolin (optional)

1 Peel the cucumber and cut in very thin slices 2 Arrange neatly on a shallow dish 3 Pour the French dressing over and sprinkle with chopped parsley
NB If the skin is thin, the cucumber need not be peeled.

Carrot Salad

1 large carrot
French dressing or mayonnaise (page 131)
chives or parsley

to serve: 1
time: 10 minutes
shredder

1 Scrape the carrot 2 Shred on a coarse shredder 3 Mix with the chosen dressing 4 Pile in a dish and sprinkle with chopped chives or parsley

Tomato Salad

2 firm tomatoes
French dressing (page 131)
chopped parsley, chives or gherkins

to serve: 1–2
time: 15 minutes

1 Skin the tomatoes and cut into thin slices 2 Arrange in a shallow dish 3 Pour the dressing over 4 Sprinkle with chosen ingredient

Orange Salad

1 large sweet orange
French dressing (page 131)
chopped parsley

to serve: 1
time: 15 minutes

1 Peel the orange and remove all the pith 2 Cut in thin slices, remove pips and arrange in a shallow dish 3 Pour the French dressing over and sprinkle with chopped parsley

Red Pepper and Orange Salad

1 large orange
1 medium red pepper
French dressing (page 131)

to serve: 2
time: 15 minutes

1 Parboil the pepper–remove seeds, cut into strips 2 Put into a basin–add chopped orange 3 Toss in French dressing 4 Pile on a dish

Orange and Tomato Salad

1 orange
1 firm tomato
small lettuce
mayonnaise (page 131)

to serve: 2–3
time: ½ hour

1 Prepare the lettuce 2 Skin tomato and orange and cut in thin slices 3 Reserve 4 slices each of orange and tomato and tender leaves and heart of lettuce for garnish 4 Cut up remaining fruit and tear up

lettuce 5 Mix and moisten with mayonnaise 6 Pile in a bowl inside a border of lettuce leaves 7 Arrange the slices of orange and tomato, overlapping round the top 8 Garnish with a small piece of lettuce heart

Potato Salad

230g/½ lb cooked new potatoes (page 111)
1 tbsp chopped or grated onion (raw)
⅛ lit/¼ pt salad cream or mayonnaise (page 131)
1 tbsp chopped chives or parsley
clove of garlic

to serve: 2
time: 15 minutes

1 Dice the potatoes, add the onion 2 Mix with the dressing 3 Rub dish with cut clove of garlic and put potato mixture in it 4 Garnish with either chopped chives or parsley

Mixed Vegetable Salad

cooked vegetables, e.g. potatoes, carrots, peas, tomatoes, etc.
mayonnaise (page 131)
lettuce

to serve: 2–3
time: ½ hour

1 Prepare as for potato salad (page 126) 2 Pile in a bowl and garnish with lettuce leaves round the outside and the heart of the lettuce in the centre, or serve without the lettuce as part of an hors-d'œuvre variés

Green Salad

lettuce
watercress
small cress
endive
chicory
French dressing (page 131)

to serve: 2–4
time: ½ hour
tea-cloth

1 Wash lettuce, using as much as possible–drain on a cloth 2 Wash watercress, removing yellow leaves and small roots–drain 3 Wash small cress in bunches–drain 4 Divide chicory–wash and drain 5 Wash endive in small pieces–drain 6 Break up some of the coarser leaves and put into a bowl 7 Arrange the better leaves round, avoiding a heavy or flat appearance–decorate with remaining prepared salad 8 Pour the dressing over just before serving, or serve separately

Tossed Green Salad with Herbs

½ lettuce
young spinach
dandelion
½ clove garlic

to serve: 2–3
time: 20 minutes

chicory
watercress
pinch basil, marjoram, chervil (if fresh use ½ tsp of each)
French dressing (page 131)

1 Rub salad bowl with garlic 2 Prepare ingredients, breaking up larger leaves 3 Put French dressing into the bowl and add salad—toss with wooden spoons 4 Serve immediately

Cole-slaw or Raw Cabbage Salad

1 heart of white cabbage
1 dessert apple
celery
nuts
French dressing or mayonnaise (page 131)
chives

to serve: 2–3
time: 25 minutes
vegetable-brush
tea-cloth

1 Prepare cabbage, cut in quarters—slice thinly, dry thoroughly 2 Slice apple thinly, prepare and slice celery 3 Toss prepared ingredients and nuts in onion-flavoured French dressing or mayonnaise 4 Pile on a dish or serve in a salad bowl, sprinkle with chopped chives

Summer Cauliflower (Choux-fleur d'été)

1 medium-sized cooked cauliflower (page 103)
1 carrot
3 cooked new potatoes (page 111)
1 hard-boiled egg
⅛ lit/¼ pt mayonnaise (page 131)
finely-chopped tarragon, chervil or parsley

to serve: 3–4
time: 25 minutes
shredder

1 Dice potatoes and chop hard-boiled egg 2 Season the mayonnaise using 1 tsp tarragon vinegar 3 Arrange cauliflower, egg and potatoes in a vegetable dish 4 Coat with the mayonnaise 5 Sprinkle with coarsely-grated raw carrot mixed with the herbs

Pineapple and Prune Salad

1 slice of pineapple
2 cooked prunes
2 almonds
French dressing (page 131)
green salad plant to garnish

to serve: 1
time: 10 minutes

1 Stone the prunes and replace stones with almonds—marinade in French dressing 2 Break up some salad plant, lettuce, chicory, endive, etc. 3 Arrange in an individual dish 4 Coat the pineapple with dressing and place on the salad 5 Garnish with the prunes and some small pieces of green salad

Pear and Grape Salad

1 small ripe pear (or tinned pear)
1 dessertsp chopped walnuts
60g/2 oz cream cheese
a little endive or watercress
90g/3 oz green or black grapes

to serve: 2
time: ½ hour
kitchen roll

1 Peel the pear and cut in half lengthwise. Scoop out the core. Dry the pear **2** Beat the cheese, adding cream or mayonnaise if it requires softening **3** Add the walnuts and seasoning **4** Use this mixture to fill the core space and to coat the outside of the pear **5** Remove grape pips cutting grapes in half lengthwise **6** Cover the pears with the grapes, skin-side up, to look like a bunch of grapes **7** Place on a dish or small plate and decorate with a little watercress or endive
These may be served individually or on one plate

Grapefruit and Chicory Salad

1 grapefruit
1 head chicory
15g/½ oz sultanas
French dressing (page 131)

to serve: 2
time: 15 minutes

1 Prepare the grapefruit (page 2) **2** Soak the sultanas in hot water to 'plump' them **3** Prepare the chicory **4** Mix grapefruit segments, sultanas and some chicory with the dressing **5** Put into skins or glasses **6** Garnish with small pieces of chicory

Orange, Melon and Tomato Salad

1 small ripe melon
1 orange
2 firm tomatoes
30g/1 oz mixed nuts
French dressing (page 131)
lettuce or chicory to garnish

to serve: 3–4
time: 35 minutes
1 flat oval dish
ball-cutter (optional)

1 Cut the melon with a large ball-cutter, or into dice **2** Peel orange and cut into thin slices **3** Skin tomatoes and cut into thin slices **4** Chop nuts roughly **5** Wash salad garnish **6** Arrange the melon at the back of the dish **7** Place orange slices overlapping in front and tomatoes in front of orange **8** Put nuts in front of the dish **9** Garnish lightly with the salad **10** Serve dressing separately or pour it over just before serving

Banana and Cream Cheese Salad

1 banana
30g/1 oz cream cheese
small piece of lettuce
15g/½ oz chopped nuts (walnuts, almonds, etc.)

to serve: 2
time: 15 minutes

seasoning
mayonnaise (page 131)

1 Skin the banana and cut in half both ways (four pieces) 2 Moisten the cheese with a little mayonnaise 3 Spread over the banana and coat with the nuts 4 Arrange on a bed of lettuce and garnish with lettuce hearts, small cress, etc.

Ham and Rice Salad

to serve: 1–2
time: 20 minutes plus cooling time

60g/2 oz patna rice
60g/2 oz lean thinly-sliced ham
30g/1 oz diced carrots
30g/1 oz peas
2 tomatoes
1 tsp chopped parsley
1 tsp chopped chives or onions
French dressing (page 131)
watercress

1 Boil rice, rinse and drain well–dry (see Misc. Processes)–cool 2 Shred or dice ham 3 Boil vegetables until tender 4 Skin tomatoes–cut in quarters 5 Add ham, peas and carrots to rice–stir lightly adding parsley and chives and dressing to moisten 6 Pile in the centre of an oval dish, arrange quartered tomatoes round the sides and watercress at the ends

Salade à la Waldorf

to serve: 3–4
time: 25 minutes

2 small cooked turnips
2 potatoes (cooked)
3 artichokes (cooked)
1 slice pineapple
1 banana
4 tbsp mayonnaise (page 131)
1 tbsp cream
seasoning–sugar
chopped parsley or tarragon

1 Dice the vegetables 2 Add cream to the mayonnaise and season–add sugar 3 Mix in the prepared vegetables 4 Pile into a bowl 5 Sprinkle with the parsley or tarragon

NB This salad may also be garnished with shredded celery.

Salade à la Dumas

to serve: 2–3
time: 20 minutes
sieve
tea-cloth

1 gherkin
1 small cooked beetroot
3 small cooked potatoes
3 firm tomatoes
1 small lettuce

Dumas dressing

1 hard-boiled egg

1 tbsp tartar sauce (page 95)
2 tbsp olive oil
1 tbsp vinegar
1 dessertsp anchovy essence
seasoning

1 Skin tomatoes and beetroot 2 Cut vegetables into strips 3 Mix with the dressing and pile in a bowl 4 Garnish with the heart of a lettuce and sprinkle with chopped hard-boiled egg, parsley and capers

To make the dressing–
1 Sieve the hard-boiled egg and add ⅔ to the tartar sauce 2 Add the olive oil and vinegar, gradually 3 Add seasoning and anchovy essence–

Carmen Salad (Salade Carmen)

to serve: 2–3
time: 15 minutes

1 red sweet pepper
2 tbsp diced chicken or ham
1 tbsp peas
60g/2 oz cooked patna rice
2 firm skinned tomatoes
1 hard-boiled egg
chopped parsley and capers
French dressing (page 131)

1 Mix the prepared vegetables with the well-seasoned French dressing 2 Cut the tomatoes and egg into thin slices and put in a bowl 3 Circle with sliced tomatoes, putting chopped parsley and capers in the centre

Fish Salad

to serve: 1
time: 15 minutes
tea-cloth

110g/4 oz cooked fish, e.g. salmon, haddock
salad vegetables
mayonnaise (page 131)

1 Place fish on a dish and coat with mayonnaise 2 Garnish with salad vegetables

Alternative method
1 Flake fish–mix with mayonnaise–put into a mould 2 Turn out and garnish with salad vegetables

Tomato Ring Salad

to serve: 2–3
time: 2 hours
tea-cloth
1 ring-mould or baba-tins or dariole-moulds

¼ lit/½ pt tomato juice (tinned or raw rubbed through a sieve
15g/½ oz gelatine
salt
pepper
sugar
Worcester sauce

potato salad (page 126)
salad garnish

Any of the following may be added–
peas, chopped cooked carrot, asparagus tips, olives, chopped ham, chopped chicken, shrimps, prawns, chopped egg, anchovies and pineapple.

1 Heat the tomato juice and add the gelatine–stir until dissolved 2 Season–add other chosen ingredients 3 Stir until thickening and pour into a wetted mould 4 Leave in a cool place to set 5 Turn out on to an oval dish–garnish with potato salad in the centre and salad vegetables

Russian Salad

aspic jelly (page 211)
60g/2 oz cooked fish, e.g. sole, haddock, lobster, shrimps, prawn
cooked vegetables cut into dice
lettuce
anchovies
French dressing (page 131)

to serve: 2–3
time: 1½ hours
tea-cloth
ice
medium-sized border-mould

1 Line and decorate the bottom of the border mould 2 Set layers of fish and vegetables alternately with jelly. Leave to set 3 Turn out 4 Toss lettuce and other ingredients in the dressing and pile in centre of the mould 5 Arrange chopped jelly round

SALAD DRESSINGS

French Dressing

1 tbsp vinegar
2 tbsp salad oil
salt, pepper, mustard, grated onion (optional), sugar

time: 10 minutes
screw-top jar

1 Put all ingredients into the jar. Shake vigorously 2 Serve in a sauce-boat on a stand or use as required

Mayonnaise

1 egg-yolk
¼ tsp salt
pepper
dry mustard
⅛ lit/¼ pt salad oil
vinegar–(chilli, malt, tarragon, garlic)
sugar
grated onion or garlic (optional)

time: by hand, approx. 15 minutes
by machine, 5 minutes
grater
whisk or liquidizer

1 Put egg-yolk and seasonings into a basin–whisk 2 Add slightly-warmed oil drop by drop at first, whisking well until mixture thickens 3 Continue adding oil steadily and more quickly as the

mixture continues to thicken (if too thick to whisk, thin with vinegar and then add remaining oil) **4** Adjust flavour and consistency with vinegar and sugar **5** If too thick when seasoning is correct, thin with a little boiling water
NB For larger quantities, use a liquidizer in which case all the ingredients may be put in together and full speed used for about ½ minute. Should the mixture curdle, add curdled mixture *slowly* to another egg-yolk.

Mayonnaise verte

time: as for mayonnaise plus 5 minutes
muslin

1 Add 1 tbsp spinach or watercress purée to mayonnaise **2** Colour if necessary. Tammy

Cooked Mayonnaise

⅛ lit/¼ pt flowing white sauce
1 tsp castor sugar
½ tsp mustard, made
1–2 tbsp vinegar
salt and pepper
grated onion

time: 5 minutes

1 Add vinegar gradually to the sauce **2** Add seasoning and other ingredients

Cream Dressing (Thick) (A good substitute for Mayonnaise)

1 tsp French or English mustard
½ tsp salt
1 tsp sugar
¼ tsp pepper
⅛ lit/¼ pt evaporated milk
⅛ lit/¼ pt salad oil
3 tbsp white vinegar

time: 10 minutes
liquidizer

1 Mix seasonings and milk **2** Put into liquidizer and switch on **3** Add oil fairly slowly **4** Add vinegar **5** Check seasonings
NB The dressing will thicken when vinegar is added—how quickly depends on the acidity of the vinegar.

Cream Dressing with Horse-radish

⅛ lit/¼ pt thick cream dressing (page 132)
1 tbsp freshly grated horse-radish
lemon-juice
1 tsp sugar
salt and pepper

time: 10 minutes
grater or liquidizer

1 Mix all ingredients and flavour carefully with the horse-radish **2** Add a little extra cream if necessary

Cream Salad Dressing

2 tbsp single cream or top of milk
1 tbsp vinegar
pepper, salt, mustard
¼ tsp sugar

time: 10 minutes
whisk

1 Add ½ tbsp vinegar to the cream and whisk till thick and frothy 2 Stir in the other ingredients until suitably seasoned 3 Add remainder of vinegar 4 Serve in a sauce-boat

NB Evaporated milk may be used instead of cream.

Condensed Milk Dressing

3 tbsp sweetened condensed milk
½ tsp salt
1 dessertsp oil
1 tsp made mustard
5 tbsp white vinegar
1 tsp chopped herbs (parsley, tarragon, fennel, chives, etc.)

time: 15 minutes
liquidizer

1 Put all ingredients except herbs into the liquidizer 2 Liquidize for ½ minute 3 Add herbs to taste

NB This can be made using one herb as flavouring, e.g. fennel with fish, chives, etc.

Mayonnaise Rémoulade

⅛ lit/¼ pt mayonnaise (page 131)
1 tsp made mustard
1 tsp chopped capers
1 tsp chopped gherkins
½ tsp chopped parsley and tarragon
1 tsp anchovy essence
seasoning

time: 15 minutes

1 Add all the ingredients to the mayonnaise 2 Season well

NB 1 If fresh tarragon is not available, a little tarragon vinegar may be used.

2 This dressing is excellent served with fried fish.

Andalouse Dressing

⅛ lit/¼ pt mayonnaise (page 131)
1 tbsp tomato purée
1 tbsp red pepper (tinned or fresh)
seasoning

time: 15 minutes

1 Cut pepper into julienne strips (if using fresh pepper, blanch first) 2 Add tomato purée to the mayonnaise—season well 3 Add pepper.

Apple Dressing

⅛ lit/¼ pt mayonnaise (page 131)
1 tsp sugar
1 medium-sweet apple
1 tbsp chopped green pepper (optional)
1 tsp onion-juice or garlic

time: 15 minutes
grater

1 Grate apple and add to mayonnaise with the green pepper **2** Add onion or garlic **3** Check seasoning

NB Any type of mayonnaise may be used. This dressing is suitable with green salads or with a beetroot-and-apple salad.

Thousand Island Dressing

⅛ lit/¼ pt mayonnaise (page 131)
2 tsp sugar
2 tbsp chopped olives
2 tsp chopped capers
½ tsp paprika
1 tsp onion-juice or crushed garlic

time: 15 minutes
grater

1 Add olives, capers and paprika to the mayonnaise **2** Check seasoning and add onion or garlic

NB Any type of mayonnaise may be used. May be served with green salad.

Orange Dressing

grated rind of ½ an orange
garlic (optional)
4 tbsp cream
4 tbsp French dressing (page 131)
salt and pepper

time: 15 minutes
liquidizer

1 Crush the garlic and put into the liquidizer with the dressing **2** Add cream, orange-rind and a little of the juice **3** Liquidize for ½ minute **4** Check seasoning

NB This dressing may be made with lemon instead of orange—both are good with a chicory salad.

Spanish Dressing

1 medium onion
½ fresh green pepper (blanched)
1 clove garlic
1½ tinned red pimentos
salt, pepper, sugar
1 tsp French mustard
1 tbsp Worcester sauce
4 tbsp salad oil
lemon-juice

time: 15 minutes
liquidizer

1 Chop onion roughly **2** Remove seeds from peppers and chop **3** Crush

garlic 4 Put into the liquidizer 5 Add other ingredients and liquidize for ½ minute 6 Check seasoning and add a little sugar if liked
NB This is a good dressing for potato and other root vegetable salads.

Hard-boiled Egg Dressing

1 yolk of hard-boiled egg
1 tbsp salad oil
⅛ tsp made mustard
2 tsp vinegar
1 tsp Worcester sauce
½ tsp grated onion
2 tbsp cream or evaporated milk
salt and pepper

time: 10 minutes
grater
sieve
whisk

1 Sieve the egg-yolk 2 Add the seasonings and oil gradually 3 Whip the cream and fold it in 4 Check the seasoning and if too acid add a little castor sugar

Beetroot Salad Dressing (1)

1 hard-boiled yolk
½ tsp made English mustard
½ tsp made French mustard
1½ tbsp oil
1 tbsp cream
salt and cayenne
lemon-juice
sugar, if liked

time: 10 minutes
liquidizer

1 Put all ingredients into the liquidizer 2 Liquidize for ½ minute 3 Season to taste

Beetroot Salad Dressing (2)

1 raw yolk
1 tsp made mustard
1½ tbsp oil
1 tbsp white vinegar
½ tsp tarragon vinegar
1 dessertsp onion-juice
salt, cayenne, sugar
2 tbsp cream

time: 10 minutes
liquidizer

1 Put the yolk into the liquidizer and switch on 2 Add other ingredients 3 Liquidize for ½ minute 4 Add seasonings and sugar

Potato Salad Dressing (with Wine)

1 raw yolk
1 hard-boiled egg
2 tsp French mustard
1 clove garlic
3 tbsp oil

time: 10 minutes
liquidizer

2 tbsp white vinegar
2 tbsp white or red wine
1 tbsp cooked beetroot
1 tbsp gherkin
1 tbsp cream
seasoning

1 Put all the ingredients except cream into the liquidizer **2** Liquidize for ½ minute **3** Check seasoning and add a little sugar if liked **4** Add cream to taste

7
Vegetarian

Vegetable Curry

mixed vegetables (about 230g/½ lb)
e.g. tomatoes, cauliflower, celery, pulses, carrot, etc. (cooked)
curry sauce (page 99) (use vegetarian stock)
lemon juice
salt
110g/4 oz patna rice
lemon and gherkin to garnish

to serve: 2
time: 45 minutes

1 Make the curry sauce 2 Simmer gently about 20 minutes 3 Add the vegetables cut into neat pieces and re-heat gently without boiling for 10–15 minutes 4 Add lemon-juice and salt 5 Dish on a hot dish and garnish with lemon and gherkin 6 Serve the boiled rice separately

Cheese Pudding

90g/3 oz fresh breadcrumbs
¼ lit/½ pt milk
90g/3 oz grated Cheddar cheese
30g/1 oz margarine
1 egg
1 tsp grated onion
seasoning
1 dessertsp Parmesan cheese
(or finely-grated Cheddar)
parsley

to serve: 2
time: 45 minutes
grater (whisk)
¼ lit/½ pt pie or gratin-dish
bain-marie
oven No. 4 or 180 °C/355 °F.

1 Heat the milk, add the breadcrumbs and bring to the boil 2 Add margarine, yolk of egg, cheese, onion and seasoning 3 Fold in whisked white of egg 4 Bake 20–30 minutes in a bain-marie 5 Sprinkle with a little cheese 6 Serve on plate or dish on a plain paper–garnished with parsley

Roman Pie

110g/4 oz short-crust pastry (page 229)
170g/6 oz mixed vegetables, cooked
(fresh or frozen)

to serve: 3
time: 1½ hours
grater

30g/1 oz macaroni or pulse—cooked
45g/1½ oz grated cheese
seasonings (cayenne pepper)
1 tbsp vegetable stock or white sauce
raspings
tomato sauce (page 99)

150 mm/6 in. cake-tin greased
foil
oven No. 6 or 205 °C/400 °F

1 Chop vegetables or shred 2 Mix with seasoning, sauce or vegetable stock, cheese and macaroni (save a few peas, etc., for garnish) 3 Line the tin with the raspings and then ¾ of the pastry 4 Add filling—press down well 5 Cover with remaining pastry—press edges down with a knife 6 Cover with foil 7 Bake ¼–1 hour 8 Turn on to a dish—float tomato sauce round 9 Add garnish—hand new potatoes

Lentil Cutlets or Croquettes

110g/4 oz lentils
1 onion
1 egg
60g/2 oz breadcrumbs or 1 small potato
salt and pepper
30g/1 oz margarine or butter
¼ tsp mixed herbs or 1 tsp chopped parsley
¼ lit/½ pt water
raspings
parsley and macaroni garnish
tomato sauce (page 99)

to serve: 3–4
time: 1¼ hours
kitchen roll
deep-fat pan
thermometer

1 Wash the lentils and put into a pan with chopped onion, and potato (if used) and water 2 Cook gently—lid off, till much drier—stir continually 3 Add fat, herbs, salt and pepper and 1 dessertsp egg 4 Stir well—turn on to a plate to cool 5 Divide for cutlets (4 or 6) shape (mould in raspings not flour) 6 Coat twice with egg and raspings and reshape 7 Fry in very hot fat at 190 °C/380 °F to crisp only for 2 minutes 8 Drain well, put a small piece of macaroni in each cutlet to simulate the bone 9 Serve on a hot dish—plain paper. Hand tomato sauce separately

Macaroni and Cheese Cutlets or Croquettes

60g/2 oz macaroni
30g/1 oz butter or margarine
45g/1½ oz flour
¼ lit/½ pt milk and macaroni water
60g/2 oz grated cheddar cheese
salt and cayenne
egg and raspings
parsley

to serve: 2
time: 1 hour 10 minutes
kitchen roll
grater
deep-fat pan
thermometer

1 Cook the macaroni, drain and chop finely 2 Make a sauce with the fat, flour and liquid 3 Add the macaroni and cheese—season 4 Turn on to a plate to cool 5 Form into cutlets or croquettes 6 Coat twice with egg and raspings 7 Fry in deep fat at 190 °C/380 °F 8 Drain well—put a small piece of macaroni in each cutlet to simulate the bone 9 Serve

on a dish on a plain paper, the cutlet bone facing to the left **10** Garnish with fresh or fried parsley and serve tomato sauce separately

Nut Cutlets or Croquettes

110g/¼ lb mixed nuts	*to serve:* 3–4
60g/2 oz fresh breadcrumbs	*time:* 1¼ hours
⅛ lit/¼ pt milk } sauce	kitchen roll
30g/1 oz margarine } sauce	grater
30g/1 oz flour } sauce	deep-fat pan
1 tsp grated onion	thermometer
1 tsp chopped parsley	liquidizer
salt and cayenne	
tomato sauce (page 99)	
macaroni } to garnish	
parsley } to garnish	

1 Liquidize the nuts **2** Make the sauce and add nuts, breadcrumbs, onion and parsley–season **3** Put on a plate to cool **4** Divide into 4 or 6 pieces **5** Form into cutlets or croquettes **6** Coat twice with egg and raspings **7** Fry in deep fat at 190 °C/380 °F **8** Drain, place a piece of macaroni in each cutlet to simulate the bone **9** Dish on a plain paper with the bone to the left **10** Garnish with fresh or fried parsley and serve tomato sauce separately **NB** The cutlets may be served on mashed potato and the sauce poured round.

Variation: Liquidized chestnuts may be used for chestnut cutlets.

Vegetarian Scotch Eggs (See recipe and method for Scotch Eggs (page 151)

1 Substitute lentil-cutlet mixture or a nut-cutlet mixture for sausage-meat **2** Egg and crumb twice

Savoury Rolls (See Sausage Rolls (page 59)

Substitute nut-cutlet mixture (page 139) or lentil-cutlet mixture (page 138) for sausage-meat

Summer Croustade

stale bread } croustade	*to serve:* 3
60g/2 oz butter } croustade	*time:* 1 hour
garlic } croustade	150 mm/6 in. sandwich tin
vegetables, peas, carrots, beetroot, etc.	buttered paper
French dressing (page 131)	baking beans
	oven No. 4 or 180 °C/355 °F

1 Crush garlic with salt and work into the butter **2** Cut bread into thin slices and remove crusts **3** Spread with the butter and cut into approx. 50 mm/2 in. squares **4** Butter the sandwich tin and line bottom and sides with the squares overlapping **5** Line with buttered paper and beans as for a flan **6** Bake to a golden brown, 15–20 minutes **7** Remove paper and return to oven to dry–5 minutes **8** Prepare and cook vegetables **9** Marinade in French dressing for 10 minutes **10** Put croustade on a flat dish and arrange vegetables in it.

8
Pasta

Pasta

170g/6 oz flour
90g/3 oz dry mashed potato or potato-powder
1 egg-yolk
1 tsp salad-oil
salt

time: 1 hour
sieve

1 Sieve salt and flour 2 Add potato, yolk and oil 3 Knead to a pliable dough 4 Leave to stand for ½ hour and use as required
NB For green pasta (pasta verde) add 100g/¼ lb cooked spinach (which has been liquidized and dried in a pan to evaporate excess moisture.) This paste may be used for noodles, etc.

Ravioli

pasta (page 140)
filling
brown or tomato sauce (page 95, 99)
grated cheese

to serve: 3–4
time: 1 hour
kitchen roll
grater

1 Roll pasta out into a square–brush with water 2 Mark with a knife 50 mm/2 in. squares 3 In the centre of each square place a small piece of the chosen filling 4 Cover with a square of pasta, seal round filling and cut into squares 5 Allow to dry for at least 1 hour 6 Cook in boiling, salted water or stock for 6 to 7 minutes 7 Drain and serve coated with brown or tomato sauce 8 Sprinkle well with grated cheese

Fillings–

1 60g/2 oz minced meat or poultry
chopped parsley, seasoning–bind with egg
2 30g/1 oz minced veal or poultry
25g/½ oz grated Parmesan cheese
grated lemon-rind–garlic
seasoning–bind with egg
3 60g/2 oz minced ham
4 tbsp dried spinach purée

Seasoning–

egg to bind
15g/½ oz Parmesan cheese

Cannelloni

Pasta (plain or verde) (page 140)
spinach à la crème (page 123)
seasoning
grated cheese
cheese sauce (page 89)

to serve: 3–4
time: 1 hour
kitchen roll
grater
fireproof dish
grill

1 Roll pasta out and cut into 75 mm/3 in. squares 2 Boil in salted water and drain 3 Spread with the spinach 4 Roll and arrange in a fireproof dish on mornay sauce 5 Coat lightly with the same sauce 6 Sprinkle with the grated cheese and brown under the grill

Macaroni or Spaghetti bolonaise

1 onion
1 tbsp oil
60g/2 oz liver (chicken, calf or pig)
15g/½ oz flour
⅛ lit/¼ pt stock or stock cube
bouquet garni
1 tsp tomato purée
½ clove garlic
1 tbsp sherry
110g/¼ lb macaroni or spaghetti
chopped parsley
grated Parmesan cheese

to serve: 3
time: ½ hour

1 Chop onion and sauté in the oil 2 Add sliced liver and cook for a few minutes–add flour 3 Add stock and bring to the boil 4 Add garlic, tomato purée and bouquet garni–simmer gently until thick 5 Remove bouquet garni, check seasoning, and add sherry 6 While sauce is cooking, cook the macaroni or spaghetti, drain and toss in a little butter 7 Pile in a hot dish and pour the sauce over 8 Sprinkle with chopped parsley 9 Serve grated cheese separately

Spaghetti or Macaroni à la milanaise

110g/¼ lb spaghetti or macaroni
30g/1 oz butter
30g/1 oz sliced mushrooms
30g/1 oz lean ham
30g/1 oz tongue
⅛ lit/¼ pt tomato sauce (page 99)
seasoning
15g/½ oz grated Parmesan cheese

to serve: 3
time: 20 minutes
grater

1 Cook the macaroni or spaghetti 2 Melt the butter and cook the mushrooms 3 Add ham and tongue, cut in julienne strips 4 Add the cooked pasta, tomato sauce and seasoning–heat and add the cheese 5 Serve at once with a dish of additional cheese

NB Garlic may be used to flavour the tomato sauce.

Spaghetti with Aubergines

1 aubergine
110g/¼ lb spaghetti
15g/½ oz butter
1 green pepper
1 clove garlic
1 tbsp salad oil
2 anchovy fillets (or anchovy essence)
110g/¼ lb tomatoes
4 tbsp white wine
seasoning
chopped basil
grated Parmesan cheese

to serve: 3
time: 30 minutes
grater

1 Cut aubergine in short strips without skinning **2** Sprinkle with salt and leave to drain for 15–20 minutes **3** Cook spaghetti–and put into a pan with the butter **4** Shred pepper removing the seeds **5** Fry in the oil with the aubergine **6** Add garlic, anchovies, tomato (skinned and cut in slices) **7** Season, add a good sprinkling of basil and the wine **8** Simmer for about 7 minutes **9** Pile spaghetti on a hot dish and pour the vegetable mixture over **10** Serve with a dish of grated Parmesan cheese

Macaroni with Oysters

110g/¼ lb macaroni
1 small tin of oysters
1 tsp grated Parmesan cheese
Sauce
1 tsp chopped onion
1 blade mace
2 peppercorns
¼ lit/½ pt milk
1 bay-leaf
15g/½ oz butter
15g/½ oz flour
seasoning
1 tbsp cream

to serve: 2–3
time: ½ hour
grater
strainer

1 Cook the macaroni **2** Put onion, mace, peppercorns and bay-leaf in the milk and bring to the boil **3** Stand for 10 minutes and strain **4** Make the sauce with the butter, flour and flavoured milk **5** Add the cream and oysters–season **6** Stir the macaroni into this mixture and pile on to a dish and sprinkle with the cheese **7** Brown under the grill
NB This dish may be served using prawns or shrimps instead of oysters.

Macaroni Cheese (or Spaghetti)

60g/2 oz macaroni or spaghetti
90g/3 oz grated cheese (mixture of Parmesan and Cheddar cheese)
¼ lit/½ pt liquid (½ milk, ½ macaroni water or all milk)

to serve: 2
time: 20 minutes
gratin-dish
grill

¼ tsp mustard
30g/1 oz butter
15g/½ oz flour
1 tsp grated onion or ½ clove crushed garlic
seasoning
triangular croûtons of toast or fried bread
parsley

1 Cook the pasta in boiling salted water until tender—strain **2** Make a roux sauce, mixing the mustard with the flour **3** Add the pasta, ⅔ of the cheese, and onion or garlic **4** Season and put into the dish **5** Sprinkle with remaining cheese and brown under the grill **6** Arrange croûtons round the edge—garnish with parsley **7** Stand on a dish on a plain paper

NB 1 This dish may be made substituting tomato for white sauce.
2 Slices of skinned tomatoes may be arranged on top before sprinkling with cheese.

Gnocchi parisienne

to serve: 3
time: ½ hour
tea-cloth
gratin-dish
grill

60g/2 oz butter
⅛ lit/¼ pt water
100g/3¼ oz flour
2 eggs
30g/1 oz grated cheese
seasoning
⅛ lit/¼ pt mornay sauce (page 89)

1 Bring water and butter to boil and proceed as for choux pastry (page 232) **2** Add cheese and seasoning **3** Poach in dessertspoons for 8 minutes taking care that the water does not boil and that the mixture is very smooth **4** Drain on a cloth and put into the buttered dish **5** Coat with the well-seasoned mornay sauce **6** Sprinkle with cheese and brown under the grill

Gnocchi à la Romana

to serve: 3
time: ½ hour
grill
gratin-dish

1 small onion
1 bay-leaf
¼ lit/½ pt milk
2½ tbsp semolina
30g/1 oz grated cheese
15g/½ oz butter
½ tsp French mustard
extra cheese for sprinkling
seasoning

1 Put onion and bay-leaf in the milk and bring to the boil **2** Remove flavourings and sprinkle the semolina into the boiling milk **3** Simmer 15–20 minutes stirring **4** Remove from the heat and stir in butter, cheese and mustard season **5** Spread out about 25 mm or 1 in. thick and allow to cool **6** When quite cold, cut into squares **7** Arrange in the buttered dish **8** Sprinkle thickly with cheese and brown in the oven or under the grill

Fried Gnocchi

gnocchi à la Romana (page 143)
tomato sauce (page 99)
egg and raspings
parsley

to serve: 3
time: ½ hour
deep-fat pan
thermometer

1 Spread out about 25 mm/1 in. thick and allow to cool **2** Cut into fingers 50 mm/2 in. long and 25 mm/1 in. wide **3** Flour lightly, brush with egg and coat with raspings **4** Fry at 180 °C/355 °F **5** Dish on a plain paper, garnish with parsley and serve with highly-seasoned tomato sauce

Risotto (Plain)

170g/6 oz rice (Italian rice is best)
45g/1½ oz butter
1 onion
1 clove garlic
½ lit/1 pt stock or stock cube
pinch nutmeg
bouquet garni
seasoning
45g/1½ oz grated cheese

to serve: 3–4
time: 35 minutes
gratin-dish
oven No. 3 or 170 °C/335 °F

1 Heat butter and add chopped onion and crushed garlic and sauté until soft but not brown **2** Add unwashed rice and cook till all fat is absorbed **3** Add stock, bouquet garni and seasoning **4** Bring to boil, cover and put into the oven **5** Cook for about 20 minutes **6** Remove bouquet garni and add cheese and butter–season **7** Serve piled up on the dish

NB This risotto is very good plain, but can be enriched by adding: *(a)* mushrooms; *(b)* tomato sauce (page 99); *(c)* kidneys–liver–ham–prawns–shrimps.

Risotto à la milanaise

170g/6 oz Italian rice
30g/1 oz beef marrow
45g/1½ oz butter
1 chopped onion
1 crushed clove garlic
60g/2 oz sliced mushrooms
⅜ lit/¼ pt white wine
pinch saffron
⅛ lit/¾ pt stock or stock cube
60g/2 oz grated cheese
seasoning

to serve: 3–4
time: 35 minutes
gratin-dish
oven No. 3 or 170 °C/335 °F

1 Sauté onion and garlic in melted marrow and half the butter 2 Add rice and cook until fat is absorbed 3 Add sliced mushrooms, wine, saffron and stock 4 Bring to boil, cover and put in the oven for 20 minutes 5 Add remaining butter and cheese 6 Cover and leave for a few minutes 7 Stir lightly with a fork and check seasoning 8 Serve at once piled on the dish

Pilaff aux fruits de mer

to serve: 3
time: 1 hour
medium Savarin mould
oven No. 3 or 170 °C/335 °F

30g/1 oz butter
1 onion (chopped)
110g/¼ lb rice (Patna or Italian)
⅜ lit/¾ pt white stock or stock cube
1 scallop
4 tbsp white wine
bouquet garni
6 prawns
30g/1 oz sliced and sautéd mushrooms
⅛ lit/¼ pt coating sauce (made with fish stock)
4 tbsp cream
1 tsp paprika butter (page 102)
seasoning

1 Sauté ¾ of the onion in the butter 2 Add the rice and sauté for a few minutes 3 Add stock, bring to the boil, cover and put in the oven for 20 minutes 4 Add the paprika butter and put into the oiled mould 5 While rice is cooking prepare the fish 6 Put the scallop in to a pan with a little water, the white wine, the remaining onion, bouquet garni and seasoning 7 Cook very gently for 5 minutes–remove and slice 8 Toss prawns in the liquid 9 Make sauce with this liquid–add cream and fish 10 Colour with paprika butter and check seasoning 11 Turn out the pilaff and pile the fish in the centre 12 Pour the sauce round and decorate with prawn heads

9
Eggs

EGG COOKERY

To boil eggs–

1 Put into boiling water to cover and boil gently for 3–4½ minutes according to freshness and individual taste.
2 Put into boiling water, bring back to boil, put on lid, remove from heat and leave for 5 minutes (coddled egg).
3 *To coddle–*
   (i) Bring water to the boil
   (ii) Put in egg–cover
   (iii) Remove from heat and leave 10 minutes
   or coddle in a patent coddler
4 Put into cold water, bring slowly to boiling-point and remove at once.

To hard-boil eggs–

1 Put into boiling water and boil gently for 10 minutes.
2 Put at once into cold water and crack the shell.

NB If the eggs are not very fresh, they may be put into cold water and brought slowly to the boil and boiled for 5–7 minutes. In this case the eggs should be turned during cooking to avoid the yolk dropping.

Scrambled Egg

1 egg
1 tbsp milk
knob of butter
salt, pepper
parsley
buttered toast

to serve: 1
time: 5 minutes
grill
non-stick or enamel saucepan

1 Make toast, butter, remove crusts or cut into a round. Keep hot **2** Break egg into a basin, beat, add seasoning and milk **3** Melt butter in a small pan, add the egg mixture **4** Stir gently with a wooden spoon over low heat until the egg is lightly set **5** Pile on toast–garnish with parsley

Poached Egg

1 egg
boiling, salted water
1 round buttered toast

to serve: 1
time: 5 minutes
frying-pan
plain cutter

1 Boil a little water in a frying-pan—reduce heat **2** Place cutter in water—add salt **3** Break egg into a cup or saucer and pour into the cutter, holding it down **4** Allow the egg to set in simmering water, then baste with water to cook the surface **5** Drain very well and put on to the toast **6** Serve at once

NB A patent poacher may be used. This is then a steamed egg.

Poached Egg on Spinach

110g/¼ lb creamed spinach, fresh or frozen (page 123)
2 eggs
seasoning
triangles of fried bread

to serve: 2
time: ¼ hour
gratin-dish

1 Prepare and cook the spinach **2** Poach the eggs (page 147) **3** Serve the eggs on a bed of spinach **4** Arrange the croûtons round

To Fry Eggs

To each egg allow 2 tsp bacon fat, or butter or oil.

time: 5 minutes
a thick frying-pan

1 If using bacon, fry it first and keep it warm **2** Add extra fat if there is not enough from the bacon **3** Slide the egg into the pan, cover with a lid **4** Cook slowly until the white is opaque and just set **5** Lift out carefully with a fish-slice and serve with the bacon

NB The eggs may be turned over and cooked on the other side. These are known as 'turned' eggs.

To Bake Eggs

1 egg per dish
butter or cream
seasoning

time: 5 minutes
ramekin-dishes
oven No. 3 or 170 °C/335 °F

1 Grease the dishes with the butter **2** Break an egg into each dish **3** Season, and add a small pat of butter or 1 tsp of cream to each egg **4** Bake until just set

Omelets

kitchen roll
150 mm/6 in. omelet-pan
spoon
fork

To prove the pan

1 Heat the pan over low heat.
2 Sprinkle the pan with salt and heat.
3 Rub well with paper and tip out the salt.
4 Wipe out with paper.

After use

1 Rub the pan with soft paper.

Basic recipe

1 egg
15g/½ oz butter or margarine
salt and pepper
1 dessertsp cold water
parsley

to serve: 1
time: 5 minutes

1 Beat egg, add water and seasoning 2 Melt the fat, skim and heat till smoking 3 Add egg mixture and stir rapidly with a fork, over low heat 4 When mixture has almost set, smooth the surface, remove from heat 5 Tilt pan away from handle and fold over top $\frac{1}{3}$ of omelet. Press the omelet towards the bottom of the pan with the back of a spoon 6 Heat for a few seconds and turn over on to a dish 7 Garnish with parsley

Variations

1 *Cheese Omelet*
Add 30g/1 oz grated Parmesan cheese to the basic recipe. Add ½ cheese to the egg, sprinkle the remainder on top.

2 *Kidney Omelet*
Add 1 sheep's kidney to the basic recipe, sauté the cut-up kidney in butter, serve some folded in the omelet, the remainder as a garnish.

3 *Tomato Omelet*
Add 1 skinned tomato. Cut up tomato, sauté in butter. Serve some folded in the omelet, some round the omelet or save a ring of tomato and serve this on top of the omelet.

4 *Ham Omelet*
Add 30g/1 oz chopped ham to the basic recipe. Fold in some ham, use the remainder as a garnish.

5 *Onion Omelet*
Add 1 small onion. Chop the onion finely and sauté in butter. Fold into the omelet, garnish with a little onion.

6 *Mixed Herbs Savoury Omelet or Omelet Fines Herbes*
Add ½ tsp chopped parsley or mixed fresh herbs or a good pinch of dried herbs to the egg mixture.

7 *Asparagus Omelet*
Add 6 asparagus tips fresh or tinned. Prepare the fresh asparagus and sauté in butter. Fold in some tips, garnish with the remainder. If tinned asparagus is used, drain well, sauté in butter and use as fresh.

8 *Mushroom Omelet*
Add 30g/1 oz button mushrooms. Save 2 whole for garnish, sauté the remainder, chopped, in butter, fold these in.

9 *Shrimp or Prawn Omelet*
Add 30g/1 oz peeled shrimps or prawns—sauté in butter—fold in ¾, garnish with remainder.

Puffed Omelets

2 eggs
½ tsp vanilla essence
15g/½ oz butter
15g/½ oz castor sugar

to serve: 1
time: 20 minutes
whisk
kitchen roll
150 mm/6 in. omelet-pan lined
oven No. 4 or 180 °C/355 °F

1 Separate the yolks and whites **2** Beat the yolks and sugar until thick—add the flavouring **3** Whisk the whites stiffly and fold very lightly into the yolks **4** Heat the butter, pour the omelet mixture into the pan, hold the pan over the heat and stir a few times **5** Put the pan into the oven and leave for about 8 minutes before opening the door **6** When firm (10–12 minutes) turn on to sugared paper **7** Spread ½ the omelet with the filling (warmed), turn the other half over with a palette knife **8** Serve on a hot plate sprinkled with sugar

Fillings
1 Jam.
2 Fruit purée, sweetened.
3 Chopped fresh fruit heated in syrup, rum or a liqueur may be added.

Omelet Soufflé

2 eggs
1 tsp flour
30g/1 oz castor sugar
vanilla essence

to serve: 1
time: 20 minutes
150 mm/6 in. omelet-pan (lined)
oven No. 6 or 205 °C/400 °F

1 Follow the method for a puffed omelet (page 149) adding the flour to the beaten yolks and sugar **2** Cook for 12–15 minutes **3** Fill as for puffed omelet

NB This mixture may be used for omelette en surprise.

Eggs Mornay

2 hard-boiled or poached eggs	*to serve:* 1–2
⅛ lit/¼ pt white coating sauce	*time:* ½ hour
60g/2 oz grated cheese	grater
230g/½ lb mashed potato (page 107)	grill, gratin-dish
	nylon bag
	No. 8 vegetable-forcer

1 Prepare mashed potato–season, put into the bag and pipe round the edge of the dish **2** Cut hard-boiled eggs lengthwise, across or in slices–arrange in the dish **3** Prepare the sauce–add ⅔ cheese, season, check consistency and coat the eggs **4** Sprinkle remaining cheese over eggs and brown under the grill **5** Serve on a dish with plain dish paper, accompanied by vegetables as a supper dish or as a vegetarian dish

NB Fillets or boned cutlets of white fish may be used instead of eggs.

Curried Eggs

2 hard-boiled eggs	*to serve:* 1–2
1 small onion	*time:* ½ hour
small piece apple	gratin-dish
15g/½ oz dripping	
1 tsp flour	
1 tsp curry powder	
⅛ lit/¼ pt stock	
1 tsp sultanas	
1 tsp treacle	
1 tsp coconut	
lemon-juice and seasoning	
90g/3 oz boiled patna rice	
gherkin and chutney	

1 Chop onion finely and sauté in the fat **2** Add flour and curry powder and cook for a few minutes **3** Add stock and bring to boil **4** Add chopped apple, sultanas, treacle and coconut **5** Bring to the boil and simmer gently 15–20 minutes and add seasoning, lemon-juice and one chopped egg **6** Make a border with the rice and pour in the sauce **7** Cut the other egg in wedges and arrange inside the rice **8** Garnish with cut gherkin and serve with a small dish of chutney

Egg Cutlets

2 hard-boiled eggs		*to serve:* 3
15g/½ oz butter or margarine	sauce	*time:* ½ hour
45g/¾ oz flour	sauce	kitchen roll
⅛ lit/¼ pt milk	sauce	deep fat
1 tsp curry-powder	sauce	thermometer
egg and raspings		

seasoning and lemon-juice
parsley and lemon for garnish
macaroni

1 Mix flour and curry-powder and make the sauce **2** Add the finely-chopped eggs **3** Season well and add lemon-juice **4** Spread on a plate to cool **5** Divide into 6 even-sized pieces and shape into cutlets **6** Coat twice with egg and raspings **7** Fry at 180 °C/355 °F for 2–3 minutes **8** Drain and arrange in a semicircle on a plain paper **9** Stick a small piece of macaroni in the 'bone' end of the cutlet **10** Garnish with fried parsley and small lemon wedges

Egg Fritters

1 hard-boiled egg
1 tsp anchovy essence
lemon-juice
egg and raspings
croûtons of fried bread
parsley, cress or watercress garnish

to serve: 1–2
time: 20 minutes
kitchen roll
small cutter
tea-cloth
deep-fat pan
thermometer

1 Cut egg in half across **2** Remove yolk, add anchovy essence and lemon-juice and cream together **3** Press back into the whites **4** Flour egg lightly and coat with egg and raspings twice **5** Fry in hot fat at 180 °C/355 °F until golden brown **6** Drain well–stand on the croûtons **7** Dish on an oval dish on a plain paper with salad garnish

Scotch Eggs

2 hard-boiled eggs
2–3 pork sausages–or 170g/6 oz sausage-meat
egg, raspings, flour
round croûtons of fried bread
tomato sauce (page 99).

to serve: 2
time: served hot, 40 minutes
served cold, 40 minutes plus cooling time
small plain cutter
kitchen roll
deep-fat pan
thermometer

1 Roll egg in flour (to dry) **2** Half sausage meat and flatten **3** Cover egg with meat–moulding well **4** Roll on the table–flatten the ends **5** Coat with egg and crumbs, firm on, reshape **6** Fry in deep fat at approx. 170 °C/335 °F for 8 minutes–drain **7** Cut in half–stand on the croûtons on a hot dish and pour the sauce round 8 *Or* Allow to cool, cut and serve with salad

Stuffed Eggs

1 hard-boiled egg
15g/½ oz margarine or butter
15g/½ oz grated cheese
seasoning
sliced beetroot, cucumber or tomato
cress for garnish

to serve: 1
time: 20 minutes
sieve
nylon bag
No. 8 vegetable-forcer

1 Cut egg in half, cut a small slice off the bottom **2** Remove yolk, cream with the fat and cheese **3** Season–rub through a sieve **4** Put into the bag and force into the whites **5** Stand on a round of thinly-sliced vegetable **6** Garnish with cress

Alternative fillings

Sardine
Anchovy
Anchovy essence
Pastes

Egg Mayonnaise

2 hard-boiled eggs	*to serve:* 1–2
4 tbsp mayonnaise (page 131)	*time:* ½ hour
4 tbsp aspic jelly (page 209)	muslin
salad garnish	decorating-pins
red and green peppers } for decoration	cooler
black olives } for decoration	
cucumber and tomato skins } for decoration	
aspic for coating	

1 Cut eggs lengthwise, roughen the surface with a little flour and place on a cooler **2** Mix mayonnaise and aspic–tammy **3** Stir until on point of setting **4** Coat the eggs quickly **5** Decorate with neatly-cut pieces of decoration material dipping each piece in liquid aspic **6** Glaze with cool aspic **7** Dish and garnish lightly with cress, etc.
NB These may be served as an hors-d'œuvre or savoury..

Variations

1 Add liquidized spinach or watercress to the mayonnaise and aspic-colour if necessary–tammy.
2 Add 1 tsp of tomato purée and ½ tsp of paprika–tammy.
3 Add 1 tsp curry-powder or paste and a few drops of lemon-juice–tammy.

Soufflés aux œufs pochés

2 eggs	*to serve:* 2
30g/1 oz butter }	*time:* ½ hour
30g/1 oz flour }	whisk
⅛ lit/¼ pt milk }	¼ lit/½ pt gratin-dish
60g/2 oz grated cheese	oven No. 5 or 190 °C/380 °F
1 tbsp grated cheese and bread-crumbs	
2 eggs (for poaching)	

1 Grease the gratin-dish **2** Make the sauce and add egg-yolks and cheese-season **3** Poach the eggs **4** Whisk whites and fold into the sauce **5** Put ½ this mixture into the dish **6** Put the poached eggs on top and cover with remaining mixture **7** Sprinkle top with the breadcrumbs and grated cheese **8** Bake for about 20 minutes **9** Serve on a plain paper and garnish with parsley

10

Batters

Pancake or Yorkshire Pudding Batter

¼ lit/½ pt milk and water
110g/¼ lb flour
1 egg
pinch of salt

time: 1 hour
sieve

1 Sieve the flour and salt **2** Make a well in the centre **3** Pour in half the liquid and egg **4** Mix gradually to avoid lumps and beat well **5** Stir in the remaining liquid **6** Stand for ½–1 hour **7** Use as required
NB Beat with spoon, rotary whisk, whisk on machine or in a liquidizer.

COATING BATTERS

Economical No. 1

60g/2 oz flour
1 tsp baking-powder
4 tbsp milk and water
pinch of salt

time: 5 minutes

1 Mix flour and liquid gradually and stir until it is a smooth mixture coating the back of the spoon **2** Use as required, adding the baking-powder just before frying

Fritter Batter No. 2

60g/2 oz flour
3–4 tbsp tepid water
2 tsp oil
pinch of salt
1 egg-white

time: 10 minutes
sieve
whisk

1 Sieve flour and salt into a small bowl **2** Make a well in the centre and add the oil and water **3** Mix gradually to a smooth batter–it should coat the back of a spoon thickly **4** When ready to fry, fold in the stiffly-whisked white of egg

Yeast Batter No. 3

110g/¼ lb flour
pinch of salt
15g/½ oz butter or margarine
a walnut of yeast
⅛ lit/¼ pt milk and water
½ tsp castor sugar

time: ½ hour
sieve
tea-cloth

1 Sieve flour and salt and rub in the fat **2** Cream the yeast with the sugar and add the tepid liquid **3** Add to the dry ingredients and beat well for 3–4 minutes **4** Cover with a damp cloth and put in a warm place to rise to double its size **5** Check the consistency. Use as required

Savoury Fritter-cases

coating batter 2 or 3 (pages 153–154)
savoury filling
salad garnish

time: 45 minutes
kitchen roll
deep-fat pan
thermometer
plain fritter-iron
tea-cloth

1 Heat the fat at 180 °C/355 °F **2** Prepare the cases as for sweet fritters (page 170) **3** Fill with the chosen filling and decorate with salad, etc.

Suggested fillings

1 White sauce base with chopped chicken, ham or veal. Garnish with salad.
2 White sauce base with chopped prawns or shrimps. Garnish with salad and prawn heads.
3 White sauce base with chopped lobster, crab or salmon. Garnish with salad and lobster or crab feelers.
4 Any of the above with a mayonnaise base.
5 Any of the above set in aspic and piled into the cases. Cucumber-skin could be used to form a handle.

Serve on a dish or plate with a plain paper and garnished with salad.

11

Puddings and sweets

Fruit Crumble

340g/¾ lb fruit	*to serve:* 3
water according to fruit up to 1 tbsp	*time:* ¾ hour
sugar to taste	sieve
110g/¼ lb flour } crumble	castor sugar dredger
75g/2½ oz margarine or butter } crumble	½ lit/1 pt pie-dish
30g/1 oz castor sugar } crumble	oven No. 6 or 205 °C/400 °F

1 Prepare the fruit–put into the pie-dish and add sugar and water if necessary 2 Sieve flour, add sugar, rub in the fat till like breadcrumbs 3 Press the mixture on top of the fruit 4 Dredge with castor sugar 5 Bake up to 30 minutes till pale golden brown 6 Serve on a fancy paper or an oval dish with custard sauce, junket or cream

Fruit Pie

450g/1 lb fruit	*to serve:* 3
110g/¼ lb short crust or biscuit crust pastry (page 229)	*time:* 1 hour
2 tbsp sugar	sieve
water according to fruit	½ lit/1 pt pie-dish
	oven No. 6 or 205 °C/400 °F

1 Prepare the fruit 2 Half fill the pie-dish, add sugar, water, flavouring, then remaining fruit 3 Knead pastry lightly–turn over–roll out 10 mm/½ in. bigger than top of dish 4 Damp the edges of the pie-dish–put a strip all round the edge–press down well 5 Damp the pastry rim and put pastry on top 6 Trim–knock up edges and mark with small lines 7 Lift pastry at ends to let steam out 8 Bake ½ hour 9 Take out of the oven, brush lightly with water and sprinkle with castor sugar–return for 1 minute to dry off 10 Dish on an oval dish, on a fancy paper 11 Serve with custard, cream or junket

NB Brown sugar may be used when making apple pie or with a dark fruit.

Apple Dumplings

For each medium-sized apple–	*to serve:* 1

60g/2 oz short crust pastry (page 229)
15g/½ oz sugar
1 clove

time: 45 minutes
greased and floured baking-tray
oven No. 6 or 205 °C/400 °F

1 Peel and core apple 2 Knead the pastry into a round, roll thinly into a circle–turn over 3 Stand the apple on the pastry and fill up the hole with sugar and clove 4 Cover with pastry, moulding without stretching–seal the edges 5 Turn dumpling upside down on to the baking sheet 6 Brush with water and sprinkle with castor sugar 7 Bake 20–30 minutes 8 Serve on a round plate with a fancy paper with custard sauce, cream or junket

NB Dates, raisins, etc., may be used with the sugar to fill up core cavity of apple.

Toffee Fruit Pudding

110g/¼ lb short crust pastry (page 229)
340g/¾ lb fruit
water according to fruit
60g/2 oz demerara sugar
butter or margarine

to serve: 3
time: 1 hour
foil
125 mm/5 in. round cake-tin
oven No. 6 or 205 °C/400 °F

1 Make the pastry 2 Grease the cake-tin very thickly with butter or margarine 3 Coat the side and base with brown sugar–tip out surplus 4 Roll ¾ of the pastry into a circle and line bottom and side of tin 5 Fill with fruit adding sugar and water if a hard fruit 6 Roll remaining pastry out, damp edges and cover the fruit 7 Cover the tin with greased paper or foil 8 Bake for 40 minutes 9 Turn out immediately on to a hot plate and serve with caramel sauce, or custard sauce, or cream or junket

Baked Jam Roll

110g/¼ lb short-crust pastry (page 229)
3 tbsp jam

to serve: 2–3
time: 45 minutes
greased and floured baking-tray
oven No. 6 or 205 °C/400 °F

1 Knead pastry lightly and roll into an oblong–turnover 2 Spread with the jam 3 Turn up sides about 10 mm/½ in. 4 Damp bottom and roll down 5 Brush with water and sprinkle with sugar 6 Bake 20–30 minutes 7 Serve on a fancy paper with a suitable sauce or cream

Variations

1 2 tbsp golden syrup
1 tbsp fresh breadcrumbs

2 230g/½ lb chopped apples
60g/2 oz chopped dates
1 tbsp brown sugar

3 2 tbsp lemon curd

4 3 tbsp mincemeat

Apple Strudel

strudel pastry (page 233)
1 kg/2 lb apples
60g/2 oz currants
60g/2 oz sultanas
60g/2 oz brown or white sugar
½ tsp cinnamon
½ tsp mixed spice
3 tbsp browned crumbs
60g/2 oz butter
oil

to serve: 8–10
time: 1¾ hours
greased baking-tray
icing-sugar dredger
oven No. 6 or 205 °C/400 °F

1 Roll out the strudel pastry and brush with the oil **2** Peel, core and slice the apple thinly **3** Mix with the fruit, sugar, spices and half the crumbs **4** Dab half the butter over the pastry and sprinkle with the remaining crumbs **5** Sprinkle the apple mixture over the pastry **6** Tear away the extreme edge of the pastry all round **7** Pull down the cloth and roll the pastry over the filling to form a fairly close roll **8** Roll off the cloth and on to the baking-tray **9** Brush with the remaining butter (melted) and bake about ¾ hour until golden brown **10** Turn on to a board, cut in slices slantwise, and dredge with icing-sugar **11** Serve hot with cream

Steamed Pudding (Rubbing-in Mixture)

110g/¼ lb basic rubbed-in mixture (page 237)
For flavouring–see rock cakes (page 237)

to serve: 2–3
time: 1¼ hours
steamer
greased ½ lit/1 pt basin
foil

1 Prepare rubbed-in mixture and mix with egg and milk to a dropping consistency **2** Put into the basin and cover with foil **3** Steam 1 hour **4** Serve on a round plate, sprinkled with castor sugar **5** Hand a suitable sauce separately

NB Jam or dried fruit may be put into the basin before adding the mixture.

Fruit Pudding

110g/¼ lb suet crust (page 229)
340–450g/¾–1 lb fruit
60g/2 oz brown or white sugar
water according to fruit

to serve: 3
time: steamed, 2½ hours; boiled, 2 hours; pressure-cooked, 1¼ hours
steamer or pressure-cooker
greased basin
foil

1 Knead the pastry and roll into a round **2** Flour thickly and fold in half **3** Pull up each end to make a crescent shape **4** Roll out lightly keeping the shape of the basin (no wrinkles) **5** Line the basin **6** Half fill with fruit—add sugar **7** Add remaining fruit and water **8** Cover with the pastry sealing with water **9** Cover with foil,and steam 2 hours **10** Turn on to a round or oval dish—sprinkle with castor sugar **11** Serve accompanied by custard or cream

NB If to be boiled, cook for 1½ hours. If cooked in a pressure-cooker allow vent to steam for 20 minutes. Apply 15 lb pressure and cook for a further 25 minutes.

Suet Roll

110g/¼ lb suet-crust pastry (page 229)
3 tbsp jam

to serve: 2–3
time: baked, 1 hour; steamed, 2 hours
foil
steamer of greased baking-tray
oven No. 6 or 205 °C/400 °F

1 Roll pastry into an oblong **2** Spread evenly with jam **3** Turn up sides about 10 mm/½ in. **4** Damp the bottom and roll down **5** Wrap in foil and steam 1½ hours **6** Turn on to a hot dish and serve with a suitable sauce

NB To bake, put on to the tray and bake ½ hour.

Variations

1 Fruit, e.g. currants, sultanas, raisins, dates.

2 2 tbsp syrup
1 tbsp fresh breadcrumbs
lemon-rind

3 Lemon curd—2 tbsp

4 230g/½ lb chopped apple
1 tbsp brown sugar
1 lemon-rind

5 3 tbsp mincemeat

Christmas Pudding

340g/¾ lb flour
340g/¾ lb fresh breadcrumbs
450g/1 lb suet
1 kg/2 lb raisins
450g/1 lb brown sugar
340g/¾ lb sultanas
340g/¾ lb currants
230g/½ lb peel
170g/6 oz almonds
1 tsp nutmeg
1 tsp cinnamon

quantity: approx 5 kg/10 lb cooked pudding
time: as table
kitchen roll
grater
whisk
steamers
pudding-basins
foil

2 apples (medium size)
2 carrots (medium size)
½ lit/1 pt stout
1 tsp salt
2 tbsp marmalade
2 tbsp treacle
4 eggs

1 Chop or shred suet if using butchers' suet **2** Wash the fruit and drain on paper **3** Grate apples and carrots **4** Chop almonds **5** Beat eggs **6** Mix all ingredients thoroughly **7** Put into greased basins and cover with foil **8** Steam for at least 12 hours **9** Turn out and serve with brandy butter (page 100) cream or custard

Alternative Methods of cooking

1 Pressurized steamer: 8 hours
2 Boiled: 8 hours
3 Pressure-cooker: blowing-time plus 4 hours

Snowdon Pudding

90g/3 oz raisins
90g/3 oz suet
110g/¼ lb fresh breadcrumbs
3 tsp ground rice
90g/3 oz marmalade
rind of ½ lemon
4 tbsp milk
90g/3 oz castor sugar
2 eggs

to serve: 3
time: 3 hours 20 minutes
liquidizer
½ lit/1 pt pudding-basin
steamer
foil

1 Make a caramel with the granulated sugar (page 92)—add milk **2** Cut **2** Mix the suet, crumbs, ground rice and lemon-rind **3** Beat the eggs and add the marmalade and milk **4** Add to dry ingredients **5** Mix well and put into the basin **6** Cover with foil and steam for 2½–3 hours **7** Turn on to a hot dish **8** Serve with marmalade sauce (page 96)

Viennoise Pudding (Pudding à la viennoise)

90g/3 oz bread
45g/1½ oz sultanas
15g/½ oz peel
45g/1½ oz castor sugar
30g/1 oz granulated sugar (for caramel)
¼ lit/½ pt milk
2 eggs
1 tbsp sherry
a little lemon-rind

to serve: 3
time: 2¼ hours
strainer
steamer
¼ lit/½ pt fancy or plain greased mould
foil

1 Make a caramel with the granulated sugar (page 92)–add milk **2** Cut the bread into small dice **3** Add peel, sultanas, castor sugar and lemon-rind **4** Beat eggs and add milk and caramel **5** Strain on to the bread **6** Allow to stand at least ½ hour–pour into the mould and cover with foil **7** Steam 1–1¼ hours **8** Turn out and serve with custard, wine or sherry sauce (page 97)

Canary Pudding

1 egg quantity creaming mixture (page 243)
1 lemon

to serve: 3–4
time: in darioles, 50 minutes; in basin, 1 hour 20 minutes
sieve
mixer
125 mm/5 in. greased pudding-basin or 4 dariole-moulds
steamer
foil

1 Cream fat and sugar—add egg **2** Add finely-grated lemon-rind **3** Fold in sieved flour and baking-powder—add cold water to make a dropping consistency **4** Put into the basin or darioles—cover **5** Steam for 30 minutes in dariole-moulds or 1 hour in a basin **6** Turn on to a hot plate **7** Hand custard or lemon sauce (pages 96, 97), separately

Variation

Orange pudding may be made in the same way.

Castle Puddings

Make as for canary pudding (page 160) omitting lemon.

to serve: 2
time: in darioles, 40 minutes; in basin, 1 hour

Cooking

Steam as for canary pudding—serve with jam sauce (page 96) floated round.

or

Bake—oven No. 4 or 180 °C/355 °F for 20 minutes in dariole-moulds—for 30–40 minutes in basin. Serve custard or jam sauce separately.

Mince Pies

110g/¼ lb biscuit crust (page 229)
110g/¼ lb mincemeat

to serve: 3
time: 40 minutes
6 patty-tins
60 mm/2½ in. plain cutter
50 mm/2 in. plain cutter
castor-sugar dredger
oven No. 4 or 170 °C/355 °F

1 Roll biscuit crust big enough to cut out 6 larger rounds (for tops) **2** Roll out remaining pastry and cut another 6 large rounds (thinner for bottoms) **3** Put these into the patty-tins and divide mincemeat between the 6 tins **4** Damp edges of tops and place over the mincemeat **5** Seal with the turned side of the smaller cutter **6** Brush with water and sprinkle with castor sugar **7** Bake 15–20 minutes **8** Serve hot

NB If the mince pies are to be kept, heat before serving.

Apple Amber

450g/1 lb apples
110g/¼ lb biscuit crust (page 229)
1 tbsp sugar
strip of lemon-rind
1 egg
30g/1 oz butter
60g/2 oz castor sugar for meringue
cherries
angelica

to serve: 2–3
time: 2 hours
whisk
liquidizer
small fancy cutter
½ lit/1 pt pie-dish
castor-sugar dredger
nylon bag } optional
No. 8 vegetable star-forcer } optional
oven No. 4 or 180 °C/355 °F
oven No. ½ or 115 °C/265 °F (for meringue)

1 Prepare the apples and put in a pan with the sugar, lemon-rind and butter **2** Cook very gently until tender with the lid on **3** Liquidize after removing the rind **4** Add yolk of egg **5** Half line the pie-dish with the pastry **6** Roll out cuttings and cut into rounds **7** Damp the edge and arrange the rounds overlapping on this edge **8** Pour the apple purée into the prepared pie-dish **9** Bake about 20 minutes **10** Whisk egg-white and sugar until stiff and pile or pipe on top **11** Dredge with sugar and decorate with cherries and angelica **12** Bake until crisp—at least 1 hour

NB This may be made using gooseberries or apricots.

Strawberry Shortcake

110g/¼ lb flour
60g/2 oz rice flour
110g/¼ lb butter
90g/3 oz ground almonds
90g/3 oz castor sugar
1 egg-yolk
Filling—
230g/½ lb strawberries
sugar to taste
⅛ lit/¼ pt whipped cream

to serve: 3–4
time: 1¾ hours
2 × 150 mm/6 in. sandwich-tins greased and floured
No. 8 vegetable star-forcer
nylon forcing-bag
icing-sugar dredger
oven No. 4 or 170 °C/335 °F

1 Rub butter into flour and rice flour **2** Add sugar and ground almonds **3** Bind with egg-yolk **4** Divide mixture into 2 (or 3) portions **5** Roll into rounds 10 mm/½ in. thick and press into the sandwich-tins **6** Bake 30–40 minutes **7** Prepare the strawberries—select 6–8 of the best for decoration—mix the remainder, cut up, with ¾ of the cream **8** Spread one round with strawberry mixture, cover with the second round—dredge with icing-sugar **9** Decorate the top round with piped cream and whole strawberries **10** Serve on a fancy paper on a plate

Chocolate Profiteroles

75g/2½ oz choux pastry (page 232)
⅛ lit/¼ pt cream
⅛ lit/¼ pt hot chocolate sauce (page 97)

to serve: 4–6
time: 1¼ hours
greased and floured baking-tray

10 mm/½ in. forcer
nylon bag
icing-sugar dredger
oven No. 7 or 220 °C/425 °F

1 Make the choux pastry 2 Pipe in balls on to the baking-tray 3 Bake 30 minutes 4 Open and dry and cool 5 Fill with cream 6 Pile in a pyramid on a dish—pour hot sauce over just before serving—or serve separately and sprinkle the balls with icing-sugar

Beignets soufflés

choux pastry (page 232)
vanilla essence
jam or wine sauce (pages 96, 97)

to serve: 6–8
time: ¼ hour
kitchen roll
deep-fat pan
thermometer
icing-sugar dredger

1 Heat the fat to 170 °C/335 °F 2 Drop the choux pastry into the fat in dessertsps 3 Fry for 8–10 minutes, turning all the time, until golden brown 4 Drain 5 Pile up on a plate on a fancy paper 6 Dredge with icing-paper and serve the sauce separately

Gâteau Saint-Honoré

110g/¼ lb biscuit crust (page 229)
75g/2½ oz quantity choux pastry mixture (page 232)
230g/½ lb strawberries
⅛ lit/¼ pt whipped cream
apricot glaze (see Misc. Processes)
colouring
chopped pistachio nuts or green chopped almonds
sugar

to serve: 3–4
time: 2 hours
baking-sheet
forcing-bag
10 mm/½ in. plain forcer
No. 8 vegetable-forcer
oven No. 5 or 190 °C/380 °F

1 Roll the biscuit crust into a 175 mm/7 in. circle 2 Pipe choux pastry round the edge of this circle—cover with a second layer of piped choux pastry 3 Pipe the remainder on to the baking-sheet in small balls 4 Bake for 25–30 minutes—cool 5 Fill the choux balls with whipped and sweetened cream 6 Prepare strawberries, save 8 for decoration, cut and mix remainder with ⅔ remaining cream and 1 tbsp sugar 7 Put this mixture into the centre 8 Glaze choux balls, sprinkle with nuts, place round choux pastry ring 9 Decorate edge between choux balls and centre with remaining strawberries and piped cream

French Fruit Tart

110g/¼ lb rough puff pastry or puff pastry (pages 230, 231) or frozen pastry
fruit, e.g. apricots
⅛ lit/¼ pt syrup from fruit

to serve: 2–3
time: 1½ hours
baking tray
icing-sugar dredger

1 scant tsp arrowroot
colouring
cherries
angelica

oven No. 7 or 220 °C/425 °F

1 Roll the pastry into a thick oblong—trim sides and ends—put on to a baking sheet **2** Cut halfway through the thickness of the pastry 25 mm/1 in. from the edge, parallel with the edges **3** Rest in a refrigerator for 10 minutes **4** Bake 25 minutes—remove top—return to oven at No. 3 or 170 °C/335 °F, to dry—about 10 minutes—cool **5** Dust sides with icing-sugar and pack with fruit—glaze **6** Decorate with cherries and angelica **7** Serve on a plate with fancy paper

NB Fresh fruit may be used either stewed or raw and glazed with a jam glaze.

Gâteau jalousie

110g/¼ lb puff pastry or rough puff pastry (page 231, 232) or frozen pastry
3 tbsp jam
egg-white
castor sugar

to serve: 4–6
time: 1¼ hours
baking-tray
castor-sugar dredger
oven No. 7 or 220 °C/425 °F

1 Roll pastry very thinly into an oblong and 100 mm/4 in. wide **2** Cut in two across, one slightly longer than the other **3** Roll the smaller one to the same size as the other and place on the baking tray **4** Trim the edges and damp a 25 mm/1 in. border all the way round **5** Spread the centre with the jam **6** Fold the other piece of pastry in half lengthwise **7** Cut across the fold, leaving 25 mm/1 in. of pastry uncut along the cut length and at each end. The cuts should be 10 mm/½ in. apart **8** Open out and place over the prepared piece **9** 'Knock up' the edges **10** Brush with beaten egg-white and dredge with castor sugar **11** Bake 25–30 minutes **12** Cut into 35 mm/1½ in. fingers for serving

Gâteau mille-feuilles

230g/½ lb puff or rough puff pastry (pages 231, 232) or frozen pastry
apricot glaze (see Misc. Processes)
¼ lit/½ pt cream
230g/½ lb fresh fruit or jam
almonds or chopped pistachio nuts
crystallized fruits

to serve: 4–6
time: 1½ hours
baking-tray
dessert-plate or flan-ring
oven No. 7 or 220 °C/425 °F

1 Roll out pastry thinly and cut 5 or 6 rounds the size of a dessert-plate **2** Cut out the centre leaving a large ring of pastry **3** Cut a plain round of pastry a little larger and thicker than the rings—this forms the base **4** Bake 8–12 minutes **5** When pastry is cool, brush each ring with apricot glaze **6** Mount the rings on the base, one on top of the other **7** Brush top and sizes with more glaze **8** Decorate the top with tiny shapes of pastry, crystallized fruits and almonds or pistachio nuts

9 Just before serving, fill with fruit or jam and piped cream

NB 1 This may be made with solid rings, with fruit and cream between each.

2 It may be oblong instead of round when it is iced.

Stewed Fruit (fresh)

⅛ lit/¼ pt water
60g/2 oz sugar
lemon-juice
230g/½ lb fruit

to serve: 1–2
time: ½ hour plus cooling time

1 Boil dissolved sugar and water till a syrup is formed—add lemon-juice 2 Add prepared fruit—cover and simmer very gently until fruit is tender, but still whole 3 Cool and serve cold in a glass dish or individual glasses

NB 1 When stewing pears and apples, cinnamon stick and cloves may be added when making the syrup. They should be strained out before stewing the fruit.

2 The syrup may be coloured for pale fruits.

Stewed Fruit (Dried)

230g/½ lb dried apricots, prunes, etc.
⅛ lit/¼ pt syrup
flavouring

to serve: 2–4
time: overnight plus ½ hour plus cooling time

1 Wash the fruit and soak in cold water overnight 2 Make syrup as for fresh fruit using the soaking water 3 Proceed as for fresh fruit

NB Brown sugar may be used for syrup when preparing dark fruits.

Fruit Salad

1 pear
1 orange
1 banana
60g/2 oz grapes
60g/2 oz cherries
whipped cream
Syrup—
⅛ lit/¼ pt water
60g/2 oz sugar
sherry
lemon-juice

to serve: 2
time: 1½ hours

1 Boil dissolved sugar and water till a syrup is formed 2 Prepare fruit according to kind 3 Add lemon-juice and sherry to syrup 4 Pour over the fruit whilst hot—cool 5 Serve very cold in a glass dish or in sundae-glasses, piped with cream 6 Serve with sponge fingers (page 241) or shortbread biscuits (page 273)

NB Tinned or bottled fruits may be used, making the syrup from the liquid.

Fruit Fool

230g/½ lb rhubarb or any fresh fruit
60g/2 oz sugar
⅛ lit/¼ pt cream

to serve: 2
time: 1½ hours
forcing-bag
No. 8 icing-forcer
liquidizer

1 Prepare fruit, put in a pan with the sugar and cook with the lid on till tender 2 Liquidize—cool 3 Whip the cream and mix with the fruit purée 4 Add colouring if necessary 5 Serve very cold in a glass dish or sundae-glasses—pipe with cream

Variations
Any tinned fruit or frozen fruit may be substituted for fresh fruit.

Eve's Pudding

340g/¾ lb fresh fruit
1 egg quantity creaming mixture (page 243)
sugar for fruit

to serve: 2–3
time: 1¼ hours
mixer
½ lit/1 pt pie-dish
oven No. 4 or 180 °C/355 °F

1 Prepare fruit and put in the pie-dish 2 Sprinkle with sugar 3 Cover with the creamed mixture 4 Bake for 30–40 minutes 5 Serve on an oval dish on a fancy paper 6 Serve custard, cream or junket separately

Baked Apples

2 large cooking apples
2 dessertsp brown sugar
2 cloves

to serve: 2
time: 40 minutes
baking-tray
apple-corer or -peeler
oven No. 5 or 190 °C/380 °F

1 Wash the apples and remove the core 2 Slit through the skin round the apple 3 Place on the baking-tray and fill the centres with the sugar and the clove 4 Pour a little water round the apples 5 Bake until tender (time will vary according to the kind of apple) 6 Serve on a dish, pouring any liquid round the fruit. These may be served with cream, milk pudding, etc.

Variations
1 Add currants, sultanas, prunes or dates to the sugar.
2 Add marmalade or honey.
3 If required savoury, sausage-meat or chopped bacon or ham may be used.

Apples Meringue (Pommes à la meringue)

3 medium cooking apples
⅛ lit/¼ pt syrup (page 164)
2 egg-whites
90g/3 oz castor sugar
whipped cream
cherries
angelica
lemon-juice
sherry
colouring

to serve: 3
time: 1½ hours
whisk
greased baking-sheet
forcing-bag
No. 8 vegetable-forcer
casserole or pie-dish and foil
castor-sugar dredger
oven No. 3 or 170 °C/335 °F

1 Peel and core apples 2 Put into the casserole or pie-dish–pour syrup over–cover and bake till just tender (but still whole) 3 Lift on to the baking-sheet 4 Whisk whites stiffly with the sugar 5 Pipe over the apples and pile roughly. Dredge with castor sugar 6 Bake till crisp–about 45 minutes–oven No. ½ or 130 °C/265 °F 7 Colour the syrup, add lemon-juice and sherry 8 Put apples on a dish, pour syrup round 9 Pipe cream in centre of the apples and decorate with cherries and angelica

NB Pears or peaches may be served in the same way.

Apple Snow

1 medium cooking apple
1 egg
sponge fingers or cakes (page 241)
⅛ lit/¼ pt milk
sugar to sweeten
cherries–angelica
colouring

to serve: 2
time: 1½ hours
whisk
2 sundae-glasses
liquidizer

1 Prepare the apple, slice and stew slowly with sugar until tender 2 Make egg custard with yolk, milk and sugar (page 97) 3 Break up 4 sponge fingers and arrange in 2 sundae glasses 4 Pour the custard over and allow to cool 5 Liquidize the apple–chill 6 Whisk white stiffly and fold in coloured purée 7 Pile on top of the custard–decorate with cherry and angelica 8 Serve on a fancy paper on a saucer or plate

Apple Jelly

230g/½ lb cooking apples
½ lemon
45g/1½ oz sugar
⅛ lit/¼ pt water
1 tsp gelatine (scant)
colouring
cherries
angelica
whipped cream

to serve: 2
time: 1½–2 hours
liquidizer
sundae-glasses
 or dariole-moulds
 or border-mould
forcing-bag
No. 8 icing-forcer

1 Prepare the apples, slice and stew with sugar, water and lemon-rind 2 Liquidize 3 Add gelatine and heat–colour 4 Pour into wetted moulds and set 5 Turn out and decorate with cream, cherries and angelica
NB If set in sundae-glasses do not turn out.

Orange Jelly

⅛ lit/¼ pt water	*to serve:* 2
⅛ lit/¼ pt orange-juice	*time:* 1½–2 hours
juice of 1 lemon	strainer
rind of 2 oranges thinly peeled	dariole moulds or
45g/1½ oz sugar	sundae-glasses or
1 tsp gelatine	wetted mould
	No. 8 icing-forcer
	nylon bag

1 Wash the oranges 2 Put water, sugar, orange-rind and gelatine into a pan and stir until dissolved 3 Cover and infuse for 30 minutes away from heat 4 Add juices, strain and colour 5 Pour into the mould or glasses and set 6 Turn out of mould–decorate with piped cream 7 Serve sponge fingers (page 241), shortbread (page 273) or macaroon biscuits (page 279) separately

Lemon Cream

1 large lemon	*to serve:* 2
1 egg	*time:* 1½–2 hours
110g/¼ lb sugar	grater
1 tsp gelatine	strainer
yellow colouring if necessary	dariole-moulds or
4 tbsp whipped cream	sundae-glasses or
⅛ lit/¼ pt water	100 mm/4 in border mould
	forcing-bag
	No. 8 icing-forcer

1 Grate the lemon 2 Put into a pan with the juice and all other ingredients 3 Bring slowly to the boil stirring all the time 4 Strain and add colouring 5 Put into sundae-glasses, mould or moulds 6 When set turn out and decorate with the whipped cream, cherries and angelica 7 Serve with an accompaniment of sponge fingers (page 241) or small biscuits
NB If set in sundae-glasses do not turn out.

Summer Pudding

stale bread or sponge cake	*to serve:* 2–3
450g/1 lb soft fruit	*time:* 30 minutes plus overnight
170g/6 oz sugar	¼ lit/½ pudding basin
4 tbsp water	forcing-bag
custard or cream	No. 8 icing-forcer
	saucer and weight

1 Stew the fruit in the sugar and water 2 Line the basin with slices of bread or cake 3 Pour in the *hot* fruit making sure the lining is well soaked 4 Cover with a round of bread or cake 5 Stand a saucer and weight on top 6 Allow to stand overnight 7 Turn out on to a dish and serve coated with custard of pipe with whipped cream

Apple Charlotte (1)

450g/1 lb apples
110g/¼ lb suet
170g/6 oz fresh breadcrumbs
110g/¼ lb sugar
1 lemon
raspings

to serve: 3
time: 1½ hours
liquidizer
½ lit/1 pt pie-dish
foil
oven No. 5 or 190 °C/380 °F

1 Grease the pie-dish and line with raspings **2** Peel, core and cut up the apples **3** Mix the sugar, suet, breadcrumbs, lemon-rind and -juice **4** Fill the pie-dish with alternate layers of the above mixture and apples **5** Press down well and cover with foil **6** Bake for 1 hour **7** Turn out on to a hot dish and serve with custard

NB Gooseberries, apricots and plums may also be used.

Apple Charlotte (2)

450g/1 lb apples
110g/¼ lb granulated sugar
rind and juice of ½ lemon
stale bread
melted butter

to serve: 3
time: 1½ hours
¼ lit/½ pt charlotte-mould
oven No. 5 or 190 °C/380 °F

1 Peel, core and cut up apples **2** Put them in a pan with the sugar and grated lemon-rind **3** Cook until tender **4** Beat until smooth and add lemon-juice **5** Dip a round of bread in melted butter and put in the bottom of the mould **6** Cut strips of bread, dip in the butter and put round the sides of the mould **7** Fill with the apple mixture **8** Cover with a second round of dipped bread **9** Bake for ¾–1 hour **10** Turn out on to a hot dish **11** Serve with custard or cream

NB Gooseberries, apricots or plums may be used.

Apple and Almond Pudding

4 large cooking apples
2 tbsp honey
60g/2 oz ground almonds
60g/2 oz brown breadcrumbs
60g/2 oz brown sugar
1 egg
cream
blanched almonds

to serve: 3–4
time: 1 hour
liquidizer
soufflé-dish or
½ lit/1 pt pie-dish
oven No. 4 or 180 °C/355 °F

1 Cook apples–liquidize or beat to a pulp with honey **2** Mix ground almonds, breadcrumbs, brown sugar, egg and 1 tbsp cream to a paste

3 Put apple into the dish, cover with mixture 4 Bake for 30 minutes until golden brown 5 Decorate with blanched almonds 6 Serve on a fancy paper on a plate 7 Hand cream separately

Bread and Butter Pudding

¼ lit/½ pt milk	*to serve:* 2
1 egg	*time:* 1¼ hours
30g/1 oz currants or sultanas	strainer
30g/1 oz castor sugar	½ lit/1 pt pie-dish
3 small thin slices bread	bain-marie
butter	oven No. 3 or 170 °C/335 °F
nutmeg (optional)	

1 Spread the thin slices of bread with butter 2 Beat egg and sugar–add heated milk 3 Place half the bread in the pie-dish–sprinkle with fruit–cover with remaining bread 4 Strain egg and milk over the bread–sprinkle with the nutmeg–soak 30 minutes 5 Bake in the bain-marie for 30 minutes until set and crisp on top 6 Serve on a fancy paper on an oval dish. This pudding can be served hot or cold

Alternate flavouring
Marmalade may be spread on the bread and butter before soaking in the milk. The fruit may then be omitted.

Queen of Puddings

90g/3 oz fresh breadcrumbs	*to serve:* 2
1 egg	*time:* 35 minutes plus time for meringue
¼ lit/½ pt milk	castor-sugar dredger
1 tbsp sugar	whisk
grated lemon-rind	liquidizer (optional)
30g/1 oz margarine or butter	grater
30g/1 oz castor sugar (for meringue)	½ lit/1 pt pie-dish
	bain-marie
1 tbsp jam	oven No. 3 or 170 °C/335 °F

1 Heat the milk, add crumbs and lemon-rind and bring to the boil 2 Add sugar, fat and yolk of egg 3 Mix well, put into the pie-dish, stand in the bain-marie 4 Bake till set, about 20 minutes 5 Warm the jam and spread on the top of the pudding 6 Whisk the white of egg very stiffly, *fold* in the sugar very gently, pile on top of the pudding and dredge with castor sugar for a crisp finish 7 Bake at No. ½ or 130 °C/265 °F for 1 hour or until meringue is crisp all through 8 Serve on an oval dish on a fancy paper

Cabinet Pudding

90g/3 oz sponge cake	*to serve:* 2
4 ratafia biscuits or macaroons	*time:* 1½ hours
¼ lit/½ pt milk	strainer

2 eggs
15g/½ oz castor sugar
vanilla essence
cherries and angelica
⅛ lit/¼ pt jam sauce (page 96)

¼ lit/½ pt charlotte-mould
steamer
greaseproof paper
foil

1 Grease the mould, and put a round of greaseproof paper in the bottom 2 Decorate with a bold design of cherries and angelica 3 Cut cake in slices and line the tin 4 Crumble remaining cake and biscuits 5 Bring the milk to the boil and add sugar and cake-crumbs 6 Pour on to beaten egg and add vanilla 7 Strain into the mould and leave until cool–cover 8 Steam gently until firm–about 45 minutes 9 Turn out and pour the jam sauce round, straining if necessary

Baked Egg Custard

¼ lit/½ pt milk
2 eggs
1 tbsp sugar
vanilla
nutmeg (optional)

to serve: 2
time: ½ hour
strainer
bain-marie
½ lit/1 pt pie-dish
oven No. 3 or 170 °C/335 °F

1 Break the eggs into a basin, add the sugar–beat to mix 2 Heat the milk, pour on to the eggs–stir–add vanilla 3 Strain into the dish–sprinkle with nutmeg 4 Bake, standing in the bain-marie till set–about 20–25 minutes 5 Serve hot or cold

Steamed Custard

¼ lit/½ pt milk
2 eggs
vanilla
1 tbsp sugar

to serve: 2
time: in a mould, 1 hour hot; in darioles, 40 minutes hot; cold as above plus cooling time
strainer
foil
pan of water
¼ lit/½ pt mould or dariole moulds

1 Prepare as for baked custard (page 170) 2 Strain into the mould, or dariole-moulds 3 Cover with foil 4 Cook over simmering water for 20 minutes for a dariole-mould and 40 minutes in a single mould–cool a little 5 Turn on to a hot dish 6 Serve with jam or syrup sauce (page 96).

or *To Serve cold*

Allow to cool–turn out and serve with stewed fruit (page 164). A little cream may be piped on top of each mould.

Caramel Custard

steamed custard (page 170)
60g/2 oz sugar } Caramel
4 tbsp water }

to serve: 2
time: hot–in a mould 1¼ hours; hot–in darioles 1 hour; cold–plus cooling time

1 Make the caramel (page 92) 2 Pour into a heated mould or darioles and coat quickly, strain in the custard 3 Cover, steam and serve as for steamed custard
NB These may be cooked in a bain-marie in the oven.

Crème brûlée

2 egg-yolks
½ tbsp castor sugar
¼ lit/½ pt single cream
vanilla
castor sugar for dredging

to serve: 6
time: ½ hour and overnight
double saucepan
strainer
6 ramekins
grill

1 Mix the yolks and sugar 2 Heat the cream to scalding-point in the double saucepan and pour on to the yolks 3 Return to the pan and heat carefully till thick, stirring. Add vanilla to taste 4 Strain into the ramekins and allow to stand overnight 5 Dredge evenly with castor sugar, but not thickly 6 Grill till the sugar has melted and colours 7 Chill and serve

Fruit Cream

⅛ lit/¼ pt fruit purée
⅛ lit/¼ pt cream or evaporated milk
30g/1 oz castor sugar
½ tsp lemon-juice
2 tsp gelatine
4 tbsp fruit syrup
Decoration
pistachio nuts or angelica, glacé cherries, small pieces of fruit
lemon jelly (page 177) or 1 packet

to serve: 2–3
time: 40 minutes plus setting time
liquidizer
ice
¼ lit/½ pt charlotte-mould
decorating pins

1 Mask and decorate the mould and cover with jelly 2 Half whip the cream 3 Add fruit purée, sugar and lemon-juice 4 Dissolve the gelatine in the syrup–cool and add to the cream mixture, stir until thickening–mould 5 Turn out when set and decorate with chopped jelly (see misc. processes).

Trifle

1 egg whisked sponge (page 240) cooked in ⅛ lit/¼ pt mould or fingers
⅛ lit/¼ pt egg custard (page 97)
4 tbsp whipped and sweetened cream

to serve: 2
time: 45 minutes
nylon bag
No. 8 icing-forcer
glass dish or sundae-glasses

fruit–tinned, fresh or frozen
almonds,
cherries and angelica
sherry
lemon-juice
jam

1 Split the sponge and spread with jam or crumble the fingers 2 Make a syrup or use the fruit syrup and add lemon juice and sherry to taste 3 Put the fruit in the bottom of a bowl and stand the sponge on it 4 Soak thoroughly with the syrup and coat with the custard 5 Decorate with spikes of almonds, cherries and angelica and a little of the fruit used 6 Pipe with the cream

NB 1 Tiny meringues (page 187) or ratafia biscuits may be used in the decoration.
2 Stale sponge may be used if crumbled.

Zabaglione

4 egg-yolks
4 tbsp sweet sherry or marsala
30g/1 oz castor sugar
pinch salt
wafers (optional)

to serve: 2–3
time: 20 minutes
whisk
double saucepan
coupe glasses

1 Whisk egg-yolks and sugar well, add wine and salt–whisk 2 Cook in the double pan until the mixture begins to thicken. Do not boil–whisk continually 3 Remove from the heat and pour into the glasses–cool 4 Serve on a plate on a fancy paper. Hand wafers separately

Milk Puddings
Large, Fine and Powdered grains

Basic recipe

½ lit/1 pt milk
45g/1½ oz grain
30g/1 oz sugar (or to taste)
15g/½ oz butter
Flavourings
Vanilla or almond essence
Chocolate powder or instant coffee
Nutmeg, cinnamon, bay-leaf
lemon- or orange-rind
1–2 eggs (optional)

Large grain, e.g. pudding rice, flaked rice, pearl barley, barley kernels, bullet tapioca and sago.

to serve: 2–3
time: 3½ hours
½ lit/1 pt pie-dish
oven No. 1 or 140 °C/290 °F

1 Wash the grain if necessary and put in to the pie-dish 2 Add sugar and milk and stir 3 Add butter and sprinkle with nutmeg (optional) 4 Stand for 1 hour or as long as possible and bake 2½ hours 5 Serve on an oval dish on a fancy paper

NB Macaroni may be cooked this way, but should never be washed.

Fine grain, e.g. semolina, pearl sago or tapioca. See basic recipe (page 172).

1 Sprinkle in the grain, stirring well. 2 Cook, stirring all the time until the grain is suspended in the milk. 3 Add sugar, butter and flavouring. 4 Pour into the pie-dish and bake or grill until golden brown. 5 Serve as for large grain pudding.

To serve cold. Pour into sundae-glasses and decorate when cold.

To enrich with egg

1 Add yolk with sugar and flavouring. 2 Whisk white and fold into the mixture. 3 Finish according to directions given for hot or cold puddings.

Powdered grains, e.g. arrowroot, cornflour, ground rice. See basic recipe (page 172).

to serve: 2–3
time: ½ hour hot plus cooling time
½ lit/1 pt pie-dish
oven No. 3 or 170 °C/335 °F
or heated grill

1 Blend the powder to a smooth paste with a little of the milk 2 Heat remaining milk and pour on to the mixture, stirring well 3 Return to the pan and bring to the boil 4 Boil for about 2 minutes, stirring all the time 5 Add sugar, butter and flavouring 6 Pour into the pie-dish and bake or grill until golden brown

NB Egg may be added in the same way as for fine grains.

To serve cold as a mould

1 Colour the mixture if liked.
2 Pour into a wetted mould.
3 When set, turn on to a dish or plate and decorate or serve with stewed fruit (page 164) or a suitable sauce.

To add flavourings

1 *Essences.* At end of method.
2 *Lemon-rind or orange-rind, or bay-leaf.* At the beginning of the method and remove at the end.

3 *Chocolate powder.* Dissolve in the milk and finish according to grain used.
4 *Instant coffee.* As for chocolate or may be dissolved in water and added at the end.

Quantities
Essences: ¼ tsp
Bay-leaf: 1
Lemon or orange: rind of ½
Chocolate: 1 tbsp
Coffee: 1 tsp

Honeycomb Mould

¼ lit/½ pt milk
1 egg
15g/½ oz sugar
1 tsp gelatine
4 tbsp water
Flavouring
½ tsp vanilla or ½ tsp instant coffee or rind and juice of ½ lemon
cream
cherries, angelica

to serve: 2
time: 30 minutes plus setting plus decorating time
whisk
¼ lit/½ pt mould
nylon bag
No. 8 icing-forcer

1 Make a custard with the yolks and milk (page 97) **2** Add sugar and flavouring, if used–and gelatine dissolved in the water **3** Stir in lemon-juice–if used–and fold in stiffly-beaten egg-white **4** Mould when on point of setting **5** Turn on to a dish and decorate with piped cream, cherries and angelica
NB If lemon-rind is used, infuse in the milk when making the custard–remove.

Rice Mould

½ lit/1 pt milk
45g/1½ oz pudding rice
sugar to taste
lemon-rind, vanilla, or chocolate powder
1–2 eggs (optional)

to serve: 2–3
time: ½ hour plus setting time
½ lit/1 pt mould

1 Wash the rice **2** Cook slowly in the milk with the lemon-rind–if used–until tender and the milk absorbed **3** Add sugar and remove the rind or add other flavourings **4** Pour into the wetted mould **5** When set turn out on to a dish or plate **6** Serve with jam, stewed fruit (page 164) or a suitable sauce
NB To use egg–Add beaten whole egg to the cooked rice and heat without boiling for one minute.

Fruit Condé

30g/1 oz sugar
¼ lit/½ pt milk
3 tsp pudding rice
2 dessert pears cut into halves, or chosen fruit
cherries
angelica
vanilla essence
apricot glaze (see Misc. Processes)
colouring

to serve: 2
time: 1 hour
plate or sundae-glasses

1 Blanch the rice—cook in the milk—simmer for about ½ hour—leave to cool **2** Prepare the fruit and poach gently—leave to cool **3** Put the rice on a round dish **4** Drain the fruit and arrange round **5** Coat with apricot glaze suitably coloured **6** Decorate with angelica and cherries and serve cold
NB Condé may be served in individual glasses if small fruit is used and piped with cream.

Alternative fruits. Apples, apricots, peaches, tinned fruits, gooseberries.

Pineapple Meringue

3 tsp cornflour
⅛ lit/¼ pt milk
⅛ lit/¼ pt pineapple juice
1 egg
pineapple pieces
2 tbsp castor sugar
cherries and angelica

to serve: 2
time: 1¼ hours approx.
whisk
½ lit/1 pt pie-dish
castor-sugar dredger
oven No. 1 or 130 °C/265 °F

1 Blend the cornflour with a little of the milk **2** Heat remaining milk and pour over cornflour **3** Return to heat and boil for 1 minute **4** Cool slightly, add the egg-yolk, half the sugar and the juice **5** Put pieces of pineapple on the bottom of the dish and pour the cornflour mixture over **6** Whisk the egg-white till stiff, fold in remaining sugar **7** Pile on top of the pudding, dredge with castor sugar **8** Bake 1 hour or until meringue is crisp all through—decorate **9** Serve on a dish with fancy paper

Pancakes

⅛ lit/¼ pt pancake batter (page 153)
30g/1 oz lard or oil
lemon-juice
castor sugar
lemon wedges

to serve: 2–3
time: ½ hour plus standing time
kitchen roll
150 mm/6 in. frying-pan
a plate over a pan of hot water
castor-sugar dredger

1 Make the batter—stand 1 hour **2** Prove the pan (page 148) **3** Heat the lard or oil thoroughly—pour off into a china basin or measure **4** Pour a very thin layer of batter quickly over the pan—return pan to low heat and cook till set and golden brown on underside **5** Shake pan to loosen pancake and slip pancake down the pan–toss **6** Cook on the second side **7** Turn on to sugared paper **8** Sprinkle with lemon-juice and sugar **9** Roll–keep hot on a plate over a pan of water **10** Repeat from No. 3 **11** Serve on a fancy paper with lemon wedges

Variations

1 **Jam**–Spread with jam and roll.
2 **Lemon Curd**–as above.
3 **Fruit**–Stewed or tinned or frozen–place fruit on pancake and roll.
4 **Chocolate**–Spread with grated, plain chocolate. Hand chocolate sauce (page 97).
5 **Honey or syrup**–Keep pancakes flat–spread with honey or syrup and pile one on top of the other. Cinnamon may be added after spreading with syrup.

Black Cap Pudding (Steamed Batter)

¼ lit/½ pt pancake batter (using 140g/5 oz of flour)
45g/1½ oz currants
⅛ lit/¼ pt syrup sauce (page 96)

to serve: 2–3
time: 1½ hours plus standing time
steamer
¼ lit/½ pt pudding-basin, greased
foil

1 Clean the currants and arrange in the bottom of the prepared basin **2** Pour in the batter and cover with foil **3** Steam 1–1¼ hours **4** Turn on to a hot dish and pour the sauce round

Fruit Fritters

fritter batter (page 154)
fruit, e.g. apple, banana, pineapple, etc.

time: ½ hour
sieve
kitchen roll
deep-fat pan
thermometer
castor-sugar dredger

1 Make the batter and prepare the fruit, sprinkling with lemon-juice and sugar **2** Dip in the batter and drain well **3** Fry at 180 °C/355 °F till batter is crisp and fruit soft **4** Drain very well–sprinkle with castor sugar **5** Serve on a fancy paper on an oval dish

Fritter-cases for Sweet Mixtures

coating batter 2 or 3 (pages 153, 154)
¼ tsp vanilla essence
⅛ lit/¼ pt cream
fruit
angelica

to serve: 1–2 baskets per person
time: 45 minutes
kitchen roll
deep-fat pan
thermometer
fancy fritter-iron
nylon bag and No. 8 icing-forcer

1 Heat the fat to 185 °C/360 °F 2 Dip the fritter-iron into the hot fat and then in the batter 3 Coat very thinly 4 Put into hot fat and fry until crisp–shake off and drain 5 When cool fill with fruit and cream 6 Pipe with cream and decorate with small pieces of fruit 7 Serve on a plate with a fancy paper

French Pancakes

30g/1 oz butter or margarine
30g/1 oz flour
⅛ lit/¼ pt milk
1 egg
30g/1 oz castor sugar
jam

to serve: 3–4
time: 45 minutes
kitchen roll
large greased patty-tins
castor-sugar dredger
oven No. 6 or 205 °C/400 °F

1 Cream the butter and sugar–add egg and flour–beat well in. 2 Stir in *hot* milk 3 Fill the tins and bake 10–15 minutes 4 Turn on to sugared paper 5 Put 1 tsp of hot jam on each 6 Either fold each in half or put two together 7 Serve on a fancy paper

Lemon Jelly (Clear)

¾ lit/1½ pt water
¼ lit/½ pt lemon-juice (5 lemons) (or tinned)
rind of 2 lemons
170g/6 oz granulated sugar
1 in. cinnamon stick
2 cloves
whites and shells of 2 eggs
75g/2½ oz gelatine

time: 1 hour
whisk
large pan
jelly-cloth and stand

1 Put all the ingredients into the rinsed pan 2 Whisk until the mixture boils 3 Allow to come to the top of the pan three times 4 Stand for 10 minutes; over very low heat 5 Strain through the scalded jelly-cloth three times or until clear. Use as required

NB If the jelly is to be used for masking moulds or for chopping, use 90g/3 oz gelatine.

Fruit in Jelly

lemon jelly (page 177)
mixed fruits
whipped cream (sweetened and flavoured)

to serve: 2
time: 2 hours
ice
150 mm/6 in. border-mould
¼ lit/½ pt charlotte-mould or dariole-moulds
decorating-pins
nylon bag
No. 8 icing-forcer

1 Set a thin layer of jelly in the bottom of the chosen mould
2 Arrange some of the prepared fruit on the jelly, dipping each piece

3 Cover with jelly and allow to set 4 Continue in layers of jelly and fruit until the mould is full 5 When set firmly, turn out 6 Decorate with chopped jelly and piped cream

Muscovite of Prunes (Prune Mould)

110g/¼ lb prunes
4 tbsp red wine
4 tbsp water
rind and juice of ¼ lemon
1 tsp gelatine } dissolve
4 tbsp water }
sugar
lemon jelly
almonds
cream

to serve: 2
time: overnight plus 40 minutes plus setting time
liquidizer
ice
nylon bag
No. 8 icing-forcer
¼ lit/½ pt border-mould

1 Soak the prunes in the wine and water overnight 2 Cook with a little sugar and the lemon rind 3 Remove stones and liquidize 4 Mask the mould and decorate with almonds 5 Add dissolved gelatine to purée 6 Add more sugar if necessary 7 Stir until on point of setting–mould and set 8 Turn out–decorate with chopped lemon jelly and whipped cream piped in the centre

Banana Chartreuse

lemon jelly (page 177) or 1 packet
2 bananas
cherries
pistachio nuts
almond cream (page 178)

to serve: 2–3
time: 2 hours
ice
¼ lit/½ pt charlotte-mould and 1 dariole-mould
decorating-pins

1 Set a layer of jelly in the charlotte-mould 2 Set decoration of nuts and cherries–cover with thin layer of jelly 3 Set a layer of sliced banana round the edge of the mould, set a second layer inside and a third layer outside 4 Place the dariole-mould in the centre 5 Make further settings outside this to the top of the mould 6 *When set*–pour hot water into the dariole-mould–remove 7 Put almond cream in the banana border. Set 8 Unmould and serve on a plate surrounded by chopped jelly

NB Other fruits may be used–e.g. mandarin oranges.

Almond Cream

15g/½ oz whole almonds
sugar
2 tbsp cream
2 tbsp stiff jelly
1 tsp lemon-juice

to serve: see Banana Chartreuse
time: 45 minutes
liquidizer
1 dariole-mould
oven No. 3 or 170 °C/335 °F

1 Blanch the almonds–brown in the oven–liquidize 2 Half whip the cream–add the almonds 3 Add sugar, jelly and lemon-juice–mould 4 Turn out when set

Charlotte Russe

10 sponge fingers (page 241)
or 1 packet
$\frac{1}{8}$ lit/¼ pt cream
4 tbsp milk
vanilla sugar to sweeten
1 tsp gelatine
4 tbsp water
lemon jelly (page 177) or 1 packet
cherries and angelica

to serve: 2–3
time: 45 minutes plus setting time plus making of sponge fingers
ice
¼ lit/½ pt charlotte-mould
decorating-pins

1 Set a thin layer of jelly at the bottom of the mould **2** Decorate with cherries and angelica, and cover with jelly **3** Straighten sides of sponge fingers and cut off one end **4** Dip this end into jelly and arrange the fingers round side of mould **5** Mix cuttings of fingers with enough jelly to make a paste and use to seal the joins between the fingers **6** Half whip the cream–add the milk–sweeten **7** Dissolve gelatine in the water–cool **8** Add to the cream and stir until on point of setting **9** Pour into the mould **10** Turn out when set and decorate with chopped jelly **11** A narrow ribbon may be tied round if liked

Variations

1 **Charlotte St. José.** Add 60g/2 oz of chopped pineapple to cream–dissolve gelatine in pineapple syrup and use pineapple in decoration.
2 **Charlotte aux fraises.** Add 90g/3 oz cut up strawberries to cream and use in decoration.

NB The mould may be filled with the cream as in charlotte aux meringues (page 179).

Velvet Cream

¼ lit/½ pt cream
sugar to sweeten
4 tbsp sherry or rum
1 tsp gelatine } dissolve
4 tbsp water }
For decoration
lemon jelly (page 177) or 1 packet
cherries and angelica

to serve: 2–3
time: ½ hour plus setting time
ice
¼ lit/½ pt charlotte-mould
decorating-pins

1 Mask and decorate the mould **2** Half whip the cream–add sugar and sherry or rum **3** Add gelatine and stir until beginning to set–mould **4** Turn out when set and decorate with lemon jelly, chopped or cut into fancy shapes

Charlotte aux meringues

2 whites of egg } for meringues
110g/¼ lb castor sugar }
$\frac{1}{8}$ lit/¼ pt milk } for custard
2 egg-yolks }
vanilla sugar }

to serve: 4
time: 2 hours
ice
125 mm/5 in. charlotte-mould
oiled baking-tray

⅛ lit/¼ pt cream
1 tsp gelatine } dissolve
4 tbsp water }
rum
cherries and angelica

nylon bag
No. 8 vegetable-forcer
decorating-pins
castor-sugar dredger
oven No. ½ or 130 °C/265 °F

1 Make the meringue mixture and pipe on to the tray in 'fingers' 10 mm/ ½ in. deeper than the mould **2** Dredge with castor sugar and put into the oven until dry and crisp **3** Make custard (page 97) and allow to cool **4** Half whip the cream and mix with custard, sweeten and add rum to taste **5** Add gelatine, and when on point of setting pour into the mould **6** Turn out when set **7** Arrange the meringue fingers round the mould, sticking them on with cream **8** Pipe cream round the base and top and decorate with cherries and angelica

NB The cream may be made with equal quantities of fruit purée and cream and decorated with some of the whole fruit, which should be glazed. Raspberries and strawberries would be an excellent choice.

Cold Cabinet Pudding

6 sponge fingers
30g/1 oz ratafia biscuits or macaroons
⅛ lit/¼ pt milk
1 tsp gelatine
4 tbsp water
2 eggs
4 tbsp cream
15g/½ oz castor sugar
vanilla essence
cherries, angelica

to serve: 2
time: 1 hour plus setting time
strainer
ice
¼ lit/½ pt charlotte-mould
decorating-pins

1 Decorate the bottom of the mould with cherries and angelica **2** Cut sponge fingers in half and arrange round the inside of the mould **3** Crumble any sponge left and the biscuits **4** Bring the milk to the boil and add sugar and vanilla–add to eggs **5** Strain on to the crumbs **6** Return to pan and cook gently for a few minutes–cool **7** Dissolve the gelatine in the water **8** Add to the custard mixture and stir until on point of setting–mould **9** Turn out when set **10** Serve with a fruit purée

Bavarois of Chocolate (Bavaroise au chocolat)

lemon jelly (page 177) or 1 packet
1 tbsp cream }
2 tbsp jelly } for re-masking
carmine colouring }
rum
lemon jelly } for decoration
pistachio nuts or angelica }

to serve: 2–3
time: 1 hour plus setting time
strainer
ice
¼ lit/½ pt charlotte-mould
decorating-pins

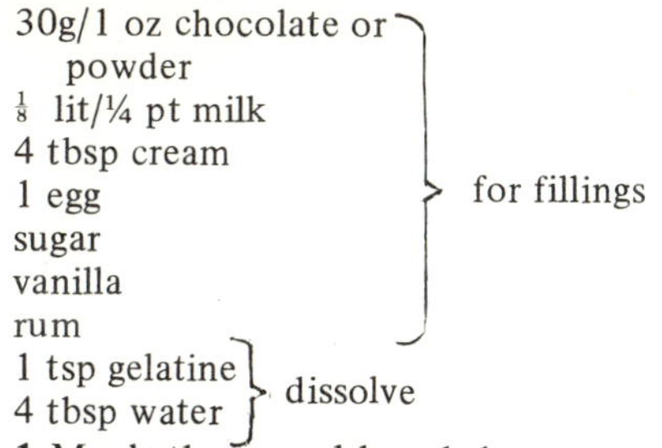
30g/1 oz chocolate or powder
⅛ lit/¼ pt milk
4 tbsp cream
1 egg
sugar
vanilla
rum
} for fillings

1 tsp gelatine
4 tbsp water
} dissolve

1 Mask the mould and decorate with pistachios or angelica **2** Re-mask with the cream and jelly, coloured, and flavoured with rum **3** Dissolve the chocolate in the milk **4** Make custard with above and cool **5** Half whip the cream, and add the custard **6** Add sugar and flavour with rum **7** Add gelatine and stir until starting to set–mould **8** Turn out when set, and decorate with jelly chopped or cut into fancy shapes

For Vanilla Bavarois. Omit chocolate.

Coffee Cream

⅛ lit/¼ pt egg custard (page 97)
⅛ lit/¼ pt cream
1 level tsp instant coffee
sugar to sweeten
1 tsp gelatine
4 tbsp water
lemon jelly (page 177) or 1 packet
cherries and angelica

to serve: 2–3
time: 45 minutes
strainer
ice
¼ lit/½ pt charlotte-mould
decorating-pins

1 Mask the mould with lemon jelly and decorate with cherries and angelica **2** Cover the decorations with jelly **3** Make the custard–cool **4** Half whip the cream and mix with the custard **5** Sweeten, and flavour with the coffee dissolved in 1 tsp of water **6** Dissolve the gelatine in the water–cool to correct temperature and add to cream **7** Stir until on point of setting–mould **8** Turn out when set and decorate with chopped jelly

Variations

Chocolate cream: 45g/1½ oz chocolate powder dissolved in the milk–a few drops of vanilla.

Vanilla cream: 1 tsp vanilla essence or sweeten with vanilla sugar.

Coffee Mousse (Mousse au café)

2 eggs
2–3 dessertsp liquid instant coffee
30g/1 oz walnuts
⅛ lit/¼ pt cream
15g/½ oz gelatine

to serve: 2–3
time: 1 hour plus setting time
whisk
125 mm/5 in. soufflé-mould
nylon bag

60g/2 oz castor sugar
4 tbsp water
chocolate medallions

No. 8 icing-forcer
waxed paper or foil

To make medallions–1 Soften chocolate in a bowl of hot water. Mark circles on a piece of paper or foil the size of a penny. Spread chocolate evenly on the circles and put aside to cool 2 Whisk yolks and sugar with coffee until thick (over hot water)–cool 3 Add chopped walnuts and whipped cream 4 Melt gelatine in the water–cool and stir in 5 Whisk egg-whites and when mixture is on point of setting, fold in 6 Put into the mould–when set decorate with chocolate circles and whipped cream

Chocolate Mousse

Use 2 tbsp liquid chocolate instead of coffee.

Lemon Soufflé (Soufflé à la milanaise)

2 lemons (rind and juice)
2 eggs
90g/3 oz castor sugar
⅛ lit/¼ pt cream
1 tsp gelatine
4 tbsp water
For decoration
4 tbsp cream
chopped pistachios
cake crumbs or crushed nuts

to serve: 2–3
time: ¾ hour plus setting time
strainer
whisk
125 mm/5 in. soufflé-mould
foolscap paper
decorating-pins
rubber bands
No. 8 icing-forcer
nylon bag

1 Fix a double band of foolscap paper round the outside of the soufflé-mould, reaching 50 mm/2 in. above the dish 2 Put rind and juice of lemons, sugar and egg-yolks into a small pan 3 Whisk until boiling–strain and cool 4 Half whip cream–mix with the above 5 Dissolve the gelatine and water over heat 6 Add to cream and lemon mixture 7 Stir until on point of setting and fold in the whisked whites 8 Pour into the soufflé-mould 9 When set remove the paper 10 Decorate with piped cream, finely-chopped pistachios, and cake crumbs or crushed nuts 11 Serve on a plate with a fancy paper

NB Cold soufflés should be served with petit fours (page 261)

Orange soufflé–as lemon using oranges.

Fruit purées ⅛ lit/¼ pt fruit purée may be used instead of lemons.

Chocolate Soufflé

⅛ lit/¼ pt milk, 2 eggs, 60g/2 oz chocolate } custard
⅛ lit/¼ pt cream
15g/½ oz gelatine
4 tbsp water
vanilla

to serve: 2–3
time: 45 minutes plus setting time
strainer
whisk
125 mm/5 in. soufflé-mould
foolscap paper
nylon bag

4 tbsp cream for piping
chopped pistachio nuts and cake crumbs

No. 8 icing-forcer

1 Prepare soufflé—mould (see Lemon soufflé, page 182) 2 Bring chocolate and milk to the boil—pour on to yolks—cool 3 Mix with cream—add vanilla—sweeten 4 Dissolve the gelatine in the water cool and add to the mixture—stir until beginning to set 5 Fold in stiffly-whisked egg whites—mould 6 When set remove the paper and decorate with piped cream, chopped pistachios and cake crumbs

Variations

1 *Coffee soufflé*—2 tsp instant coffee added to milk.
2 *Praline*—60g/2 oz almond rock crushed and added to cream mixture before gelatine and egg whites. Home-made nougatine may be used instead of almond rock (page 256).
3 *Vanilla soufflé* (cold)—add ½ tsp vanilla essence to cream mixture or sweeten with vanilla sugar.

Vanilla Soufflé (hot)

30g/1 oz flour } sauce
30g/1 oz butter } sauce
⅛ lit/¼ pt milk } sauce
1 dessertsp sugar
vanilla essence
4 eggs

to serve: 4
time: 1¼ hours
whisk
½ lit/1 pt charlotte-mould
greased paper
large pan with water to the top of a cutter

1 Prepare the mould by greasing well and tie a band of greased paper round the outside 50 mm/2 in. higher than the mould 2 Make the sauce. Add vanilla and egg-yolks 3 Fold in the whisked whites 4 Put into the mould, put a square of paper over the top and stand on the cutter in the pan and cover with a lid 5 Simmer *very gently* until firm in the centre—about 40 minutes 6 Turn out and serve with a wine sauce (page 97)

Variations

Chocolate. Add 45g/1½ oz of chocolate powder to the milk and proceed as above—serve with a custard or sherry sauce (page 97).
Coffee. Make as above using strong coffee instead of milk. Serve with a suitable sauce.
Pineapple, Ginger, etc. Use 60g/2 oz of chopped fruit and 15g/½ oz extra flour. Make as above. Serve with wine sauce with chopped fruit added.
All these soufflés may be steamed or baked.

Rice Cream (Riz à l'impératrice)

lemon jelly (page 177) or 1 packet
cherries and angelica

to serve: 2–3
time: 45 minutes plus setting time

¼ lit/½ pt milk
3 tsp pudding rice
⅛ lit/¼ pt cream whipped
1 tsp gelatine
2 tbsp water
sugar and vanilla pod
To dish
fruit
chopped jelly

ice
medium border-mould or
4 dariole-moulds
decorating-pins

1 Mask and decorate the chosen mould **2** Blanch the rice, then cool in the milk and vanilla pod until soft and milk is absorbed **3** Cool–add the half-whipped cream and sugar to sweeten **4** Dissolve the gelatine in the water–cool and add **5** Stir until on the point of setting–mould **6** Turn out when set and decorate with fruit, fruit purée or chopped jelly

Border of Pears

3 small ripe pears or ½ tin pears
¼ lit/½ pt milk
2 eggs
90g/3 oz cake crumbs
¼ lit/½ pt water } syrup
90g/3 oz sugar } syrup
or fruit syrup
15g/½ oz sugar
Colouring: lemon-juice and 1 tbsp sherry
4 tbsp sweetened and flavoured whipped cream

to serve: 3
time: 1¼ hours
bain-marie
175 mm/7 in. border mould or 150 mm/6 in. sandwich-tin
nylon bag
No. 8 icing-forcer
oven No. 4 or 180 °C/355 °F

1 Make the syrup and colour **2** Poach the fresh pears in this or lay the tinned ones in it **3** Beat the eggs and pour on the heated milk **4** Add the cake crumbs, sugar and colouring and pour into the greased tin **5** Stand in the bain-marie and bake until firm–about ½ hour **6** Turn on to a dish **7** Arrange the pears on top **8** Reduce the syrup, add lemon-juice and sherry–glaze the pears and pour round the dish **9** Decorate with piped cream and angelica
NB This may be made using fresh or tinned peaches.

Pêches à la chevreuse

3 whole peaches or 6 tinned halves
5 tsp semolina } for base
4 tbsp white wine or cider } for base
4 tbsp water } for base
30g/1 oz sugar } for base
1 white of egg } for base
vanilla } for base
2 tbsp apricot glaze (see misc. processes)
jam sauce (page 96)
colouring } sauce
water if necessary or fruit syrup } sauce

to serve: 3
time: 1 hour
whisk
nylon bag
No. 8 icing-forcer
bain-marie
150 mm/6 in. sandwich-tin
oven No. 4 or 180 °C/355 °F

1 Put wine and water in to a pan–bring to the boil 2 Shake in the semolina and cook for 2–3 minutes 3 Stir in the sugar and vanilla 4 Fold in whisked white 5 Put into the tin, which has been greased and sugared 6 Stand in the bain-marie and bake about ½ hour–allow to cool and turn on to a dish 7 Arrange the peaches on this base 8 Decorate with piped cream, cherries and angelica 9 Pour the jam sauce round
NB If fresh peaches are used–remove skins and cut in half–poach lightly in a syrup

Syllabub

60g/2 oz castor sugar
juice ½ lemon
grated rind of ¼ lemon
pinch ground cinnamon
2 tbsp sherry or madeira
few drops almond essence
¼ lit/½ pt cream
5 ratafia biscuits or macaroons

to serve: 3
time: ½ hour plus chilling time
grater
whisk
3 wineglasses

1 Mix the sugar, lemon-juice and -rind, cinnamon and wine 2 Add few drops of the essence and stir until sugar has dissolved 3 Add cream and whip to a froth 4 Arrange biscuits in bottom of the glasses 5 As froth is formed skim it off–place on biscuits until all the mixture has been reduced to a froth and is piled on the biscuits 6 Chill and serve

Strawberry Waflen (Crème waflen aux fraises)

100 mm/4 in. circle of genoese or sponge cake (pages 248, 239)
16 wafers
60g/2 oz ratafias or macaroons
30g/1 oz castor sugar
230g/½ lb royal icing (page 258)
450g/1 lb strawberries
¼ lit/½ pt cream
1 tbsp sherry or brandy
angelica

to serve: 4–5
time: 1 hour
board
ribbon
No. 8 icing-forcer
nylon bag
plate with fancy paper

1 Put aside 12 strawberries for decoration 2 Cut up the remainder and mix with crushed biscuits, sugar and wine 3 Sandwich together wafer biscuits with royal icing to make 8 pairs–press under a board 4 Put the sponge on the plate–pipe royal icing round the side. Fix the wafers round the sponge and pipe the joins inside and out–decorate with stars on top and round base–allow to set–tie the ribbon round 5 Mix the strawberry mixture with ⅔ of the cream–fill the case with the mixture 6 Pipe top with the remaining cream–decorate with strawberries and angelica

Variations
1 Raspberries.
2 Tinned fruit.
3 Frozen fruit.

Savarin Chantilly

125g/4½ oz flour
15g/½ oz yeast
15g/½ oz castor sugar
2 eggs
4 tbsp tepid milk
60g/2 oz butter
110g/¼ lb granulated sugar } syrup
¼ lit/½ pt water } syrup
2 tbsp rum or sherry } syrup
mixed fruit
4 tbsp cream
apricot glaze (see Misc. Processes)

to serve: 4–6
time: 1½ hours
sieve
tea-cloth
greased and floured 175 mm/7 in. border-mould
nylon bag
vegetable star-forcer
oven No. 6 or 205 °C/400 °F

1 Sieve the flour and break the eggs into it **2** Cream the yeast with 1 tsp of the sugar–add the tepid milk **3** Pour on to flour and eggs–mix and beat thoroughly **4** Cover with the damp cloth and put in a warm place until double the size–15–20 minutes **5** Add the remaining sugar, and softened butter a little at a time **6** Put into the mould and 'prove' until the mixture rises to *nearly* the top of the tin **7** Bake about ½ hour **8** Make the syrup, add the sherry or rum and prepared fruit **9** Turn out the savarin and soak with the hot syrup **10** Put on to a dish and glaze **11** Fill the centre with the fruit **12** Decorate with some nice pieces of fruit and with piped cream
NB This may be made using one kind of fruit, e.g. strawberries, apricots, etc.

Rum Babas

125g/4½ oz flour
a walnut of yeast
1 tsp castor sugar
4 tbsp tepid milk
2 eggs
75g/2½ oz butter
30g/1 oz currants
¼ lit/½ pt water } syrup
110g/¼ lb sugar } syrup
1 tbsp rum } syrup
jam glaze (see Misc. Processes)
⅛ lit/¼ pt cream–whipped

to serve: 4–6
time: 1 hour
sieve
tea-cloth
12 baba- or dariole-moulds, greased and floured
nylon bag
No. 8 vegetable-forcer
oven No. 6 or 205 °C/400 °F

1 Cream the yeast and sugar, add the tepid milk **2** Add to the sieved flour with the eggs, mix into a batter and beat **3** Cover with the damp cloth, and put into a warm place till risen to double its size **4** Add the softened butter, beating in a little at a time 5 Half fill the moulds, which have been sprinkled with currants 6 Prove until nearly to the top 7 Bake for 15 minutes 8 Turn out into the hot syrup 9 Arrange on a dish–glaze–pipe centres with cream when cool

Meringues

Basic mixture

2 egg whites
110g/4 oz castor sugar

time: 10 minutes
electric mixer

1 Whisk the egg whites and half the sugar stiffly 2 Add the remaining sugar and whisk till the mixture will hold its shape

Uses: 1 *Meringues*

basic mixture
whipped cream
pistachio nuts or green coloured, chopped almonds

time: 4 hours
oiled baking-sheet
nylon bag
No. 8 vegetable-forcer
No. 8 icing-forcer
castor-sugar dredger
cake-cases
oven No. ½ or 130 °C/265 °F

1 Put the meringue mixture into the forcing bag with the larger forcer 2 Pipe on to the baking sheet 3 Dredge with castor sugar 4 Bake until firm enough to hold 5 Knock a hole in the underside and put back in oven to dry

When cold

1 Fill with sweetened and flavoured whipped cream 2 Sandwich together in twos 3 Pipe round the join with a little cream and No. 8 icing-forcer 4 Sprinkle with chopped nuts 5 Put into a cake-case

Uses: 2 *Meringue fingers–petits fours*

1 Proceed as for meringues but pipe in fingers or in small spirals 2 Finish as for meringues

Uses: 3 *Meringue rings*

basic mixture
rice paper
filling

1 Pipe the mixture on to rice paper on an oiled baking-tray, in a ring 75 mm/3 in. in diameter for individual rings or 150 mm/6 in. in diameter for a large ring 2 Dredge with castor sugar 3 Bake as for meringues

Fillings

1 *Cream and fruit*
⅛ lit/¼ pt cream–whipped

fresh or tinned fruit

2 *Charlotte russe filling*—see Charlotte russe (page 179)
Add rum—pipe with cream when set

3 *Almond cream filling*—see filling for Banana Chartreuse (page 178)
Pipe with cream

4 *Fruit cream,* e.g. strawberry, apricot.
See recipe for fruit cream (page 171)

Meringues using Albumen Powder

30g/1 oz albumen powder	electric mixer
$\frac{1}{8}$ lit/¼ pt water	nylon bag
290g/10 oz castor sugar	No. 8 vegetable-forcer

1 Mix the powder and water (tepid) 2 Add sugar and whisk in the electric mixer until the mixture will hold its shape 3 Proceed as for meringues made with egg-white (page 187)

12
Ices

Custard for cream ices

½ lit/1 pt milk
2 eggs and 2 yolks or 3 whole eggs

time: ½ hour

Make the custard (page 97) and leave to cool—do not add the sugar. (The custard must not be so rich that it sets when cold)

Syrup for water ices

230g/½ lb granulated sugar
½ lit/1 pt water
rind and juice of ½ lemon

time: ½ hour
muslin
lemon-squeezer
grater

1 Put the sugar, water, lemon-rind and -juice in to a pan. Dissolve sugar **2** Bring to boiling-point and remove the scum **3** Boil for 10 minutes **4** Strain through muslin and cool

Fruit ice cream (Glace à la crème de fruits)

⅛ lit/¼ pt fruit purée
⅛ lit/¼ pt cream
sugar
lemon-juice and colouring if necessary

to serve: 2–3
time: 1½–2 hours
liquidizer
freezer of refrigerator

1 Mix the fruit purée and the half-whipped cream **2** Sweeten—remember that too much sugar will prevent freezing **3** Colour if necessary **4** Put into cold compartment of the refrigerator **5** When the cream begins to thicken beat well with a spatula (this should be done every 20 minutes to prevent formation of ice) **6** Serve when firm enough to keep its shape with ice wafers or petits fours (page 261)

NB To prevent ice crystals forming and spoiling the smooth texture of the ice cream, add to the mixture before freezing: ½ white of egg half beaten, ½ tsp gelatine dissolved in 1 dessertsp of water.

Custard Ice Cream

⅛ lit/¼ pt cream
¼ lit/½ pt custard (page 189)

to serve: 3–4
time: 1½–2 hours

sugar
flavouring
½ egg-white or ½ tsp gelatine dissolved
in 1 dessertsp water

freezing-tray
freezer of refrigerator

1 Mix the cold custard with the half-whipped cream **2** Add the sugar and flavouring **3** Add white of egg or gelatine **4** Freeze as for fruit cream ices (page 189) **5** Serve with ice wafers or petits fours (page 261)

NB If using chocolate, dissolve 60g/2 oz of chocolate powder in the milk before making the custard.

To make coffee ice cream dissolve 2 tsp instant coffee in the milk before making the custard.

Water Ices

⅛ lit/¼ pt cold syrup (page 189)
⅛ lit/¼ pt fruit juice or purée
colouring if necessary
½ egg-white or ½ tsp gelatine dissolved
in 1 dessertsp water

to serve: 2
time: 1½–2 hours
freezing-tray
freezer of refrigerator

1 Mix the syrup and juice or purée **2** Add white of egg or gelatine **3** Add colouring **4** Freeze as for cream and custard ices **5** Serve as for other ices

NB Water ices may be served as a 'sorbet,' which is a partially-frozen water ice, served before the roast in a full dinner. It may be either sweet or savoury.

Ice Pudding (Pouding glace)

⅛ lit/¼ pt cream
¼ lit/½ pt cold custard (page 189)
sugar
60g/2 oz crystallized fruits
chopped pistachio nuts
round of genoese sponge (page 248)
brandy or maraschino
½ egg-white or ½ tsp gelatine dissolved
in 1 dessertsp water
ice wafers

to serve: 4
time: 4 hours
bomb-mould
deep-freeze
nylon bag
No. 8 icing-forcer

1 Decorate the top of the bomb-mould with chopped pistachio nuts and fruits **2** Mix the custard and the half-whipped cream **3** Add the sugar, brandy, chopped fruits and white of egg or gelatine **4** Half freeze and pack into the prepared mould **5** Put into the deep-freeze for about 3 hours **6** Decorate the edge of the genoese sponge with chopped pistachio nuts **7** Turn the pudding on to the sponge standing on a plate with a fancy paper **8** Decorate quickly with piped cream and ice wafers **9** When moulding ices, pack mixture into a wet mould, and seal lid with lard. Wrap in greaseproof paper. When ready to unmould, dip in cold water, scrape off the lard and remove top and bottom

Pouding à la praline

⅛ lit/¼ pt cream
¼ lit/½ pt cold custard (page 189)
90g/3 oz crushed nougat (page 256)
sugar
1 tsp instant coffee
round of genoese sponge (page 248)

see ice pudding (page 190)

1 Prepare and freeze as for pouding glacé, adding the coffee and nougat to the cream and custard mixture 2 Decorate the sponge with crushed nougat 3 Dish, pipe with the cream and decorate with small pieces of nougat in rounds or triangles

Soufflé Ices

Chocolate Soufflé Ice

Recipe for Chocolate Soufflé (page 182)
Omit the gelatine
cream for piping

to serve: 5
time: 3½ hours
rubber bands
foolscap paper
No. 8 icing-forcer

5 ramekins
deep-freeze
nylon bag

1 Prepare the moulds as for a cold soufflé 2 Prepare the soufflé mixture and put into the moulds 3 Pack into a biscuit- or cake-tin with a lid 4 Put into deep freeze for 2–3 hours 5 Remove the paper and pipe cream on top

NB These may be made from any cold soufflé mixture, in each case omitting the gelatine.

Omelette soufflé en surprise (Baked Alaska)

omelet soufflé mixture (page 149)
¼ lit/½ pt stiffly-frozen ice cream
piece of genoese sponge (page 248)
rum or sherry

to serve: 2
time: 15 minutes
whisk
oven No. 9 or 240 °C/470 °F

1 Soak the sponge with the rum or sherry 2 Put on a fireproof glass or china dish 3 Place the ice cream on top 4 Cover with the soufflé mixture 5 Dredge with sugar 6 Bake for 5 minutes 7 Serve at once

NB A meringue mixture may be used for the covering of the ice cream.

Fruit Coupe (Coupe glacée)

fruit salad (page 164)
water ice, e.g. lemon, orange or pineapple (page 189)
whipped cream

time: 10 minutes
coupe glasses
nylon bag
No. 8 icing-forcer

1 Put the fruit salad into the glasses 2 Place ice cream on top 3 Decorate with piped cream, a cocktail cherry and angelica

NB Rum or sherry may be added to the fruit salad.

Varieties

Strawberry or raspberry ice with strawberries or raspberries.

Vanilla Ice Cream with Hot Chocolate Sauce

Vanilla ice cream (page 189)
110g/¼ lb plain chocolate
2 tbsp castor sugar
⅛ lit/¼ pt water
60g/2 oz butter
rum or vanilla essence

to serve: 3–4
time: 15 minutes
coupe-glasses

1 Melt the chocolate in the water with the sugar over low heat 2 Raise the heat and continue cooking until syrupy 3 Beat in the butter a little at a time and flavour 4 Put the ice cream into the glasses 5 Pour the hot sauce over and serve at once

Pear Belle Hélène

As Vanilla ice cream with hot chocolate sauce (page 192)

1 Prepare 2 pears–cut in half and remove core–poach–cool 2 Put on top of ice cream–coat with the hot chocolate sauce

Meringue Glace

Vanilla ice cream (page 189)
meringue-cases or small meringu-baskets (page 187)
cream for piping
cherries, angelica

to serve: 3–4
time: 15 minutes
nylon bag
No. 8 icing-forcer

1 Place a meringue-case each side of piled ice cream 2 Decorate with piped cream cherries and angelica *or* 3 Fill meringue-baskets with ice cream 4 Pipe with cream and decorate with an angelica handle

Pêche Melba

2 fresh ripe peaches
⅛ lit/¼ pt raspberry purée
vanilla essence
60g/2 oz sugar
⅛ lit/¼ pt vanilla ice cream (page 189)
wafers

to serve: 2
time: 45 minutes
foil
2 sundae-glasses
oven No. 3 or 170 °C/335 °F

1 Skin the peaches, cut in half and remove the stone 2 Add vanilla to the purée and sweeten with sugar to taste 3 Poach the peaches in this purée until tender but not broken 4 Drain the peaches and cool 5 Put the ice cream into the sundae-glasses and arrange the peaches on top 6 Coat with the purée 7 Serve with wafers

Evaporated Milk Ice Cream

1 large tin evaporated milk
2 tbsp sugar
vanilla essence

to serve: 4
time: 2 hours
whisk
freezing-tray
freezer of refrigerator

1 Chill the tin of milk in the refrigerator overnight 2 Whisk the milk until it doubles its bulk and becomes very thick 3 Fold in the sugar and vanilla 4 Add the other flavouring if desired 5 Turn into trays and freeze for 1½–2 hours 6 Stir about every 20 minutes

13
Flans and tartlets

Flan-cases

flan-ring
baking-tray

For savoury dishes use plain rings.
For sweet dishes use fluted rings.

Method of lining
1 Place the ring on a flat baking-sheet 2 Roll pastry into a circle just larger than the flan-ring 3 Lift the pastry on a rolling-pin and turn over on to the flan-ring 4 Ease into the ring pressing well to the bottom where the flan-ring meets the tray 5 Press the pastry against the sides of a plain ring or into each flute of a fluted ring—turn remaining pastry outwards over the top of the ring—roll across the top with a rolling-pin 6 Remove small pieces of pastry from the outside of flutes with a pointed knife

Baking
Either bake with filling or bake "blind"

To bake "blind"

baking-bean
greased paper
oven No. 4 or 180 °C/355 °F

1 Place a piece of greased paper over the base and up the sides of the flan 2 Add 2 tbsp of baking beans, or macaroni, or crusts of bread 3 Bake for 15 minutes 4 Remove the beans and paper and brush the inside with egg and return to the oven reduced to No. 3 or 170 °C/335 °F for 10–15 minutes to dry 5 Remove and use as required

Tartlet-cases

tartlet-tins
oven No. 3 or 170 °C/335 °F

1 Line the tins—prick well all over 2 Bake till pale golden brown 3 Brush with egg whilst very hot 4 Cool

Fruit Flan

110g/¼ lb biscuit crust (page 227)
fruit–mandarins, peaches, cherries, etc.
⅛ lit/¼ pt fruit syrup
1 tsp arrowroot
colouring
cherries and angelica

to serve: 3–4
time: 50 minutes
150 mm/6 in. fluted flan-ring
oven No. 4 or 180 °C/355 °F

1 Line the flan-ring with the pastry and bake "blind" (page 193) **2** Drain the fruit and arrange neatly in the flan-case **3** Blend the arrowroot and fruit syrup–bring to boil **4** Colour to suit fruit being used and coat with the syrup **5** Decorate suitably–cherries, angelica, etc. **6** Serve on a plate with a fancy paper

Strawberry Flan

110g/¼ lb biscuit crust (page 227)
450g/1 lb strawberries
castor sugar
apricot glaze (see Misc. Processes)
colouring

to serve: 3–4
time: 50 minutes
150 mm/6 in. fluted flan-ring
castor-sugar dredger
oven No. 4 or 180 °C/355 °F

1 Line the flan-ring and bake blind (page 193) **2** Prepare the strawberries and pile in a dome in the case **3** Dredge with castor sugar and put in the oven 1–2 minutes No. 2 or 155 °C/310 °F **4** Coat with the glaze (coloured) **5** Serve on a round plate on a fancy paper

NB Raspberries may be used in the same way.

For tartlets or boats– Line tartlet- or boat-shaped tins (page 193) and proceed in the same way.

Apple Flan (1)

110g/¼ lb biscuit crust (page 227)
filling:
450g/1 lb cooking apples
1 strip lemon-rind
60g/2 oz sugar
30g/1 oz butter
1 red eating apple
colouring
1 tbsp apricot glaze (see Misc. Processes)
cherries–angelica

to serve: 3–4
time: 1 hour
150 mm/6 in. fluted flan-ring
liquidizer
oven No. 4 or 180 °C/355 °F

1 Line the flan-ring and bake blind (page 193) **2** Peel, core, cut up and cook the apples with sugar, lemon-rind and butter, lid on, very slowly **3** Liquidize the apples–put into the flan **4** Slice the red apple *very* thinly and arrange round the flan **5** Coat with glaze and decorate with cherries and angelica **6** Serve on a round plate on a fancy paper

Apple Flan (2)

110g/¼ lb biscuit crust (page 227)
450g/1 lb cooking apples
1 tbsp castor sugar

to serve: 3–4
time: 50 minutes
150 mm/6 in. fluted flan-ring

2 tbsp apricot glaze (see Misc. Processes)

castor-sugar dredger
oven No. 5 or 190 °C/380 °F

1 Line the flan ring (page 193) 2 Prepare the apples, slice thinly and put into the case 3 When the case is nearly full arrange an overlapping layer of apples to cover the top 4 Dust with the castor sugar and bake 30 minutes 5 Heat the glaze correcting the consistency, glaze the top, and sides of the flan 6 Serve hot or cold on a plate with a fancy paper

Apricot Bourdaloue Flan

110g/¼ lb biscuit crust (page 227)
1 tin apricots
filling:
1 egg
⅛ lit/¼ pt milk
15g/½ oz flour
1 tsp semolina, cornflour or ground rice
30g/1 oz castor sugar
15g/½ oz ground almonds
1 tbsp white wine
apricot glaze (see Misc. Processes)

to serve: 3–4
time: 50 minutes
150 mm/6 in. fluted flan-ring
oven No. 4 or 180 °C/355 °F

1 Line the flan ring with the pastry and bake 'blind' (page 193) 2 Beat the egg and sugar until thick 3 Add the flours 4 Heat milk and add to the above 5 Return to the pan, bring to the boil and cook for about 3 minutes 6 Add the wine and pour into the flan 7 Arrange the apricots over the top in a dome 8 Coat with the glaze 9 Serve on a plate with a fancy paper

NB If fresh apricots are used, remove the stones and poach in a syrup (page 164).

Sponge Fruit Flan

2 egg whisked sponge (page 239)
fruit
apricot glaze (see Misc. Processes)
colouring
4 tbsp cream

175 mm/7 in. sponge flan-tin
greased and floured
greaseproof disc on the bottom
oven No. 5 or 190 °C/380 °F

1 Put the whisked sponge into the prepared tin 2 Bake about 20 minutes–cool a little–turn out 3 When cool arrange the fruit neatly 4 Coat with the apricot glaze, coloured if necessary 5 Decorate with cherries and angelica and piped whipped cream

NB A gelatine or arrowroot glaze may be used

Lemon Meringue Pie (1)

110g/¼ lb biscuit crust (page 227)
filling:
1 lemon
1 egg
1 dessertsp custard powder
⅛ lit/¼ pt water
1 tbsp sugar
30g/1 oz butter

to serve: 3–4
time: 1¾ hours
whisk
grater
150 mm/6 in. fluted flan-ring
castor-sugar dredger
oven No. 4 or 180 °C/355 °F; for

30g/1 oz castor sugar for meringue | meringue No. ¼ or 115 °C/240 °F

1 Make the flan-case, bake 'blind' (page 193) 2 Blend the custard powder with water 3 Add the lemon-rind and bring to the boil, stirring all the time—allow to boil thoroughly 4 Add sugar, lemon-juice, egg-yolk and butter 5 Pour into the flan-case 6 Whisk the egg-white, and the sugar and continue whisking until stiff 7 Pile on top of the flan and dredge with castor sugar 8 Dry the meringue for *at least* 1 hour 9 Serve on a plate with a fancy paper

Lemon Meringue Pie (2)

110g/¼ lb biscuit crust (page 227)
1 lemon, zest and juice
1 egg
60g/2 oz butter
60g/2 oz castor sugar
1 tsp cornflour
1 tbsp castor sugar for meringue (page 187)

to serve: 3–4
time: 1¾ hours
grater or zester
150 mm/6 in. fluted flan-ring
baking-tray
castor-sugar dredger
whisk
oven No. 4 or 180 °C/355 °F

1 Line the flan ring with the pastry and bake 'blind' (page 193) 2 Put the butter, sugar, zest and juice, and egg yolk into a pan and add the cornflour blended to a smooth paste with a little water 3 Bring slowly to the boil, stirring 4 Pour into the flan ring and pile the meringue on top. Dredge with sugar 5 Bake till crisp, about 1 hour, oven No. ¼ or 115 °C/240 °F 6 Serve hot or cold, on a plate on a fancy paper

Banana Flan

110g/¼ lb biscuit crust (page 227)
⅛ lit/¼ pt milk } custard (page 97)
1 egg } custard (page 97)
1 dessertsp sugar } custard (page 97)
1½ bananas
apricot glaze (see Misc. Processes)
cherries–angelica

to serve: 3
time: 1 hour
strainer
150 mm/6 in. fluted flan-ring
oven No. 4 or 180 °C/355 °F

1 Line the flan-ring and bake 'blind' (page 193)—cool 2 Make the custard—add ½ banana 3 Pour into the flan-case—cool 4 Slice remaining banana and arrange on top of the custard 5 Coat with glaze, decorate 6 Serve on a round plate with fancy paper
NB Pineapple may be used instead of banana.

Syrup Flan

110g/¼ lb biscuit crust (page 227)
3 tbsp syrup } filling
1½ tbsp fresh breadcrumbs } filling
grated rind and juice of ¼ lemon } filling

to serve: 3
time: 45 minutes
liquidizer (optional)
grater
lemon-squeezer
150 mm/6 in. fluted flan-ring
oven No. 4 or 180 °C/355 °F

1 Line the flan-ring with the pastry 2 Mix syrup, crumbs and lemon 3 Put into the flan and bake 30 minutes 4 Serve on a plate with a fancy paper

Butterscotch Flan

110g/¼ lb biscuit crust (page 227)
1 small tin condensed milk boiled for 3 hours
90g/3 oz plain chocolate
1 tbsp rum
4 tbsp whipped cream

to serve: 3–4
time: 1 hour
150 mm/6 in. fluted flan-ring
nylon bag
No. 8 icing-forcer
oven No. 4 or 180 °C/355 °F

1 Line the flan-ring and bake 'blind' (page 193) 2 Fill the flan-case with the milk 3 Melt the chocolate in a basin over hot water and flavour with rum and float over the milk–set 4 Pipe with cream 5 Serve on a round plate on fancy paper

Chocolate and Rum Flan

110g/¼ lb biscuit crust (page 227)
60g/2 oz chocolate powder or grated chocolate
4 tbsp whipped cream
rum
90g/3 oz green glacé icing (page 258)

to serve: 3–4
time: 45 minutes
grater
150 mm/6 in. fluted flan-ring or 12–18 50 mm/2 in. round deep-tartlet-tins
oven No. 4 or 180 °C/355 °F

1 Line the flan-ring and bake 'blind' (page 193) 2 Mix the cream and chocolate and flavour with the rum 3 Put into the case 4 Coat with the icing and decorate with a narrow band of grated chocolate round the edge 5 Serve on a plate with a fancy paper

For tartlets

paper cases

1 Line the tartlet-tins with the pastry and bake 'blind' about 10 minutes (page 193) 2 Fill to just below the top with the chocolate mixture 3 Coat with the icing 4 Put into paper cases and serve on a plate with a fancy paper

Fruit Cream Flan

110g/¼ lb biscuit crust (page 227)
⅛ lit/¼ pt cream
1 small tin pineapple, mandarin oranges, etc.
90g/3 oz glacé icing (page 258)
colouring
chopped pistachio nuts or coloured chopped almonds

to serve: 4
time: 45 minutes
150 mm/6 in. fluted flan-ring or 12–18 50 mm/2 in. round deep-tartlet-tins
oven No. 4 or 180 °C/355 °F

1 Line the flan ring and bake 'blind' (page 193) 2 Whip the cream stiffly and add finely-chopped, well-drained, fruit 3 Fill the flan-case 4 Coat with glacé icing (made with the fruit syrup and suitably

coloured) **5** Decorate with fruit and chopped nuts **6** Serve on a round plate on a fancy paper

For Strawberry or Raspberry cream flan

1 Mix 170g/6 oz chopped strawberries or raspberries with cream.
2 Coat with pink glacé icing.
3 Decorate with nuts.

For tartlets paper cases

1 Line the tartlet-tins with the pastry and bake 'blind' (page 193) **2** Fill to just below the top with the fruit and cream mixture **3** Coat with the icing **4** Decorate with angelica or fruit **5** Put into paper cases and serve on a plate with a fancy paper

Bakewell Tart

110g/¼ lb biscuit crust (page 227)
60g/2 oz castor sugar
30g/1 oz butter
1 egg
60g/2 oz ground almonds
30g/1 oz cake crumbs
almond essence or lemon-rind
} filling
1 tbsp jam or lemon curd
chopped almonds
apricot glaze (page xxii)

to serve: 3–4
time: 1½ hours
150 mm/6 in. fluted flan-ring
oven No. 3 or 170 °C/335 °F

1 Line the flan-ring–spread with jam or curd **2** Cream the butter and sugar–add egg, cake crumbs, ground almonds and essence **3** Put into the flan-case–sprinkle with nuts **4** Bake for 1 hour **5** Brush with the glaze whilst hot–cool **6** Serve on a round plate with fancy paper

Balmoral Tart

110g/¼ lb biscuit crust pastry (page 227)
60g/2 oz butter
60g/2 oz castor sugar
1 egg
30g/1 oz cherries, chopped
15g/½ oz peel–chopped
1 tsp cornflour
30g/1 oz cake crumbs
} filling
apricot glaze (see Misc. Processes)

to serve: 3–4
time: 1 hour
150 mm/6 in. fluted flan-ring or 12 50 mm/2 in. round deep-tartlet-tins
oven No. 4 or 180 °C/355 °F

1 Line the flan-ring **2** Cream the butter and sugar–beat in the egg **3** Fold in all the dry ingredients and put into the flan-case **4** Bake 30-40 minutes **5** Glaze whilst hot **6** Serve on a round plate with a fancy paper

For Tartlets

1 Line the tins with the pastry **2** ¾ fill with the mixture **3** Bake and finish as for the tart

Nougatine Flan

110g/¼ lb biscuit crust (page 227)
60g/2 oz butter
30g/1 oz ground almonds
1 egg
few drops almond essence
60g/2 oz castor sugar
30g/1 oz cake crumbs
1 tbsp apricot glaze (see Misc. Processes)
15g/½ oz chopped almonds

to serve: 3–4
time: 1 hour
150 mm/6 in. fluted flan-ring or 12 50 mm/2 in. round deep tartlet-tins
oven No. 4 or 180 °C/355 °F

1 Line the flan-ring **2** Cream the butter and sugar and beat in the egg and essence **3** Fold in the ground almonds and cake crumbs **4** Put into the case, sprinkle with the chopped almonds and bake 30–40 minutes **5** Coat with the apricot glaze while hot **6** Serve on a plate with a fancy paper

For tartlets

paper cases

1 Line the tins with the pastry **2** ¾ fill with the mixture and sprinkle with almonds **3** Bake and finish as for the flan **4** Put into paper cases and serve on a plate with a fancy paper

Gâteau espagnole

110g/¼ lb biscuit crust (page 227)
75g/2½ oz castor sugar
2 eggs
75g/2½ oz ground almonds
30g/1 oz butter
105g/3½ oz ground almonds } piping mixture
105g/3½ oz castor sugar } piping mixture
white of egg } piping mixture
apricot glaze (see Misc. Processes) } to finish
split almonds } to finish

to serve: 3–4
time: 1½ hours
150 mm/6 in. flan-ring
nylon bag
No. 8 vegetable-forcer
oven No. 4 or 180 °C/355 °F

1 Line the flan-ring with the pastry **2** Brush the inside with apricot glaze before filling **3** Melt the butter **4** Whisk the sugar with 1 egg and 1 yolk until thick **5** Fold in the ground almonds and melted butter **6** Lastly fold in stiffly-whisked white of egg **7** Put this mixture into the flan-case **8** Bake for 25–30 minutes until firm **9** Lift off the flan-ring leaving the flan on the baking-tray **10** Mix the sugar and ground almonds **11** Add enough white of egg to make the mixture a piping consistency **12** Pipe over the top of the flan in a lattice design **13** Pipe stars round the edge and return to the oven and allow to brown lightly–cool **14** Fill the lattice with apricot glaze **15** Put a split browned almond in each section of the lattice **16** Serve on a plate on a fancy paper

Gâteau italienne

110g/¼ lb biscuit crust (page 227)
60g/2 oz castor sugar
2 egg-yolks
almond essence
60g/2 oz ground almonds
Meringue
2 egg-whites
4 tbsp water
110g/4 oz castor sugar
1 tbsp of red-currant jelly

to serve: 3–4
time: 1½ hours
whisk or electric mixer
No. 8 vegetable-forcer
nylon piping-bag
thermometer
150 mm/6 in. fluted flan-ring
oven No. 4 or 180 °C/355 °F

1 Line the flan-ring **2** Mix almonds, sugar and essence **3** Add egg yolks one at a time and mix well **4** Put into the flan-case and bake for 30 minutes **5** Coat with ¾ of the meringue **6** Pipe the remainder in ovals **7** Put into the oven to become pale brown for approx. 4–5 minutes **8** Warm the jelly and put into the ovals

To Make Meringue
1 Put the sugar and water into a small pan, boil to 115 °C/240 °F **2** Whisk whites very stiffly **3** Pour the syrup on to whites gradually, whisking **4** Continue whisking until stiff **5** Use as required

Vegetable Flan

110g/4 oz biscuit crust (page 227, omit sugar)
mixed cooked vegetables, frozen or fresh
tomato, mushrooms, peas, carrot, asparagus } garnish
⅛ lit/¼ pt coating cheese sauce (60g/2 oz cheese)

to serve: 2–3
time: 35 minutes
grater
plain 150 mm/6 in. flan-ring
greased paper
baking-beans
oven No. 4 or 180 °C/355 °F

1 Line the flan-ring and bake 'blind' (page 193) **2** Prepare the vegetables–cook if necessary **3** Mix ⅔ vegetables with the sauce. Pour into the flan-case **4** Garnish with pieces of vegetables **5** Serve on a round plate–plain paper

Bacon and Egg Flan

110g/¼ lb biscuit crust (page 227, omit sugar)
3 streaky rashers bacon
2 eggs
seasoning
1 tsp chopped parsley

to serve: 3–4
time: 1 hour
baking-tray
150 mm/6 in. plain flan-ring
oven No. 4 or 180 °C/355 °F

1 Line the flan-ring (page 193) **2** Prepare the bacon, chop and add to the beaten eggs–season well, add the parsley **3** Pour into the flan-case and bake until set–about 30–35 minutes **4** Serve hot or cold on a plain paper on a round plate

Cheese Flan (Flan au fromage)

110g/¼ lb biscuit crust with cheese (page 227)
30g/1 oz butter
30g/1 oz flour
⅛ lit/¼ pt milk
60g/2 oz Gruyère cheese
15g/½ oz Parmesan cheese
1 egg
seasoning–salt, black pepper, nutmeg

to serve: 3–4
time: 1 hour
grater
whisk
150 mm/6 in. plain flan-ring
oven No. 6 or 205 °C/400 °F

1 Line the flan-ring with the pastry **2** Make a sauce with the butter, flour and milk–beat in the yolk of egg **3** Add grated cheese and seasoning **4** Fold in the whisked white of egg, put into the case and bake 25–30 minutes **5** Sprinkle the top with the grated Parmesan and serve on a plate with a plain paper

Danish Cheese Flan

110g/¼ lb biscuit crust with cheese (page 227)
60g/2 oz Danish blue cheese
110g/4 oz cream or cottage cheese
15g/½ oz butter
2 tbsp cream
1 egg
seasoning
1 dessertsp chopped chives
egg for brushing
parsley

to serve: 3–4
time: 1 hour
150 mm/6 in. plain flan-ring
baking-tray
oven No. 4 or 180 °C/355 °F

1 Line the flan-ring and brush with egg **2** Mix cheese, butter and cream thoroughly and add the beaten egg–add chives and season **3** Pour into the flan-case and bake 30–40 minutes **4** Serve on a plate with a plain paper garnished with parsley

Alternatives
Camembert–Brie (removing outside crusts) or a mixture.

Bacon, Cheese and Mushroom Flan

170g/6 oz biscuit crust with cheese (page 227)
170g/6 oz cottage cheese
110g/4 oz mushrooms
1 egg
30g/1 oz butter
salt, pepper, paprika
4 lean streaky rashers of bacon

to serve: 4
time: 1¼ hours
sieve
baking-tray
175 mm/7 in. plain flan-ring
oven No. 4 or 180 °C/355 °F

1 Line the flan-ring 2 Prepare the bacon, make 4 bacon rolls–chop and fry the remainder till crisp–remove from the pan 3 Prepare the mushrooms. Keep 4 whole–slice remainder and fry in the melted butter and bacon fat–cool and put into the flan-case with the fried bacon 4 Sieve the cheese and mix with the beaten egg, salt and pepper and pour over the mushrooms and bacon 5 Bake for 35 minutes 6 Place whole mushrooms and bacon rolls on top and bake for a further 10 minutes 7 Sprinkle each mushroom with paprika pepper 8 Serve on a plain paper on a round plate

Cream Cheese and Bacon Flan (Quiche au fromage blanc)

110g/¼ biscuit crust with cheese (page 227)
4 rashers streaky bacon
2 eggs
110g/4 oz cream cheese
⅛ lit/¼ pt cream
seasoning

to serve: 3–4
time: 1 hour
whisk
150 mm/6 in. plain flan-ring
oven No. 4 or 180 °C/355 °F

1 Line the flan-ring with the pastry 2 Cut the bacon into strips and fry lightly and cover the inside of the flan 3 Whip the cream until thick and mix with the well-beaten cream cheese 4 Stir in the whisked egg and add seasoning and pour into the flan-case 5 Bake for about 30–40 minutes 6 Serve on a plate with a plain paper

Quiche Lorraine

110g/¼ lb biscuit crust (page 227, add 1 oz cheese, omit sugar)
1 egg
45g/1½ oz grated cheese
seasoning
½ onion
60g/2 oz bacon
⅛ lit/¼ pt single cream or top of the milk
15g/½ oz butter

to serve: 3
time: 1 hour
grater
150 mm/6 in. plain flan-ring
oven No. 3 or 170 °C/335 °F

1 Line the flan-ring 2 Beat the eggs–add cheese, seasoning and milk or cream 3 Sauté blanched, diced bacon and chopped onion in butter–add to the egg mixture 4 Pour into the flan-case 5 Bake till firm and golden brown, about 30 minutes 6 Serve on a plain paper on a plain paper on a plate, either hot or cold

For vegetarians
Omit bacon–add mushrooms and/or sweet pepper.

Spanish Flan

110g/¼ lb biscuit crust with cheese (page 227)

to serve: 3–4
time: 1 hour

egg for brushing
30g/1 oz butter or margarine
1 onion
½ green or red pepper
3 tomatoes
1 level tbsp tomato purée
seasoning
1 small tin anchovy fillets
black or stuffed green olives

150 mm/6 in. plain flan-ring
baking-tray
oven No. 4 or 180 °C/355 °F

1 Line the flan-ring and brush the inside with egg **2** Chop the onion, skin and chop the tomatoes, remove seeds and chop blanched pepper **3** Sauté in the fat and cook to a pulp **4** Add tomato purée and season well (a pinch of curry powder or nutmeg may be added) **5** Pour into the flan-case and bake for 30–40 minutes **6** Decorate with a lattice of anchovy fillets filled with olives **7** Serve on a plate with a plain paper

Italian Flan

170g/6 oz biscuit crust
(page 227, 1 oz cheese, omit sugar)
15g/½ oz butter
½ onion
¼ lit/½ pt tinned tomatoes or
220g/½ lb fresh
2 eggs
salt and pepper
a little curry-powder
cheese–sliced

to serve: 4
time: 1 hour
whisk
175 mm/7 in. plain flan-ring
oven No. 4 or 180 °C/355 °F

1 Line the flan-ring **2** Fry the chopped onion in butter till golden brown–add curry-powder **3** Add to the tomatoes **4** Add 2 whisked eggs and seasoning–pour into the flan-case and bake for 25 minutes
5 Place sliced cheese on top and return to the oven for 5 minutes
6 Serve on a plain paper on a plate
This may be served hot or, if preferred, cold with a salad.

Prawn and Asparagus Flan

110g/¼ lb biscuit crust with
cheese (page 227)
⅛ lit/¼ pt coating white sauce
1 tbsp cream
½ tin asparagus tips
110g/4 oz peeled prawns
15g/½ oz butter
seasoning
egg for brushing

to serve: 3–4
time: 1 hour
baking-tray
150 mm/6 in. plain flan-ring
oven No. 4 or 180 °C/335 °F

1 Line the flan-ring, brush the inside with egg, and bake 'blind' (page 193)
2 Save 6 prawns and 6 tips for decoration–chop the remainder and add to the sauce **3** Add cream, season well, pour into the flan-case and reheat in the oven **4** Sauté the prawns and tips in melted butter and use to decorate the hot flan **5** Serve on a plate with a plain paper

Cream and Leek Flan

110g/¼ lb biscuit crust with cheese (page 227)
⅛ lit/¼ pt cream
4 leeks
60g/2 oz ham or bacon
15g/½ oz butter
2 eggs
seasoning
egg for brushing
parsley

to serve: 3–4
time: 1 hour
whisk
150 mm/6 in. plain flan-ring
baking-tray
oven No. 5 or 180 °C/355 °F

1 Line the flan-ring and brush the inside with egg **2** Sauté the chopped white part of the leeks in the butter and add the chopped bacon or ham **3** Cook gently until soft–season and put into the flan-case **4** Whip the cream until thick and add the well-beaten eggs–season **5** Pour over the leeks and bake for about 30–40 minutes. Garnish with parsley **6** Serve on a plate with a plain paper
NB Onions may be used instead of leeks.

Sea Fruit Flan

110g/¼ biscuit crust (page 227, omit sugar)
1 tbsp chopped onion
30g/1 oz butter
90g/3 oz fresh picked or tinned crab, lobster, shrimps or prawns
1 tbsp dry white wine
1 egg
2 tbsp cream
½ tbsp tomato purée
seasoning
egg for brushing
paprika

to serve: 3–4
time: 45 minutes
150 mm/6 in. plain flan-ring
baking-tray
oven No. 4 or 180 °C/355 °F

1 Line the flan-ring, brush with egg and bake 'blind' (page 193) **2** Sauté the onion in butter until soft but not brown–add the fish, seasoning and wine and boil for 2 minutes and allow to cool a little **3** Add the egg, cream and purée–check the seasoning **4** Pour into the flan-case and heat for 10 minutes **5** Sprinkle with paprika and serve on a plate on a plain paper

14
Savouries

Welsh Rarebit

A cheese savoury on a whole square of toast
or 1 slice in 4
or 1 slice in 2

1 slice buttered toast
1 tbsp milk, water, beer or cider
¼ tsp mustard
60g/2 oz grated cheese
15g/½ oz butter or margarine
salt and pepper
parsley

to serve: 1, 2 or 4
time: 10 minutes
grater
grill

1 Butter (thin) toast **2** Put mustard, liquid and fat in a pan and boil **3** Cool slightly–add cheese, salt and pepper **4** Mix well–pile on the toast **5** Brown quickly under the grill **6** Serve on a hot dish with parsley garnish
NB Buck rarebit is served as above with the addition of a poached egg.

Cheese Straws

30g/1 oz cheese pastry (page 228)
paprika
parsley

to serve: 4
time: 40 minutes
35 mm/¾ in. plain cutter
60 mm/1½ in. plain cutter
greased and floured baking-tray
oven No. 4 or 180 °C/355 °F

1 Make the pastry **2** Roll into an oblong 5 mm/¼ in. thick–trim the ends and sides **3** Cut into straws about 75 mm/3 in. long and 5 mm/¼ in. wide **4** Roll out the cuttings and cut out rings using the plain cutters **5** Put on to the tray and bake about 10 minutes–cool **6** Dip each end of the straws into paprika **7** Put four straws into each ring **8** Serve on a plain paper, with parsley garnish
NB For cocktail savouries, cut 35 mm/1½ in. long.

Cheese Butterflies

30g/1 oz cheese pastry
(pastry, page 228)

to serve: 4
time: 40 minutes

1 small packet cream cheese
paprika
parsley

No. 8 icing-forcer
nylon bag
50 mm/2 in. plain cutter
25 mm/1 in. plain cutter
greased and floured baking-tray
oven No. 4 or 180 °C/355 °F

1 Roll out the pastry fairly thinly **2** Cut into rounds with the larger cutter **3** Roll out the cuttings left from the above and cut into rounds with the smaller cutter–cut these small rounds in half **4** Bake about 10 minutes **5** When cool pipe down the centre of the larger rounds using the cream cheese **6** Arrange the small pieces each side of the line of piping to stand up like 'wings' **7** If liked the 'butterflies' may be decorated with paprika and finely chopped parsley

NB This size may be used as savouries. If to be used as cocktail savouries, use the smaller cutter.

Cheese Soufflé

30g/1 oz butter
15g/½ oz flour
⅛ lit/¼ pt milk
2 eggs
90g/3 oz Parmesan cheese (grated)
paprika

to serve: 4
time: 45 minutes
grater
whisk
100 mm/4 in. soufflé-mould or 4 individual moulds greased and lined
oven No. 6 or 205 °C/400 °F

1 Make a sauce with the butter, flour and milk **2** Add the yolks of egg, cheese and seasoning **3** Fold in the whisked whites and put into the prepared moulds **4** Bake 20–30 minutes for the larger size or 15–20 minutes for the smaller ones **5** Remove the paper and stand on a plate with a plain paper **6** Sprinkle with grated cheese and paprika and serve at once

Cold Cheese Soufflés

45g/1½ oz grated Cheddar or Gruyère cheese
30g/1 oz grated Parmesan cheese
⅛ lit/¼ pt cream
⅛ lit/¼ pt aspic jelly (page 209) or 1 packet
¼ tsp French mustard
1 tsp tarragon vinegar
seasoning
paprika

to serve: 4
time: 1 hour
grater
4 ramekin-cases with paper tied round the outside

1 Half whip the cream **2** Mix the cheese and seasonings **3** Whisk the aspic until frothy and cool but not set–add to the cheese **4** Fold in the cream and check the seasoning **5** Put into the ramekin cases, allowing the mixture to come a little above the rim **6** When set, cover with a thin layer of aspic jelly—set—remove the paper and sprinkle with a little grated Parmesan cheese and paprika pepper **7** Serve on a plate with a plain paper

Cheese Aigrettes

2 egg choux pastry mixture (page 230)
45g/1½ oz Parmesan cheese (grated)
seasoning

to serve: 4–5
time: ½ hour
grater
kitchen roll
deep fat
thermometer (optional)

1 Add the cheese to the choux pastry—season carefully **2** Heat the fat to 170 °C/335 °F **3** Drop the mixture into the fat in teaspoonsful **4** Fry for 8–10 minutes turning all the time. Drain well **5** Serve piled up on a plain paper **6** Sprinkle with grated Parmesan cheese
NB The mixture may be piped into the fat using a plain 10 mm/½ in. vegetable-forcer or rolled in wetted hands into small balls.

Savoury Eclairs

2 egg choux pastry (page 230)
savoury filling (page 230)
glaze
chopped pistachio nuts
parsley or cress

to serve: 4–5
time: 45 minutes
baking-tray, greased and floured
5 mm/¼ in. plain forcer
nylon bag
oven No. 7 or 220 °C/425 °F

1 Pipe the pastry into lengths of 50 mm/2 in. or into small balls **2** Bake about 20 minutes **3** Cut the sides to let out the steam and return to the oven to dry. Cool **4** Fill with the chosen filling **5** Glaze and sprinkle with the chopped nuts **6** Dish on a plain paper garnished with parsley or cress

Cheese d'Artois

1 egg
30g/1 oz butter
45g/1½ oz Parmesan cheese (grated)
seasoning
egg for brushing
cuttings of puff pastry or a small packet of frozen puff pastry
parsley

to serve: 4–6
time: ½ hour
grater
baking-tray
50 mm/2 in. plain cutter
oven No. 6 or 205 °C/400 °F

1 Beat the egg **2** Melt the butter and add to the egg with the cheese—season **3** Roll the pastry out thinly and cut in half **4** Spread the cheese mixture over one half and cover it with the other half—cut into rounds **5** Brush with egg—sprinkle with cheese **6** Bake about 10 minutes **7** Serve on a plain paper, garnished with parsley
NB These may be cut into fingers instead of rounds.

York Slices

110g/¼ lb rough puff pastry (page 229) or frozen puff pastry
45g/1½ oz cheddar cheese
1–2 streaky rashers
made mustard
egg glaze
parsley

to serve: 4–6
time: ½ hour
grater
baking-tray
oven No. 7 or 205 °C/425 °F

1 Roll the pastry into an oblong–trim the edges **2** Cut through centre lengthwise **3** Spread one length lightly with the mustard and cover with diced bacon and grated cheese **4** Cover with the second strip of pastry **5** Roll lightly–glaze with egg **6** Cut into fingers 25 mm/1 in. wide **7** Bake for 12–15 minutes–cool **8** Serve on plain paper on an oval dish garnished with parsley

Talmouse of Haddock

30g/1 oz cheese pastry (page 228)
1 tbsp white sauce
2 tbsp flaked smoked haddock
15g/½ oz Parmesan cheese
seasoning–paprika pepper
egg glaze
parsley or cress

to serve: 4–6
time: 40 minutes
grater
greased and floured tray
75 mm/3 in. cutter or 50 mm/2 in. cutter
oven No. 4 or 180 °C/355 °F

1 Roll the pastry out thinly and cut into rounds using the smaller cutter for a cocktail savoury, the larger for a dinner savoury **2** Mix the fish with the sauce, add cheese and seasoning **3** Put 1 tsp on each round of pastry **4** Brush the edges with egg and draw up into a triangular shape–glaze **5** Bake for 15 minutes **6** Sprinkle with paprika pepper **7** Serve hot on a plain paper garnished with parsley or cress

Little Baskets of Vegetables (Petits paniers à la jardinière)

110g/¼ lb biscuit crust (without sugar) (page 227)
small packet frozen mixed vegetables
French dressing (page 131)
aspic jelly (page 209) or 1 packet
black olives
seasoning
parsley or cress garnish

to serve: 9
time: ¾ hour
9 small tartlet-tins or boat-moulds
oven No. 4 or 180 °C/355 °F

1 Line the tins with the pastry and bake 'blind' (page 193) **2** Cook the vegetables in a little butter **3** When cool toss in very well-seasoned French dressing and little aspic jelly **4** Fill the pastry-cases and glaze with the aspic **5** Decorate with small rounds of the jelly and pieces of black olives **6** Dish on a plain paper and garnish with parsley or cress

NB If liked these baskets may be decorated with handles of thinly-cut cucumber-skin.

Anchovy Straws (Pailles au parmesan à la Yarmouth)

110g/¼ lb biscuit crust
(page 227, without sugar)
15g/½ oz grated Parmesan
ground mace
anchovy fillets
egg to glaze

to serve: 6
time: ½ hour
grater
baking-tray
oven No. 4 or 180 °C/355 °F

1 Roll the pastry into an oblong **2** Sprinkle with half the cheese, fold in three and roll out **3** Repeat No. 2 again **4** Trim the ends and sides– glaze **5** Cut into strips 100 mm/4 in. long and 10 mm/½ in. wide **6** Put an anchovy fillet along each strip **7** Twist and flatten each end **8** Bake about 10 minutes **9** Dish on a plain paper and serve hot

NB **1** Strips cut from a kipper may be used instead of anchovy fillets.
2 These may be made half the size and used as a cocktail savoury.

Aspic Jelly

¾ lit/1½ pt stock or stock cube
⅛ lit/¼ pt sherry
⅛ lit/¼ pt mixed vinegars
rind and juice of 1 lemon
1 carrot
1 onion
piece of celery or celery salt
bouquet garni
½ tsp salt
whites and shells of 2 eggs
60–90g/2–3 oz gelatine

time: 1 hour
whisk
lemon-squeezer
large pan
jelly-cloth
string

1 Put all the ingredients into a large clean pan, leaving the vegetables in large pieces **2** Whisk until boiling **3** Allow to boil up three times (without whisking) **4** Infuse over low heat for 15 minutes **5** Strain 2–3 times through the scalded cloth **6** Skim off any froth
Use as required.

Amount of gelatine depends on
(a) use for which aspic is intended
(b) temperature–in hot weather use more
(c) kind of gelatine (for loose gelatine, use the larger quantity)

Small Foie Gras Aspics (Petits aspics de foie gras)

1 small tin foie gras
aspic jelly (page 209) or 1 packet
black olives
port wine

to serve: 4
time: 1½ hours
4 dariole-moulds
ice
cutters

1 Mask the moulds with aspic that has been flavoured and coloured with the port wine **2** Decorate with black olives and cover with aspic **3** Cut the foie gras into neat cubes and fill the moulds with layers of aspic and foie gras, allowing each layer to set before starting the next **4** Turn out when set and garnish with chopped or cut-out aspic

NB **1** These may be served as an hors-d'œuvre or a cold savoury.
2 Pâté may be used instead of foie gras.

Parmesan Boats (Petites gondoles au Parmesan)

60g/2 oz cassolette pastry (page 231)
1 tbsp white sauce
1 tbsp aspic jelly (page 209) or 1 packet
1 tbsp cream
15g/½ oz grated Parmesan cheese
15g/½ oz grated Cheddar
seasoning
salad garnish, cream
paprika

to serve: 6
time: 1 hour
grater
6 75 mm/3 in. boat-moulds
paper forcing-bag
No. 8 icing-forcer
oven No. 4 or 180 °C/355 °F

1 Line the moulds with the pastry and bake **2** Warm the sauce, add aspic (melted), seasoning and cheese **3** When nearly cold, add cream half whipped **4** When beginning to thicken fill the cases **5** When quite firm glaze with aspic, pipe with seasoned cream and sprinkle with paprika **6** Serve on a plain paper on a plate **7** Garnish with parsley, cress, watercress or endive

NB For cocktail savouries, use smallest size moulds.

Devils on Horseback

6 large prunes
½ bay-leaf
water or red wine to cover
filling of–
  (a) Anchovy fillet round an almond
  (b) Chopped mango chutney
  (c) Olive stuffed with pimento
3 rashers
croûtes of fried bread
watercress

to serve: 6
time: 1¼ hours
baking-tray
small oval-cutter
oven No. 4 or 180 °C/355 °F

1 Pour boiling water or hot wine over the prunes and leave for ½ hour **2** Simmer in the same liquid until all is absorbed, cool and stone **3** Fill with the chosen filling **4** Remove rind from bacon, stretch and cut in half **5** Roll the prunes in the bacon and bake for 10–15 minutes **6** Place on croûtes **7** Dish on a plain paper and garnish with watercress

Devilled Chicken Livers (Foie de volaille à la diable)

1 chicken's liver
2 rashers
fried croûtes
cayenne
parsley
onion or garlic salt

to serve: 4
time: ½ hour
baking-tray
small oval-cutter
oven No. 4 or 180 °C/355 °F

meat glaze (page 10)

1 Steep the liver in tepid, salted water–drain 2 Cut into 4 or 5 pieces and season 3 Remove rind from bacon–stretch and cut each rasher in 2 or 3 (according to length) 4 Wrap the liver in the bacon 5 Put into the oven for 5–7 minutes 6 Place on the croûtes 7 Glaze and decorate with chopped parsley 8 Serve on a plain paper and garnish with whole parsley

NB May be used as a cocktail savoury.

Olive à la Madras

4 Spanish olives	*to serve:* 4
2 anchovy fillets	*time:* ½ hour
30g/1 oz anchovy butter (page 101)	25 mm/1 in plain cutter
4 small round fried croûtes	forcing-bag
cress	No. 8 icing-forcer

1 Stone the olives and place on the croûtes 2 Fill with piped anchovy butter 3 Cut anchovies in halves lengthwise and twist them round the olives 4 Serve on a plate with a plain paper and garnish with cress

NB These may be used as hors-d'œuvres or cocktail savouries.

Sardines à la piémontaise

4 sardines	*to serve:* 4
4 croûtes of fried bread (finger-shape)	*time:* ½ hour
paprika pepper	whisk
finely-chopped parsley	
watercress or parsley	

sauce for coating:
- 2 yolks
- walnut of butter
- ½ tsp tarragon vinegar
- ½ tsp white malt vinegar
- ¼ tsp made mustard

1 Remove tails from the sardines and place on the fried bread–warm 2 For the sauce, whisk yolks and seasonings over hot water until thick 3 Coat the sardines 4 Decorate 2 with a line of paprika, and 2 with the chopped parsley 5 Dish on a plate as a star and garnish with parsley or watercress in the centre

NB Should the sauce get too thick add a little hot water and whisk. These may be served as hors-d'œuvre, omitting the croûtes.

Crème Joséphine

2 tbsp cooked, smoked haddock	*to serve:* 8
30g/1 oz butter	*time:* 35 minutes
1 egg	kitchen roll
1 tbsp cream	8 greased boat-moulds
seasoning	bain-marie

egg } coating
raspings }
parsley

tea-cloth
flour-dredger, deep fat-pan
thermometer
oven No. 4 or 180 °C/355 °F

1 Remove the skin and bones from the fish and chop finely 2 Add the melted butter, beaten egg, cream and seasoning 3 Fill the moulds, put into the bain-marie and bake until set–about 10–15 minutes 4 Turn out on to the cloth and dredge with flour 5 Coat with egg and raspings, and fry at 180 °C/355 °F 6 Drain and serve on a plate on a plain paper in the form of a star, garnish with fried or fresh parsley

Butter Balls (Cassolettes à la chasseur)

90g/3 oz butter
egg and white raspings
mayonnaise or white sauce
prawns, gherkins, seasoning

to serve: 4
time: 1 hour
ice
deep fat
thermometer
10 mm/½ in. plain cutter

1 Divide the butter into four and shape into balls 2 If the weather is hot, put into iced water or refrigerator 3 Coat *four* times in egg and raspings 4 Mark the top with the cutter 5 Fry at 180 °C/355 °F until golden brown 6 Remove the tops and pour out the liquid butter 7 Fill, put back the tops and decorate with prawn heads 8 Serve on a plain paper–garnish with parsley

Cheese Board

Aim to offer a selection of cheeses of differing flavours and textures, e.g. cheeses from different countries or a selection of English cheeses.

Serve small cuts of cheese, clearly labelled in original covering, e.g. Camembert in a box–Gorgonzola in its own foil.

The board should be firm, easily handled and large enough to hold a good selection, e.g. 7–8 varieties and should include a cheese-knife.

Accompaniments

1 Biscuits, e.g. crackers, oat, digestive, water, etc.
2 Butter–serve on a dish, whole, in balls or in cubes, with a butter-knife.
3 Celery–serve in a glass.

Garnishes

Grapes, olives, gherkins, cocktail cherries, nuts, tomato and radishes. These may be impaled on cocktail-sticks with pineapple, in an orange, grapefruit or apple.

Storage

NB If cheese is stored in a refrigerator it should be removed in time to allow it to reach room-temperature before serving—at least 1 hour.

15
Cocktail savouries

Puff Pastry Base

Use cuttings from puff pastry or frozen puff pastry.

1 Bouchées (page 229)

2 Horns

time: ½ hour
baking-tray
cornet-moulds greased
oven No. 6/205 °C/400 °F

(a) Roll pastry very thinly.
(b) Trim–glaze–cut in 5 mm/¼ in. strips.
(c) Wind round moulds to a depth of 35 mm/1½ in.
(d) Bake about 15 minutes.
(e) Fill as for bouchées.

3 Sausage Rolls (page 59)

to make: 16 rolls
time: 45 minutes

(a) Roll pastry very thinly.
(b) Make rolls–miniature in size.

4 Anchovy Eclairs

time: ½ hour
baking-tray
oven No. 7 or 220 °C/425 °F

(a) Roll the pastry very thinly.
(b) Marinade anchovy fillets in French dressing (page 131).
(c) Put on to strips of pastry.
(d) Turn over to form allumettes.
(e) Glaze–sprinkle with Parmesan cheese.
(f) Bake about 10 minutes.

5 Cheese Tartlets

time: ¾ hour
small tartlet-tins
baking-tray
oven No. 6 or 205 °C/400 °F

(a) Line the tins with thin puff pastry.
(b) Put 1 tsp cheese soufflé mixture in each (page 206).
(c) Bake 10–15 minutes.
(d) Sprinkle with cheese and paprika.
NB Cheese pastry may also be used.

Cheese Pastry Base

1 Cheese Straws (page 205)
Cut smaller than normal.

2 Cheese Butterflies (page 205)

3 Almond Biscuits

time: 20 minutes
small cutter

(a) Cut cheese pastry into small oval biscuits.
(b) Place a whole almond on each.
(c) Glaze with egg.
(d) Bake at No. 4 or 170 °C/335 °F for 10 minutes.

4 Walnut Biscuits

time: ½ hour
small cutter
paper forcing-bag
No. 8 icing-forcer

(a) Cut cheese pastry in to small rounds and bake as above.
(b) When cool pipe a rosette of cream cheese on each and top with a walnut, *or* pipe a ring round the edge and fill the centre with chopped walnut.

5 Barquettes

time: ¾ hour
small boat-moulds

(a) Line the moulds with cheese pastry and bake 'blind' about 10 minutes, at No. 4 or 180 °C/335 °F.
(b) Fill with any savoury mixture and decorate suitably.

6 Cheese Canapés

time: ½ hour

(a) Cut rounds, squares, etc., out of cheese pastry and bake as above.
(b) Put various savouries on top and decorate suitably, e.g. a sardine, prawns dipped in curry dip, etc.

Ham Horns

110g/¼ lb biscuit crust without sugar (page 227)
⅛ lit/¼ pt white coating sauce
60g/2 oz minced ham
1 tsp tomato purée
seasoning
garnish—black olives or chopped yolk or white of egg, chopped parsley, paprika, etc.

to serve: 12
time: 1 hour
cornet-moulds
oven No. 3 or 170 °C/335 °F

1 Roll out the pastry rather thinly **2** Glaze with egg and cut into strips about 150 mm/6 in. long and 10 mm/½ in. wide **3** Roll round the moulds **4** Bake 10–15 minutes to a pale golden brown **5** Mix the ham with the sauce, add the purée and seasoning **6** Fill the horns and garnish **7** Serve on a plain paper and garnish with parsley
NB Any savoury filling may be used.

Anchovy Toast

1 hard-boiled egg
30g/1 oz butter
croûtes of fried bread
anchovy paste or essence
cress

to serve: 6
time: ½ hour
sieve
50 mm/2 in. plain cutter
paper forcing-bag
No. 8 icing-forcer

1 Mix butter, paste or essence and yolk of egg—season—sieve **2** Chop the white of egg finely **3** Pipe the mixture on the fried croûtes **4** Decorate with the white of egg **5** Serve on a plain paper and garnish with cress

Glazed Canapés

time: ½ hour
cooler
paper forcing-bag
No. 8 icing-forcer

1 Slice and butter brown and white bread **2** Cut into small shapes and place on the cooler **3** Decorate with various savoury pieces, e.g. smoked salmon, pâté, ham, sardines, hard-boiled egg, prawns, shrimps, crab, lobster **4** Pipe with various savoury butters (pages 101, 102) **5** Glaze with cool aspic (packet)

Stuffed eggs (page 151)

sieve

1 Cut hard-boiled eggs into quarters and remove yolks.
2 Stand the whites on croûtes of fried bread
3 Make the filling with sieved yolk, butter and flavouring (e.g. anchovy paste, curry-powder, sardine, etc.).
4 Sieve and pipe into the whites.

Yeast Base

Bridge Rolls or Bread Rolls

Basic rich yeast dough (page 282)

time: 1 hour
baking-tray
35 mm/1½ in. plain cutter
oven No. 7 or 220 °C/425 °F

1 Knead, roll out, cut into rounds or knead into bridge rolls–prove, glaze 2 Bake 6 minutes–cool–cut in half and spread with a savoury mixture (see sandwiches, page 292) 3 Decorate suitably

Smoked Salmon or Ham Cornets

time: 15 minutes
cornet-moulds
paper forcing-bag
No. 8 icing-forcer
50 mm/2 in. plain-cutter

1 Cut ham or smoked salmon into small rounds 2 Shape round or in a cornet-mould 3 Pipe savoury butter or pâté into the centre

Stuffed Grapes

black grapes
cheese–Gorgonzola or cream cheese

time: ½ hour
sieve
paper forcing-bag
No. 8 icing-forcer
petits-fours cases

1 Wash the grapes, cut in half and remove the pips 2 Sieve the Gorgonzola and beat to a piping consistency with the addition of cream or milk 3 Put the grape together with the cheese and pipe a little on the outside 4 Serve in petits-fours cases 5 If using cream cheese, sprinkle with chopped nuts

Stuffed Dates or Prunes

dates–cheese–nuts

time: 15 minutes
petits-fours cases

1 Remove the stone and put a cheese and nut mixture in its place

2 Press a whole nut on the outside 3 Serve in petits-fours cases
NB Prunes (pre-cooked) may be used instead of dates.

Mushroom Princess

12 small mushrooms
60g/2 oz butter
90g/3 oz cream cheese
12 rounds toast or fried bread
paprika pepper

to serve: 6–12
time: ½ hour
kitchen roll
paper forcing-bag
No. 8 icing-forcer
35 mm/1½ in. cutter

1 Prepare the mushrooms and remove the stalks and cook in the butter, drain and cool 2 Pipe a rosette of cream cheese in the centre of each mushroom 3 Dust with paprika pepper and put the stalk in position 4 Serve on a round of toast or fried bread

Chestnut Croquettes (Croquettes de marrons)

110g/¼ lb chestnut purée (tinned)
15g/½ oz butter
¼ egg
salt and cayenne
chopped parsley or marjoram
egg and raspings

to serve: 12
time: 1 hour
kitchen roll
deep fat
thermometer
cocktail-sticks

1 Melt the butter–beat in the purée 2 Add the egg and heat thoroughly 3 Add herbs and seasoning and shape into small balls or rolls 4 Coat twice with egg and raspings 5 Fry at 180 °C/355 °F to a golden brown 6 Serve on cocktail-sticks with a well-seasoned dip (pages 219, 220)
NB These may be served as an accompaniment to chicken or turkey.

Fish Croquettes (Petites croquettes de poisson)

90g/3 oz cooked fish
15g/½ oz butter
15g/½ oz flour
4 tbsp milk
60g/2 oz fresh breadcrumbs
½ tsp curry-powder
salt, pepper, nutmeg
lemon-juice
egg and raspings

to serve: 12
time: 1 hour
kitchen roll
liquidizer
deep fat
thermometer
cocktail-sticks

1 Flake the fish and remove skin and bones 2 Make a sauce with the butter, flour and milk 3 Add fish, crumbs and seasonings 4 Spread on a plate to cool 5 Shape into *small* balls or rolls 6 Coat twice in egg and raspings 7 Fry at 180 °C/355 °F until golden brown 8 Serve on cocktail-sticks with a well-seasoned dip (pages 219, 220)

Salted Almonds

110g/¼ lb Jordan almonds

to serve: 2–6

2 tbsp oil
salt or celery salt

time: 45 minutes
kitchen roll
heavy frying-pan
sieve (wire)

1 Blanch and dry the almonds 2 Heat the oil and add the almonds 3 Cook very gently keeping the almonds moving all the time, until a very pale brown 4 Turn on to paper sprinkled with the salt or celery salt (or a mixture) 5 Leave for a few minutes 6 Shake in the sieve to remove surplus salt 7 When cold put into a screw-topped jar

NB 1 Devilled almonds may be made in the same way adding a pinch of cayenne pepper to the salt.
2 Cashew-nuts, pea-nuts and pine-kernels may be treated in the same way.

Dips

1 Cheese and Smoked Roe

60g/2 oz jar smoked roe
110g/¼ lb cream cheese
3 tbsp cream
1 tbsp onion juice (grated onion)
Worcester sauce

time: 15 minutes
grater

Beat all these ingredients together and season well.

2 Cheese Dip with yoghurt

1 carton plain yoghurt
110g/¼ lb cream cheese
1 tbsp mayonnaise (page 131)
seasoning

time: 15 minutes

Beat all these ingredients together and season well.

3 Cheese and Tomato Dip

⅛ lit/¼ pt tomato sauce (page 99)
110g/¼ lb cream cheese
1 tsp Worcester sauce
garlic salt–seasoning

time: 15 minutes

Mix all these ingredients together and season well.

4 Avocado Dip

1 ripe avocado pear
110g/¼ lb cream cheese
3 tsp Worcester sauce
1 tbsp mayonnaise (page 131)
3 tbsp cream
seasoning

time: 15 minutes
liquidizer

1 Cut the pear in half, remove the stone and scoop out the flesh
2 Liquidize all the ingredients–season well

NB All dips are served in a bowl and food arranged round it, e.g. crisps, vegetables, fish balls, prawns, etc.

Swiss Cheese Fondue

230g/½ lb grated Gruyère or Cheddar cheese
4 tbsp dry cider or white wine
1 egg
salt, pepper, mustard
pinch of cayenne pepper
Worcester sauce
crushed garlic (optional)

time: ½ hour
grater or liquidizer
double saucepan or fondue-pan
fondue-dish

1 Melt the cheese slowly in the pan or double saucepan **2** Add the wine gradually, stirring all the time over gentle heat **3** Add beaten egg, a little at a time **4** Cook gently until thickened–season to taste **5** Serve in a fondue-dish with cubes of bread
NB Bread is dipped into the fondue on a long fork.

Savoury Butters (pages 101, 102)

'Things on Sticks'

cheese in cubes
cubes of pâté
stuffed olives
gherkins
pineapple
cocktail onions (all colours)
cocktail sausages
cocktail cherries

cocktail-sticks

The above can be used singly on sticks or combined, e.g. cheese and pineapple, pâté and onions, etc.
The sticks look attractive stuck into grapefruit, red apples, cabbage heart, etc.

16
Beverages

To Make Tea

Personal taste must be taken into account when making tea. The usual amount is–

1 level tsp per person 1 level tsp for the pot or 1 tea-bag per person	allowing at least ⅛ lit/¼ pt water per person	kettle tea-pot

1 Fill the kettle with cold water 2 Heat the tea-pot, and measure the tea into it 3 Pour on freshly-boiling water 4 Infuse 3–5 minutes
5 Serve with milk or thinly-sliced lemon and sugar
NB Tea used may be Indian or China or a mixture.

Iced Tea

time: 10 minutes
plus chilling time
strainer

1 Make tea using China tea 2 Infuse for 3 minutes–strain 3 Add thin slices of lemon and orange, a little sugar and, if liked, a few crushed mint-leaves–chill 4 Serve with straws

Variation
Make as above–omit mint and add 1 tbsp rum or brandy to each pint or tea.

To Make Coffee

60g/2 oz freshly-ground coffee to
½ lit/1 pt water
small pinch of salt

Jug Method

jug
muslin

1 Warm the jug and put the coffee into it 2 Pour on boiling water–stir 3 Stand for 4 minutes–strain through muslin 4 Re-heat and serve

Pan Method

time: 15 minutes
muslin

1 Put the coffee into a pan and 'freshen' over heat 2 Add cold water and bring to the boil 3 Allow to boil up three times 4 Stand for 8–10 minutes 5 Strain through muslin, re-heat and serve

Percolator method

time: 15 minutes

Use a percolator of metal or glass.
1 Put cold water into the lower container and bring to the boil 2 Put the coffee into the upper part and fix into the lower 3 Allow to percolate 6–8 minutes 4 The coffee may be re-heated and served in the usual coffee-pot, or in the lower container of the percolator

The Vacuum Method, e.g. Expresso

1 Fill the lower container with water to within 10 mm/½ in. of the top 2 Fill the filter loosely with coffee and screw on the top tightly 3 Heat until the water rises into the top container and remove from heat at once 4 Serve in a coffee-pot or in the lower container having removed the coffee

To serve Coffee

Whichever method is used, the coffee must be served very hot with hot milk or single cream, and sugar, either brown, loaf or coffee crystals.

Iced Coffee

¼ lit/½ pt strong coffee
⅛ lit/¼ pt creamy milk
sugar to sweeten
1 tbsp brandy (optional)

time: 10 minutes
plus chilling time
liquidizer

1 Mix coffee, milk and a little sugar 2 Liquidize and add the brandy, if used 3 Put into a jug and chill thoroughly 4 Serve with a little whipped cream on top flavoured lightly with vanilla 5 Serve with straws

Lemonade

1 lemon
¼ lit/½ pt water
sugar to sweeten (or glucose)

to serve: 1–2
time: 10 minutes
plus cooling time
zester (optional)
lemon-squeezer
strainer

1 Wash the lemon and peel the rind off very thinly 2 Pour on boiling water–cool 3 Add lemon-juice and sweeten–strain 4 Serve very cold

with a thin slice of lemon on top
NB Ice-cubes may be added.

Alternative Method

to serve: 3–4
time: 10 minutes
liquidizer
muslin

1 Wash the lemon and cut into quarters **2** Put into the liquidizer with ½ lit/1 pt of water **3** Liquidize for one minute **4** Strain through muslin, sweeten and serve as Method 1
NB If for immediate use, liquidize for a few seconds, add ice and sugar and blend on maximum speed for 1 minute.

Orangeade

1 orange
¼ lit/½ pt water
¼ lemon
sugar or glucose to sweeten

to serve: as lemonade
time: as lemonade

Method 1 and 2
As for lemonade (page 222).

Milk Shakes

¼ lit/½ pt cold milk
2 tsp sugar or to taste
2 ice-cubes or a scoop of ice cream
flavouring and colouring if required
Flavour use
- **1** 1 banana or
- **2** few drops vanilla or any essence
- **3** 2 tsp powdered coffee
- **4** 3 tsp chocolate powder
- **5** 2 tsp any concentrated fruit syrup, e.g. Ribena
- **6** 2 tbsp canned or stewed fruit
- **7** 2 tbsp fresh berries (add extra sugar and strain)
- **8** 1 tbsp jam
- **9** 1 small Crunchie bar
- **10** 2 tsp Nesquik in different flavours

to serve: 1–2
time: 5 minutes
liquidizer

1 Place all ingredients in the liquidizer and blend 30 seconds on maximum speed **2** Serve chilled with straws

Malted Milk Drinks (e.g. Horlicks)

⅛ lit/¼ pt water, milk or milk and water

to serve: 1
time: 5 minutes

3–4 heaped tsp of powder or to taste

liquidizer or Horlicks mixer

1 Mix the powder with a little cold water **2** Add the liquid and stir briskly or use a liquidizer or a Horlicks mixer **3** Serve hot or chilled **NB** Horlicks may be served slightly sweetened if liked.

Egg Flip

⅛ lit/¼ pt milk
1 egg
sugar to sweeten
1 dessertsp sherry, brandy or rum

to serve: 1
time: 5 minutes
whisk

1 Heat the milk and pour on to the egg-yolk **2** Add sugar and flavouring **3** Fold in the whisked egg-white **4** Serve hot or cold with straws

Protein drinks, e.g. Complan

3 dessertsp powder
¼ lit/½ pt water

liquidizer (optional)

1 Put the powder into a bowl or jug **2** Add a little of the water and mix to a smooth cream **3** Add the remaining liquid **4** Serve hot or chilled **5** Flavouring may be added, e.g. instant coffee or chocolate, meat extracts, fruit juices, etc.

Golden Punch (non-alcoholic)

¼ lit/½ pt lemon juice } fresh or tinned
¼ lit/½ pt orange juice }
230g/½ lb sugar
¼ lit/½ pt water
4 lit/4 qt ginger-ale chilled
ice-cubes

to serve: 20–30
time: ¾ hour
large bowl or jug
lemon-squeezer
punch-bowl
ladle

1 Put the juices, sugar and water into the large bowl or jug **2** Allow to stand for 30 minutes **3** When ready to serve, add the ginger-ale **4** Serve in a punch-bowl, with ice-cubes, plain or decorated

Wine Punch (Hot)

1 lemon
110g/¼ lb loaf sugar
⅛ lit/¼ pt rum
¼ lit/½ pt tea
1 bottle white wine

to serve: 6–8
time: ½ hour
enamel pan
lemon-squeezer
strainer
punch-bowl
ladle

1 Put thinly-peeled lemon-rind and strained juice into the pan 2 Add sugar, rum, tea and wine 3 Heat gently, but do not boil 4 Strain into a bowl and serve at once

Mulled Wine

¼ lit/½ pt water
6 cloves
small piece cinnamon stick
pinch of ground nutmeg
½ lemon
1 bottle port or claret
sugar

to serve: 7–8
time: 20 minutes
enamel pan
strainer

1 Put spices and water into the pan 2 Add thinly-peeled lemon-rind and bring to the boil and simmer for 10 minutes 3 Strain into a bowl 4 Add the wine, sweeten to taste–add the lemon-juice 5 Reheat without boiling 6 Serve at once in a warmed bowl

Champagne Cup

1 bottle champagne or sparkling white wine
1 bottle soda-water (large)
2 tbsp brandy
1 tbsp maraschino
1 tsp castor sugar
a few strips of lemon-rind

to serve: 10
time: 1 hour 5 minutes

1 Chill the wine and soda-water for one hour 2 When ready to serve, put the lemon-rind, sugar, brandy and maraschino into a jug or bowl 3 Add the wine and soda-water 4 Serve at once

Cider Cup

½ lit/1 pt cider
4 tbsp orange squash
4 tbsp lemon squash
4 tbsp sherry
cucumber
crushed mint
ice

to serve: 4
time: 10 minutes plus chilling time

1 Mix all the ingredients and allow to stand for 15 minutes 2 Chill thoroughly 3 Serve with a little cucumber and mint, adding some ice-blocks just before serving in a bowl or jug

Claret Cup

1 bottle claret
rind of 1 lemon

to serve: 8
time: 1 hour 10 minutes

4 tbsp sherry
2 tbsp brandy
2 tbsp liqueur—Cointreau, Orange Curaçao, Cherry Brandy, Apricot Brandy, etc.
a few strips of cucumber-rind
spriggs of balm, borage or verbena (optional)
1 large bottle soda-water
sugar to sweeten
ice-cubes

1 Put claret, lemon-rind and sugar into a bowl and chill for at least one hour 2 Add all the other ingredients 3 Serve very cold in a jug or bowl, adding a few ice-cubes

17
Pastry

Suet-crust Pastry

110g/¼ lb flour
1 tsp baking-powder
pinch salt
45g/1½ oz beef or prepared suet
cold water

time: 10 minutes
sieve

1 Sieve the flour, baking-powder and salt 2 Add the prepared suet or the beef suet shredded in a little of the flour 3 Mix to a moderately stiff dough 4 Roll out and use as required

Uses
Fruit puddings, meat puddings, suet rolls steamed or baked, dumplings.

Short-crust Pastry

Proportions– ½ fat to flour
110g/¼ lb flour
pinch salt
30g/1 oz lard
30g/1 oz margarine or butter
cold water

time: 10 minutes
sieve
oven No. 6 or 205 °C/400 °F

1 Sieve the flour and salt 2 Add fats, cut up, rub in with the finger-tips, lifting well, till like breadcrumbs 3 Mix with a *little* cold water to a stiff dough 4 Knead till smooth on a lightly-floured table. Use as required

Biscuit-crust Pastry

110g/¼ lb flour
75g/2½ oz margarine or butter
15g/½ oz castor sugar
¼– ⅓ egg

time: by hand, 15 minutes; by machine, 10 minutes
sieve
electric mixer (optional)
oven No. 4 or 180 °C/355 °F

1 Sieve the flour—add the sugar **2** Rub in the fat firmly **3** Mix to a stiff dough with the egg **4** Knead. Use as required
Or—place all ingredients in a mixer, and blend using the beater.

Uses
Mince-pies, flans, fruit-pies, jam-tarts, etc.

NB For savoury uses substitute ½ oz sugar with 15g/½ oz Parmesan cheese or 45g/1½ oz Cheddar.

Cheese Pastry

30g/1 oz flour
30g/1 oz butter or margarine
15g/½ oz Cheddar cheese
15g/½ oz Parmesan cheese
salt, pepper, mustard
1 tsp egg

time: 15 minutes
grater
sieve
oven No. 4 or 180 °C/355 °F

1 Grate the cheese finely **2** Mix with sieved flour and seasonings **3** Put on to the table and *chop* in the fat **4** Return to the basin, add the egg and knead into a stiff dough. Use as required

Uses
Savoury flans, cocktail savouries, etc.

Flaky Pastry

110g/¼ lb flour
pinch salt
45g/1½ oz margarine or butter
45g/1½ oz lard
1 tsp lemon-juice
cold water

time: 45 minutes
sieve
oven No. 7 or 220 °C/425 °F

1 Sieve the flour and salt **2** Mix the fats on a plate and divide into 4 **3** Rub one quarter into the flour **4** Mix to a soft dough with water and lemon-juice **5** Roll into an oblong, flake one quarter of the fat in small pieces over ⅔ of the pastry, fold in 3 with alternate layers of pastry and fat. Seal the edges and turn one quarter **6** Repeat No. 5 twice more **7** Roll and fold twice more without the addition of fat
NB Relax the pastry in a cool place between rollings.

Uses
As for rough puff pastry (page 229).

Rough Puff Pastry

230g/½ lb strong flour
pinch salt
90g/6 oz butter
lemon-juice
cold water

time: 1–1¼ hours
sieve
tea-cloth
oven No. 7 or 220 °C/425 °F

1 Sieve the flour and salt **2** Add a few drops of lemon-juice and mix to a soft dough with cold water **3** Knead until smooth and elastic **4** Shape the butter in the corner of the floured cloth **5** Roll out the dough into an oblong and place butter in centre **6** Fold the dough over in three, seal edges, and turn one ¼ turn **7** Roll out as thinly as possible **8** Fold ends to the centre and fold in half again, seal the edges–turn–roll and fold 5 times in all **9** Roll out and use as required
NB Allow pastry to relax 10–20 minutes between rollings

Uses
Meat pies, meat patties, mince pies, banbury cakes, bouchées, vol-au-vent, jam puffs, etc.

Puff Pastry

Make as for rough puff, using equal quantities of butter and flour. Roll 7 times in all. Use as for rough puff.

Vol-au-Vent Case

230g/½ lb puff pastry (page 229)
or frozen puff pastry
egg glaze

time: 35 minutes
baking-tray
large oval-cutter and smaller oval-cutter
or large and smaller round-cutter
oven No. 7 or 220 °C/425 °F

1 Roll out the pastry 5 mm/¼ in. thick **2** Cut with the larger cutter **3** Mark with the smaller cutter **4** Glaze with egg **5** Bake 20 minutes, remove the top, remove any uncooked pastry, return to the oven to dry

Bouchée Cases

time: 30 minutes
50 mm/2 in. round-cutter
25 mm/1 in. round-cutter
baking-tray
oven No. 7 or 220 °C/425 °F

1 Roll out pastry very thinly **2** Cut into rounds with the larger cutter **3** Mark with the smaller cutter **4** Glaze with egg **5** Bake 10–15 minutes–remove the top and dry as for vol-au-vent **6** Fill with any savoury mixture

Savoury Fillings

To a $\frac{1}{8}$ lit/¼ pt of coating sauce, e.g.
white, tomato (page 99),
espagnole (page 92), etc.
add–
60g/2 oz grated cheese
110g/4 oz sautéed mushrooms
60g/2 oz shrimps or prawns
60g/2 oz cooked ham or chicken, etc.

Sweet Fillings

Omit glazing, dredge with icing-sugar after cooling, add: jam, lemon curd, fruit and cream.

Hot-water Crust

110g/¼ lb flour
salt
30g/1 oz lard
4 tbsp milk and water

time: 10–15 minutes
sieve
pan of hot water

1 Sieve the flour and salt **2** Melt the lard in the liquid, boil **3** Pour on to the flour **4** Mix well with a wooden spoon **5** Knead on a floured table until smooth **6** Put into a mixing bowl over a pan of hot water until required

Uses
Raised pies of all kinds.

Choux Pastry

75g/2½ oz strong flour
60g/2 oz butter
2 eggs
$\frac{1}{8}$ lit/¼ pt water

time: 15 minutes
sieve
oven No. 7 or 220 °C/425 °F

1 Put the butter and water into a small pan and bring to the boil **2** Shoot in the sieved flour and remove from the heat **3** Beat until the mixture leaves the sides of the pan **4** Add eggs one at a time, beating well between each **5** Use as required

Uses
1 Eclairs (page 252)
2 Chocolate Profiteroles (page 161)

3 Beignets Soufflé (page 162)
4 Gâteau St. Honoré (page 162)
5 Savoury éclairs (page 207)
6 Cheese aigrettes (page 207)

Cassolette Pastry

Basic Proportion–¼ fat to flour
110g/¼ lb flour
30g/1 oz butter
1 tsp lemon juice
1 dessertsp egg
approx. 2 tbsp water

time: 15 minutes
sieve

1 Sieve the flour and rub in the fat 2 Add the liquid and mix to a stiff dough 3 Knead until smooth 4 Use as required

Uses
Filled tartlets, sweet and savoury.

Almond Pastry (Pâté frolle)

110g/¼ lb flour
90g/3 oz butter
45g/1½ oz castor sugar
½ egg
45g/1½ oz ground almonds
vanilla essence

time: 40 minutes
sieve
electric mixer
oven No. 4 or 180 °C/355 °F

1 Sieve the flour 2 Put all the ingredients into a bowl 3 Mix in the mixer at slow speed until the dough is formed 4 Cool for ½ hour before using

Uses
For flans and tartlets, or as a base for petits fours.

Strudel Paste

230g/½ lb flour
pinch salt
1 small egg
⅛ lit/¼ pt tepid water
1 tbsp oil
oil for brushing
60g/2 oz melted butter

sieve
tea-cloth
oven No. 5 or 190 °C/380 °F

1 Beat the egg with the water and add the oil 2 Sieve the flour and salt and add the liquid to make a soft dough adding more water if necessary 3 Beat or knead until smooth and elastic 4 Put into a bowl, cover and leave in a warm place for 15 minutes 5 Roll out the pastry as thinly as

possible **6** Lift on to the floured cloth, brush with oil and leave for 10–15 minutes **7** Pull gently from all sides until the paste is as thin as paper **8** Brush with melted butter. The paste is now ready for filling

Uses

Apple strudel is the best known but other uses may include savoury ones.

18
Scone mixtures and baking-powder breads

Scones

110g/¼ lb flour
30g/1 oz margarine or butter
pinch of salt
1 tsp baking-powder
4 tbsp sour milk

makes: 7
time: 20 minutes
sieve
greased and floured baking-tray
50 mm/2 in. cutter
oven No. 8 or 230 °C/445 °F

1 Sieve the flour, salt, and baking-powder and rub in the fat **2** Add the milk to make a soft dough—knead lightly **3** Roll or press out to 10 mm/½ in. thickness **4** Cut into rounds **5** Bake 6–7 minutes

NB Sour milk improves the flavour and lightness, but fresh milk may be used.

Variations

1 Wholemeal scones
60g/2 oz wholemeal flour
60g/2 oz white flour

2 Cheese scones
Add 45g/1½ oz grated cheese

3 Fruit scones
Add 30g/1 oz currants or sultanas
1 tsp sugar

4 Potato scones
Use 60g/2 oz freshly cooked, sieved potato instead of 60g/2 oz flour and slightly less liquid

Baking-powder Bread

230g/½ lb flour
60g/2 oz lard or margarine
level tsp salt

time: ½ hour
sieve
150 mm/6 in. cake-tin

⅛ lit/¼ pt sour milk
1½ tsp baking powder

greased and floured
oven No. 7 or 220 °C/425 °F

1 Sieve the flour, salt and baking-powder and rub in the fat **2** Add the milk and mix into a soft dough **3** Put into the tin and bake 10–15 minutes

Variation in shape

1 Shape into small rolls and bake 6–8 minutes.
2 Make into a cottage loaf and bake 10–15 minutes.

Dropped Scones

230g/½ lb flour
level tsp salt
2 tsp baking-powder
90g/3 oz castor sugar
1 tbsp oil
1 egg
¼ lit/½ pt milk

to serve: 8
time: ½ hour
sieve
hot greased girdle
tea-cloth

1 Sieve the flour, salt and baking-powder–add the sugar **2** Make a well and add the beaten egg, oil and milk, and beat to a thick cream **3** Pour from a tablespoon on to the girdle and cook till the mixture has set and the underside is golden brown **4** Turn with a knife and cook the second side **5** Cool in the folded tea-towel **6** Spread with butter and serve on a fancy paper on a round plate

Malt Bread (without Yeast)

230g/½ lb self-raising flour
1 level tsp bicarbonate of soda
60g/2 oz butter or margarine
2 tbsp golden syrup
2 tbsp malt extract
⅛ lit/¼ pt milk
1 egg
60g/2 oz sultanas or raisins

time: 1 hour
sieve
230g/½ lb bread-tin (greased and and floured)
oven No. 6 or 205 °C/400 °F

1 Sieve the flour and soda, rub in the fat and add the fruit **2** Melt the syrup and malt with the milk **3** Add to the dry ingredients with the beaten egg **4** Mix well and put into the tin **5** Bake 40–50 minutes, reducing the heat the last 20 minutes if necessary

Date and Walnut Loaf

230g/½ lb flour
pinch of salt
110g/¼ lb chopped dates
60g/2 oz sugar
60g/2 oz margarine or butter
½ egg
30g/1 oz chopped walnuts

time: 45 minutes
sieve
greased and floured 230g/½ lb bread-tin
oven No. 6 or 205 °C/400 °F

1 level tsp bicarbonate of soda
½ tsp vanilla essence
6 tbsp boiling water

1 Sieve the flour and salt **2** Put the chopped dates, sugar, fat and soda into a bowl and pour on the boiling water **3** Add egg, flour, walnuts and essence and beat well **4** Put into the tin **5** Bake about 1 hour reducing heat to No. 4 or 180 °C/355 °F after 30 minutes

Variations

1 Use chopped nuts and raisins or sultanas.
2 Use chopped peel and raisins or sultanas.
3 Use chopped nuts and mashed banana.

Mincemeat Loaf

230g/½ lb plain scone mixture (page 233)
230g/½ lb mincemeat

time: 1 hour
230g/½ lb greased and floured bread-tin
sieve
oven No. 5 or 190 °C/380 °F

1 Sieve the flour, salt and baking-powder **2** Rub in the fat and add the mincemeat **3** Mix using approximately half the liquid **4** Put into the tin and bake for ¾ hour **5** Cool and serve sliced, spread with butter

Girdle Scones

110g/¼ lb flour
30g/1 oz margarine or butter
pinch of salt
¼ tsp bicarbonate of soda
½ tsp cream of tartar
½ tsp castor sugar
4 tbsp milk

to serve: 7
time: 20 minutes
sieve
50 mm/2 in. plain round-cutter
a heated and greased girdle or hot-plate or heavy frying-pan

1 Sieve the dry ingredients rub in the fat and add the sugar **2** Mix to a soft dough, knead lightly **3** Roll out 5 mm/¼ in. thick **4** Cut into rounds or triangles **5** Cook on the girdle for 5 minutes until golden brown **6** Turn and cook the other side for about 5 minutes **7** When cool, split and butter

NB For fruit scones, add 30g/1 oz currants or sultanas.

Potato Scones

230g/½ lb cooked potatoes
30g/2 oz butter or margarine
30g/1 oz flour
¼ tsp salt
½ tsp baking powder

makes: 10–12
time: ½ hour
sieve
60 mm/2½ in. round cutter
oven No. 7 or 220 °C/425 °F or a greased girdle

1 Dry and mash the potatoes–beat in the fat **2** Sieve the flour, salt and baking-powder and add to the potatoes **3** Knead and roll out to 5 mm/¼ in. thickness–cut **4** Bake 8–10 minutes or cook on the hot girdle for about 15 minutes, turning frequently

19
Cakes

Rubbed-in Mixture

230g/½ lb flour
pinch salt
90g/3 oz butter or margarine
90g/3 oz sugar
1 egg
2 tsp baking-powder
milk to mix

time: 15 minutes
sieve

1 Sieve the flour, salt and baking-powder 2 Rub in the fat—add the sugar 3 Mix to the required consistency with egg and milk

Fruit Cake (Rubbed-in Mixture)

230g/½ lb cake flour
90g/3 oz fat (butter or margarine)
90g/3 oz castor sugar
1 egg
2 tsp baking-powder
milk to mix
170g/6 oz currants and sultanas
30g/1 oz peel

time: 1¼ hours
sieve
150 mm/6 in. lined tin
oven No. 4 or 180 °C/350 °F

1 Make rubbed-in mixture 2 Add the fruit and peel 3 Mix to a dropping consistency with egg and milk 4 Put into prepared tin and sprinkle with castor sugar 5 Bake 40–50 minutes
For alternative flavours see Recipe for Rock Cakes (page 236).

Rock Cakes

110g/¼ lb basic rubbed-in mixture (page 236)
45g/1½ oz currants
15g/½ oz peel
pinch mixed spice (sieved with flour)

makes: 6–8
time: 25 minutes
sieve
greased and floured baking-tray
oven No. 6 or 205 °C/400 °F

1 Add cleaned fruit and peel to the rubbed-in mixture—add the egg
2 Add the milk and mix to a stiff consistency 3 Divide into 6–8 and

put on to the tray in rough heaps **4** Bake for 15 minutes–cool **5** Serve on plate on a fancy paper

Alternative flavourings

45g/1½ oz cherries
45g/1½ oz sultanas
45g/1½ oz chopped dates
30g/1 oz coconut
lemon-rind
30g/1 oz chocolate powder
{ 30g/1 oz crystallized ginger
{ 1 tsp ground ginger
30g/1 oz chopped walnuts

Raspberry Buns

110g/¼ lb basic rubbed-in mixture (page 236)
raspberry jam
castor sugar
milk

makes: 6
time: ½ hour
sieve
greased and floured baking-tray
castor-sugar dredger
oven No. 6 or 205 °C/400 °F

1 Make the rubbed-in mixture **2** Mix with egg and milk to a moderately stiff dough that can be handled **3** Divide into 6 and knead into rounds –flatten **4** Place ½ tsp jam in the centre and knead the dough over the jam. Turn over **5** Put on to the tray–brush with milk–sprinkle with castor sugar **6** Bake 15 minutes till set and pale golden brown–cool **7** Serve on a plate with a fancy paper

Jam Turnovers

110g/¼ lb short-crust pastry flaky or rough puff (pages 227, 228, 229) or frozen pastry
jam

makes: 6–8
time: 20 minutes
greased and floured baking-tray
castor-sugar dredger
oven No. 6 or 205 °C/400 °F

1 Roll the pastry out very thinly–turn over **2** Cut into rounds or squares **3** Place the jam in the centre and damp the edges–fold into triangles or oblongs **4** Brush with cold water–sprinkle with castor sugar–bake 10 minutes **5** Cool and serve on a round plate with a fancy paper

NB Sliced apple, sweetened, may be used instead of jam. Cook for 15 minutes.

Jam Tarts

110g/¼ lb short-crust pastry (page 227) or frozen pastry
jam

makes: 12
time: ½ hour
fluted cutter
bun-tins or patty-tins
oven No. 6 or 205 °C/400 °F

1 Roll out the pastry very thinly–turn over **2** Cut in rounds with the cutter and press into the tins–prick **3** Fill with jam and bake 10 minutes

4 Cool and serve on a round plate with a fancy paper
NB For lemon curd, bake cases 'blind' and well pricked for about 7 minutes. Fill when cold and serve as for jam tarts.

Banbury Cakes

110g/¼ lb rough puff or flaky pastry (page 229) or frozen pastry
Filling
30g/1 oz butter or margarine
30g/1 oz castor sugar
¼ egg
15g/½ oz cake-crumbs
30g/1 oz peel
60g/2 oz currants
¼ tsp spice

makes: 6–8
time: 40 minutes
baking-tray
100 mm/4 in. plain cutter
castor-sugar dredger
oven No. 7 or 220 °C/425 °F

1 Cream the fat and sugar and add the egg **2** Add remaining prepared ingredients **3** Roll the pastry out thinly, turn over and cut into rounds **4** Put 1 tsp of the filling on to each round, damp and draw up edges, turn over **5** Roll into an oval, score diagonally **6** Brush with water and sprinkle with sugar **7** Bake for 20 minutes–cool **8** Serve as for eccles cakes (page 238)
NB Egg-white or whole-egg may be used for brushing, instead of water.

Eccles Cakes

110g/¼ lb rough puff or flaky pastry (page 229) or frozen pastry
Filling
30g/1 oz margarine or butter
30g/1 oz moist brown sugar
15g/½ oz chopped peel
45g/1½ oz currants

makes: 6–8
time: 40 minutes
baking-tray
100 mm/4 in. plain cutter
castor-sugar dredger
oven No. 7 or 220 °C/425 °F

1 Melt or cream the fat **2** Add the other ingredients **3** Roll out the pastry very thinly, turn over and cut into rounds **4** Put a good teaspoonful of the filling on to each round **5** Damp the edges and draw together firmly **6** Turn over, and roll into circles till the fruit can just be seen through the pastry **7** Score diagonally **8** Brush with egg or water and dredge with castor sugar **9** Put on to the tray and allow to relax for 10 minutes **10** Bake just above the centre of the oven for 15–20 minutes **11** Cool and serve on a plate on a fancy paper

Gingerbread

170g/6 oz flour
110g/¼ lb treacle (or syrup or honey or a mixture)
60g/2 oz brown sugar
60g/2 oz margarine
1 egg

time: 1½ hours
sieve
greased and lined Yorkshire-pudding tin 225 x 150 mm/9 x 6 in., or 150 mm/6 in. square tin

1 tsp ground ginger
1 level tsp bicarbonate of soda
⅛ lit/¼ pt milk (scant)
Additions (optional)
30g/1 oz sultanas
30g/1 oz crystallized ginger
30g/1 oz glacé cherries
15g/½ oz mixed peel
15g/½ oz split almonds for top

oven No. 3 or 180 °C/335 °F

1 Sieve the flour, ginger and soda 2 Prepare the fruit–add to the flour 3 Melt the margarine, sugar and treacle. *Do not boil!* 4 Beat the egg, add to the dry ingredients with the melted mixture and milk to make a soft batterlike consistency. Mix well 5 Pour into the prepared tin and arrange the almonds on top 6 Bake for 1 hour in the middle of the oven –cool 7 Store for one week before cutting 8 Serve whole or cut into squares, on a fancy paper

Yorkshire Parkin

230g/½ lb plain flour
pinch salt
1 tsp bicarbonate of soda
30g/1 oz mixed spice
110g/¼ lb coarse oatmeal
170g/6 oz moist sugar
110g/¼ lb butter or margarine
110g/¼ lb treacle
⅛ lit/¼ pt milk

makes: 24 pieces
time: 1¼ hours
sieve
greased and lined oblong tin 300 x 200 mm/12 x 8 in.
oven No. 3 or 180 °C/335 °F

1 Sieve the flour, salt, soda and spice 2 Add the oatmeal and mix thoroughly 3 Melt the sugar, treacle and fat and add to the dry ingredients with the milk–mix well 4 Spread evenly in the tin and bake in the middle of the oven 45–50 minutes 5 Cool–keep for several days before using 6 Cut into squares and serve on a plate with a fancy paper

Basic Whisked Sponge Mixture

1 egg
30g/1 oz flour
30g/1 oz castor sugar

time: 10 minutes
whisk or mixer
sieve

1 Whisk eggs and sugar until thick and light (by hand or in an electric mixer at full speed 2 Fold in the sieved flour 3 Use as required

Whisked Sponge Sandwich

2 eggs
60g/2 oz castor sugar
60g/2 oz flour

time: ½ hour plus cooling time
greased and lined tin 150 mm/6 in.
oven No. 4 or 180 °C/355 °F

1 Make the whisked mixture (page 239) 2 Pour into the prepared tin 3 Bake for 20 minutes till elastic to the touch 4 Turn out and cool 5 Split and fill as desired

Iced Sponge

2 egg whisked sponge (page 239)
170g/6 oz sieved icing-sugar
water
flavouring
colouring
} glacé icing (page 258)
filling (page 254)
decorations

time: ½ hour
cooling-tray

1 Cut the cake in half and spread with the chosen filling 2 Place on the cooling-tray over a plate 3 Coat with the glacé icing over the top and sides 4 Decorate before the icing has set

NB Butter icing (page 254) may be used instead of glacé icing to coat the cake, or as piped decoration.

Fruit Basket

2 egg whisked sponge baked in a
  150 mm/6 in. lined tin (page 239)
apricot jam
cake crumbs
  or chopped almonds
  or coconut
  or chopped walnuts
  or crushed praline (page 256)
230g/½ lb strawberries, raspberries
  tinned or frozen fruit
⅛ lit/¼ pt cream
angelica

to serve: 3–4
time: ½ hour
100 mm/4 in. round-cutter
nylon bag
No. 8 vegetable-forcer

1 Cut a round from the centre of the cake to the depth of half the cake 2 Brush the cake and lid with the hot jam and press on nuts or crumbs 3 Fill the centre with sweetened strawberries, saving a few for decoration –cover with sweetened, whipped cream 4 Put on the lid and decorate with piped cream and strawberries 5 Fix an angelica handle 6 Serve on a plate with fancy paper

NB 1 The strawberries and cream may be mixed before filling.
2 1 tbsp sherry added to the strawberries improves the flavour.

Sponge Fingers (1)

1 egg
30g/1 oz flour
30g/1 oz castor sugar

makes: approximately 9
time: ½ hour
greased sponge-finger tins dredged with equal quantities of flour and castor sugar
castor-sugar dredger
oven No. 4 or 180 °C/355 °F

1 Make the whisked mixture (page 239) 2 Put into the tins from a metal spoon 3 Dredge with castor sugar and bake for 7–10 minutes 4 Cool for 5 minutes–knock out of the tins. Use as required

Uses

1 Serve with fools or cold sweets.
2 Use to line charlotte-moulds.
3 Use as a basis for trifles or fruit snows.
4 Use sandwiched together with jam and/or cream.
5 Use iced or dipped in chocolate.

Sponge Fingers (2)

75g/2½ oz flour
pinch salt
15g/½ oz cornflour
75g/2½ oz castor sugar
2 eggs (separated)
vanilla essence

makes: 20
time: 45 minutes
sieve
whisk
greased baking-tray
nylon bag
10 mm/½ in. plain-forcer
castor-sugar dredger
oven No. 4 or 180 °C/355 °F

1 Whisk the egg whites stiffly, add the sugar and whisk again 2 Fold in the beaten egg-yolks 3 Fold in the sieved flour 4 Put the mixture into the forcing-bag and pipe in 75 mm/3 in. lengths on the tray 5 Dredge with castor sugar 6 Bake for 10 to 20 minutes. Use as for sponge fingers (1)

Swiss Roll

60g/2 oz flour
60g/2 oz castor sugar
2 eggs
jam

time: ½ hour
whisk or electric mixer
175 x 275 mm/6 x 11 in. lined tin
castor-sugar dredger
oven No. 6 or 205 °C/400 °F

1 Make the whisked mixture (page 239) 2 Pour into the tin–tip to level 3 Bake for 12 minutes till the cake feels elastic when touched 4 Turn on to a lightly-floured paper 5 Trim the sides and spread with jam–make a dent with the back of a knife 10 mm/½ in from the top or bottom 6 Roll from the dent pulling the paper–finishing with the end underneath 7 Cool–dredge with castor sugar

For a cream or lemon-curd filling–

1 Allow the sponge to cool on the paper.
2 Spread with the filling and then proceed as for jam.

Yule-log

1 Swiss roll (page 241)
90g/3 oz butter
170g/6 oz icing sugar
Divide– ⅓ flavour coffee, ⅔ flavour chocolate

time: ½ hour
nylon bag
No. 8 icing-forcer
icing-sugar dredger
log-board

1 Coat the top and sides of the roll with chocolate cream. Mark with a fork to represent bark 2 Pipe the ends with coffee cream 3 Dust with icing sugar and decorate with holly, etc.

Creaming Mixture

Basic recipe

The weight of one egg in fat, flour and sugar
110g/¼ lb flour
110g/¼ lb castor sugar
110g/¼ lb margarine or butter
2 eggs
¾ tsp baking-powder
2 tbsp cold water

time: 20 minutes
sieve

1 Beat the fat–add the sugar and cream till light and fluffy 2 Beat in the beaten eggs, a little at a time 3 Add the sieved flour and baking-powder (all at once) and cold water. *Fold* in with a metal spoon or palette-knife. The mixture should be a soft dropping consistency. Use as required

Victoria Sandwich

2 egg quantity creaming mixture (page 242)
jam

time: 1¼ hours
2 150 mm/6 in. greased and floured tins
2 greaseproof discs
castor/or icing-sugar dredger
oven No. 5 or 190 °C/380 °F

1 Make the creamed mixture (page 242) 2 Divide between the tins–smooth 3 Bake for 20 minutes till firm 4 Remove from the tins and cool 5 Sandwich together with the jam 6 Dust with castor or icing-sugar 7 Serve on a plate with a fancy paper

Variations

1 *Chocolate Sandwich*

Add 60g/2 oz chocolate powder, dissolve in the cold water after adding the egg.

2 *Coffee Sandwich or Coffee Walnut Sandwich*

(a) Add 3 tsp instant coffee dissolved in the cold water after adding the eggs.

(b) Add 60g/2 oz chopped walnuts to the above.

3 *Mocha Sandwich*

(a) Add 30g/1 oz chocolate powder and 1 tsp instant coffee. Dissolve the chocolate in the water and add the coffee. Add to the mixture after the eggs.

4 *Fruit and cream gâteau*

1 Fill the sandwich with 110g/¼ lb fruit and 4 tbsp whipped cream
2 Dredge with icing-sugar.

Using ⅛ lit/¼ pt cream

1 Sandwich the cake with 4 tbsp whipped cream.
2 Spread sides with cream and coat with chopped nuts.
3 Pipe the top with the remaining cream and decorate with fruit or nuts.

Orange Sandwich Cake

2 egg quantity creamed mixture (page 242)
grated rind of ½ orange
Filling: see Fillings (pages 254, 255)
Glacé icing: see Icing (page 258)

time: 1½ hours
2 greased and floured tins 15 mm/6 in.
2 greaseproof discs
oven No. 5 or 190 °C/380 °F

1 Make the creaming mixture (page 242)—add the rind 2 Fold in the remaining ingredients 3 Put into the tins and smooth 4 Bake for 20–25 minutes 5 Remove from tins and cool; *or* bake in small cake-cases or greased and floured bun-tins 6 Fill and decorate as for iced sponge (page 240)

Lemon Sandwich

Substitute rind of ½ lemon for orange-rind.

Madeleines

60g/2 oz flour
60g/2 oz margarine
60g/2 oz castor sugar
1 egg
¼ tsp baking powder
1 tbsp cold water
coconut
jam
cherries

makes: 5
time: 1 hour
kitchen roll
5 greased and floured 50 mm/2 in. diameter dariole-moulds
skewer
oven No. 5 or 190 °C/380 °F

1 Make the creaming mixture (page 242) 2 Half fill the moulds 3 Bake for 10–15 minutes—turn out and cool 4 Brush with heated jam whilst holding the cake on a skewer and roll in the coconut 5 Decorate with half a cherry 6 Serve on a round plate on a fancy paper

Queen Cakes

To a 1-egg basic creaming mixture (page 242) add—

30g/1 oz currants
or sultanas
or cherries

makes: 8
time: 45 minutes
greased and floured bun-tins or cake-cases
oven No. 5 or 190 °C/380 °F

1 Make the creamed mixture and add the prepared fruit **2** Put into tins or cases and bake for 15 minutes **3** Turn out and cool **4** Serve on a plate on a fancy paper

Butterfly Cakes

As Queen Cakes (page 243, omit fruit)

makes: 8
time: 1 hour
greased and floured bun-tins or cake-cases
nylon bag—No. 8 icing-forcer
sieve
icing-sugar dredger
oven No. 5 or 190 °C/380 °F

Cream and bake as for queen cakes

Decoration

90g/3 oz sieved icing-sugar
45g/1½ oz butter
½ tsp vanilla essence
or 4 tbsp sweetened and whipped cream

1 When the cakes are cool, cut a round off the top **2** Cut this round in half **3** Pipe a large star on the top of the cake—replace the 2 slices at an angle to look like wings—decorate with small stars **4** Dust with icing-sugar **5** Serve on a round plate on a fancy paper

Madeira Cake

230g/½ lb flour
1 tsp baking-powder
a little finely-grated lemon-rind
150g/5 oz castor sugar
150g/5 oz butter
3 eggs
milk
citron-peel—2 slices

time: 1½ hours plus cooling time
grater
sieve
lined cake-tin 150 mm/6 in.
castor-sugar dredger
oven No. 3 or 170 °C/355 °F

1 Use creaming method (page 242) **2** Put into the tin—place the citron slices on top—dredge with castor sugar—bake for about 1 hour **3** Turn out—cool **4** Serve on a plate on a fancy paper

Alternatives

Cherry cake
Omit peel and lemon—add 110g/4 oz cherries cut in half.

Ginger cake
Add 1 level tsp ground ginger with flour and 90g/3 oz roughly-chopped crystallized ginger.

Dundee Cake

230g/½ lb flour
230g/½ lb butter
230g/½ lb castor sugar
4 eggs
340g/12 oz sultanas and currants
60g/2 oz cherries
60g/2 oz peel
split almonds for the top

time: 2 hours plus cooling time
lined cake-tin 150 mm/6 in.
oven No. 3 or 170 °C/335 °F

1 Use the creaming method (page 242) **2** Mix to a dropping consistency and put into the tin **3** Cover the top generously with the almonds **4** Bake for 1½ hours **5** Turn out and cool **6** Serve on a fancy paper on a plate

Battenburg Cake

2-egg creaming mixture (page 242)
pink colouring
1 tbsp apricot glaze (see Misc. Processes)
230g/½ lb almond paste (page 259)

time: 1½ hours
2 greased and floured square tins 150 mm/6 in.
oven No. 5 or 190 °C/380 °F

1 Put half the mixture into one tin **2** Colour the second half pink and put into the second tin **3** Bake for 15 minutes–turn out and cool **4** Trim the sides–cut into three strips **5** Sandwich together with apricot glaze, arranging the colours alternately **6** Roll out the almond paste the length of the cake and wide enough to wrap around. Brush the paste with the glaze, stand the cake in the centre and press the paste round, joining at the corner **7** Decorate the top with crossed markings and crimp the edges **8** Trim the ends and serve on a fancy paper on a plate

Rich Chocolate Cake

110g/¼ lb chocolate or chocolate powder
90g/3 oz flour
110g/¼ lb butter
30g/1 oz ground rice
90g/3 oz castor sugar
½ tsp baking powder
2 eggs
vanilla
4 tbsp milk

time: 2½ hours
lined tin 140 mm/5½ in. square or 150 mm/6 in. round
oven No. 4 or 180 °C/355 °F

1 Dissolve the chocolate in the milk–cool **2** Cream the butter and sugar until light and beat in the eggs **3** Add the chocolate and vanilla **4** Fold in the dry ingredients and put into the tin **5** Bake for 1¼ hours **6** Turn out, cool. Ice and decorate as liked
This being a very rich mixture does not need a cream filling.

Walnut Cake

150g/5 oz flour
1 tsp baking-powder
60g/2 oz butter
125g/4½ oz castor sugar
2 eggs
vanilla essence
4 tbsp milk or milk and water
30g/1 oz chopped walnuts

time: 1½ hours
sieve
2 150 mm/6 in. sandwich-tins greased and floured
2 greaseproof discs
oven No. 5 or 190 °C/380 °F

1 Chop the walnuts and mix with the sieved flour and baking powder **2** Cream the butter and sugar—add the essence—beat in the eggs **3** Fold in the dry ingredients and milk—put into the tins **4** Bake for about 20 minutes **5** Turn out, cool, sandwich together, and ice

NB This cake can be made with ginger or pineapple instead of walnuts. For pineapple use pineapple essence instead of vanilla. For ginger use ½ tsp ground ginger sieved with the flour and baking powder.

Simnel Cake

110g/¼ lb flour
30g/1 oz rice flour
110g/¼ lb sultanas
60g/2 oz currants
60g/2 oz cherries
30g/1 oz peel
110g/¼ lb butter
110g/¼ lb castor sugar
2 eggs
1 level tsp spice
60g/2 oz almond paste (page 259)

time: 2 hours for cake
to finish: 1 hour
sieve
175 mm/7 in. lined cake-tin
oven No. 3 or 170 °C/335 °F

1 Make the cake using the creaming method (page 242) **2** Put half the mixture into the tin **3** Add the paste in balls **4** Cover with the remaining cake mixture **5** Bake 1¼–1½ hours—turn out and cool

To finish

110g/4 oz almond paste (page 259)
apricot glaze (see Misc. Processes)
90g/3 oz glacé icing (page 258)
egg to glaze
marzipan fruits
Easter eggs
chickens
ribbon
} decorations

greaseproof paper

1 Divide the paste in half. Roll into a round the size of the cake. Cut out centre leaving a 25 mm/1 in. border **2** Divide the remaining paste into 12 and roll into balls **3** Brush the border with apricot jam and put on to the cake **4** Mark the border with crossing lines **5** Brush with the egg—place the balls evenly round the border and brush with egg **6** Put into the oven at No. 6 or 205 °C/400 °F for 10 minutes—or until browned 7 Fill the centre with thick glacé icing 8 Decorate with fruits, etc. 9 Circle the cake with a band of greaseproof paper the width of the ribbon–tie on the ribbon

Genoa Cake

230g/½ lb butter
230g/½ lb moist sugar
4 eggs
290g/10 oz flour
salt
450g/1 lb mixed fruit, e.g. currants and sultanas
110g/¼ lb glacé cherries
90g/3 oz candied peel
60g/2 oz split almonds for the top

time: round, 3½ hours; oblong, 2 hours
sieve
200 mm/8 in. round lined tin or 300 x 200 mm/12 x 8 in. oblong lined tin
oven No. 2 or 155 °C/310 °F

1 Make the cake use the creaming method (page 242) 2 Put into the tin–smooth 3 Place the almonds on top 4 Bake oblong cake 1¼ hours. Bake round cake 2½–3 hours 5 Allow to cool in the tin–turn out

Christmas Cake

230g/½ lb flour
230g/½ lb moist sugar
230g/½ lb butter
4 eggs
450g/1 lb currants
230g/½ lb sultanas
230g/½ lb raisins
110g/¼ lb peel
60g/2 oz cherries
60g/2 oz chopped almonds
60g/2 oz crystallized ginger (optional)
1 tbsp treacle
1 tbsp mixed spice

time: 4½–5 hours
sieve
225 mm/9in. round cake-tin lined or 175 mm/7in. square cake-tin lined brown paper or newspaper
electric mixer
oven No. 2 or 155 °C/310 °F

1 Cream the fat and sugar, add the eggs, and treacle 2 Add the prepared fruit, cherries cut in half, nuts and ginger roughly chopped 3 Add the sieved flour and spice–mix thoroughly 4 Put into the tin lined with 3 layers of paper 5 Smooth with the back of a metal spoon 6 Tie brown paper or newspaper round the outside 7 Bake 1 hour, reduce to No. 1 or 140 °C/290 °F for 1 hour, reduce to No. ½ or 130 °C/265 °F for 1½ hours (total 3½ hours approximately)

NB To make a richer mixture for a

Wedding Cake

Increase fruit as follows–

500g/1¼ lb currants
230g/½ lb sultanas
340g/¾ lb raisins
170g/6 oz peel

to bake: add ½ hour to cooking time

90g/3 oz cherries
90g/3 oz crystallized ginger (optional)
1½ tbsp spice

Quick-method Victoria Sandwich

110g/¼ lb butter
110g/¼ lb castor sugar
2 large eggs
110g/¼ lb flour
1 tsp baking-powder
jam for filling

time: 35 minutes plus cooling time
sieve
2 175 mm/7 in. greased and floured sandwich-tins
2 greaseproof discs
castor- or icing-sugar dredger
oven No. 3 or 180 °C/335 °F

1 Soften the butter 2 Sieve the flour and baking-powder 3 Add all the ingredients and beat by hand or machine 2–3 minutes 4 Put into the tins–bake 25–30 minutes 5 When cool, put together with the jam and dust with castor- or icing-sugar

For variations see Victoria Sandwich (page 242).

Genoese Sponge

4 eggs
110g/¼ lb castor sugar
90g/3 oz flour
90g/3 oz butter

time: sandwich, 50 minutes; oblong, 35 minutes
whisk or electric mixer
sieve
oven No. 5 or 190 °C/380 °F

1 Whisk the eggs and sugar until thick and light (by hand or in an electric mixer at full speed) 2 Fold in the flour quickly and lightly 3 Fold in the warm, skimmed, melted butter 4 Use as required

Uses

Sponge sandwiches Gâteaux of all kinds	2 lined 175 mm/7 in. sandwich tins–bake 25–30 minutes.
Fancies of all kinds Petits Fours	lined Swiss roll tin 200 x 350 mm/8 x 14 in.–bake 12–15 minutes.

Gâteau à l'ananas

1 genoese sandwich (page 248)
crème au beurre mousseline (page 255)
60g/2 oz glacé pineapple
apricot glaze (see Misc. Processes)
pineapple rings
glacé cherries
angelica
chopped nuts

time: 1 hour
2 175 mm/7 in. sandwich-tin greased and floured
200 mm/8 in. cake-board
2 greaseproof discs
oven No. 5 or 180 °C/355 °F

1 Chop the pineapple and add to the crème au beurre 2 Use as a filling for the genoese 3 Brush the sides with apricot glaze and coat with the chopped nuts 4 Glaze the top and decorate with the pineapple

rings, glacé cherries and angelica leaves 5 Brush over with apricot glaze 6 Serve on the cake-board

Swedish Hazel-nut Cake

100g/3½ oz flour
1 tsp baking powder
100g/3½ oz ground hazel-nuts
110g/¼ lb castor sugar
2 eggs
60g/2 oz melted butter
4 tbsp milk or cream
glacé icing (page 258)

time: mould, 1½ hours; tin, 1¾ hours
sieve
whisk or electric mixer
greased and floured border-mould or 175 mm/7 in. lined tin
oven No. 5 or 190 °C/380 °F

1 Whisk the eggs and sugar till thick 2 Mix the flour, baking powder and nuts and fold into eggs and sugar 3 Fold in the cooled melted butter and cream or milk 4 Put into the prepared mould 5 Bake for 30 minutes in the mould or 40–45 minutes in the tin 6 When cool, coat with white glacé icing and decorate with nuts, cherries and angelica 7 Serve on a cake-board or a plate with a fancy paper

Gâteau nougatine

1 genoese sandwich cooked in two 175 mm/7 in. tins
crème au beurre à la meringue (page 254)
nougatine (page 256)
coffee flavouring

time: 1½ hours
small round-cutter
paper bag
No. 8 icing-forcer
200 mm/8 in. cake-board

1 Flavour the crème au beurre with instant coffee (approximately 1½ tsp) 2 Roll out the nougatine and cut out rounds, etc. 3 Crush down the remainder into praline 4 Divide the crème in half 5 To one half add half the praline 6 Use half this mixture to sandwich the two cakes together 7 Spread the remaining praline cream round sides of the cake and coat with the crushed nougatine 8 Spread the top with the crème and pipe with remaining crème 9 Decorate with the cut-out shapes of nougatine 10 Serve on the cake-board

Gâteau aux marrons

1 genoese sandwich (page 248)
½ quantity crème au beurre à la meringue (page 254)
2 tbsp sweetened chestnut purée (tinned)
230g/½ lb fondant or glacé chocolate icing (pages 259, 258)
60g/2 oz almond paste (page 259)
1 dessertsp chocolate powder

time: 1½ hours
200 mm/8 in. cake-board

1 Mix the chestnut purée with the crème au beurre 2 Sandwich the genoese with this mixture 3 Coat with the icing 4 Make three

chestnut leaves from the almond paste—green tinged with yellow or orange **5** Make a cluster of small chestnuts from the remaining paste and dip in the chocolate powder **6** Decorate cake with these **7** Serve on the cake-board

Gâteau champignons

1 genoese sandwich (page 248)	*time:* 2 hours
crème au beurre (page 254)	oiled baking-tray
sponge fingers (page 240)	nylon bag
Meringue mushrooms	small plain forcer
2 egg whites	castor-sugar dredger
110g/¼ lb castor sugar	ribbon
grated chocolate or chocolate powder	200 mm/8 in. cake-board
	oven No. ½ or 130 °C/265 °F

1 Make the meringue mixture and force on to the tray in 'caps' for mushrooms and stalks—keeping them small but in a variety of sizes—dust with sugar and bake until dry and crisp **2** Sandwich the cakes with the crème—coat the sides **3** Press sponge fingers round the sides, keeping the tops rounded and slightly higher than the depth of the cake **4** Pile the 'mushrooms' on top at varying levels, sticking them on with crème **5** Dust with chocolate **6** Tie the ribbon round the cake **7** Serve on the cake-board or plate with a fancy paper **8** A few 'mushrooms' may be arranged round the base

Gâteau carrelé au chocolat

1 genoese sandwich (page 248)	*time:* 1 hour
crème au beurre chocolate flavoured (page 254)	waxed paper
	icing-sugar dredger
110g/¼ lb plain chocolate	200 mm/8 in. cake-board

1 Sandwich the cake together with crème au beurre **2** Melt the chocolate in a basin over a pan of water **3** Pour on to waxed paper or an oiled surface. Mark in squares just before set. Cool thoroughly **4** Spread the top and sides of the cake with chocolate cream and stick on the squares **5** Dust with icing-sugar **6** Serve on the cake-board

NB Bought squares may be used.

Gâteau cone

1 genoese sandwich (page 248)	*time:* 1¼ hours
Filling	whisk
230g/½ lb coffee-flavoured crème au beurre mousseline (page 255) or crème au beurre à la meringue (page 254)	cornet-moulds
	greased baking-tray
	paper bag
	No. 8 icing-forcer
For cornets	200 mm/8 in. cake-board
½ egg-white	oven No. 5 or 205 °C/400 °F
1 tbsp sugar	

1 tbsp ground almonds
1 tbsp softened butter
1 dessertsp flour
1 tsp vanilla sugar
To finish
chopped, browned almonds

To make the cornets

1 Beat the white of egg with the sugar until thick **2** Add the ground almonds, flour and butter **3** Put on the tray in thin rounds about 75 mm/3 in. in diameter–bake 4–5 minutes **4** Remove whilst hot and shape into cones inside the cornet-moulds **5** Sandwich the cakes together with a thick layer of the crème au beurre **6** Coat the sides with a thin layer and cover with the almonds **7** Cover the top with a thin layer **8** Arrange the cones on the top, pointed ends to the centre, and one standing upright in the centre, put the remaining cream into the bag and pipe into the cones and round the edge of the gâteau

Gâteau Charlemagne

1 genoese sandwich (page 248)
crème au beurre mousseline (page 255)
30g/1 oz chopped walnuts
1 tbsp honey
coffee-flavoured glacé or fondant icing (pages 258, 259)
walnuts for decoration

time: 1 hour
paper bag
No. 8 icing-forcer
200 mm/8 in. cake-board

1 Make the crème au beurre and put ¼ of it aside for decoration **2** Add the honey and chopped nuts to the remaining crème **3** Sandwich the cakes with this filling **4** Coat with the icing **5** Decorate with piped crème and walnuts

Gâteau Java

1 genoese sandwich (page 248)
2 tbsp finely chopped peel
orange marmalade
mandarin orange sections dipped (page 270)
glacé or fondant orange icing (pages 258, 259)

time: 1¼ hours plus cooling time
sieve
whisk or electric mixer
2 175 mm/7 in. sandwich-tins
200 mm/8 in. cake-board

1 When making the genoese fold the peel in with the flour–bake and cool **2** Make the dipped sections **3** Sandwich the cakes together with the marmalade **4** Coat with the orange-flavoured and coloured icing **5** Decorate with the dipped orange sections

Gâteau pomme au rhum

genoese sandwich cooked in 2 tins (page 248)

time: 1¼ hours
paper bag

Filling
crème au beurre à la meringue (page 254)
45g/1½ oz glacé cherries soaked in 1½ tsp rum
To finish
3 tbsp chopped nuts
110g/¼ lb apple jelly

No. 8 icing-forcer
No. 3 icing-forcer
200 mm/8 in. cake-board

1 Mix the cherries with 2 tbsp of the filling and sandwich the cakes together **2**. Use half of the remaining filling to coat the sides of the cake–cover with the nuts **3** Pipe a border round the edge of the cake using the last of the filling **4** Melt the apple jelly with 1 tbsp of rum–cool and spread over the top of the cake **5** Put into the refrigerator to get thoroughly cold **6** Pipe 'Rhum' across the top using the No. 3 forcer **7** Serve on the cake-board

Lemon Curd Cake

1 genoese sponge cooked in 2 tins (page 248)
lemon curd (page 256)
royal icing (page 258)

time: 1 hour
paper bag
No. 8 icing-forcer
200 mm/8 in. cake-board

1 Sandwich the cakes together with some of the lemon curd **2** Pipe the icing in stars round the join **3** Put the cake on to the board and pipe round the bottom **4** Pipe round the top edge and divide the top into 4–allow to set **5** Fill the sections with lemon curd

Eclairs

2-egg quantity choux pastry (page 230)
⅛ lit/¼ pt whipped and sweetened cream
110g/¼ lb chocolate or coffee glacé icing (page 258)

time: 1 hour
greased and floured baking-tray
nylon bag
small plain forcer
paper cases
oven No. 7 or 220 °C/425 °F

1 Pipe the choux on to the baking tray in 75 mm/3 in. lengths **2** Bake 30 minutes **3** Take out, slit the sides to let out the steam, and put back into the oven to dry (about 5 minutes) **4** Cool–fill with the cream **5** Coat with the icing **6** Put into the paper cases and serve on a fancy paper

Jap Cakes

170g/6 oz ground almonds
170g/6 oz castor sugar
3 egg-whites
230g/½ lb coffee butter cream (page 254)
60g/2 oz pink glacé icing (page 258)

time: 1½ hours
electric mixer
oiled and floured swiss-roll tin
35 mm/1½ in. plain cutter
cake-cases
oven No. 6 or 205 °C/400 °F

1 Whisk the whites and sugar together stiffly **2** Fold in the ground almonds and spread evenly on the tin **3** Bake until set–about 10 minutes **4** Cut and return to the oven till crisp **5** Remove the rounds–put the cuttings back into the oven until crisp and slightly browned–cool and crush **6** Sandwich together 2 rounds with the butter cream and coat the top and sides–roll in the crumbs **7** Make a dent in centre–fill with a dot of the icing **8** Serve in the cake-cases

NB To make petits fours use a smaller plain cutter.

Gâteau Rolla

4 whites of egg
260g/9 oz castor sugar
crème au beurre à la meringue (page 254)
110g/¼ lb chocolate
60g/2 oz chopped browned nuts
60g/2 oz icing-sugar

time: 3 hours
wet baking-tray
greaseproof paper
electric mixer
strips of paper 10 mm/½ in. wide
nylon bag–paper bag
plain vegetable-forcer
No. 8 icing-forcer
200 mm/8 in. cake-board
castor- and icing-sugar dredgers
oven No. ½ or 130 °C/250 °F

1 Cut four rounds of greaseproof paper 150 mm/6 in. in diameter and put on the tray **2** Whip the whites stiffly and fold in the sugar **3** Pipe evenly on to the round of paper–dredge with sugar **4** Bake 1½ to 2 hours–turn the rounds over, remove the paper and dry thoroughly **5** Make the crème au beurre and add the softened chocolate with the butter **6** Put the meringue rounds together with this filling **7** Coat the sides and cover with the nuts–do the same on the top **8** Arrange the strips of paper on the top in a lattice design **9** Dust thickly with the icing-sugar and remove the paper **10** Pipe round the edge and leave to harden **11** Serve on the cake-board

20

Fillings

Butter Cream

230g/½ lb sieved icing-sugar
110g/¼ lb butter
colouring
flavouring

time: 15 minutes
sieve
electric mixer (optional)

1 Cream the butter and sugar until light and soft **2** Add the flavouring–essences, etc.

Coffee–1 tsp instant coffee in 1 tsp water
Chocolate–60g/2 oz chocolate or chocolate powder.
Heat the powder in 1 tbsp water–cool and add to the butter cream.

Use as required, e.g. for *(a)* For coating a cake, *(b)* as a filling, *(c)* for piping.

For further flavourings see crème au beurre à la meringue (below).

Crème au beurre à la meringue

2 whites of egg
110g/4 oz icing sugar
230g/½ lb butter (unsalted may be used)

time: 25 minutes
sieve
electric mixer

1 Whisk the sieved sugar and egg-whites until very stiff **2** Soften the butter **3** Add to the meringue a little at a time **4** Flavour as required
NB The whisking is best done by machine but if done by hand over hot water, mixture must be quite cold before adding butter.

Flavourings
Add as required–
1 Vanilla essence–1 tsp.
2 Almond essence–½ tsp.
3 Coffee essence–1½ tsp in 2 tsp hot water.
4 Chocolate powder 60g/2 oz dissolved in 2 tbsp water, or melted block

chocolate.

5 Rum—1 tbsp.

6 Liqueurs—to taste.

7 Lemon or orange—rind or juice

8 Marron, 2—3 tbsp chestnut purée—a little rum may also be added.

9 Pineapple—2 tbsp pineapple conserve or chopped glacé pineapple plus rum if liked.

10 Cherry, Strawberry, Raspberry, Red Currant — 2 tbsp of jam plus liqueur if liked

11 Crushed praline—3 tbsp finely crushed praline or nougat (page 256).

12 Chopped nuts—walnuts, hazel nuts, almonds—3 tbsp.

Crème au beurre mousseline

150g/5 oz butter
75g/2½ oz castor sugar
2 yolks of egg
4 tbsp water

time: 25 minutes
electric mixer
thermometer (optional)

1 Put the sugar and water in to a small pan **2** Dissolve and bring to boil and boil until it forms a thread when tested between finger and thumb at 105 °C/220 °F **3** Pour slowly on to egg-yolks and beat until thick and fluffy **4** Add the butter, a little at a time

NB If the mixture should curdle, hold the basin over the water for a minute or two, or add a little more butter. Flavour as for crème au beurre à la meringue (page 254).

Frangipane

60g/2 oz butter
60g/2 oz castor sugar
60g/2 oz ground almonds
1 egg
15g/½ oz flour
vanilla essence, kirsch, lemon-juice or rum

time: 15 minutes

1 Soften the butter **2** Add the sugar and beat together until light and fluffy **3** Beat in the egg—add the flavouring **4** Fold in the flour and ground almonds. Use as required

Pithiviers Filling

35g/1½ oz ground almonds
20g/¾ oz butter
35g/1½ oz castor sugar
½ egg
rum to flavour

time: 15 minutes

1 Cream the butter and sugar and beat in the egg **2** Fold in the ground almonds—add about 1 tbsp of rum. Use as required

Crème Chantilly

⅛ lit/¼ pt cream
1 dessertsp vanilla sugar or
  1 dessertsp sugar and ¼ tsp
  vanilla essence

time: 10 minutes
whisk

1 Whisk all the ingredients in a cold basin until the cream thickens. Use as required

Walnut Filling

1 tbsp apricot jam
1 tbsp ground almonds
15g/½ oz chopped walnuts
lemon-juice

time: 10 minutes

1 Mix these ingredients together and use as a filling for a walnut cake
NB If the jam is rich in fruit–sieve.

Nougat

110g/4 oz castor sugar
90g/3 oz chopped almonds

time: ½ hour
oiled rolling-pin
small cutters

1 Melt the sugar over very gentle heat **2** Continue heating until pale golden brown **3** Add the almonds and mix quickly **4** Turn on to an oiled surface–roll out **5** Cut into rounds or fancy shapes–work quickly as the nougat sets very rapidly

NB 1 Any cuttings may be crushed and used to flavour or decorate cakes.
2 This mixture may also be moulded round a small oiled basin and used as a basket in which to serve petits fours.
3 For use in a filling see crème au beurre à la meringue (page 254).

Lemon Curd

1 lemon
60g/2 oz butter
1 egg
90g/3 oz granulated sugar

time: 15 minutes
grater or zester
strainer
lemon-squeezer
jars
covers
labels

1 Grate the lemon rind thinly–put into a pan with the juice **2** Add the well-beaten egg, sugar and fat **3** Stir over *gentle* heat–bring to the boil–boil 1 minute **4** Strain, pot, cover and label

Orange Filling

2 egg yolks
30g/1 oz butter
15g/½ oz cake-crumbs
110g/¼ lb castor sugar
rind and juice of 1 orange
1 tsp lemon-juice

time: 15 minutes
grater or zester
lemon-squeezer

1 Put the butter, sugar, yolks and grated rind and fruit juices into a pan 2 Stir over gentle heat until the mixture thickens 3 Add the cake-crumbs 4 Allow to cool–use as required

21

Icings

Coffee Glacé Icing

110g/¼ lb sieved icing-sugar
1 level tsp instant coffee
1 tsp hot water
warm water

time: 10 minutes
sieve

1 Dissolve the coffee in the water and add to the sieved icing-sugar **2** Add extra warm water using enough to make a thick coating consistency **3** Beat well and use as required

NB Lemon, orange- or pineapple-juice may be used instead of coffee, and suitably coloured.

Chocolate Glacé Icing

110g/¼ lb sieved icing-sugar
60g/2 oz plain chocolate or chocolate powder
1 tsp oil
2 tbsp water approximately

time: 15 minutes
sieve

1 Boil the chocolate and water **2** Pour on to the sieved icing-sugar **3** Mix, beat well and add the oil **4** Correct the consistency if necessary before using

Royal Icing

450g/1 lb sieved icing-sugar
3–4 tbsp liquid egg albumen or egg-white

time: 20 minutes
sieve
whisk
electric mixer (optional)

1 Put the liquid into a bowl **2** Add the sugar gradually, beating all the time until the peaks are smooth. Use as required

NB Sprinkle 30g/1 oz albumen powder on to ¼ lit/½ pt tepid water–whisk.

Almond Paste

230g/½ lb ground almonds
110g/¼ lb icing-sugar
110g/¼ lb castor sugar
1 tsp vanilla essence
2 tsp lemon-juice
½ tsp almond essence
1 small egg (approximately)

time: 15 minutes
sieve

1 Sieve the sugars and add to the ground almonds—add the flavourings
2 Add enough beaten egg to make a stiff (not dry) paste. Use as required

American Icing

230g/½ lb granulated or demerara sugar
1 white of egg
4 tbsp water

time: ½ hour
sugar-thermometer
whisk

1 Dissolve the sugar in the water 2 Bring to boil and boil quickly to 115 °C/240 °F 3 Whisk the white of egg and add the syrup *very* gradually 4 Continue whisking until thick enough to coat 5 Use very quickly and decorate at once

Fondant Icing (Uncooked)

1 egg-white
450g/1 lb icing-sugar
60g/2 oz liquid glucose

time: 15 minutes
sieve
icing-sugar dredger

1 Sieve the sugar into a bowl 2 Add the softened glucose and egg-white and mix to a stiff paste 3 Turn on to a table dusted with icing-sugar and knead till smooth. Use as required

Modelling Fondant

340g/¾ lb icing-sugar
1 tsp white vegetable fat
1 tsp gelatine
1½ tbsp water

time: 15 minutes
sieve

1 Put the fat, gelatine and water into a small pan over gentle heat
2 Sieve ⅔ of the sugar into a basin and add the cooled mixture—mix
3 Turn on to a table—knead in enough of the remaining sugar (sieved) to make a good moulding consistency. Use as required

Fondant Icing (Boiled)

450g/1 lb loaf or castor sugar
⅛ lit/¼ pt water
90g/3 oz liquid glucose or a pinch of cream of tartar

time: 1.hour
sugar-thermometer
pastry-brush

1 Put the sugar and water in to a pan and heat gently until the sugar has dissolved **2** Bring to boil and boil to 114 °C/238 °F, brushing down the sides of the pan with a wet brush **3** Cool the pan in cold water to stop the cooking **4** Pour the syrup on to an enamel- or plastic-topped table **5** Cool to blood heat, until a skin forms over the surface **6** Using a metal scraper or wooden spatula work the mixture thoroughly, until it becomes thick and white **7** Knead till smooth and shiny. Store in a polythene bag

NB If it becomes too hard to knead, cover with a damp cloth and leave for ½ hour.

22

Petits fours

BISCUIT-CRUST BASE

Magali

110g/¼ lb biscuit-crust (page 227)
crème ganache (page 272)
glacé icing coloured green (page 258)
shredded browned almonds
browned ground almonds

makes: 24
time: 45 minutes
24 small tartlet-tins
oven No. 4 or 180 °C/355 °F

1 Line the tins and bake 'blind' (page 193) for 10 minutes **2** When cold fill with the crème ganache **3** Coat the top with the green glacé icing **4** Decorate the edge with the browned ground almonds **5** Put a thin shred of the browned almonds in the centre

Conversations

110g/¼ lb biscuit-crust or puff pastry (pages 227, 229)
crème frangipane (page 255)
royal icing (page 258)

makes: 24
time: 1 hour
24 small tartlet-tins or boat-moulds
oven No. 4 or 180 °C/355 °F

1 Line the tins with thin biscuit-crust **2** Fill with crème frangipane **3** Cover with a very thin layer of pastry, sealing well **4** Brush the top with royal icing **5** Arrange 4 very narrow strips of pastry criss-cross over the top **6** Bake 12–15 minutes **7** Serve on a plate with a fancy paper

NB They may be made larger and used at tea-time when they should be baked for 20 minutes.

Meringue Boats (Barquettes meringues)

110g/¼ lb biscuit-crust (page 227)
frangipane (page 255)
meringue (page 187)
icing sugar
apricot glaze (see Misc. Processes)

makes: 24
time: 50 minutes
electric mixer (optional)
24 small boat-moulds
paper bags
oven No. 3 or 170 °C/335 °F

1 Line the moulds with thin pastry **2** Fill with frangipane and bake for about 10 minutes **3** Make the meringue by beating 2 egg whites with 110g/¼ lb of castor sugar until stiff enough to keep its shape **4** Cover the cakes, shaping up into a point with a palette knife **5** Pipe each with a scroll of meringue **6** Put back into the oven to set and brown slightly **7** Put apricot glaze into a paper bag and pipe a thin line over the meringue scroll

Fruit Tartlets (Tartlettes aux fruites)

110g/¼ lb biscuit-crust (page 227)
grapes, strawberries
raspberries, cherries
apricot glaze coloured pink (see Misc. Processes)

makes: 24
time: 45 minutes
paper cases
24 small tartlet-tins or boat-moulds
oven No. 4 or 180 °C/355 °F

1 Line the tins with the biscuit-crust and bake 'blind' for 10 minutes **2** When cool, brush the inside carefully with the apricot glaze and leave to set **3** Arrange the fresh fruit in the pastry-cases and again brush with glaze **4** Serve in small paper cases
NB For tea use larger tins.

Almond Tartlets (Tartlettes amandines)

110g/¼ lb biscuit-crust (page 227)
frangipane (page 255)
flaked almonds
apricot glaze coloured pink (see Misc. Processes)
praline (page 331)

makes: 24
time: 45 minutes
24 small tartlet-tins or boat-moulds
oven No. 4 or 180 °C/355 °F

1 Line the tins with the biscuit-crust **2** Fill with the frangipane **3** Sprinkle with the flaked almonds **4** Bake 12–15 minutes **5** Remove from the tins and brush with the apricot glaze **6** Decorate the edge with the praline
NB This may be made in large tins or served as a flan.

Strawberry Cream Cheese Tartlets (Tartlettes fraise à la crème)

110g/¼ lb biscuit-crust (page 227)
60g/2 oz Petit Suisse cream cheese
castor sugar
small ripe strawberries
apricot glaze coloured pink (see Misc. Processes)

makes: 24
time: 40 minutes
24 small tartlet-tins or boat-moulds
sieve
oven No. 4 or 180 °C/355 °F

1 Line the tins with the biscuit-crust and bake 'blind' for 10 minutes **2** Sieve the cream cheese and sweeten to taste **3** When the cases are cool, fill with the cream mixture and cover with the strawberries **4** Brush over with the apricot glaze
NB These may be made in larger tins or in a flan-case.

Marie-Louise Boats (Barquettes Marie-Louise)

110g/¼ lb biscuit-crust (page 227)
60g/2 oz chestnut purée (tinned)
rum

makes: 24
time: 40 minutes
24 small boat-moulds

white fondant or glacé icing (pages 259, 258)
sweet-cases
oven No. 3 or 170 °C/335 °F

1 Line the moulds with the paste and bake 'blind' for 10 minutes **2** When cool, fill with the chestnut purée, sweetened if necessary and flavoured with the rum **3** Glaze with the icing **4** Serve in sweet-cases
NB For tea use larger tins.

Pot-pourri

110g/¼ lb biscuit-crust (page 227)
60g/2 oz cake-crumbs or trimmings
1 dessertsp apricot glaze (see Misc. Processes)
45g/1½ oz chopped glacé fruits
15g/½ oz chopped peel
rum to flavour
fondant or glacé icing (pages 258, 259)
sultanas or raisins

makes: 24
time: 45 minutes
24 small tartlet-tins
sweet-cases
oven No. 3 or 170 °C/335 °F

1 Line the tins with thin pastry and bake 'blind' for 10 minutes **2** Mix the crumbs with the fruit and peel **3** Moisten with the apricot glaze and flavour with the rum **4** Fill the pastry-cases and ice with glacé or fondant icing flavoured with rum **5** Place a sultana in the centre of each **6** Serve in sweet-cases

PUFF PASTRY BASE

Sacristans

trimmings of puff pastry (page 229)
finely-chopped almonds
beaten egg

time: ½ hour
baking tray
icing-sugar dredger
oven No. 7 or 220 °C/425 °F

1 Roll out the pastry thinly and trim to an oblong 175 mm/7 in. wide **2** Brush with the egg and mark a band 100 mm/4 in. wide down the centre **3** Sprinkle this band with the almonds and dredge with icing sugar **4** Cut into strips 25 mm/1 in. wide **5** Twist 2 or 3 times and put on the tray **6** Bake 8–10 minutes **7** Cool and serve on a small plate on a fancy paper

Allumettes glacées

puff pastry (page 229)
royal icing (page 258)

time: ½ hour
baking tray
oven No. 7 or 220 °C/425 °F

1 Roll out the pastry thinly to an oblong 125 mm/5 in. wide **2** Add a good pinch of flour to the icing **3** Trim the edges of the pastry and coat with a thin layer of the icing **4** Cut into 35 mm/1½ in. fingers, put on to the tray and bake for 8–10 minutes **5** Cool and serve on a small plate on a fancy paper

CHOUX PASTRY BASE

Tyroliens

choux pastry (page 230)
pithiviers filling (page 255)
110g/¼ lb sugar
4 tbsp water
oil

time: 45 minutes
greased and floured baking-tray
nylon bag with small plain forcer
thermometer
sweet-cases
oven No. 6 or 205 °C/400 °F

1 Pipe the choux pastry on to the tray in very small balls **2** Bake until crisp 10–15 minutes **3** When cool fill with the pithiviers filling **4** Dissolve the sugar in to water–boil to 130 °C/265 °F **5** Dip the balls quickly in the syrup **6** Drain on an oiled surface **7** Serve in sweet-cases

Japonais

choux pastry (page 230)
crème au beurre mousseline (half quantity) (page 254)
chocolate fondant or glacé icing (pages 259, 258)
hazel-nuts

time: 35 minutes
nylon bag with a small plain forcer
greased and floured baking-tray
sweet-cases
oven No. 6 or 205 °C/400 °F

1 Pipe the choux pastry on to the tray in very small balls **2** Bake until crisp–10–15 minutes **3** When cool, fill with the crème au beurre mousseline **4** Dip into the icing **5** Decorate with a hazel-nut

Salambos

choux pastry (page 230)
⅛ lit/¼ pt crème Chantilly (page 256)
30g/1 oz sugar–2 tbsp water
chopped pistachio nuts or coloured almonds

time: 45 minutes
greased and floured baking-tray
nylon bag and small plain forcer
sweet-cases
thermometer
oven No. 6 or 205 °C/400 °F

1 Pipe the choux pastry in very small balls on to the tray **2** Bake until crisp–about 10–15 minutes **3** When cool fill the balls with crème Chantilly **4** Dissolve the sugar in the water and boil to 105 °C/220 °F **5** Dip each ball in this and at once roll in very finely chopped and dried pistachio nuts **6** Serve in sweet-cases

Suprêmes pralinées

choux pastry (page 230)
beaten egg
almonds
icing-sugar
crème au beurre (page 254)
praline (page 331)

time: 45 minutes
icing sugar dredger
greased and floured baking-tray
nylon bag and small plain forcer
sweet-cases
oven No. 6 or 205 °C/400 °F

1 Pipe the choux pastry on to the tray in very small balls **2** Brush each ball with egg and sprinkle with very finely chopped almonds and icing sugar **3** Bake until crisp–about 10–15 minutes **4** When cool, fill with crème au beurre flavoured with crushed praline 5 Dust with icing-sugar and serve in sweet cases

Carolines

choux pastry (page 230)
⅛ lit/¼ pt cream
110g/¼ lb chocolate or coffee glacé icing (page 258)

time: 40 minutes
greased and floured baking-tray
nylon bag and small plain forcer
sweet-cases
oven No. 6 or 205 °C/400 °F

1 Pipe the choux pastry into tiny éclairs on to the tray (page 252) 2 Bake until crisp—about 15–20 minutes 3 When cool, fill with sweetened and flavoured whipped cream 4 Coat with the icing and when set, serve in sweet-cases

GENOESE BASE

Bichettes

1 slab genoese (page 248)
crème au beurre (page 254)
vanilla essence
chocolate fondant or glacé icing (pages 258, 259)

time: 35 minutes
nylon forcing-bag
15 mm/¾ in. plain forcer
sweet-cases
oven No. 4 or 180 °C/355 °F

1 Cut the genoese into strips 25 mm/1 in. wide 2 Pipe two rolls of crème au beurre side by side down the strips 3 Pipe a third on top 4 Put into the refrigerator to cool and harden 5 Coat with the icing 6 When firm cut into 10 mm/½ in. slices and put into the cases

NB The crème au beurre may be flavoured with strawberry jam.

Printanier

1 slab geonese (page 248)
crème au beurre (page 254)
vanilla
instant coffee
sieved strawberry jam
pink colouring
fondant or glacé icing (pages 259, 258)

time: 45 minutes
sieve
nylon bag 10 mm/½ in. plain forcer
sweet-cases
oven No. 5 or 190 °C/380 °F

1 Trim the slab and cut into 25 mm/1 in strips 2 Divide the crème au beurre into three 3 Flavour *(a)* with vanilla; colour *(b)* with coffee; colour and flavour *(c)* with pink colouring and sieved strawberry jam 4 Pipe 2 rolls side by side in vanilla and coffee 5 Pipe one roll on top in pink 6 Put into the refrigerator to harden 7 Ice with thin white fondant or glacé icing 8 When set, cut on the bias into sections 10 mm/½ in. thick 9 Serve in the cases

NB Almond paste may be used instead of crème au beurre.

Mokatines

genoese slab (page 248)
crème au beurre mousseline au café or au chocolat (page 255)

time: 35 minutes
paper icing-bag with small star-forcer
small cutter (round)

finely-chopped nuts
sweet-cases

1 Cut the genoese into rounds 2 Split and fill with the crème au beurre 3 Coat the top and sides with the same crème 4 Coat with the chopped nuts 5 Pipe a small star in the centre 6 Serve in the sweet-cases

NB If chocolate-flavoured these are called chocolatines.

Mignonnes

genoese slab (page 248)
apricot glaze coloured red (see Misc. Processes)
white fondant or glacé icing (page 258, 259)
flavoured with kirsch or rum

time: 30 minutes
25 mm/1 in. round-cutter
10 mm/½ in. round-cutter
sweet-cases

1 Cut round of genoese with the larger cutter 2 Cut a piece out of the centre of each using the smaller cutter 3 Coat the whole with the red apricot glaze 4 Fill the centre with the icing 5 Serve in the sweet-cases

Marron

genoese slab (page 248)
crème au beurre mousseline (page 255)
2 tbsp chestnut purée (tinned)
rum
finely-chopped nuts
chocolate fondant or glacé icing (pages 259, 258)

time: 40 minutes
small round plain cutter
paper icing-bag
No. 2 writing-forcer
sweet-cases

1 Cut the genoese into rounds or squares 2 Add the chestnut purée to the crème and flavour with the rum 3 Cut the rounds and fill with the crème 4 Coat the sides with crème and then with nuts 5 Cover the top with the chocolate icing 6 Pipe neatly with the crème 7 Serve in the sweet-cases

NB This may be made into a gâteau.

Small Pineapple Fancies (Petits ananas)

genoese slab (page 248)
apricot glaze (see Misc. Processes)
crème au beurre mousseline (page 255)
2 tbsp pineapple jam
rum
finely-chopped nuts
glacé pineapple and cherries

time: 40 minutes
small round-cutter or small oval-cutter
sweet-cases

1 Cut the genoese into rounds or ovals 2 Flavour the crème with the pineapple and rum 3 Split the cake and fill with the flavoured crème 4 Brush the sides with apricot glaze and coat with the nuts 5 Decorate the top with small piece of glacé pineapple and cherries 6 Brush the decoration thickly with apricot glaze 7 Serve in the sweet-cases

Small Cherry Fancies (Cerises)

genoese slab (page 248)
crème au beurre mousseline (page 255)
60g/2 oz chopped glacé or cocktail-cherries
1 tbsp kirsch
chocolate and white fondant icing (page 259)

time: 45 minutes
small plain cutter, round or oval
paper icing-bag and a No. 2 writing-forcer
sweet-cases

1 Cut the genoese into rounds or ovals 2 Add the cherries and kirsch to the crème 3 Split the genoese and fill with the crème 4 Coat with white icing 5 Using the writing-forcer and chocolate icing pipe two stalks on each cake 6 Top these with small rounds to look like cherries 7 Serve in the sweet-cases

Rose Cakes (Rosée)

genoese slab (page 248)
almond paste coloured pink (page 259)
apricot glaze (see Misc. Processes)
cake-crumbs
chopped pistachio nuts or greened almonds or crushed mimosa balls

time: 45 minutes
small plain cutter
5 mm/¼ in. plain forcer
sweet-cases

1 Cut out rounds of genoese 2 Brush the sides with apricot glaze and coat with the cake-crumbs 3 Roll out the paste thinly and cut small rounds using the plain forcer 4 Brush the tops of the cakes with apricot glaze 5 Arrange the rounds of paste overlapping round the edge of the cakes 6 Put the chopped nuts or mimosa balls in the centre 7 Serve in sweet-cases

NB For tea cut with a 50 mm/2 in. cutter.

Greengage Petits Fours

genoese slab (page 248)
green almond paste (page 259)
apricot glaze (see Misc. Processes)
angelica

time: 40 minutes
10 mm/½ in. round-cutter
35 mm/1½ in. round-cutter
sweet-cases
castor-sugar dredger

1 Cut the genoese into rounds, using the smaller cutter 2 Roll out the paste thinly and cut into rounds with the larger cutter, allowing two rounds to each cake 3 Brush these with apricot glaze and place a cake on one and cover with the second 4 Mould into the shape of a greengage 5 Put a 'stalk' of angelica at one end 6 Dust with castor sugar 7 Serve in sweet-cases

NB For tea make larger.

Almond and Cherry Petits Fours

genoese slab (page 248)
almond paste (page 259)
apricot glaze (see Misc. Processes)

time: 40 minutes
small round-cutter
small fluted cutter

cake-crumbs
cocktail-cherries
sweet-cases

1 Cut the genoese into rounds using the plain cutter 2 Brush the sides with apricot glaze and coat with the cake-crumbs 3 Brush the top with glaze and place a cherry in the centre 4 Roll out the paste thinly and cut into rounds using the fluted cutter 5 Place on top of the cakes, cutting a cross in the centre which opens and shows the cherry 6 Serve in sweet-cases

NB For tea make larger.

MISCELLANEOUS

Frangipane Boats (Barquettes frangipane)

frangipane (page 255)
glacé icing (page 258)
glacé or cocktail cherries

makes: 24
time: 45 minutes
24 small boat-moulds
sweet-cases
oven No. 3 or 170 °C/335 °F

1 Grease and flour the moulds 2 Fill with frangipane and bake 10–12 minutes 3 Turn out and when cool, place ½ a cherry on each 4 Coat with a thin white glacé icing 5 Serve in sweet-cases on a plate with a fancy paper

Meringues

2 egg-whites
110g/¼ lb castor sugar
cream or butter cream (page 254)
pistachio nuts

time: 1 hour 20 minutes
castor-sugar dredger
oiled tray
nylon bag and No. 8 vegetable star-forcer
sweet cases
oven No. ¼ or 115 °C/240 °F

1 To make meringues (page 187) 2 Pipe in very small 'stars' or 'fingers' and dredge with castor sugar 3 Bake until crisp–about 30–40 minutes 4 When cool put two together with cream or flavoured butter cream

Fours aux amandes

60g/2 oz ground almonds
45g/1½ oz castor sugar
1 egg-white
vanilla essence
split almonds
glacé cherries
angelica
bun-glaze (page 281)

time: 45 minutes
whisk
baking-tray
rice paper
nylon bag and vegetable star forcer
sweet-cases
oven No. 3 or 170 °C/335 °F

1 Whisk the egg-white until stiff and fold in the almonds, sugar and flavouring 2 Put into the bag and pipe on to the rice-paper in stars, fingers, etc. 3 Decorate each with an almond, or cherry and angelica

4 Bake about 15 minutes 5 Brush with the glaze whilst hot 6 Serve in sweet-cases on a plate with a fancy paper

Muscadins

60g/2 oz ground almonds
75g/2½ oz castor sugar
15g/½ oz flour
2 egg-whites
praline (page 331)
melted plain chocolate

time: 55 minutes
baking-tray and rice-paper sweet-cases
nylon bag and small plain forcer
oven No. 4 or 180 °C/355 °F

1 Fold the ground almonds, sugar and flour into the stiffly beaten egg-whites 2 Pipe on to the rice-paper in very small rounds and bake about 5 minutes–cool 3 Sandwich two together with a little pounded praline 4 Dip in the melted chocolate 5 When quite set put into the sweet-cases

Printaniers au chocolat

110g/¼ lb almond paste (page 259)
green and pink colouring
melted plain chocolate
apricot glaze (see Misc. Processes)

time: 50 minutes
sweet-cases

1 Divide the almond paste into 3 and colour *(a)* pink, *(b)* green, *(c)* leave plain 2 Roll each colour into thin rolls and place 2 side by side and brush with thin apricot glaze 3 Place the third roll on top and glaze 4 When the glaze has cooled, cut on the bias in 25 mm/1 in. pieces and coat with the melted chocolate 5 When quite set, put into the sweet cases

Rum and Almond

110g/¼ lb almond paste (page 259)
30g/1 oz peel
1 tbsp rum
fondant or glacé icing flavoured with rum (pages 259, 258)
citron-peel

time: 50 minutes
sweet-cases

1 Make the almond paste incorporating the finely-chopped peel and the rum 2 Roll into very small balls 3 Coat with thin white fondant or glacé icing 4 Place a small piece of citron-peel on top of each one 5 When set, serve in the sweet-cases

Florentines

60g/2 oz butter (scant weight)
60g/2 oz castor sugar
15g/½ oz glacé cherries
45g/1½ oz chopped almonds
30g/1 oz flaked almonds
45g/1½ oz peel
1 tbsp cream
60g/2 oz plain chocolate

time: 1 hour
greased baking-tray
oven No. 4 or 180 °C/355 °F

1 Melt the butter in a pan, add the sugar and bring slowly to the boil 2 Stir in the chopped cherries, peel and both kinds of almonds 3 Whip the cream until thick and fold into the mixture 4 Leave to cool and set 5 Put on the tray in *(a)* tsps: for tea-time size, *(b)* ½ tsps: for petits-fours size—bake about 7 minutes 6 After 4 minutes take the tray from the oven and pull together the edges of each biscuit with a plain cutter and return to the oven 7 Leave for a few minutes on the tin—remove and cool on the rack 8 Melt the chocolate on a plate over a pan of hot water and work well with a knife 9 When the biscuits are quite cold spread the smooth side with the chocolate and when on the point of setting, mark with a 'comb' or fork in wavy lines

Dipped Fruits (Fruits glacés)

grapes
cherries
sections of oranges or tinned mandarins
strawberries
stuffed dates
Syrup
110g/4 oz granulated sugar
4 tbsp water
1 tsp liquid glucose or a pinch of cream of tartar

time: 30 minutes
oiled cooler
thermometer
sweet-cases

1 Prepare the fruit, making sure it is ripe and quite dry 2 Dissolve the sugar in the water and bring to the boil 3 Add the glucose or cream of tartar 4 Boil rapidly to 135 °C/275 °F 5 Stand the pan in cold water 6 Dip the fruit quickly and put on to the cooler 7 When hard put into the cases
NB Do not move the fruit about in the syrup as this will cause it to granulate quickly

Langues de chat

60g/2 oz butter
60g/2 oz castor sugar
60g/2 oz flour
2 egg-whites

time: ½ hour
sieve
greased and floured baking-tray
nylon bag and 10 mm/½ in. plain forcer
oven No. 6 or 205 °C/400 °F

1 Cream the butter and sugar until light and fluffy 2 Add the unbeaten whites and beat 3 Fold in the sieved flour and put this mixture into the bag 4 Pipe in finger-lengths and bake about 5 minutes 5 Remove from the tray and cool

Palets au chocolat

60g/2 oz ground almonds
45g/1½ oz castor sugar
60g/2 oz plain chocolate

time: 50 minutes
greased and floured baking-tray
35 mm/1½ in. round-/or oval-cutter

1 egg-white
½ tsp vanilla sugar

oven No. 4 or 180 °C/355 °F

1 Mix the almonds, sugar and vanilla sugar and add enough egg-white to make a stiff paste 2 Roll out on a sugared board and cut into rounds or ovals 3 Place on the baking-tray and bake for 10–15 minutes–cool 4 Melt the chocolate in a bowl over hot water and spread a thick layer over half the biscuits 5 Sandwich with the plain ones and serve on a fancy paper

Pâté au berrichon

60g/2 oz castor sugar
60g/2 oz ground almonds
2 egg-whites
½ tsp flour
crème au beurre (page 254)
fondant or glacé icing (pages 259, 258)

time: 1 hour
whisk
baking-tray greased and floured
nylon bag and 10 mm/½ in. plain forcer
oven No. 4 or 180 °C/355 °F

1 Whisk the egg-whites stiffly and fold in the sugar, almonds and flour 2 Pipe on to the baking-tray in rounds the size of a 5 new penny piece or in fingers, 35 mm/1½ in. long 3 Bake 10–15 minutes or until a light golden brown 4 Remove carefully and cool

NB If they have cooked unevenly they may be trimmed with a sharp knife.

To finish

1 Pipe each base according to shape with a coloured and flavoured crème au beurre.
2 Place in the refrigerator until the crème is very firm.
3 Coat with the coloured and flavoured icing.
4 Finish with a suitable decoration on top, or in some cases, under the icing.

Flavourings

Coffee: Coffee icing, crème and decoration of chopped browned almonds.

Chocolate: Chocolate icing, crème decoration of violets and angelica.

Marron: Crème au beurre aux marrons. White icing with rum flavouring. Pipe 'marrons' on top.

Brésiliens: Sandwich two together with crème au beurre mousseline au café. Coat all over with the crème and roll in finely chopped nuts.

Colette

60g/2 oz plain chocolate
crème ganache (see below)

time: 1¼ hours
sweet-cases

pistachio nuts

1 Melt the chocolate over warm water 2 Cool, and dipping in a finger, line the sweet-cases 3 Leave to harden at room temperature 4 Remove the paper and pipe in the crème and decorate with a shred of pistachio nut

Crème ganache

75 g/2½ oz plain chocolate
15g/½ oz butter
4 tbsp cream
rum

1 Break the chocolate into a small pan 2 Add the butter and cream and cook until thick beating all the time 3 Flavour with the rum and cool before using

NB Should the mixture separate, stir in a few drops of cold water.

Chamonix

2 egg-whites
110g/¼ lb castor sugar
chestnut purée (tinned)
grated chocolate
4 tbsp crème Chantilly (page 256)

time: 1¼ hours
grater
whisk
oiled and floured baking-tray
nylon bag and very small plain forcer
castor-sugar dredger
oven No. ½ or 130 °C/265 °F

1 Whisk the egg-whites and sugar until stiff 2 Pipe on to the tray in spirals 25–50 mm/1–2 in. in diameter 3 Dredge with sugar and bake until crisp and dry 4 When cool, pipe chestnut purée round the edge 5 Pipe cream in the centre and dust with the grated chocolate

23
Biscuits

Shortbread Fingers

170g/6 oz flour
110g/¼ lb butter
60g/2 oz castor sugar
15g/½ oz ground rice

to make: 16 biscuits
time: ½ hour
sieve
greased and floured baking-tray
castor-sugar dredger
oven No. 3 or 170 °C/335 °F

1 Sieve the flour and rice—add the sugar 2 Rub in the fat and knead to a pliable dough 3 Roll in to a thick oblong—prick 4 Trim the sides and ends and cut into fingers 75 x 25 mm/2½ x 1 in. 5 Lift with a knife on to the baking-tray without turning over 6 Roll out the trimmings and cut to size 7 Bake for 15 minutes till pale golden brown 8 Dredge with castor sugar—cool 9 Serve on a round plate with fancy paper

Shortbread Slab

370g/13 oz flour
230g/½ lb butter
110g/¼ lb castor sugar
30g/1 oz ground rice

to make: 24–36
time: 1¼ hours
sieve
electric mixer (optional)
greased Swiss-roll tin 300 x 200 mm/ 12 x 8 in.
castor-sugar dredger
oven No. 3 or 170 °C/335 °F

1 Sieve the dry ingredients 2 Rub in the fat and knead to a pliable dough 3 Press into the tin—smooth with a knife and prick all over—dredge with castor sugar 4 Bake for 40 minutes till pale, golden brown 5 Cut whilst hot into 24 or 36 fingers 6 Turn out when cool 7 Serve on a round plate on a fancy paper

Variations

To basic mixture add the following—

1 90g/3 oz finely-chopped walnuts.

2 90g/3 oz finely-chopped crystallized ginger and 1 tsp ground ginger.

3 90g/3 oz finely-chopped peel.

4 90g/3 oz finely-chopped cherries and grated rind of 1 lemon.

Bourbon Biscuits

75g/2½ oz flour
15g/½ oz custard powder
60g/2 oz butter
1 tbsp chocolate powder
30g/1 oz castor sugar
a little egg
water
vanilla essence
chocolate or coffee butter cream (page 254)

to make: 8
time: ½ hour
sieve
greased and floured baking-tray
castor-sugar dredger
oven No. 3 or 170 °C/335 °F

1 Sieve the flour, chocolate powder and custard powder **2** Rub in the fat–add the essence and sugar **3** Mix to a stiff dough with the egg and water **4** Roll very thinly into an oblong–prick and cut into fingers 75 x 25 mm/3 x 1 in. **5** Bake 7–10 minutes. Dredge with castor sugar **6** Cool. Sandwich together with the butter cream **7** Serve on a plate with a fancy paper

Cherry Quickies

90g/3 oz butter
90g/3 oz flour
30g/1 oz icing sugar
½ tsp vanilla essence
glacé cherries

to make: 12–16
time: ½ hour
sieve
greased and floured baking-tray
oven No. 4 or 180 °C/355 °F

1 Cream the fat and sugar–add the essence and the sieved flour **2** Form into walnut-sized balls in the hands **3** Put on the baking-tray and flatten with a fork dipped in flour **4** Place a piece of glacé cherry in the centre **5** Bake 7–10 minutes–cool **6** Serve on a plate with a fancy paper

Melting Moments

110g/¼ lb flour
60g/2 oz castor sugar
60g/2 oz butter
1 egg
rolled oats or corn flakes

to make: 12–16
time: ¾ hour
sieve
greased and floured baking-tray
oven No. 4 or 180 °C/355 °F

1 Cream fat and sugar–beat in the egg **2** Fold in the sieved flour **3** Damp the hands–roll the mixture into balls and toss in oats or flakes **4** Put on to the baking-tray–flatten slightly **5** Bake for 15–20 minutes till golden–cool **6** Serve on a round plate on a fancy paper

Variation
1 tbsp chocolate powder may be added.

Easter Biscuits

110g/¼ lb flour
60g/2 oz butter or margarine
60g/2 oz castor sugar
¼ tsp baking-powder
½ egg
30g/1 oz currants

to make: 8
time: ½ hour
greased and floured baking-tray
60 mm/2½ in. fluted cutter
castor-sugar dredger
oven No. 4 or 180 °C/355 °F

1 Sieve the flour and baking-powder—rub in the fat **2** Add the sugar cleaned currants and egg—work into a dough **3** Roll out 5 mm/¼ in. thick and cut out **4** Bake for 15 minutes **5** Sprinkle with castor sugar whilst hot

Variations—Add 30g/1 oz of any of the following—
(a) chopped crystallized ginger and a level tsp ground ginger.
(b) chopped glacé cherries.
(c) chopped glacé pineapple.
(d) chopped walnuts.
(e) chopped hazel-nuts.
(f) chopped peel and almonds.

Priory Biscuits

60g/2 oz flour
pinch of baking-powder
pinch of cream of tartar
¼ tsp bicarbonate of soda
pinch of salt
60g/2 oz butter or margarine
60g/2 oz castor sugar
60g/2 oz rolled oats
1 tsp hot water
1 tbsp golden syrup

to make: 12–16
time: 1 hour
sieve
greased and floured baking-tray
oven No. 4 or 180 °C/355 °F

1 Sieve the flour and raising agents **2** Cream the butter and sugar—stir in the oats **3** Stir in the golden syrup—add water if necessary **4** Stand the mixture for half an hour **5** Put in tsps on to the baking-tray **6** Bake 8–10 minutes or until golden brown—cool **7** Serve on a plate with a fancy paper

Traffic-light Biscuits

110g/¼ lb biscuit-crust (page 227)
2 tbsp apricot jam
green and pink colouring

to make: 8–10
time: ½ hour
greased and floured baking-tray
medium-sized plain cutter
10 mm/½ in. cutter
icing-sugar dredger
oven No. 4 or 170 °C/335 °F

1 Roll out the biscuit-crust thinly **2** Cut into rounds or ovals **3** Leave ½ plain and cut three small rounds out of the other half **4** Bake for about 10 minutes 5 Divide the jam into three and colour ⅓ red, ⅓ green, leaving ⅓ natural 6 When cool, put two biscuits together and dust with icing-sugar 7 Put coloured jams into the three holes–red, green and amber 8 Serve on a round plate on a fancy paper

Almond Ring Biscuits

110g/¼ lb biscuit-crust (page 227)
60g/2 oz ground almonds
30g/1 oz castor sugar
red-currant jelly
chopped pistachio nuts
1 white of egg

to make: 20 approximately
time: ¾ hour
whisk
greased and floured baking-tray
50 mm/2 in. plain cutter
No. 8 icing forcer
nylon bag
oven No. 3 or 170 °C/335 °F

1 Roll out the biscuit-crust very thinly–cut into rounds **2** Whisk the white of egg and fold in the sugar and almonds **3** Pipe round the edge of each biscuit **4** Bake for 10–15 minutes **5** When cold fill the centre with the jelly and sprinkle with the pistachio nuts

NB 1 These biscuits may be cut small and use as petit fours.
2 Lemon curd may be used instead of red-currant jelly.
3 Chopped almonds coloured green may be used instead of pistachio nuts.

German Biscuits

110g/¼ lb biscuit-crust (page 227)
apricot jam
110g/¼ lb pink or white glacé icing (page 258)
cherry, etc., for decoration

to make: 8–10
time: ½ hour
greased and floured tray
60 mm/2½ in. cutter
oven No. 4 or 180 °C/355 °F

1 Roll out pastry very thinly **2** Cut in to rounds and bake for about 10 minutes **3** When cool put 2 together with a little of the apricot jam **4** Ice with pink or white glacé icing, putting a small decoration in the centre, e.g. cherry, etc.

Variations

1 *(a)* Cut a small hole in the centre of half the rounds,
(b) Bake and put together as above.
(c) Dust with icing sugar and fill the hole with pink or white glacé icing.

2 *(a)* Brush the rounds with white of egg and sprinkle with sugar and chopped almonds or walnuts.
(b) Bake as before. These may be cut in fingers instead of rounds.

3 *(a)* Cut and bake as before and spread thinly with apricot jam.
(b) Arrange almonds curved side up and points to the centre, round the biscuit.
(c) Put a mimosa ball in the centre.

NB The almonds may be lightly browned if liked.

Chocolate Almond Biscuits

110g/¼ lb biscuit-crust (page 227)
60g/2 oz ground almonds
30g/1 oz castor sugar
30g/1 oz icing-sugar
egg–flavourings
} almond paste
110g/¼ lb chocolate glacé icing (page 258) or melted chocolate
apricot jam
hazel-nuts, almonds or chocolate vermicelli

to make: 16
time: ¾ hour
greased and floured baking-tray
50 mm/2 in. round-cutter
oven No. 4 or 180 °C/355 °C

1 Roll out the biscuit-crust thinly and cut into rounds **2** Bake for about 10 minutes **3** Make the almond paste, roll out thinly and cut into rounds **4** When the biscuits are cold, brush with a little warm jam and cover with rounds of paste **5** Coat with the icing or chocolate **6** Decorate in the centre with the nuts or vermicelli
NB These may be cut with a 25 mm/1 in. cutter and served as petits fours.

Chocolate Meringues

110g/¼ lb biscuit-crust (page 227)
12 meringues (page 187)
110g/¼ lb plain chocolate (melted)
⅛ lit/¼ pt cream

to make: 12
time: 2½ hours
nylon bag
No. 8 vegetable-forcer
oiled baking-tray
50 mm/2 in. cutter
oven No. 3 or 170 °C/335 °F

1 Roll out the biscuit-crust and cut into rounds **2** Bake 10–15 minutes **3** Make meringues and bake **4** When cool dip or coat with the chocolate –set **5** Place on the biscuits and pipe the cream round
NB Cream may be omitted or alternatively the meringues may be filled with cream before coating with chocolate.

Piped Biscuits

110g/¼ lb flour
110g/¼ lb butter
30g/1 oz castor sugar
vanilla essence

to make: 20–30
time: ¾ hour
sieve
greased and floured tray
electric mixer
large star-forcer
nylon bag
icing-sugar dredger
oven No. 3 or 170 °C/335 °F

1 Sieve the flour and sugar **2** Soften the butter and add the flour to it a little at a time–add the vanilla **3** Continue beating until the mixture is of a piping consistency **4** Pipe in stars and fingers **5** Bake about 10 minutes—the biscuits should be firm and pale brown in colour **6** When cool *(a)* Store or *(b)* Dip the ends in melted chocolate and/or *(c)* Put two together with jam, chocolate or butter cream *(d)* Dredge with icing sugar

Variations

1 *Swiss tarts*

(a) Pipe the mixture into small paper cases leaving a depression in centre.

(b) Bake 20–25 minutes. When cool dredge with icing-sugar.

(c) Fill the centre with a little raspberry jam.

2 *Petits Fours*

(a) Pipe the same shapes making them half the size.

(b) Small pieces of cherry may be put in the centre of the round ones.

Gingernuts

110g/¼ lb flour
60g/2 oz butter
1 tbsp syrup
1 tsp ground ginger
¼ tsp bicarbonate of soda
pinch of salt

to make: 20 approximately
time: 40 minutes
sieve
greased and floured baking-tray
oven No. 4 or 180 °C/355 °F

1 Melt the sugar, fat and syrup in a pan and stir in the sieved dry ingredients **2** Mix thoroughly—when cool enough to handle, roll in damp hands into balls **3** Put on to the baking-tray—flatten slightly **4** Bake 10–15 minutes till pale golden brown—cool **5** Serve on a round plate on a fancy paper

Flapjacks

90g/3 oz butter
90g/3 oz castor or brown sugar
150g/5 oz rolled oats
2 level tbsp golden syrup

to make: 8 pieces
time: ¾ hour
150 x 150 mm/6 x 6 in. greased tin or 175 mm/7 in. round tin
oven No. 4 or 180 °C/355 °F

1 Melt the butter and add the syrup and sugar **2** When blended add to the oats, mix well **3** Press into the tin and bake about 25 minutes **4** Cut into squares or triangles whilst still warm **5** Serve on a plate with a fancy paper

Brandy Snaps

60g/2 oz syrup
60g/2 oz butter
50g/1¾ oz flour

to make: 12
time: ½ hour
greased trays

45g/1½ oz castor sugar
½ tsp ground ginger
a few drops lemon-juice

greased handles of wooden spoons
oven No. 5 or 190 °C/380 °F

1 Melt the sugar, butter and syrup 2 Add the flour, ginger and lemon-juice 3 Put on to the trays in teaspoonsful (not more than four on a tin allowing room for spreading) 4 Bake for about 10 minutes 5 Take off the tray with a palette-knife and roll round the handle of the spoon 6 When cool and set, store or serve plain or filled with whipped sweetened cream 7 Serve on a plate with a fancy paper

Macaroon Biscuits

110g/¼ lb ground almonds
230g/½ lb castor sugar
15g/½ oz ground rice
2 egg-whites
vanilla essence
split almonds

to make: 10–12
time: ¾ hour
electric mixer (optional)
oiled baking-tray
rice-paper
10 mm/½ in. plain forcer
nylon bag
oven No. 3 or 170 °C/335 °F

1 Put the almonds, sugar, ground rice, essence and egg whites into a basin–beat till light 2 Put rice-paper on the baking-tray–pipe in 60 mm/2½ in. rounds and put half an almond on each 3 Bake for about 25 minutes. Cool 4 Remove excess rice-paper 5 Serve on a round plate on a fancy paper
If egg-whites are not sufficient a little water may be necessary to make a moderately soft texture.

NB If to be used as petits fours or for decorations for trifles, etc., make about half the size.

Coconut Meringues

1 egg-white
75g/2½ oz castor sugar
½ tsp ground rice
75g/2½ oz desiccated coconut
pink colouring

to make: 12–16
time: 1¼ hours
whisk or electric mixer
baking-sheet
rice-paper
oven No. 1 or 140 °C/290 °F

1 Whip the egg-white making a meringue with the castor sugar 2 Fold in the coconut and colour as required 3 Put in small heaps on the dry baking-tray covered with the rice-paper 4 Bake until crisp, about 40 minutes 5 Cool and remove excess rice-paper 6 Serve on a plate with a fancy paper

24
Yeast mixtures

White Bread

230g/½ lb flour
15g/½ oz yeast
15g/½ oz lard
1 tsp castor sugar
¼ tsp salt
⅛ lit/¼ pt tepid water

time: 1½ hours
sieve
electric mixer (optional)
greased and floured bread-tin 150 x 100 mm/6 x 4 in.
oven No. 8 or 230 °C/445 °F

1 Sieve the flour and salt—rub in the lard **2** Cream the yeast and sugar—add the water **3** Make a well in the flour—pour in the liquid and cover with some of the flour **4** Cover with a plate and put in a warm and draughtproof place **5** Leave for 20 minutes or until the surface is covered with bubbles, 'setting the sponge' **6** Mix and knead until smooth and elastic (this may be done by a machine using a dough-hook) **7** Mould and place in the tin **8** Prove in a warm place until the dough rises to the top of the tin **9** Bake for 15 minutes—turn out of the tin on to the baking-tray and bake for a further 15 minutes, reducing the heat of the oven to No. 6 or 205 °C/400 °F **10** The loaf should sound hollow when the bottom is tapped

Alternative methods (1)

A Put the water and sugar into a basin—sprinkle on the yeast and leave till frothy.

B Add to the sieved flour and salt and proceed as above.

(2) Mix the yeast and liquid and pour into the well in the flour and proceed as from No. 4.

NB This will take longer.

Brown Bread

110g/¼ lb wholemeal flour
110g/¼ lb white fiour
15g/½ oz yeast
1 tsp treacle
¼ tsp salt

time: 1½ hours
sieve
electric mixer (optional)
greased and floured bread-tin 150 x 100 mm/6 x 4 in.

½ oz lard
⅛ lit/¼ pt *tepid* water

oven No. 8 or 230 °C/445 °F

Follow the method for white bread (page 280) with the following exceptions–

1 Sieve the white flour only **2** Cream the yeast with the treacle; or put water and treacle in a basin and sprinkle on the yeast; or add liquid, yeast and treacle to flour and mix as alternative to 2–white bread **3** Bake for 40 minutes

Yeast Buns

170g/6 oz flour
¼ tsp salt
30g/1 oz margarine or butter
½ egg
15g/½ oz yeast
1 tbsp sugar
4 tbsp milk
45g/1½ oz sultanas
15g/½ oz peel

to make: 6–8 buns
time: 1 hour
sieve
electric mixer (optional)
greased and floured baking-tray
oven No. 8 or 230 °C/445 °F

1 Sieve the flour and salt and rub in the fat **2** Cream the yeast and 1 tsp sugar–add the *tepid* milk **3** Make a well in the flour–add the egg and yeast mixture. Set to 'sponge' **4** Add the fruit and remainder of the sugar, mix, beat and knead until smooth and elastic **5** Shape and prove **6** Bake for 6–8 minutes **7** Whilst hot, brush with bun-glaze–cool and serve

Bun Glaze

1 dessertsp sugar
1 dessertsp milk

1 Heat in a pan without stirring **2** When very hot, brush over the buns
NB Alternative methods may be used as for bread.

Fruit Loaf

230g/½ lb white flour
¼ tsp salt
30g/1 oz margarine or butter
15g/½ oz yeast
½ egg
1 tbsp sugar
4 tbsp milk
45g/1½ oz sultanas
15g/½ oz peel

time: 1½ hours
sieve
electric-mixer
greased and floured bread-tin 150 x 100 mm/6 x 4 in.
oven No. 8 or 230 °C/445 °F

1 Follow the instructions for yeast buns (page 281) **2** Mould and put into the tin and prove and bake as for white bread (page 280) **3** After baking rub with a knob of butter or margarine for a shiny finish or brush with bun-glaze (page 281)

Brown Malt Bread

230g/½ lb wholemeal flour
¼ tsp salt
15g/½ oz yeast
15g/½ oz malt extract
⅛ lit/¼ pt *warm* water
30g/1 oz sultanas or raisins (optional)

time: 2 hours
greased and floured bread-tin 150 x 100 mm/6 x 4 in.
oven No. 8 or 230 °C/445 °F

1 Mix the yeast and malt extract with the water **2** Sieve the flour and salt, put into a bowl—make a well in the centre—add the liquid
3 Sprinkle a little of the flour over the top—cover and leave in a warm place ½–1 hour **4** Add the fruit and mix and knead until smooth and elastic **5** Put into the tin and prove until the dough reaches the top
6 Bake for 45 minutes, reducing the temperature at half-time and turning the bread on to a baking-tray as for white bread (page 280)
Alternative methods of adding the yeast may be used as for white bread.

Basic Rich Dough

230g/½ lb flour
¼ tsp salt
60g/2 oz margarine or butter
15g/½ oz yeast
1 egg
½ tsp castor sugar
4 tbsp tepid milk

time: 35 minutes
sieve
electric-mixer

1 Sieve the flour and salt—rub in the fat roughly **2** Cream the yeast and sugar—add the milk **3** Make a well in the flour—add the egg and yeast mixture—cover with a little of the flour and a plate—set to 'sponge'
4 Beat to a soft, smooth dough and knead until elastic or beat for 4 minutes on a machine with a dough-hook **5** Mould and use as required or add the yeast by alternative methods as for white bread (page 280)

Rolls

230g/½ lb basic rich dough (page 282)
egg-glaze

to make: 8–12 rolls
time: 1 hour
greased and floured baking-tray
oven No. 8 or 230 °C/445 °F

1 Divide the dough into 8–12 even-sized pieces **2** Knead into rolls and put on to the tray **3** Put in a warm place for about 10–15 minutes
4 Glaze with beaten egg **5** Bake for 6–8 minutes
NB This mixture may also be used for bridge rolls, in which case it is rolled, after kneading, to a 10 mm/¼ in. thickness and cut with an oval-cutter, or moulded into shape.

Swiss Buns: Make larger than bridge rolls—ice with white glacé icing (page 258) when cool.

Belgian Rings

230g/½ lb basic rich dough (page 282)
60g/2 oz ground almonds
60g/2 oz castor sugar
lemon-juice
230g/8 oz white glacé icing (page 282)
a few sliced browned almonds

to make: 4–8 rings
time: 1¾ hours
greased and floured baking-tray
oven No. 8 or 230 °C/445 °F

1 Divide the dough into 4 **2** Roll ¼ into a sausage about 225 mm/9 in. long–flatten with a rolling pin **3** Mix the ground almonds with the lemon-juice and sugar to make a paste **4** Spread the paste down the centre of the dough–fold the dough over the paste–make into a circle **5** Prove till the mixture feels light **6** Bake for 8–10 minutes **7** Coat with slack glacé icing whilst hot–sprinkle with the almonds **8** Repeat with the remainder of the dough

NB The dough may be divided into 8 so that individual rings are made.

Chelsea Buns

230g/8 oz rich dough (page 282)
add–
2 tsp sugar
60g/2 oz currants
30g/1 oz peel
pinch mixed spice
30g/1 oz butter
a little lemon-juice
egg-glaze

to make: 12
time: 1¾ hours
castor-sugar dredger
greased and floured deep-sided tin or tins
oven No. 8 or 230 °C/445 °F

1 Roll the dough into an oblong–brush with the butter **2** Sprinkle with the remaining ingredients **3** Roll up from the long side–cut into 25 mm/1 in. slices–stand in the tin on the cut side tucking the ends under **4** Prove, glaze and sprinkle with the sugar **5** Bake 10–12 minutes–cool and serve

NB 1 Buns may be iced with thin glacé icing (page 258) whilst hot or
2 Brush with bun-glaze (page 281).

Tea Wreath

230g/½ lb basic rich dough (page 282)
nuts, e.g. flaked or split almonds
cherries
170g/6 oz glacé icing (page 258)
15g/½ oz soft butter
60g/2 oz castor sugar
30g/1 oz raisins
½ tsp powdered cinnamon

to make: 1
time: 1¾ hours
greased and floured baking-tray
oven No. 6 or 205 °C/400 °F

1 Roll the dough into an oblong **2** Spread with the butter, sugar, raisins and cinnamon **3** Roll up tightly, beginning at the long side **4** Put the roll on the tray, forming it into a circle and joining the ends together **5** Cut half through the ring at 25 mm/1 in. intervals and turn each section on its side 6 Cover with a cloth and prove 7 Bake 25–30 minutes 8 Whilst still warm, brush with the slack icing and decorate with the nuts and cherries

Tea Rings

230g/½ lb basic rich dough (page 282)
30g/1 oz melted butter
30g/1 oz currants
30g/1 oz sultanas
15g/½ oz peel
15g/½ oz castor sugar
flaked almonds
egg-glaze

to make: 1
time: 1¾ hours
pastry brush
greased and floured baking-tray
castor-sugar dredger
oven No. 7 or 220 °C/425 °F

1 Divide the dough into 3 and roll into 3 strips 300 mm/12 in. long 2 Brush each strip with melted butter 3 Spread with the fruit and castor sugar 4 Damp one side of each strip and form into a roll 5 Make a plait, stretching the roll and plaiting firmly–join in a circle and put on to the prepared tin–prove 6 Brush with egg and sprinkle with sugar and flaked almonds 7 Bake for 12–15 minutes–cool and serve

Variations

1 *Hazel-nut rings*

Prepare as for tea rings and spread with the following mixture–
60g/2 oz ground hazel-nuts
60g/2 oz castor sugar
vanilla essence
milk or cream to form a soft paste
sprinkle with hazel-nuts instead of almonds

2 *Chestnut rings*

Prepare as for tea rings and spread with the following mixture–
60g/2 oz chestnut purée (tinned)
60g/2 oz cake-crumbs
60g/2 oz castor sugar
vanilla
milk or cream to make a soft paste
When baked, coat with glacé icing

3 *Walnut rings*

Prepare as for hazel-nut rings, using walnuts in place of hazel-nuts.

Fruit Plait

230g/½ lb basic rich dough (page 282)
230g/½ lb cooking apples } filling
60g/2 oz raisins, sultanas, } filling

time: 1¾ hours
greased and floured baking-tray
pastry-brush

currants or dates
60g/2 oz brown sugar
¼ level tsp ground cinnamon
or mixed spice } filling contd.

oven No. 7 or 220 °C/425 °F

170g/6 oz glacé icing (page 258)

1 Prepare and chop the apples–put into a pan with the ingredients for filling–cook until the fruit is soft and pulpy–allow to cool 2 Roll the dough into an oblong and spread the fruit filling down the centre 3 Make 50 mm/2 in. long cuts at 25 mm/1 in. intervals down the side of oblong–take a strip from each side and cross them over the filling to form a plait–tuck the last two underneath–prove 4 Bake for 30 minutes 5 Whilst warm brush with slack glacé icing

Variations

1 Mincemeat.

2 Any savoury filling.

Doughnuts

230g/½ lb rich yeast dough (page 282)
30g/1 oz sugar
1 tsp cinnamon
jam

to make: 12
time: 1 hour
kitchen roll
deep-fat pan
thermometer

1 Roll the dough out thinly 2 Cut into rounds or divide into 12 and knead in to rounds–press with a rolling pin 3 Place a little jam in the centre–fold up and cover the jam well 4 Fry for about 5 minutes rolling constantly at 170 °C/335 °F 5 Roll in the sugar and cinnamon –cool 6 Serve on a round plate on a fancy paper

NB Doughnuts may be cut with a hole in centre using 2 cutters or a doughnut-cutter. They then need less cooking-time.

Brioches

230g/½ lb flour
¼ tsp salt
1 tsp castor sugar
3 eggs
110g/¼ lb butter
15g/½ oz yeast
3 dessertsp tepid water

to make: 12
time: ¾ hour
sieve
electric mixer (optional)
greased and floured deep patty-tins
oven No. 7 or 220 °C/425 °F

1 Sieve the flour and salt 2 Cream the yeast and sugar and add the water 3 Make a well in the flour and add the eggs, butter and liquid 4 Mix and beat well by hand or machine 5 Divide the dough into 16 and divide 4 pieces into 3 giving 12 large and 12 small pieces 6 Put a large piece in each patty tin, make a hole in the centre and put a small ball into it 7 Prove for about 15 minutes 8 Brush with egg and bake for 8–10 minutes–cool and serve

Basic Danish Pastry Dough

230g/½ lb flour
pinch of salt
1 egg
4 tbsp cold water
140g/5 oz butter
30g/1 oz lard
1 level tbsp castor sugar
15g/½ oz yeast creamed with 1 tbsp cold water

to make: 16 approximately
time: 2¼ hours
sieve
greased and floured baking-tray
oven No. 7 or 220 °C/425 °F

1 Sieve the flour and salt and rub in the lard **2** Mix together egg, sugar and 4 tbsp water–add the creamed yeast **3** Pour into the flour mixture and mix to a rough, soft dough **4** Turn on to a table and rub down very lightly until smooth **5** Allow to relax in cool place for 10 minutes **6** Beat down the butter until soft and spreadable–shape into a thick oblong cake **7** Roll out the dough into a square a little larger than the butter-place the butter in the centre, fold the sides over, just to overlap slightly down the centres–seal in the fat **8** Roll into an oblong strip about 3 times as long as it is wide–fold evenly into 3 **9** Cover and allow to relax in cool place for 10 minutes **10** Repeat the rolling and folding twice more **11** Cover and relax in cool place for 10 minutes **12** Shape into pastries **13** Leave to prove in a slightly warm place until puffy-about 15–20 minutes **14** Bake for about 12–15 minutes **15** Ice and finish whilst hot

Varieties
Crescents
Imperial Stars
Cushions
Cartwheels
Twists
Pretzels

Fillings

1 *Spiced fat and currants*
30g/1 oz butter, 30g/1 oz castor sugar, 1 level tsp cinnamon, 60g/2 oz currants.

2 *Almond Paste*
30g/1 oz ground almonds, 30g/1 oz castor sugar, a little egg to mix, vanilla and almond essence.

3 *Glacé Icing*
170g/6 oz icing sugar and water.

NB Croissants may be made from this recipe, shaping as for crescents. Brush with egg after proving–bake for 5 minutes. Reduce heat to No. 5 or 180 °C/375 °F and continue cooking until croissants are brown–about 10 minutes.

Hot Cross Buns

170g/6 oz flour
45g/1½ oz margarine or butter
4 tbsp milk
½ egg
15g/½ oz yeast
30g/1 oz castor sugar
60g/2 oz sultanas
15g/½ oz peel
1 tsp mixed spice
pinch of salt
bun-glaze (page 281)

to make: 6–8
time: 1¼ hours
sieve
electric mixer (optional)
greased and floured baking-tray
oven No. 7 or 220 °C/425 °F

1 Sieve the flour and salt–rub in the fat **2** Cream the yeast with 1 tsp sugar–add the tepid milk **3** Make a hole in the flour–add the egg and liquid–cover and put in a warm place for 15–20 minutes **4** Prepare the fruit, peel and spice and mix with the remaining sugar–add to the yeast mixture **5** Mix and beat to a pliable dough **6** Divide into 6–8 pieces, form into buns, mark with a cross or with pastry **7** Prove for about 15 minutes **8** Bake 7–10 minutes **9** Glaze whilst still hot

Bun-glaze

1 tbs sugar dissolve in 1 tbsp water, bring to boil and use while very hot.

Bath Buns

230g/½ lb flour
¼ tsp salt
90g/3 oz butter
2 eggs
4 tbsp milk (tepid)
60g/2 oz sugar
lemon rind
15g/½ oz yeast
60g/2 oz sultanas
15g/½ oz peel
loaf sugar
egg-glaze

to make: 12
time: 1¼ hours
sieve
electric mixer
greased and floured tray
oven No. 7 or 220 °C/425 °F

1 Sieve the flour and salt–rub in the fat **2** Cream the yeast and 1 tsp of the sugar–add the milk **3** Make a well in the flour, break in the eggs and add the liquid–mix and beat **4** Put in a bowl covered with a damp cloth, in a warm place until the dough has risen to twice its bulk **5** Add the sugar, lemon-rind and fruit, and divide the dough into 12 rather rough buns **6** Prove–glaze–sprinkle with coarsely broken loaf sugar **7** Bake for 10–15 minutes–cool and serve

Sally Lunns

340g/¾ lb flour
pinch of salt

to make: 2
time: 1¼ hours

45g/1½ oz margarine or butter
15g/½ oz yeast
30g/1 oz castor sugar
1 egg
⅛ lit/¼ pt milk *(tepid)*
bun-glaze or butter

sieve
electric mixer (optional)
2 125 mm/5 in. greased and floured cake-tins
oven No. 6 or 205 °C/400 °F

1 Sieve the flour and salt and rub in the fat **2** Cream the yeast and sugar and add the milk **3** Make a well in the flour and add the egg and liquid **4** Sprinkle with some of the flour—cover and put in a warm place for about 20 minutes to 'sponge' **5** Mix and knead **6** Divide into 2, knead each lightly and put into the tins **7** Prove until the dough reaches the top of the tins **8** Bake for about 20 minutes **9** Brush the tops with melted butter or bun-glaze (page 281) **10** Cool and serve on a plate on a fancy paper

Pizza

230g/½ lb plain flour
15g/½ oz yeast
¼ tsp salt
1 tsp castor sugar
⅛ lit/¼ pt water approximately
1 tbsp oil
} bread dough (page 280)

Filling
450g/1 lb tomatoes
230g/½ lb mazzarella cheese or bel paese or strong Cheddar
¼ small tin anchovy fillets
a few black olives
a sprinkling of marjoram and basil

to serve: 8–10
time: 1¾ hours
sieve
electric mixer (optional)
2 175 mm/7 in. greased and floured sandwich-tins or flan-rings
oven No. 7 or 220 °C/425 °F

1 Make the dough, adding the oil with the liquid—'sponge,' knead and leave to rise till it doubles its bulk **2** Knead again to remove the air-bubbles **3** Roll out into 2 rounds and raise the outside edge with the fingers **4** Either place on a greased baking-tray or place in greased sandwich-tins or flan-rings **5** Brush with oil **6** Prove for 10–15 minutes in warm place **7** Slice the tomatoes, season and spread over the risen dough **8** Cut the cheese into thin slices and place over tomatoes **9** Arrange the anchovy fillets in a lattice design on the cheese **10** Decorate with the black olives and sprinkle with the herbs **11** Bake for about 20 minutes **12** Serve either hot, or cold with salad

Saffron Cake

450g/1 lb flour
1 tsp salt
90g/3 oz lard
110g/¼ lb butter
90g/3 oz sugar
1 pkt saffron
170g/6 oz currants

time: overnight and 1¾ hours
sieve
2 150 mm/6 in. greased cake-tins
oven No. 7 or 220 °C/425 °F

30g/1 oz peel
¼ lit/½ pt warm milk and water
15g/½ oz yeast
bun-glaze (page 281)

1 Steep the saffron in hot water overnight 2 Sieve the flour and salt, rub in the fats, add the yeast creamed with a little sugar and tepid liquid from the saffron made up to the required quantity with milk and water–leave to sponge about 15–20 minutes 3 Add the prepared fruit and the remainder of the sugar–beat by hand or in a mixer until smooth and elastic 4 Knead on a lightly-floured table and put into the tins 5 Prove until the mixture reaches the top of the tins 6 Bake for 25 minutes–turn out of the tin–reduce to No. 4 or 180 °C/355 °F for a further 20 minutes–brush with the glaze 7 Cool and serve on a fancy paper on a plate

Splits

230g/½ lb flour
30g/1 oz lard
½ tsp salt
15g/½ oz yeast
1 tsp sugar
⅛ lit/¼ pt warm milk and water

to make: 10–12
time: 1½ hour
sieve
greased and floured baking-tray
oven No. 8 or 230 °C/445 °F

1 Dissolve the sugar in the liquid–add the yeast–leave to sponge 2 Sieve the flour and salt, rub in the lard 3 Add the yeast mixture to the flour and beat and knead to a pliable dough 4 Cover, and leave to rise in a warm place till double the size 5 Knead into 10–12 balls and put on to the baking-tray–prove–dust with flour 6 Bake for 6–8 minutes 7 Cool under a cloth 8 Serve with jam and cream

NB The rising may be omitted, but the splits will be coarser in texture.

Crumpets

230g/½ lb flour
½ tsp salt
1 tsp sugar
15g/½ oz yeast
¼ lit/½ pt milk and water
pinch bicarbonate of soda

to make: 12–16
time: 2½ hours
sieve
greased girdle
plain cutters

1 Cream the yeast and sugar–add to the sieved flour, salt and soda 2 Mix to a batter with ½ the liquid and beat for 5 minutes–stand for 1 hour 3 Add the remaining liquid–beat again and stand ¾ hour 4 Pour into the cutters from a spoon 5 Cook until set and holey–turn and cook the other side 6 Spread thickly with butter–serve hot

25

Sandwiches and transported meals

Open Sandwiches

Bases

1 1 slice buttered white bread.
2 1 slice buttered brown bread.
3 1 slice buttered rye bread.
4 1 slice fried bread.
5 1 thin slice cheese pastry.
6 Water-biscuits.
7 Crackers.
8 Cornish wafers.
9 Crispbreads.
10 Starch-reduced crispbreads and biscuits.

Fillings

Protein

sliced ham
sliced tongue
corned beef
luncheon meat
brawns
salami
sausages
sliced sausages
frankfurters
pâté
foie gras
poultry
cheese—sliced or cubed
—herb-flavoured
—cream
—Danish blue
—smoked, etc.

tuna
pilchards
sandines
anchovies
roll mops
roes
smoked salmon
tinned salmon
shrimps
prawns
crab
lobster
egg—hard-boiled
—scrambled

Vegetable

lettuce
watercress
chicory
endive
parsley
celery
cucumber
tomato
peppers (parboiled)
gherkins
chives
capers
radishes
asparagus
mushrooms
onion
olives

nuts
peas
horse-radish
grapes
pineapple
apples–raw
–fried
sultanas
dates
banana
pears
lemon
mayonnaise
Russian salad
potato salad
spices
lemon-juice

Rolled Sandwiches

1 thin slice of buttered brown or white bread
foil

Fillings: as for open sandwiches

1 Place the filling on the bread **2** Roll fairly loosely **3** Enclose in foil and put in a refrigerator until required, allowing time to become firm **4** Serve garnished with parsley or salad

Circular Sandwiches

1 small brown or white loaf
foil

Filling: any open-sandwich filling

1 Remove all the crusts from the bread **2** Slice thinly lengthwise **3** Spread with butter and filling **4** Roll up tightly in foil and allow to set in a refrigerator **5** Cut across in thin slices **6** Serve garnished with parsley or salad

Double-decker

foil

1 Prepare the bread as for circular sandwiches and spread each slice with filling **2** Pile in a loaf shape with alternate brown and white slices **3** Enclose in foil and set as for circular sandwiches **4** Cut in fingers, squares, oblongs or triangles **5** Serve as for circular sandwiches
NB These may be cut in tiny squares for cocktail savouries.

Sandwich Fillings

Egg-base

To 1 scrambled or 1 liquidized hard-boiled egg add–

1. 30g/1 oz grated cheese or cream cheese and horse-radish.
2. 2 tsps chopped parsley.
3. 1 tsp chopped chives.
4. 1 tsp anchovy paste or sieved anchovies.
5. 1 tsp shrimp paste.
6. 1 tsp bloater paste.
7. 60g/2 oz chopped sautéd mushrooms.
8. 30g/1 oz parboiled, chopped and sautéd peppers.
9. 30g/1 oz chopped walnuts.
10. 30g/1 oz chopped ham.
11. 30g/1 oz chopped tongue.
12. 30g/1 oz sautéd chopped bacon.
13. 30g/1 oz chopped capers and/or gherkins.
14. 1 tsp tomato purée.
15. 30g/1 oz crab meat.
16. 30g/1 oz chopped prawns.
17. 1 dessertsp chutney.
18. 30g/1 oz sieved or mashed sardines.
19. 30g/1 oz corned beef.

Mayonnaise Base

To 1 tbsp mayonnaise or salad cream add–

1. 1 tbsp chopped lobster or prawns or crab meat.
2. 2 tbsp finely-chopped poultry.
3. 2 tbsp finely-chopped ham or tongue.
4. 2 tbsp grated apple and chopped walnuts or celery or hazel-nuts.
5. 1 tsp chopped capers, 1 tsp chopped gherkins, 1 tsp chopped parsley and 1 tsp blanched and chopped peppers.
6. 1 dessertsp finely-chopped dates and 1 dessertsp finely-chopped walnuts.
7. 1 tbsp flaked salmon or tuna and 1 tsp tomato purée.

Extract: Marmite or Bovril or Similar

Mix ¼ tsp marmite with 30g/1 oz butter and/or peanut butter and add–

1. 30g/1 oz grated cheese } chopped watercress or cress
2. 30g/1 oz cream cheese } may be added
3. 30g/1 oz chopped celery
4. 30g/1 oz chopped walnuts
5. 1 tsp chopped chives
6. 1 tbsp corned beef

Sauce Base

To 1 tbsp seasoned white sauce add–

1 1 tbsp mashed sardines and 1 tsp vinegar.
2 1 tbsp minced ham and 1 tsp horse-radish sauce.
3 1 tbsp minced poultry and 1 tsp gherkins or capers.
4 1 dessertsp chopped pickled walnuts and 1 dessertsp chopped walnuts.
5 1 tbsp tinned salmon or tuna and ½ tsp tarragon vinegar.

Transported Meals

1 Office lunches.
2 Picnic lunches.
3 Lunches for special occasions.

Packing

Wrappings

(a) Foil, polythene bags–waxed papers polythene sheets } plus elastic band

(b) Plastic containers with tight-fitting lids. Vacuum-flasks, tins, insulated bags.

Utensils

Plastic cups, plastic beakers, paper or plastic plates.
Unbreakable 'china,' plastic spoons and forks, knives (wrapped), plastic cruets, plastic sugar-containers.

Include

Bottle-opener, can-opener, matches, paper napkins, paper towels, flannel in a polythene bag, a large bag for rubbish, a camping stove, if used.

Office Lunches

These must be easily carried and very compact, therefore take such things as–

pies
pasties
Scotch eggs
sandwiches
hard-boiled eggs
cooked sausages
cold meats
cheeses
salads
fruit, cakes, biscuits
convenience foods
rolls, cut loaves

For drinks

Bottles
Drinks in beakers

Picnics

As above–include utensils.
Drinks–add tea–coffee–camping stove–teapot–kettle or saucepan.

Special Occasions (e.g. Ascot lunch by car)

Pack all food and utensils in a picnic-basket or hamper or insulated bag. Take ice in a wide-mouthed flask.

Include
rugs, cushions, table, chairs, sunshade, tablecloth, napkins.

Suggested menu

Cream of cucumber soup–in flask–chilled
or consommé –in flask–chilled

Galantine of chicken
Salad, Crisps, Rolls, Butter
or Chicken bouchées
Salad
Rolls and butter

Fruit salad
Shortbread biscuits
or
Strawberry sponge
or Basket

Cheese–Coffee

Wine–Rosé or Champagne

26
Confectionery

Coconut Ice

1 kg/2 lb granulated sugar	*time:* 1 hour
⅜ lit/¾ pt milk or coconut milk	large pan
pinch of cream of tartar	buttered Swiss-roll tin 300 x 200 mm/ 12 x 8 in.
170g/6 oz coconut	thermometer
colouring and flavouring	

1 Put the milk and sugar into the pan and heat without boiling until the sugar has entirely dissolved **2** Add the cream of tartar and boil hard to 112 °C/235 °F **3** Add the coconut and beat until thick **4** Pour into the tin **5** Cut into squares when nearly set **6** The ice may be– *(a)* Coloured pink; *(b)* coloured green and flavoured with 2 tsp of peppermint essence; *(c)* flavoured with 2 tsp of instant coffee

Dark Fudge

1 kg/2 lb moist sugar	*time:* 1 hour
110g/¼ lb butter	large pan
¼ lit/½ pt evaporated milk	buttered Swiss-roll tin 200 x 300 mm/ 8 x 12 in.
	thermometer

1 Put all the ingredients into the pan **2** Heat without boiling until sugar is dissolved **3** Bring to boil and boil to 115 °C/238 °F, stirring frequently **4** Remove from heat and beat until thick **5** Pour into the tin and cut into squares when nearly set

NB *Additions*
(a) 2 tsp vanilla essence.
(b) 2 tsp peppermint essence.
(c) 60g/2 oz melted chocolate.
(d) 2 tsp instant coffee.
(e) 60g/2 oz chopped nuts.
(f) 60g/2 oz chopped dates.
(g) 60g/2 oz crystallized ginger (chopped).

(h) 60g/2 oz glacé pineapple (chopped).
(i) 1 tbsp rum.
All these ingredients are added when the fudge has finished cooking before starting the beating.

Light Fudge

1 kg/2 lb granulated sugar
110g/¼ lb butter
¼ lit/½ pt evaporated milk

time: 1 hour
large pan
buttered Swiss-roll tin 220 x 300 mm/ 8 x 12 in.
thermometer

See dark fudge (page 295)

Chocolate Fudge

1 tsp gelatine
340g/¾ lb sugar
⅛ lit/¼ pt milk
3 tbsp chocolate powder
1 tbsp butter
pinch of cream of tartar
½ tsp vanilla essence

time: 1 hour
large pan
175 x 250 mm/7 x 10 in. buttered tin
thermometer

1 Put all the ingredients, except the vanilla into the pan—dissolve the sugar **2** Bring to the boil and boil to 115 °C/238 °F **3** Remove from the heat and allow to cool slightly **4** Add the vanilla and beat until thick **5** Pour into the tin and cut into squares when nearly set
NB Chopped nuts, fruit, etc., may be added with the flavouring.

Crème de Menthe Delight

3 tsp gelatine
¼ lit/½ pt cold water
230g/½ lb granulated sugar
pinch of citric acid
1 tsp peppermint essence
green colouring
icing-sugar } for rolling
cornflour }

time: ½ hour and overnight
medium-sized pan
tin 175 x 250 mm/7 x 10 in.

1 Put the water, sugar and gelatine in the pan and stir over heat until sugar is dissolved **2** Add the citric acid, bring to the boil and boil for 15–20 minutes **3** Cool and add the peppermint essence and green colouring **4** Pour into the tin which has been wetted **5** Leave for 24 hours **6** Cut into squares using scissors **7** Roll in equal quantities of icing sugar and cornflour
NB Turkish delight can be made in the same way, substituting pink colouring and vanilla essence or rosewater for flavouring. Both these sweets are suitable for serving with coffee.

Sugared Almonds

230g/½ lb Jordan almonds
⅜ lit/¾ pt water
1½ kg/3 lbs granulated sugar
pinch of cream of tartar
colouring and flavouring

time: 1½ hours
sieve
thermometer
metal bowl

1 Blanch, dry and slightly brown the almonds 2 Dissolve the sugar in the water and bring to the boil 3 Add the cream of tartar and boil to 115 °C/230 °F 4 Add the colouring and flavouring if liked–skim 5 Put the almonds into the metal bowl and heat gently until really hot 6 Add a little of the syrup and stir gently with a spatula 7 When the almonds are quite dry add more syrup 8 Continue in this way until all the syrup is used up

NB 1 If the syrup becomes too thick, it can be warmed again.
2 During the coating process turn the almonds on to a sieve once or twice to remove the powdered sugar which collects in the bowl.
3 *Colours and flavours*
white: vanilla
pink: raspberry or rose
yellow: lemon

Apricotines

230g/½ lb apricot pulp (from tinned apricots)
230g/½ lb granulated sugar
1 tsp lemon juice

time: 1 hour and overnight
heavy saucepan
metal rings or a clean tin

1 Put the pulp and sugar in the pan and allow the sugar to dissolve slowly 2 Cook over gentle heat for about 40 minutes 3 Test a little for setting on a plate 4 If it is sufficiently cooked it should begin to set in 4 minutes 5 Pour into wet rings or tin and leave to set 6 Turn out and roll in granulated sugar

NB Tinned peaches may be used in the same way.

Spun Sugar

230g/½ lb granulated sugar
pinch of cream of tartar
⅛ lit/¼ pt water
2 drops acetic acid
colouring

time: 1 hour
thermometer
heavy pan
heavy pan
oiled rolling-pin
paper

1 Dissolve the sugar in the water and bring to the boil 2 Add the cream of tartar and acetic acid 3 Boil to 155 °C/310 °F 4 Put the pan at once into cold water to keep the temperature from rising 5 Remove from water and allow to stand for 2 minutes 6 Dip a fork

into the syrup and allow the syrup to trickle off until only a little remains **7** Shake the fork from side to side over the rolling-pin **8** The threads formed will be the spun sugar and may be used for decorating cold sweets and ices or formed into baskets for holding petits fours

NB 1 If to be coloured, add the colouring before the syrup reaches the full temperature.

2 Put paper on the floor to collect any sugar that falls—this may be used.

To Prepare Gum Arabic

110g/¼ lb gum arabic (crystals or powder)
¼ lit/½ pt cold water

time: 1 hour; or 1 week
double saucepan

Put the gum arabic and water into the top of the double saucepan and heat gently until it is all dissolved.
If there is plenty of time, the water and gum can be put into a jar and stirred occasionally. If using this method the gum will take about a week to dissolve entirely. This mixture is used to glaze sweets and decorations on cakes and also to make brillantine (or powdered gum arabic.)

Brillantine

⅛ lit/¼ pt liquid gum arabic (page 298)

time: 3 hours approximately
plates
pastry-brush
oven No. ¼ or 115 °C/240 °F

1 Brush a dish or plate with the liquid gum arabic **2** Put into very gentle heat until quite dry **3** Scrape off and keep in a tin or jar **4** The liquid may be coloured if liked **5** The brillantine is used to coat sweets and petits fours

Crystallized Mint-leaves

mint-leaves
gum-arabic glaze (page 298) or white of egg
granulated sugar

foil

1 The mint-leaves should be dry **2** Coat them with the glaze or slightly-beaten white of egg **3** Dust with the granulated sugar **4** Put the leaves on the foil and dry them in a very cool oven or in a warm place until quite dry and crisp

NB Rose petals, primroses, etc., may be treated in the same way and used as decorations for large and small cakes.

27
Preserves

FLAVOURED VINEGARS

Tarragon Vinegar

¼ lit/½ pt tarragon leaves
¼ lit/½ pt white vinegar

time: 5–6 weeks
preserving jars and bottles

1 The leaves should be dry 2 Put them into a screw top jar and pour on the vinegar and screw down tightly 3 Leave for 5–6 weeks and bottle if the flavour is strong enough

NB 1 More vinegar can be added.
2 This vinegar need not be strained.

Garlic Vinegar

8 cloves of garlic
½ lit/1 pt vinegar
salt

time: 3 weeks
strainer
preserving-jars, bottles

1 Crush the garlic with salt 2 Boil the vinegar and pour on to the garlic 3 Put into a jar and cover when cool 4 Strain and bottle after 3 weeks

Chilli Vinegar

30g/1 oz dried chillis
½ lit/1 pt vinegar

time: 6 weeks
strainer
preserving-jars, bottles

1 Pour the boiling vinegar over the chillis–cool 2 Cover and leave for 5–6 weeks 3 Strain and bottle

Spiced Vinegar

1 tsp each of allspice, celery-seed, mustard-seed, cloves, black peppers
small piece root ginger
1 fresh or dried chilli
2 cloves of garlic
1 lit/1 qt vinegar

time: 4 weeks
strainer
bottles

1 Put all the ingredients into a pan and bring slowly to boiling point 2 Simmer for 10 minutes 3 Strain after 4 weeks and bottle
NB Keep covered during the steeping period.

STORE SAUCES

Tomato Sauce

ripe tomatoes
to every ½ lit/1 pt of pulp add:
¼ lit/½ pt vinegar
15g/½ oz sugar
15g/½ oz salt
½ level tsp pepper
¼ level tsp cayenne
60g/2 oz onions
2 cloves garlic
1 bay-leaf

time: 2 hours
yield: approximately ¾ lit/1½ pt per ½ lit/1 pt of pulp
sauce bottles
liquidizer and strainer
oven No. 3 or 170 °C/335 °F

1 Wipe the tomatoes and cut up 2 Pack into a casserole and add chopped onion and garlic 3 Cover and cook in the oven until tender
4 Liquidize and strain 5 Add the other ingredients and cook gently until the consistency of cream 6 Pour into hot bottles and screw down
7 Stand the bottles in a pan of hot water and bring to boil and boil for 20 minutes
NB If liked the tops of the bottles may be dipped into melted paraffin wax.

Plum Sauce

1 kg/2 lb red plums
3 medium-sized onions
1 lit/1 qt vinegar
60g/2 oz salt
230g/½ lb granulated sugar
30g/1 oz mustard
110g/¼ lb sultanas
4 chillis
a piece root ginger
15g/½ oz allspice
1 tsp ground nutmeg

time: 1¾ hours
yield: approximately 1 lit/2 pt of sauce
liquidizer
sauce-bottles

1 Wipe and stone the plums 2 Prepare and chop the onions 3 Put the plums, onions, sultanas, chillis and crushed ginger into a pan with half the vinegar 4 Bring to the boil and simmer for 30 minutes 5 Take out the ginger and chillis–liquidize 6 Put into a pan with the remaining ingredients and add the rest of the vinegar 7 Bring to boil and simmer for 30–40 minutes 8 Finish as for tomato sauce (page 300)

CHUTNEYS

Apple and Raisin Chutney

1 kg/2 lb apples
230g/½ lb raisins
1 orange
450g/1 lb sugar
⅜ lit/¾ pt vinegar
pinch of ground cloves
110g/¼ lb chopped nuts
½ tsp salt
¼ tsp pepper

time: 50 minutes
yield: 1 kg/2 lb
grater
jam-jars
covers
labels

1 Peel, core and chop the apples 2 Chop the raisins and grate the orange rind 3 Cook the apples, raisins, nuts, spice and salt in ½ the vinegar until thoroughly cooked 4 Add the remaining vinegar, sugar, orange rind and juice 5 Cook slowly until thick 6 Put into hot jars and cover

Apricot Chutney

450g/1 lb apricots (weighed after stoning)
230g/½ lb onions
110g/¼ lb raisins
1 dessertsp mustard seed
½ level tsp cayenne
1 tsp salt
¼ lit/½ pt vinegar
grated rind and juice of ½ orange
grated rind and juice of ½ lemon
¼ tsp cinnamon
30g/1 oz chopped walnuts

time: 50 minutes
yield: approximately 1kg/2 lb
grater
jam-jars
covers
labels

1 Put all the ingredients except the walnuts in a pan and simmer until pulpy and thick 2 Add the walnuts 3 Put into hot jars–cover and label

Apricot and Date Chutney

230g/½ lb dried apricots or 450g/1 lb fresh apricots
450g/1 lb dates
2 cloves of garlic
230g/½ lb raisins
230g/½ lb brown sugar
2 tbsp salt
white vinegar to cover
110g/¼ lb preserved ginger

time: 2½ hours
yield: approximately 1½ kg/3 lb
jam-jars
covers
labels

1 Steep the apricots if dried, stone if fresh 2 Crush the garlic in the salt and chop the ginger 3 Put all the ingredients into a pan and cover with the vinegar 4 Cook gently until thick–about 2 hours
5 Put into hot jars, cover and label

Green Tomato Chutney

1½ kg/3 lb green tomatoes
340g/¾ lb apples
2 green or red peppers
340g/¾ lb onions
170g/6 oz sultanas
25g/¾ oz mustard seed
25g/¾ oz salt
1 tsp ground ginger
340g/¾ lb brown sugar
½ lit/1 pt malt vinegar
pinch of cayenne

yield: approximately 3 kg/6 lb
time: 3–3½ hours
jam-jars
preserving-pan
covers
labels

1 Remove the seeds from the peppers and chop **2** Chop the onions and apples **3** Put all the ingredients into a preserving pan and simmer gently 2–3 hours or until very soft and thick **4** Put into hot jars, cover and label

Ripe Tomato Chutney

1¼ kg/2½ lb ripe tomatoes
2 green peppers
1 large onion
15g/½ oz salt
1 tsp mustard seed
1 tsp celery seed
1 tsp whole allspice
1 piece root ginger
1 bay-leaf
(the five items above tied in muslin)
230g/½ lb granulated sugar
⅜ lit/¾ pt vinegar

yield: approximately 2 kg/4 lb
time: 3 hours
preserving-pan
jam-jars
covers
labels

1 Skin and cut up the tomatoes **2** Remove the seeds from the peppers and chop **3** Prepare and chop the onion **4** Put all the ingredients, including the spices, into the preserving-pan **5** Cook gently until thick–about 2 hours **6** Put into hot jars, cover and label

PICKLES

Sweet Pickles

2 kg/4 lb damsons, or
  morella cherries, or
  stewing pears, or
  1 kg/2 lb crab apples
½ lit/1 pt spiced vinegar (page 299)
1 kg/2 lb sugar

yield: approximately 2 kg/3½ lb
time: approximately 1¼ hours
jars
covers and labels

1 Dissolve the sugar in the spiced vinegar **2** Wash the fruit and prepare according to kind, e.g. peel, quarter and core pears. Prick the other fruit but leave whole 3 Stew the fruit in the vinegar syrup until tender (time varies according to the fruit and the degree of ripeness) 4 Half fill hot jars with drained fruit 5 Boil the vinegar syrup until it has reduced to half and pour over the fruit and cover the jars

Sour Pickles

1 Prepare the vegetables in the usual way, cutting large vegetables into suitably-sized pieces 2 Put into an earthenware or china bowl and cover with brine or pack in layers of salt. Leave for 12–48 hours 3 Drain off the brine or rinse and drain the salt-packed ones 4 Pack the drained vegetables into dry, cold jars to within 25 mm/1 in. of the top 5 Fill with cold, spiced vinegar to cover (page 299) 6 Cover and label 7 Store for 2–3 months before using

Brine: 60g/2 oz salt–½ lit/1 pt water

Beetroot Pickle

cooked beetroot (page 112)
spiced vinegar (page 299) ¼ lit/½ pt to 450g/1 lb beetroot

yield: 450g/1 lb of beetroot gives 2½ kg/5 lb
preserving-jars
covers and labels

1 Cut the beetroot into large dice or strips 2 Finish as general method (page 303) using no salt or brine

NB 'Baby' beetroot may be left whole. Time depends on the age and size of the beetroot.

Red Cabbage

red cabbage
dry salt
spiced vinegar (page 299) ¼ lit/½ pt to 450g/1 lb

time: 2 days
preserving-jars
covers and labels

1 Trim, quarter and shred the cabbage finely 2 Follow the general method (page 303)

Cauliflower

cauliflower
brine (general method, page 303)
spiced vinegar (page 299) ¼ lit/½ pt to 450g/1 lb

time: 2 days
preserving-jars
covers and labels

1 Divide the cauliflower into small sprigs 2 Follow general directions

Mixed Pickle

cauliflower
cucumber
French or runner beans

time: 2 days
preserving-jars
covers and labels

marrow
onions
dry or brine (general method, page 303)
spiced vinegar (page 299)

1 Prepare the cauliflower as for cauliflower pickle 2 Dice the cucumber—peel if liked 3 Cut the beans into 10 mm/½ in. lengths 4 Dice the marrow into small squares 5 Peel the small onions and leave whole 6 Follow the general method (page 303)

Pickled Onions

small onions for pickling
brine (page 303)
spiced vinegar to cover (page 299)

time: 2 days
preserving-jars
covers and labels

1 Follow general method, skinning after brining

NB 1 A few small chillis and bay-leaves add flavour and colour to light-coloured pickles.
2 If a slightly sweet pickle is preferred 60–110g/2–4 oz of sugar may be dissolved in the spiced vinegar.

Piccalilli

mixed vegetables (as for mixed pickle, page 303)
brine (general method, page 303)
to ½ lit/1 pt spiced vinegar (page 299) add—
60–90g/2–3 oz sugar
1 tsp turmeric powder
1 tsp dry mustard
1 tsp ground ginger
15g/½ oz cornflour

time: 2 days
preserving-jars
covers and labels

1 Prepare the vegetables as for mixed pickle (page 303) 2 Blend the powders with the vinegar and cook as for a blended sauce 3 Finish as general method using the sauce hot

JAMS

Pectin Stock

red-currants, gooseberries or apples
water 1 lit to 3 kg/2 pt to 6 lb fruit

time: approximately 2½ hours
preserving-pan
jelly-cloth
stand

1 Wash the fruit 2 Slice the apples (do not peel or core) 3 Put into the pan with the water and simmer until thoroughly tender (about 1½

hours) **4** Strain through the cloth **5** Return the mashed pulp to the pan and add enough water to make a soft mash **6** Simmer about 1 hour **7** Strain and mix the two extracts together **8** Bottle

NB If it is intended to keep this pectin, it may be sterilized in the usual way (page 318)

It is used to obtain a good set in fruit weak in pectin, e.g. strawberries, cherries.

Test for Pectin

methylated spirit

When to test

After cooking the fruit and before adding the sugar.

How to test

1 Put 1 tsp of the cooked fruit-juice into a glass and cool for one minute.
2 Add 3 tsp of the spirit and shake the glass gently and stand for 1 minute.
3 *(a)* If pectin is high there will be a complete lump of jelly.
   (b) If pectin is sufficient 2–4 clots of jelly will form.
   (c) If pectin is weak there will be many small weak clots.

If Pectin is weak

(a) Continue cooking to increase the proportion of pectin to pulp or

(b) Add extra pectin (page 304).

Raspberry Jam

2 kg/4 lb raspberries
2 kg/4 lb sugar

yield: 3½ kg/6½ lb
time: approximately 1½ hours
preserving-pan
thermometer
jars
covers and labels

1 Hull the fruit 2 Heat in the pan until the juice begins to flow 3 Add the sugar and stir until dissolved 4 Boil rapidly with an occasional stir to 105 °C/220 °F–skim or add a knob of butter 5 Stand until a skin forms and pour into hot jars 6 Cover and label

Strawberry Jam

2 kg/4 lb strawberries
2 kg/4 lb sugar

yield: 3½ kg/6½ lb
time: approximately 2 hours

¼ lit/½ pt red-currant or gooseberry pectin stock (page 304), or lemon juice

preserving-pan
thermometer
jars
covers and labels

1 Hull the fruit and put into the pan with the pectin stock or lemon juice 2 Simmer until tender 3 Add the sugar and stir until dissolved. Boil rapidly to 105 °C/220 °F 4 Skim or add a knob of butter and stand until a skin forms 5 Put into hot jars–cover and label

Blackcurrant Jam

2 kg/4 lb blackcurrants
3 kg/6 lb sugar
1½ lit/3 pt water

yield: 5 kg/10 lb
time: approximately 2½ hours
preserving-pan
thermometer
jars
covers and labels

1 Wash the fruit and remove the stalks 2 Put into the pan with the water and simmer until the skins are thoroughly tender 3 Add the sugar and stir until it is dissolved 4 Boil rapidly with only an occasional stir to 105 °C/220 °F–skim or add a knob of butter 5 Allow to stand until a skin starts to form 6 Pour into hot jars–cover and label

NB ⅛ lit/¼ pt of rum may be added before potting.

Blackcurrant Jelly Jam

1½ kg/3 lb blackcurrants
2 lit/4 pt water
3½ kg/7 lb sugar

yield: 6 kg/11–12 lb
time: 1¼ hours
preserving-pan
thermometer
jars
covers and labels

1 Prepare the fruit and put into the pan with the water 2 Simmer till really soft 3 Add the sugar, stir until dissolved and boil rapidly to 105 °C/220 °F 4 Skim or add a knob of butter–allow to stand for about 15 minutes 5 Pour into hot jars–cover and label

Gooseberry Jam

2 kg/4 lb gooseberries
3 kg/6 lb sugar
¾ lit/1½ pt water

yield: 5 kg/10 lb
time: approximately 1½ hours
preserving-pan
thermometer
jars
labels and covers

1 Prepare the gooseberries and put into the pan with the water 2 Simmer until the fruit is tender 3 Add the sugar and stir until dissolved 4 Boil rapidly with only an occasional stirring to 105 °C/220 °F–skim or add

a knob of butter **5** Allow to stand until a skin starts to form—about 15 minutes **6** Pour into hot jars—cover and label

Mulberry Jam

2 kg/4 lb mulberries
¼ lit/½ pt water or pectin stock (page 304)
*4 tbsp lemon-juice
2 kg/4 lb sugar
*If using water double the lemon-juice

yield: 3–3½ kg/6½ lb
time: approximately 1¼ hours
preserving-pan
thermometer
jam-jars
covers and labels

1 Put the prepared fruit and lemon juice, stock or water into the pan and cook until the fruit is tender **2** Add the sugar and when thoroughly dissolved bring to the boil **3** Boil to 105 °C/220 °F **4** Skim or add a knob of butter and allow to stand for about 15 minutes or until a skin is starting to form **5** Pour into the hot jars —cover and label

NB Do not have the mulberries too ripe and include some under ripe fruit in the jam

Apricot or Plum Jam

2 kg/4 lb apricots or plums (after stoning)
2 kg/4 lb sugar
⅜ lit/¾ pt water

yield: 3–3½ kg/6½ lb
time: approximately 1½ hours
muslin
preserving-pan
thermometer
jars
labels and covers

1 Wash the fruit, stone and put into the pan with the water **2** Crack some of the stones, remove the kernels, blanch and add to the fruit **3** Tie the remaining stones in the muslin and cook with the jam **4** When the fruit is tender, add the sugar and stir until dissolved **5** Boil rapidly, with only occasional stirring, to 105 °C/220 °F, skim or add a knob of butter **6** Allow to stand until a skin is forming—about 15 minutes **7** Pour into hot jars—cover and label

NB ⅛ lit/¼ pt of sherry may be added to this jam just before potting.

Dried Apricot or Peach Jam

450g/1 lb dried apricots or peaches
1¼ lit/2½ pt water
1½ kg/3 lb sugar
45g/1½ oz almonds

yield: 2½ kg/5 lb
time: approximately 2 days
preserving-pan
thermometer
jars
covers and labels

1 Wash the fruit—steep in the water 24–48 hours according to the hardness of the fruit **2** Put into the pan and simmer until the fruit is tender **3** Add the sugar and stir until it is dissolved **4** Boil rapidly, stirring only occasionally, to 105 °C/220 °F–skim or add a knob of butter **5** Allow to stand until a skin forms–about 15 minutes **6** Pour into hot jars–cover and label

NB ⅛ lit/¼ pt of sherry may be added to apricot jam just before potting, and brandy to peach jam.

Marrow and Ginger Jam

2 kg/4 lb prepared marrow
2 kg/4 lb of sugar
170g/6 oz preserved ginger
3 lemons (rind and juice)

yield: 3–3½ kg/6½ lb
time: approximately 1½ days
steamer
grater
lemon-squeezer
preserving-pan
thermometer
jars
covers and labels

1 Prepare the marrow and cut into 25 mm/1 in. cubes **2** Steam for 8 minutes (not longer) **3** Put into a bowl and add the sugar, grated lemon-rind and juice **4** Cover and stand overnight **5** Chop the ginger and put all the ingredients into the pan **6** Bring slowly to the boil **7** Boil to 105 °C/220 °F, or until the marrow is clear–skim or add a knob of butter **8** Allow to stand for about 15 minutes **9** Put into hot jars–cover and label

NB This jam will not set in the same way as other jams but will remain syrupy.

Cherry Jam (Sweet or Morella)

2 kg/4 lb cherries (after stoning)
2 kg/4 lb sugar
¼ lit/½ pt pectin stock (page 304)
1 tbsp lemon-juice

yield: 3 kg/6 lb
time: approximately 2 hours
muslin
preserving-pan
thermometer
jars
covers and labels

1 Wash and stone the cherries **2** Crack some of the stones and remove the kernels, blanch, tie the remaining stones in muslin **3** Put the fruit into the pan with the pectin stock, lemon-juice, kernels and stones –simmer until tender **4** Add the sugar and stir until dissolved **5** Boil rapidly with only an occasional stir, to 105 °C/220 °F, skim or add a knob of butter **6** Stand until a skin forms–about 15 minutes **7** Pour into hot jars–cover and label

NB ⅛ lit/¼ pt of brandy may be added to this jam just before potting.

Peach Jam (Fresh)

2 kg/4 lb peaches
¼ lit/½ pt water
2 kg/4 lb sugar

yield: 3 kg/6 lb
time: approximately 1¾ hours
muslin

4 tbsp lemon-juice
pith of 1 lemon

lemon-squeezer
thermometer
preserving-pan
jam-jars
covers and labels

1 Skin and cut up the peaches 2 Crack some of the stones and use the blanched kernels in the jam 3 Put the peaches, water, lemon-juice and lemon-pith (tied in muslin) in the pan and cook gently until tender 4 Add the sugar and when dissolved bring to the boil 5 Boil quickly to 105 °C/220° F 6 Skim or add a knob of butter and remove the bag of pith 7 Allow to stand for about 15 minutes or until a skin is beginning to form 8 Pour into the hot jars—cover and label

NB $\frac{1}{8}$ lit/¼ pt of brandy may be stirred into this jam just before potting.

Plum, Orange and Walnut Jam

2 kg/4 lb plums or greengages or damsons
2 kg/4 lb sugar
2 oranges
230g/½ lb chopped walnuts

yield: 3 kg/6 lb
time: approximately 2 hours
muslin
preserving-pan
thermometer
jars
liquidizer
covers and labels

1 Stone the fruit and tie the stones in the muslin 2 Cut the oranges in quarters, remove the pips—liquidize 3 Put the plums, stones and oranges into the pan—simmer gently until tender 4 Add the sugar and stir until dissolved 5 Boil rapidly, stirring occasionally to 105 °C/220 °F—skim or add a knob of butter 6 Allow to stand until a skin forms—about 15 minutes 7 Pour into hot jars—cover and label

Pineapple Jam

fresh pineapples (ripe)
lemon-rind and juice
sugar

yield: see below
time: approximately 2 hours
preserving-pan
thermometer
jars
covers and labels

1 Peel the pineapples, remove the core and eyes—slice 2 To every 450g/1 lb of prepared fruit allow 450g/1 lb of sugar and the grated rind and juice of 1 lemon 3 Put the fruit, lemon-rind and -juice into the pan 4 Cook gently until the juice begins to flow 5 Add the sugar and stir until dissolved 6 Boil rapidly, stirring occasionally to 105 °C/220 °F—skim or add a knob of butter 7 Allow to stand until a skin forms—about 15 minutes 8 Pour into hot jars—cover and label

NB 1 *Yield* 2 kg/4 lb of fruit and sugar should yield 3–3½ kg/6½ lb of jam.

2 $\frac{1}{8}$ lit/¼ pt of rum may be added just before potting.

Mixed Fruit Jams

Blackberry and apple	preserving-pan
Loganberry and rhubarb	thermometer
Raspberry and rhubarb	jars
Strawberry and gooseberry	covers and labels

Equal quantities of fruit can be used, or different proportions according to the desired flavour.

Use an equal weight of fruits and sugar.

1 Prepare the fruits **2** Put hard fruits into the pan with a very little water if necessary–simmer till tender **3** Add soft fruits and cook to a pulp **4** Add the sugar and follow the directions for other jams

MARMALADES

Seville Orange Marmalade (1)

12 Seville oranges	yield: approximately 7 kg/13 lb
2 sweet oranges	*time:* 1½ days
2 lemons	preserving-pan
sugar	thermometer
water	muslin
	jars
	covers and labels

1 Scrub the fruit and cut up finely, removing the pips **2** Allowing 1½ lit/3 pt water to each 450g/1 lb of pulp, steep the skin and flesh and add the pips tied in muslin–stand overnight **3** Put into the pan, bring to the boil–simmer until tender and reduced to about half the quantity –stand until cool or overnight **4** Weigh the pulp and allow 450g/1 lb sugar to each 450g/1 lb of pulp **5** Dissolve the sugar, bring to the boil and boil to 105 °C/220 °F–skim or add a knob of butter–stand for about 15 minutes **6** Pour into hot jars–cover and label

Seville Orange Marmalade. (2)

1 kg/2 lb Seville oranges	yield: approximately 4½–5 kg/9 lb
2 lemons	*time:* 2 hours
1 lit/2 pt cold water	pressure-cooker
2½ kg/5 lb sugar	preserving-pan
	thermometer
	jars
	covers and labels

1 Place the whole scrubbed fruit in the pressure-cooker–add the water **2** Bring to 8 kg/15 lb pressure–allow to reduce to zero off the heat **3** Remove the fruit and cut up finely removing the pips and steep them in a basin with a little extra water **4** Put the fruit, liquid from the pressure-cooker, sugar and strained juice from the pips into the pan

5 Stir till the sugar has dissolved 6 Boil till setting-point is reached at 105 °C/220 °F 7 Skim or add a knob of butter 8 Allow to stand for 15 minutes 9 Pot, cover and store

NB The softened fruit may be put into a liquidizer if all the pips have been removed first.

Grapefruit Marmalade

¾ kg/1½ lb grapefruit
2 lemons
1½ lit/3 pt water
1½ kg/3 lb sugar

yield: 2½ kg/5 lb
time: 1½ days
preserving-pan
muslin
thermometer
jars
cover and labels

1 Scrub the fruit–cut up finely removing the pips 2 Put into a bowl, cover with the water 3 Add the pips tied in muslin and stand overnight 4 Put into the pan and cook gently until the peel is tender 5 Add the sugar, dissolve and bring to the boil, and boil rapidly to 105 °C/220 °F 6 Skim or add a knob of butter and stand for 15 minutes 7 Pour into hot jars–cover and label

Lemon Marmalade

¾ kg/1½ lb lemons
1½ lit/3 pt water
1½ kg/3 lb sugar

yield: 2½ kg/5 lb
time: 1½ days
preserving-pan
muslin
thermometer
jars
covers and labels

1 Scrub the fruit and cut up finely tying the pips in muslin 2 Steep the fruit and pips in the water, overnight 3 Put into the pan, bring to the boil and simmer gently until the bulk is reduced by ⅓ 4 Add the sugar, allow to dissolve and bring to the boil and boil rapidly to 105 °C/220 °F 5 Skim or add a knob of butter and allow to stand 15 minutes 6 Pour into hot jars–cover and label

Grapefruit and Pineapple Marmalade

450g/1 lb grapefruit
1 small pineapple and juice of a lemon (to equal 230g/½ lb when cut)
1½ lit/3 pt water
1½ kg/3 lb sugar

yield: 2½ kg/5 lb
time: 1½ days
preserving-pan
muslin
thermometer
jars
covers and labels

1 Scrub the grapefruit and remove and skin and cut into fine shreds 2 Cut up the peeled fruit and put the pips and coarse tissue in to the

muslin 3 Cover the fruit with the water adding the pips—steep overnight 4 Peel the pineapple and remove the eyes and hard core, and cut into small pieces. 5 Put into the pan with the lemon-juice adding the steeped fruit 6 Bring to the boil and simmer until the bulk is reduced by one third 7 Add the sugar, dissolve, bring to boil and boil rapidly to 105 °C/220 °F 8 Skim or add a knob of butter and allow to stand 15 minutes 9 Pour into hot jars—cover and label

Lemon Jelly Marmalade

1 kg/2 lb lemons
1½ lit/3 pt water
1½ kg/3 lb sugar

yield: 2½ kg/5 lb
time: approximately 3½ hours
strainer
preserving-pan
scissors
thermometer
jars
covers and labels

1 Scrub the lemons thoroughly 2 Peel off the skin thinly and cut into fine shreds with the scissors 3 Cook in half the water until tender 4 Cut up the fruit roughly and cook in the remaining liquid for 2 hours with the lid on—strain 5 Put into the pan, add the sugar and allow it to dissolve—bring to the boil 6 Add the shreds and liquid and boil rapidly to 105 °C/220 °F 7 Skim or add a knob of butter and allow to stand 15 minutes 8 Pour into hot jars—cover and label

Orange Jelly Marmalade

1 kg/2 lb Seville oranges
2 lit/4 pt water
juice of 2 lemons
1½ kg/3 lb sugar

yield: 2½ kg/5 lb
time: 3½ hours
preserving-pan
scissors
thermometer
jars
covers and labels

See lemon jelly marmalade (page 312)

JELLIES

Apple or Crab Apple Jelly

apples or crab apples
water
sugar
lemon-juice

time: 1½ days
preserving-pan
jelly-stand and cloth
thermometer
jars
labels and covers

1 Wash the apples and cut up roughly 2 Just cover with water and bring to the boil and simmer until the apples are reduced to a pulp 3 Strain through the cloth and allow to drip overnight 4 A second

extraction may be made by adding water to the pulp and re-boiling 5 Measure the juice and to each ½ lit/1 pt of juice allow 450g/1 lb of sugar and 1 dessertsp lemon-juice 6 Heat the juice, add the sugar and dissolve 7 Bring to the boil and boil quickly to 105 °C/220 °F–skim or add a knob of butter 8 Pour into hot jars–cover and label

NB 1 Rum is an improvement to apple jelly, in the proportions of ⅛ lit to 2 kg/¼ pt to 4 lb sugar.

Quince or Japonica Quince Jelly

1½ kg/3 lb quinces or japonica quinces
450g/1 lb apples
sugar
water
lemon-juice

time: 1½ days
preserving-pan
jelly-stand and cloth
thermometer
jars
labels and covers

See apple jelly (page 312). Rum is not needed as quinces have a definite flavour.

Blackberry Jelly

1½ kg/3 lb blackberries
450g/1 lb apples
water
sugar
lemon-juice

time: 1½ days
preserving-pan
jelly-stand and cloth
thermometer
jars
labels and covers

See apple jelly (page 312). Rum may be used but this jelly has much more flavour than apple jelly.

Redcurrant Jelly or Cranberry Jelly

redcurrants or cranberries
sugar

time: 1½ days
preserving-pan
jelly stand and cloth
thermometer
jars
labels and covers

1 Wash the fruit, but it need not be picked 2 Heat gently in the pan and continue to cook until there is a good extraction of juice 3 Strain and allow to drip until all the juice is through 4 Measure the juice and continue as for apple jelly (page 312).

Blackcurrant Jelly

blackcurrants
water
sugar

time: 1½ days
preserving-pan
jelly-stand and cloth
thermometer
jars and labels

1 Wash the currants but do not pick 2 Put into the pan with enough water to reach half way up the fruit 3 Continue as for red-currant jelly (page 313)

Gooseberry Jelly

gooseberries	*time:* 1½ days
water	preserving-pan
sugar	jelly-stand and cloth
	thermometer
	jars
	labels and covers

1 Wash the gooseberries–they need not be topped and tailed 2 Add water as for apple jelly (page 312) 3 Continue as for apple jelly

Mint or Sage Jelly

apples	*time:* 1½ days
water	preserving-pan
mint or sage	jelly-cloth and stand
sugar	thermometer
vinegar	jars
green colouring	covers and labels

1 Wash the apples, cut up roughly 2 Put into the pan and cover with water 3 Cook gently until a pulp and strain 4 To ½ lit or 1 pt of juice allow 450g or 1 lb sugar 5 Put into the pan and allow sugar to dissolve 6 Chop a generous quantity of mint or sage–put in to a basin and cover with vinegar 7 When the sugar has dissolved boil quickly to 105 °C/ 220 °F–skim or add a knob of butter 8 Add the mint and green colouring 9 Stand until a skin is beginning to form–about 15 minutes 10 Put into hot jars, cover and label

MISCELLANEOUS

Lemon Curd

1 lemon	yield: approximately 230g/½ lb
60g/2 oz butter	*time:* 15 minutes
1 egg	lemon-squeezer
90g/3 oz granulated sugar	strainer
	grater
	jars
	covers and labels

1 Grate the lemon-rind finely, put into a pan with the juice, beaten egg, sugar and butter 2 Stir over *gentle* heat. Bring to the boil–boil 1 minute 3 Strain, pot and cover

Mincemeat

¾ kg/ 1½ lb finely-chopped beef suet
¾ kg/ 1½ lb raisins
1 kg/2 lb currants
1 kg/2 lb apples
15g/½ oz mixed spice
¾ kg/ 1½ lb castor sugar
1 saltspoon of salt
grated rind and juice of 3 lemons
230g/½ lb finely chopped mixed peel
⅛ lit/¼ pt brandy, port or sherry

yield: approximately 5 kg/9 lb
time: 1 week
lemon-squeezer
grater or shredder
jars
covers and labels

1 Wash and shred the apples 2 Mix the other ingredients and chop them fairly finely 3 Add the apples, lemon and wine 4 Stand for about a week stirring daily 5 Pot, cover and label

BOTTLING

Bottling Syrup

medium syrup
½ lit/ 1 pt water
230g/½ lb granulated sugar

muslin

1 Put the water and sugar in a pan and allow the sugar to dissolve as the water comes to the boil 2 Strain through muslin–cool. Use as required

light syrup
½ lit/ 1 pt water
60g/2 oz granulated sugar

Method–as for medium syrup

Methods of Bottling

Method 1*(a)*

Oven–Dry Pack

baking-tray
jars
foil
newspaper
oven No. ½ or 115 °C/265 °F

1 Prepare the fruit according to kind, i.e. wipe, stone or top and tail, etc. 2 Pack the jars tightly 3 Stand the jars on the tray on several thicknesses of newspaper–cover with a sheet of foil over all jars
4 Place in the oven and leave until the fruit is just beginning to crack
5 Remove from the oven one jar at a time. As the fruit shrinks it will be necessary to fill up the jars from one another 6 Fill each jar to the brim with boiling syrup (page 315) 7 Place the lid on tightly–allow to cool, tightening the lid as much as possible 8 When quite cold test the

seal and store in a cool, dark place

Method 1*(b)*

Oven–Wet Pack

equipment as for dry pack (page 315)

1 Pack the jars as for Method 1*(a)* **2** Fill to the brim with cold syrup (page 315) **3** Cover–screw the lid or band up tightly–turn back ½ a turn **4** Stand on the tray covered with several thicknesses of newspaper **5** Put into oven and leave till the bubbles rise from the fruit, which is just beginning to crack **6** Remove from the oven and screw up tightly **7** When quite cold, test the seal **8** Store in a cool, dark place

Method 2

Waterbath or Sterilizer

sterilizer or deep pan
thermometer

1 Pack the jars as for Method 1*(b)* **2** Place in a deep pan or sterilizer with a false bottom, i.e. wood or pan stand **3** Cover the jars with cold water **4** Bring to the required temperature in the time stated in the table (below) **5** Remove jars–tighten the lids **6** Allow to cool–test **7** Store in a cool, dark place

WATERBATH OR STERILIZER

Fruit	Temperature	Minutes Maintained
1 Apples 2 Apricots 3 Plums 4 Blackberries 5 Gooseberries 6 Raspberries 7 Peaches 8 Rhubarb	To reach 75 °C/165 °F in 1½ hours	10 minutes
9 Currants 10 Cherries 11 Pears	To reach 80 °C/180 °F in 1½ hours	15 minutes
12 Quinces 13 Tomatoes	To reach 90 °C/190 °F in 1½ hours	30 minutes

Method 3

Pressure-cooker

1 Place the trivet in the cooker and cover with water 25 mm/1 in. deep **2** Fill the jars as for oven Method 1*(b)* **3** Put the jars in the cooker, put the table (page 316) **5** Remove jars—tighten the lids **6** Allow to cool—minutes **4** Close the valve and bring to the pressure on chart (page 318) **5** Maintain the pressure according to the time on the chart **6** Turn the heat down and cool slowly **7** Remove the jars and screw up **8** Allow to cool—test and store

To Preserve Vegetables

NB A pressure-cooker is essential—*no vegetables should be bottled as for fruit, except tomatoes.*
Use a recognized preserving-jar—not a jam-jar—preferably 450g/1 lb size; if larger, the times below will not be correct.

pressure-cooker
jars
covers and labels

1 Fill the jars with scalded vegetables, i.e. whole vegetables dropped into boiling water, dipped in cold water, diced or shaped as required **2** Cover with boiling brine (30g/1 oz salt: 1¼ lit/2½ pt water) **3** Place the lid on—screw the band back ½ a turn **4** Place in the cooker 25 mm/1 in. water above the trivet **5** Heat until steam rises from vent-pipe, allow to steam 7–10 minutes **6** Close the valve and bring to 5½ kg–6 kg/10 lb pressure and maintain for the time shown on the chart **7** Cool very slowly to normal pressure (not less than 20 minutes) **8** Screw the bands up tightly **9** Allow to cool, test and store

NB If there is any smell or sign of decomposition the food should be destroyed at once.

TABLE FOR PRESSURE–COOKING OF VEGETABLES

Vegetable	Scalding time	Hold at pressure
Asparagus	thin stems 2 minutes	30 minutes
	thick stems 3 minutes	35 minutes
Broad Beans	3 minutes	35 minutes
Carrots	10–15 minutes	35 minutes
French or Runner Beans	2– 3 minutes	35 minutes
New potatoes	10–15 minutes	35 minutes
Peas	1– 2 minutes	40 minutes

TABLE FOR PRESSURE–COOKING OF FRUIT

Fruit	Pressure	Time
Apples	3 kg/5 lb	10 minutes
Apple purée	3 kg/5 lb	8 minutes
Apricots	3 kg/5 lb	10 minutes
Berries (except strawberries)	3 kg/5 lb	8 minutes
Cherries	3 kg/5 lb	10 minutes
Peaches	3 kg/5 lb	10 minutes
Pears	3 kg/5 lb	10 minutes
Plums	3 kg/5 lb	10 minutes
Strawberries	3 kg/5 lb	5 minutes
Rhubarb	3 kg/5 lb	5 minutes
Tomatoes	3 kg/5 lb	10 minutes

Method 4

Chemical additives

preserving-jars

Campden Tablets

1 Prepare the fruit and pack the jars as for oven Method 1*(a)* (page 315) **2** Dissolve the tablets according to the instructions on the packet **3** Fill the jars to the brim with the solution **4** Cover tightly with lids and screwtops or a patent plastic cover **5** Store as before

NB **1** The fruit will bleach in storage. To restore colour and re-oxidize–boil before using.

2 This method is very suitable for windfall apples and pears.

Method 5

Pulping

Fruit Pulp

fruit	liquidizer
sugar	large pan
	preserving-jars
	labels and covers

1 Prepare the fruit, cut up and put in to the pan with the sugar, Allowing 110g/¼ lb sugar–450g/1 lb apples **2** Heat very gently and cook until the apples are tender–liquidize **3** Heat and pour into hot jars, cover and place in a pan of hot water **4** Bring to the boil and boil for 20 minutes **5** Screw up tightly **6** When cold test for seal, label and store

Tomato Pulp

ripe tomatoes
salt
vinegar
sugar

strainer
liquidizer
large pan
preserving-jars
labels

1 Wash the tomatoes and each 450g/1 lb add ½ tsp salt, 1 tsp sugar, 1 dessertsp vinegar 2 Put into the pan and follow instructions for fruit pulp (page 318)

NB After liquidizing, strain to remove skin and pips.

OTHER METHODS OF PRESERVATION

Salting

Suitable for runner or french beans and peas

1½ kg/3 lb beans: 450g/1 lb salt

large earthernware jar

1 Put a layer of cooking salt in the bottom of the large jar 2 Place a layer of prepared and sliced beans on the salt—cover with another layer of salt 3 Repeat till the jar is full and tightly packed—finish with a layer of salt 4 Cover and tie down—store

Drying

Herbs

1 Wash the herbs—dry off the surface moisture 2 Tie in a muslin or paper bag with the stems uppermost 3 Hang in a warm dry place till thoroughly dry 4 Store in jars or tins

NB The dried herbs may be powdered.

Deep-freezing

Containers for Fruit and Vegetables

1 Screw-topped waxed cartons.
2 Waxed cartons and Polytape.
3 Polythene bags and ties.
4 Plastic boxes.

Containers for meat, poultry and fish

1 Polythene bags and ties.
2 Polythene rolls and ties.
3 Plastic bags and ties.
4 Plastic rolls and ties.
5 Foils and/or polythene.

Containers for pastry, bread, cakes, etc.

1 Waxed wrappers.
2 Polythene bags and ties.
3 Foil containers.

Deep-freezing

Fruit

To prepare

1 Wipe or wash–stone if necessary. See chart (page 321)
2 Mix with sugar or cold syrup (page 315)
3 Put into the container (page 319)
4 Seal; if a wax container, do not fill to the brim. If a plastic bag, push out the air before sealing.
5 Label and freeze rapidly.

To use

Thaw in the container or on a plate.

Vegetables

To prepare

1 Prepare vegetables in the usual way.
2 Parboil vegetables according to the chart (page 322).
3 Drain and cool under running cold water or iced water. Drain well.
4 Pack into the containers (page 319). Do not fill to the brim.
5 Push out the air and seal, when using polythene bags.
6 Label and freeze rapidly.

To use

1 Melt a little butter in a saucepan.
2 Add the frozen vegetables–cover with a lid.
3 Heat very gently until thawed, hot and cooked.
NB If a very thick pack, use a little water with the butter.

CHART FOR DEEP-FREEZING FRUIT

Fruit	Method of Preparation	Pack
1 Slices	Peel, core and slice Scald for 3 minutes	Pack with sugar (¼– ⅓ sugar to fruit)
2 Purée	Stew with sugar ½–2 kg/1–4 lb Liquidize	Pack in containers
Apricots	Wash, cut in half, stone	Pack in container with sugar, proportion as above or pack in prepared medium syrup (page 315)
Blackberries Cranberries Cherries Currants (all kinds) Gooseberries Loganberries Raspberries Strawberries	Prepare according to kind	Pack in containers with dry sugar proportion as above, or pack in medium syrup (page 315) **NB** Strawberries freeze better packed dry without sugar
Purée of above	As for apple purée	As for apple purée
Plums	As for apricots	As for apricots
Peaches	Peel, stone and slice	cover with medium syrup (page 315) or dry, with sugar

Storage Time: up to 12 months

CHART FOR DEEP-FREEZING VEGETABLES

Vegetable	Method of Preparation	Pack
Asparagus	1 Choose young fat stems 2 Trim off inedible parts 3 Arrange spears in equal lengths 4 Boil medium-sized stems for 3 minutes or steam for 4½ minutes 5 Cool under running water for 4 minutes. Drain well	Pack tips in opposite directions in waxed cartons or polythene bags
Beans–broad	1 Boil young beans for 3 minutes or steam 4½ minutes 2 Cool thoroughly	Pack in cartons or bags leaving 10 mm/½ in. air-space
Beans–runner or French	1 Choose very young beans 2 Remove tips and ends 3 If very small leave whole–if larger–slice	1 Pack in bags or cartons 2 Leave 10 mm/½ in. air-space

Vegetable	Method of Preparation	Pack
	4 Boil—whole beans 2–3 minutes sliced beans 1 minute or steam whole beans 3–4 minutes sliced beans 2 minutes 5 Cool as above	
Brocoli and Cauliflower	1 Choose tight heads 2 Trim to even lengths 3 Blanch 3–4 minutes according to thickness 4 Cool	Pack in containers leaving air-space as above
Brussels Sprouts	1 Trim and grade in sizes 2 Boil small sprouts 3 minutes. Boil medium sprouts 4 minutes	Pack in bags or cartons, leaving 10 mm/½ in. air-space
Corn on the Cob	1 Remove husk and silk 2 Grade for size 3 Boil—small 7 minutes medium 9 minutes 4 Cool	1 Wrap each separately 2 Put into bags and seal **NB** Thaw before cooking
Corn on the Cob—grain	1 Treat as before blanching on the cob 2 Remove with a knife	Pack in bag or carton leaving 10 mm/½ in. air-space
Peas	1 Pod young freshly-picked small peas 2 Blanch—1 minute 3 Cool	Pack in bag or carton leaving 10 mm/½ in. air-space
Roots	1 Must be very young	Pack as above

CHART FOR DEEP-FREEZING VEGETABLES

Vegetable	Method of Preparation	Pack
Vegetables	2 Peel, dice or slice 3 Blanch 3 minutes 4 Cool 3 minutes	
Vegetable purées	1 Cook vegetables till tender 2 Drain—sieve, liquidize or chop finely 3 Chill rapidly to 60 °C/140 °F	Pack in carton leaving 10 mm/½ in. air-space

Storage Time: up to 12 months

To Deep-freeze Meat

1 Choose only young tender meat for freezing 2 Trim off excess fat 3 Protect from drying through lack of moisture by packing in moisture-proof containers 4 If packing two or more pieces in one container,

wrap each one separately in cellophane so they do not freeze together 5 Mark each package with *(a)* Date, *(b)* Weight and kind of meat, *(c)* Price

Storage time:

Beef and Lamb	12 months
Pork	9 months
Mince and offal	2 months
Sausages and Cured Bacon	6 weeks
Smoked bacon	1 month

To use

Very small cuts may be cooked without thawing at a moderate temperature and for a longer time than fresh meat. Larger joints, allow 2–3 hours per 450g/1 lb at room temperature or 5–6 hours per 450g/1 lb in a refrigerator.

To Deep-freeze Poultry

1 Choose only the best-quality and healthy birds 2 Pack the bird in a moisture-proof container 3 Pack the giblets separately and put with the bird 4 If packing joints, wrap each one separately in cellophane and then put into a moisture-proof bag 5 Mark each package with *(a)* Date, *(b)* Weight or number, *(c)* Price

NB 1 It is unwise to keep giblets for more than three months.
2 Do not stuff before freezing.

Storage Time:

Chicken	12 months
Duck	6 months
Giblets	3 months
Game	6 months

To use

Thaw before cooking, 3 hours per 450g/1 lb at room temperature, 6 hours per 450g/1 lb in a refrigerator. For very large poultry, follow thawing directions on the pack.

To Deep-freeze Fish

1 Freeze as soon as possible after being caught 2 Scale, eviscerate, cut off heads and fins 3 Wash in cold running water 4 Dip in brine

solution (450g/1 lb salt: 5 lit/9 pt cold water) **5** Drain well **6** Pack in a moisture-proof bag or container **7** Freeze immediately

Storage Time:

White fish	6 months
Oily fish	4 months

To use

1 Thaw partially or totally–slowly, i.e. in a refrigerator or at room temperature.
2 If to be cooked rapidly, e.g. fried, thaw totally–if slowly cooked it may be used partially thawed, but allow extra cooking time.

To Deep-freeze Bread, Cakes and Pastry

Bread and Rolls
1 Allow freshly-baked bread to cool.
2 Wrap in a moisture-proof bag.

Storage Time: 6 months

To use

Thaw at room temperature. *Rolls* may be thawed in the oven.

Cakes and Scones
1 Cool, wrap and freeze.
2 Wrap large cakes singly.
3 Avoid icing cakes before freezing.

Storage Time: 6 months

To use

Thaw at room temperature.

Sandwiches
1 Wrap sandwiches individually.
2 Freeze.
3 Avoid sandwiches made with salad ingredients, hard-boiled egg and jam.

Storage Time: 3 months

To use

Thaw at room temperature for 2–3 hours.

Pastry

1 *Cooked*

   (a) Pies and tarts should be made in china or foil containers or on cardboard plates. Avoid plastic goods. Glassware tested for high and low temperatures is also suitable.

   (b) Wrap when cold–freeze.

Storage Time: 6 months.

To use

1 Thaw at room temperature.
2 Use as required.

1 *Uncooked*

   (a) Form into a small block.

   (b) Wrap in a moisture proof bag.

   (c) Freeze.

NB Do not keep longer than 2 months.
Or: make up ready for the oven and freeze in moisture-proof bag.

To use

Thaw at room temperature and use as required.

To use uncooked pies, etc.
These must be put into the oven in their frozen condition. Allow much longer cooking time.

Made-up Dishes
e.g. a whole meal on cardboard or foil plate.
soups–fruit purées
1 Cool rapidly.
2 Enclose in moisture-proof container (or if in a jar giving the lid ½ turn back).

Storage Time: 2 months

To use
Thaw at room temperature.

Chilled Eggs

Preparation

Eggs must be fresh. Wipe with a clean, dry cloth.
1 Pack the eggs on egg-trays 2 Store in a refrigerator
NB Not in a deep-freezer. This is the way eggs are imported.

To Freeze Eggs

1 Remove from the shells–whisk, 1 tsp salt or 1 tsp castor sugar may be added to each 2 eggs 2 Pack in wax containers or polythene bags. Fasten securely leaving an air space 3 Freeze

Storage Time: 10 months

To use

Thaw in packages and use immediately–3 tbsp = 1 whole egg.

28
Cookery terms

Au gratin Food coated with sauce and sprinkled with white or browned crumbs and sometimes cheese, grilled or heated in the oven and served in the dish in which it is cooked.

Bain-marie A water-bath half filled with water containing saucepans in which food may be kept hot.

Bavarois A moulded custard or custard with cream, set with gelatine.

Beignet See *Fritter*.

Beurre manié Equal quantities of butter and flour mixed together and added in small pats to liquids to thicken.

Blanch To whiten, soften and cleanse and to remove strong flavours; to remove skins.

Blanquette A white stew of poultry, rabbit or veal, the meat being cooked in a white sauce.

Bombay Duck The Bommaloe Fish dried and cured and served with curries.

Bouchée As *Vol-au-vent,* but very small.

Bouillon A brown stock made from beef and beef bones served unclarified as a soup.

Bouquet garni A collection of herbs fresh or dried, used to flavour stocks, soups, stews and sauces.

Canapés Small platforms of cheese pastry, toasted or fried bread or buttered bread, used for savouries.

Cassolettes Small cases of pastry, bread, egg and crumbs or vegetable to hold savoury fillings.

Cayenne A very hot red pepper used as a seasoning.

Chaud-froid or Chaudfroid A name given to cold dishes of poultry, game, fish or ham masked with sauce, which may be brown, white or green.

Chine The spinal bone left after the division of a carcass by the butcher; *to chine,* saw off the chine bone.

Crêpes Pancakes.

Croquettes Minced meat, poultry, fish, etc., coated with egg and raspings and fried in deep fat.

Croûte A slice of toasted or fried bread on which game, sweet-bread, etc., is served.

Croûtons Small dice of toasted or fried bread served with purée soups. May also be triangular in shape and used as a garnish.

Dariole A small mould the shape of a madeleine.

Demi-glace A brown sauce of a thinner consistency than espagnole sauce.

En papillote Food cooked enclosed in foil or oiled paper.

En tasse Served in cups, usually applied to clear soups.

Entrée The conventional term for a course which is complete with sauce and garnish–it may be hot or cold.
It used to be part of a meal, but is now often served as the main course.

Entrecôte Name given to a steak cut from the middle part of the sirloin or sometimes the rib of beef.

Entremet A hot or cold sweet or after-dinner savoury.

Escalope Thin slice of meat, usually veal

Espagnole (Spanish.) A rich brown sauce–the foundation of nearly all brown sauces.

Farce Stuffing.

Fillet Undercut of sirloin of beef—mutton, veal, pork or game.

Fines-herbes A mixture of finely-chopped herbs, used in omelets, sauces, etc.

Flambé Lighted spirit poured over a dish—or spirit poured over a dish and set alight.

Fleuron Crescents of puff pastry used as a garnish.

Foie gras Fat goose liver.

Friandises A selection of small desserts or petits fours.

Fricassée A white stew of poultry, veal, rabbit or fish, heated in a white sauce made from the stock.

Fritter Beignet—anything that is dipped in batter and fried.

Garni Dressed or garnished.

Gâteau A decorated cake—usually a sponge foundation.

Hors-d'œuvre Small side dishes generally served cold to stimulate the appetite. Sometimes a single dish.

Infuse To draw out flavour into a liquid.

Julienne Very finely-cut strips of vegetable.

Jus A gravy.

Jus lié A thickened gravy.

Kromeskis Balls or rolls of minced chicken, ham, etc., bound by a sauce, wrapped in bacon, dipped in batter and fried.

Liaison A thickening—used to prevent the separation of liquid and solid ingredients.

Macédoine A garnish of mixed vegetables evenly cut—or of fruit.

Maître d'hôtel A flavouring butter, butter mixed with chopped parsley, seasoning and lemon juice, served with all grilled foods. Dishes served "à la maître d'hôtel" mean that parsley is the principal flavouring.

Marinade To soak to improve flavour and tenderize.

Minute Steak A fillet, cut thin, taking literally a minute to cook.

Mirepoix A bed of vegetables, flavoured with bacon and meat bones, used in braising.

Mousse Literally moss: whipped cream and flavouring, sometimes set with gelatine, and without gelatine sometimes frozen.

Noisette Means a small nut or kernel, also the name of small round pieces of meat, for example, lamb or mutton cutlets with the bone removed.

Noodles A pasta used as a garnish. Egg noodles have egg added to the basic noodle mixture.

Nougat A mixture of blanched, chopped almonds and sugar. The sugar is heated slowly until a light caramel. The nuts are then added—it is poured into an oiled tin and cut into fancy shapes just before setting—*or* it may be set and crushed and used for flavouring.

Panada A thick binding sauce.

Paprika A deep, red, mild pepper used as a garnish.

Parboil To cook partially.

Pastillage Royal icing hardened by the addition of gum tragacanth.

Petits Fours See *Friandises.*

Pilau or Pilaff A dish common in the Middle and Far East, made of meat, poultry or fish with rice and garnished with raisins, almonds and onions.

Pocher To poach.

Potage Soup—especially cream and not necessarily sieved or liquidized.

Poussin A very young chicken ½–¾ kg/1–1½ lb.

Praline or Praliné A mixture of unblanched almonds, sugar and water, boiled together to 193–205 °C/380–400 °F–poured into an oiled tin and set. It may be crushed and used as flavouring.

Purée A meat, fruit or vegetable mixture that has been sieved or liquidized.

Quenelles Minced fish, meat, poultry or game bound with a very thick sauce and shaped into balls or ovals and poached. Used as a garnish or as an entrée.

Raspings Crusts and stale bread, dried in a slow oven, crushed or put in a liquidizer.

Réchauffer To reheat.

Relevé The remove course–consisting of large joints of meat or furred game and sometimes whole fish.

Risotto An Italian dish of rice, cheese and very often tomato and saffron.

Rissoles A mixture of minced meat or flaked fish and sauce, enclosed in thinly rolled pastry, half-moon shaped, and fried.

Rôti The roast.

Roux A mixture of fat and flour used for thickening soups and sauces. It may be white, fawn or brown.

Salamander An iron used red hot to brown the surface of dishes.

Salmis A rich hash of game, duck, etc.

Salpicon A mixture of minced poultry or game with ham or tongue and mushrooms used for bouchées, croquettes, rissoles, etc.

Sauté Tossed in hot fat. This may *(a)* start a process, for example, soups, stews; *(b)* finish a process, for example, vegetables; *(c)* cook entirely, for example, mushrooms.

Savarin A light, spongy yeast mixture named after the chef who originated the dish.

Sorbet A soft water ice with fruit or liqueur flavour.

Soubise Name given to a smooth onion pulp served with meat dishes.

Soufflé A sweet made from whipped cream, eggs, sugar and flavouring—baked or steamed or served iced, or served cold when it is set with gelatine and cream is added.

Syllabub A kind of milk punch.

Tammy To strain through a cloth or muslin.

Tournedos A fillet of beef 25–30 mm/1–1½ in. thick.

Truffle An underground fungus. The best come from France, where dogs and pigs are used to dig for them. Used as a garnish and sometimes chopped up in mixtures.

Vol-au-Vent An oval or round case of puff pastry.

Zest The skin of lemon or orange with no pith.

Index